BEST OF
Betty Crocker®

2011

BEST OF
Betty Crocker®
2011

For more great recipes and ideas, go to bettycrocker.com

Copyright © 2010 General Mills, Inc.
Minneapolis, Minnesota

PUBLISHED BY
Taste of Home Books
Reiman Media Group, Inc.
5400 S. 60th St., Greendale WI 53129
www.tasteofhome.com

Printed in the U.S.A.

Taste of Home® is a registered trademark of Reiman Media Group, Inc.

International Standard Book Number (10):
0-89821-821-7

International Standard Book Number (13):
978-0-89821-821-3

International Standard Serial Number:
1947-234X

CREDITS

General Mills, Inc.
EDITORIAL DIRECTOR: Jeff Nowak
PUBLISHING MANAGER: Christine Gray
COOKBOOK EDITOR: Grace Wells
PRODUCTION MANAGER: Michelle Tufts
RECIPE DEVELOPMENT AND TESTING:
Betty Crocker Kitchens
PHOTOGRAPHY: General Mills Photography Studio

. . . .

Reiman Media Group, Inc.
EDITOR: Heidi Reuter Lloyd
SENIOR EDITOR/BOOKS: Mark Hagen
ART DIRECTOR: Gretchen Trautman
CONTENT PRODUCTION SUPERVISOR: Julie Wagner
LAYOUT DESIGNERS: Nancy Novak, Kathryn Pieters
GRAPHIC DESIGN ASSOCIATE: Juli Schnuck
PROOFREADERS: Victoria Soukup Jensen,
Linne Bruskewitz
COVER PHOTOGRAPHY:
Reiman Media Group Photo Studio
PHOTOGRAPHER: Jim Wieland
FOOD STYLIST: Shannon Roum
SET STYLIST: Stephanie Marchese

. . . .

VICE PRESIDENT, EXECUTIVE EDITOR, BOOKS:
Heidi Reuter Lloyd
CREATIVE DIRECTOR/CREATIVE MARKETING:
James Palmen
VICE PRESIDENT/BOOK MARKETING: Dan Fink
NORTH AMERICAN CHIEF MARKETING OFFICER:
Lisa Karpinski
EDITOR IN CHIEF: Catherine Cassidy
PRESIDENT, NORTH AMERICAN AFFINITIES:
Suzanne M. Grimes
PRESIDENT & CHIEF EXECUTIVE OFFICER:
Mary G. Berner

Front Cover Photographs, clockwise from top:
Fruit-Topped Almond Cake, p. 182; Cranberry-Filled Sour Cream Coffee Cake with Orange Glaze, p. 30; Alfredo Chicken Pot Puff Pies, p. 106; Home-Style Chicken Dinner, p. 58; Chicken Paprika Shepherd's Pie, p. 92.

Back Cover Photographs, clockwise from upper left:
Muffuletta Slices, p. 32; Caribbean Pork with Pineapple Salsa, p. 68; Cookies 'n Cream Cupcakes, p. 216; Chocolate Chip-Pumpkin Bread, p. 19.

table
OF CONTENTS

6

28

45

84

128

105

137

158

184

230

234

278

331

A Year's Worth of Betty's Best
307 RECIPES TO MAKE ANY OCCASION A SPECIAL EVENT

Betty's back, and she's better than ever! Our first edition of *Best of Betty Crocker* was so successful that we've collected another year of great recipes from Betty Crocker's cooking magazines and compiled them in a book just for you.

The 2011 edition features 307 new recipes from the cooking expert that families have trusted in the kitchen for generations. Her recipes and products are legendary for their high quality and superb taste.

With Betty's recipes, weeknight dinners become times our families can enjoy a good meal AND good conversation. Gatherings with friends and family become special events, and holidays become memories we'll cherish for many years to come. Regardless of the occasion, Betty's there whenever we need her.

ALL NEW FOR 2011

This brand-new cookbook, *Best of Betty Crocker 2011*, features the most-requested recipes from Betty's magazines. You'll find 10 extra-special brunch dishes, 19 appetizers and quick breads, 81 mouthwatering entrees, 18 sandwiches and side dishes, 25 refreshing salads and more than 150 delicious desserts!

Giving homemade cookies for holiday gifts this year? Turn to page 231 for 41 tempting recipes. Need a luscious cheesecake for an all-girls party at your house? Flip to page 179. Would a birthday cake shaped like a purse or a dinosaur make your little one's face light up? Check out the Fun Cakes & Cupcakes chapter starting on page 213.

We've also included hundreds of Betty's best tips to simplify preparation of her recipes. You'll find how-to information, ingredient substitutions and practical suggestions for rounding out meals. These tips help you set a tasty, wholesome meal on the table for your family quickly and easily, giving you more time to spend with those you love.

ICONS TELL THE STORY

We've included at-a-glance icons so you can easily identify which recipes meet your family's needs. In a hurry? The **EASY** icon means the dish preps in just 15 minutes or less. The **QUICK** icon means the recipe goes together from start to finish in 30 minutes or less.

p. 102

p. 204

p. 64

If someone in your family is checking fat or calorie intake, the **LOW FAT** icon will help. It identifies main dishes with 10 grams of fat or less per serving and side dishes and desserts with 3 grams of fat or less per serving. In fact, nutritional information is offered with every recipe in this cookbook, so it's easy to plan a menu that meets any health concerns.

If you're looking for tasty recipes to entertain family and friends outdoors, you're set! This year's book has an entire chapter—27 scrumptious recipes—of fresh-from-the-grill favorites. How's this for a delicious dinner: Pork Tenderloin with Raspberry-Chipotle Glaze or Ham and Potatoes au Gratin. Yes, they're from the grill!

When winter comes around and your family wants to dig in to a piping-hot casserole, we've got you covered. Turn to page 93 for Loaded Baked Potato Casserole, page 102 for Beef Pot Pie with Potato Biscuit Crust or page 97 for Cheesy Tater-Topped Chicken Casserole. **Yum!** Need we say more?

brunch
FAVORITES

p. 15

12

16

9

bacon and mushroom hash brown breakfast

Prep Time: 30 Minutes
Start to Finish: 9 Hours 40 Minutes
Servings: 12

1 lb bacon, cut into 1-inch pieces
1 medium onion, chopped (1/2 cup)
1 medium red bell pepper, chopped (3/4 cup)
1 package (8 oz) sliced fresh mushrooms
2 tablespoons Dijon mustard
1/2 teaspoon salt

1/2 teaspoon pepper
3/4 cup milk
12 eggs
1 package (2 lb) frozen hash browns, thawed
2 cups shredded Cheddar cheese (16 oz)

1 In 12-inch skillet, cook bacon until crisp. Using slotted spoon, remove from pan to small bowl. Cover and refrigerate. Drain drippings, reserving 1 tablespoon in pan. Add onion, bell pepper and mushrooms; cook 4 minutes over medium heat, stirring occasionally. Stir in mustard, salt and pepper. In large bowl, beat milk and eggs with wire whisk.

2 Spray 13x9-inch (3-quart) baking dish with cooking spray. Spread half of hash browns in baking dish. Spread onion mixture evenly on top. Sprinkle with 1 cup of the cheese. Spread remaining hash browns over top. Pour egg mixture on top. Cover; refrigerate 8 hours or overnight.

3 Heat oven to 325°F. Uncover; bake 50 to 60 minutes or until thermometer inserted in center reads 160°F. Sprinkle with remaining 1 cup cheese and the bacon. Bake 3 to 5 minutes longer or until knife inserted in center comes out clean, top is puffed and cheese is melted. Let stand 5 minutes.

High Altitude (3500-6500 ft): Heat oven to 350°F.

Nutritional Info: 1 Serving: Calories 410 (Calories from Fat 220); Total Fat 24g (Saturated Fat 12g, Trans Fat 0g); Cholesterol 265mg; Sodium 740mg; Total Carbohydrate 25g (Dietary Fiber 3g, Sugars 4g); Protein 22g. % Daily Value: Vitamin A 20%; Vitamin C 20%; Calcium 25%; Iron 8%. Exchanges: 1-1/2 Starch, 2-1/2 High-Fat Meat, 1 Fat. Carbohydrate Choices: 1-1/2.

Betty's Kitchen Tip

• Other types of cheese can be used in place of the Cheddar, such as Monterey Jack, Colby or Swiss.

santa fe egg bake

Prep Time: 15 Minutes
Start to Finish: 3 Hours 5 Minutes
Servings: 6 to 8

- 4 cups frozen southern-style hash brown potatoes
- 1 can (15 oz) black beans, rinsed and drained
- 1 cup Green Giant® Niblets® frozen corn
- 1 cup frozen stir-fry bell peppers and onions (from 16-oz bag)
- 2 cups shredded Colby-Monterey Jack cheese (8 oz)
- 2 tablespoons chopped fresh cilantro
- 8 eggs
- 1-1/4 cups milk
- 1/2 teaspoon salt
- 1/4 teaspoon ground red pepper (cayenne)

1 Spray 13x9-inch (3-quart) baking dish with cooking spray. Mix potatoes, beans, corn and stir-fry peppers and onions in baking dish. Sprinkle with the cheese and cilantro.

2 Beat eggs, milk, salt and red pepper until well blended. Pour evenly over potato mixture. Cover; refrigerate at least 2 hours but no longer than 24 hours.

3 Heat oven to 350°F. Uncover; bake 45 to 55 minutes or until knife inserted in center comes out clean. Let stand 5 minutes before cutting.

High Altitude (3500-6500 ft): No change.

Nutritional Info: 1 Serving: Calories 460 (Calories from Fat 210); Total Fat 24g (Saturated Fat 10g, Trans Fat 2g); Cholesterol 240mg; Sodium 670mg; Total Carbohydrate 40g (Dietary Fiber 7g, Sugars 5g); Protein 20g. % Daily Value: Vitamin A 15%; Vitamin C 10%; Calcium 30%; Iron 15%. Exchanges: 2-1/2 Starch, 1-1/2 Medium-Fat Meat, 3 Fat. Carbohydrate Choices: 2-1/2.

EASY

Betty's Kitchen Tips

Substitution: Frozen stir-fry bell peppers and onions is a timesaving product, but if it is unavailable, substitute 1/2 cup each chopped onion and bell pepper.

Serve-With: Serve this easy dish with corn muffins and a variety of toppings, such as guacamole, salsa, sour cream, chopped fresh tomatoes and chopped fresh cilantro.

asparagus, ham and egg bake

Prep Time: 15 Minutes
Start to Finish: 9 Hours 35 Minutes
Servings: 12

EASY

1-1/2	cups chopped cooked ham (1/2 lb)
1	lb fresh asparagus spears, cut into 1-inch pieces
1	bag (30 oz) frozen shredded hash brown potatoes, thawed
1	medium onion, chopped (1/2 cup)
2	cups shredded Cheddar cheese (8 oz)
1/4	cup grated Parmesan cheese

12	eggs
1-1/4	cups milk
1	container (8 oz) sour cream
2	teaspoons lemon-pepper seasoning salt
2	teaspoons ground mustard
1	cup cornflake crumbs
2	tablespoons butter or margarine, melted

1 Spray 13x9-inch (3-quart) glass baking dish with cooking spray. In large bowl, toss ham, asparagus, potatoes, onion and cheeses. Spoon into baking dish.

2 In same bowl, beat eggs, milk, sour cream, lemon-pepper seasoning salt and mustard with fork or wire whisk until well mixed. Pour egg mixture over potato mixture. (Baking dish will be very full.) Cover; refrigerate 8 hours or overnight.

3 Heat oven to 325°F. Uncover baking dish; bake 35 minutes. Meanwhile, in small bowl, toss cornflake crumbs and butter.

4 Sprinkle cornflake mixture over partially baked casserole. Bake uncovered 30 to 35 minutes longer or until knife inserted in center comes out clean and thermometer inserted in center reads 160°F. Remove casserole from oven; let stand 15 minutes before serving.

High Altitude (3500-6500 ft): In step 3, heat oven to 350°F. Bake 55 minutes. Continue as directed.

Nutritional Info: 1 Serving: Calories 380 (Calories from Fat 190); Total Fat 21g (Saturated Fat 11g, Trans Fat 0g); Cholesterol 265mg; Sodium 920mg; Total Carbohydrate 28g (Dietary Fiber 3g, Sugars 6g); Protein 19g. % Daily Value: Vitamin A 20%; Vitamin C 10%; Calcium 20%; Iron 15%. Exchanges: 2 Other Carbohydrate, 2 Lean Meat, 1/2 High-Fat Meat, 2 Fat. Carbohydrate Choices: 2.

Betty's Kitchen Tips

Variation: Two cups small fresh broccoli florets can be substituted for the asparagus.

Purchasing: Look for precut cooked ham in your grocery store's deli department or, if they have a salad bar, see if you can purchase it there.

herbed chicken and broccoli quiche

Prep Time: 15 Minutes
Start to Finish: 1 Hours 20 Minutes
Servings: 6

- 1 Pillsbury® refrigerated pie crust (from 15-oz box), softened as directed on box
- 1 cup chopped deli rotisserie chicken (from 2- to 2-1/2-lb chicken)
- 1 cup Green Giant® frozen chopped broccoli, thawed, drained
- 4 eggs
- 1-3/4 cups half-and-half
- 1/4 teaspoon salt
- 1/2 cup garlic-and-herb whipped cream cheese spread (from 8-oz container)

1 Heat oven to 400°F. In 9-inch glass pie plate, place pie crust as directed on box for One-Crust Filled Pie. Bake 8 to 10 minutes or until light golden brown.

2 Sprinkle chicken and broccoli in partially baked crust.

3 In medium bowl, beat eggs, half-and-half and salt with wire whisk until well blended. Pour into crust.

4 Drop cream cheese by teaspoonfuls into quiche. Cover crust edge with strips of foil to prevent excessive browning. Bake 10 minutes.

5 Reduce oven temperature to 300°F. Bake 35 to 40 minutes or until knife inserted in center comes out clean. Remove foil; let stand 15 minutes before serving.

High Altitude (3500-6500 ft): In step 5, reduce oven temperature to 325°F.

Nutritional Info: 1 Serving: Calories 380 (Calories from Fat 230); Total Fat 26g (Saturated Fat 12g, Trans Fat 0.5g); Cholesterol 205mg; Sodium 430mg; Total Carbohydrate 23g (Dietary Fiber 0g, Sugars 4g); Protein 15g. % Daily Value: Vitamin A 15%; Vitamin C 8%; Calcium 15%; Iron 6%. Exchanges: 1-1/2 Starch, 1-1/2 Medium-Fat Meat, 3-1/2 Fat. Carbohydrate Choices: 1-1/2.

EASY

Betty's Kitchen Tips

Make-Ahead: This quiche is delicious cold, making it especially good for a picnic.

Special Touch: Serve this quiche with colorful spiced apple rings.

upside-down caramel latte bake

Prep Time: 25 Minutes
Start to Finish: 9 Hours 10 Minutes
Servings: 8

Caramel Base
3/4	cup packed brown sugar
1/4	cup granulated sugar
1/2	cup butter or margarine
1/4	cup maple syrup
1	tablespoon instant espresso powder
1/2	cup chopped pecans
10	slices (1/2 inch thick) French bread

Caramel Layer
1/4	cup butter or margarine, melted
1/2	cup packed brown sugar
1/2	cup chopped pecans
10	slices (1/2 inch thick) French bread

Custard
6	eggs
2	teaspoons vanilla
3/4	cup whipping cream
3/4	cup milk
1/4	cup granulated sugar

Whipped Topping
1/2	cup whipping cream
1	tablespoon sugar

1 Heat oven to 350°F. Spray 13x9-inch (3-quart) baking dish with cooking spray.

2 In 2-quart saucepan, mix 3/4 cup brown sugar, 1/4 cup granulated sugar, 1/2 cup butter, the maple syrup and espresso. Cook 4 to 6 minutes over medium heat until sugars dissolve and mixture is smooth. Pour into baking dish. Sprinkle with 1/2 cup pecans. Top with 10 slices French bread, cutting slices in half if necessary to fit in baking dish in single layer.

3 Drizzle 1/4 cup melted butter over bread in pan. Sprinkle with 1/2 cup brown sugar and 1/2 cup pecans. Top with 10 slices French bread.

4 In large bowl, beat custard ingredients with wire whisk. Slowly pour mixture over French bread. Press down on bread with spatula so all of bread absorbs egg mixture. Cover; refrigerate 8 to 24 hours.

5 Uncover; bake 35 to 40 minutes until puffed and lightly browned. Let stand 5 to 10 minutes before serving.

6 Meanwhile, in medium bowl, beat whipped topping ingredients with electric mixer on high speed until stiff peaks form. Serve each piece upside down with a dollop of whipped topping.

High Altitude (3500-6500 ft): In step 5, uncover, bake 40 to 45 minutes.

Nutritional Info: 1 Serving: Calories 760 (Calories from Fat 390); Total Fat 44g (Saturated Fat 21g, Trans Fat 1g); Cholesterol 250mg; Sodium 440mg; Total Carbohydrate 79g (Dietary Fiber 2g, Sugars 59g); Protein 12g. % Daily Value: Vitamin A 25%; Vitamin C 0%; Calcium 15%; Iron 15%. Exchanges: 1 Starch, 4 Other Carbohydrate, 1-1/2 Medium-Fat Meat, 7 Fat. Carbohydrate Choices: 5.

Betty's Kitchen Tips

Make-Ahead: Because this dish chills in the refrigerator, you can make it the previous night.

Variation: Walnuts can be substituted for the pecans in this caramel latte bake.

phyllo egg breakfast torta

Prep Time: 50 Minutes
Start to Finish: 3 Hours 55 Minutes
Servings: 8

1	lb bulk ground Italian pork sausage		3/4	cup butter or margarine, melted
1	medium red bell pepper, chopped		2	cups shredded Swiss cheese (8 oz)
1	medium onion, chopped (1/2 cup)		1	box (9 oz) Green Giant® frozen spinach, thawed and drained
6	eggs		2	tablespoons chopped fresh basil leaves
1/2	teaspoon pepper		1/4	cup grated Parmesan cheese
30	sheets frozen phyllo (filo) pastry (14x9 inch), thawed			

1 In 10-inch nonstick skillet, cook sausage over medium-high heat 6 to 8 minutes or until no longer pink. Remove sausage to medium bowl. Reserve 1 tablespoon liquid in skillet. Reduce heat to medium. Add bell pepper and onion to skillet; cook 5 to 7 minutes, stirring occasionally, until tender. Remove from skillet; add to sausage in bowl.

2 In another medium bowl, beat eggs and pepper with wire whisk. Add to skillet; cook and stir over medium heat 3 to 5 minutes or until eggs are set.

3 Spray 13x9-inch (3-quart) baking dish with cooking spray. Unroll phyllo sheets; cover with plastic wrap and damp paper towel. Place 1 phyllo sheet in baking dish; brush with melted butter. Repeat 9 times.

4 Spread half of sausage mixture over phyllo. Layer and brush with butter 10 more phyllo sheets. Sprinkle evenly with cooked eggs, Swiss cheese, spinach and basil. Layer and brush with butter 5 more phyllo sheets.

5 Top with remaining sausage mixture. Sprinkle with Parmesan cheese. Layer and brush with butter remaining 5 phyllo sheets.

6 Cover tightly; refrigerate 2 to 24 hours. Heat oven to 350°F. Uncover; bake 45 to 55 minutes or until top is golden brown. If desired, garnish with additional chopped fresh basil before serving.

High Altitude (3500-6500 ft): No change.

Nutritional Info: 1 Serving: Calories 560 (Calories from Fat 340); Total Fat 38g (Saturated Fat 20g, Trans Fat 1g); Cholesterol 255mg; Sodium 640mg; Total Carbohydrate 31g (Dietary Fiber 2g, Sugars 2g); Protein 23g. % Daily Value: Vitamin A 80%; Vitamin C 15%; Calcium 35%; Iron 15%. Exchanges: 2 Starch, 2-1/2 High-Fat Meat, 3-1/2 Fat. Carbohydrate Choices: 2.

Betty's Kitchen Tips

Success Hint: Tomato pasta sauce makes a nice topping for this casserole.
Special Touch: Serve with a tossed fruit salad.

fresh fruit medley

Prep Time: 20 Minutes
Start to Finish: 20 Minutes
Servings: 12 (about 1/2 cup each)

EASY QUICK

Dressing
1/4	cup vegetable oil
3	tablespoons honey
2	tablespoons lemon juice
1-1/2	teaspoons poppy seed

Fruits
2	cups halved seedless grapes (1 small bunch)
2	nectarines sliced, or 1-1/2 cups frozen sliced peaches, thawed
1	orange, peeled, sliced
1	medium pineapple, rind removed, cored and cut into 1-inch pieces

1 In tightly covered container, shake dressing ingredients until blended.

2 Place fruits in large bowl. Shake dressing again; pour over fruits and toss. Serve immediately, or cover and refrigerate until serving time.

High Altitude (3500-6500 ft): No change.

Nutritional Info: 1 Serving: Calories 140 (Calories from Fat 45); Total Fat 5g (Saturated Fat 1g, Trans Fat 0g); Cholesterol 0mg; Sodium 0mg; Total Carbohydrate 22g (Dietary Fiber 2g, Sugars 18g); Protein 1g. % Daily Value: Vitamin A 4%; Vitamin C 35%; Calcium 2%; Iron 2%. Exchanges: 1-1/2 Fruit, 1 Fat. Carbohydrate Choices: 1-1/2.

Betty's Kitchen Tips

Special Touch: Use a mixture of red and green grapes to add color to the fruit medley.

Do-Ahead: Make this a day ahead of time to ease prep time the day of your party.

smoked salmon-potato gratin

Prep Time: 35 Minutes
Start to Finish: 1 Hour 15 Minutes
Servings: 8

Casserole

2-1/2 lb golden potatoes, peeled and thinly sliced (6 medium), about 8 cups
2 tablespoons butter
1 cup thinly sliced leeks
2 tablespoons Gold Medal® all-purpose flour
3 cups half-and-half
1 cup shredded Gruyère or Swiss cheese

2 tablespoons chopped fresh dill weed
1/2 teaspoon salt
1/4 teaspoon pepper
12 oz smoked salmon (not lox), cut or flaked into 1/2-inch pieces

Topping

1 cup Progresso® plain bread crumbs
3 tablespoons butter or margarine, melted

1 Fill 4-quart saucepan two-thirds full with water; heat to boiling over high heat. Cook sliced potatoes in water 6 to 9 minutes or until almost tender; drain and return to saucepan.

2 Heat oven to 350°F. Spray 3-quart casserole with cooking spray.

3 In 12-inch nonstick skillet, melt 2 tablespoons butter over medium heat. Cook and stir leeks in butter about 5 minutes or until softened. Stir in flour. Gradually stir in half-and-half. Heat to boiling. Remove from heat. Stir in cheese, dill, salt and pepper until cheese is melted.

4 Pour sauce over potatoes in saucepan. Spoon half of potato mixture into casserole. Top with half the salmon. Repeat layers.

5 Stir together bread crumbs and melted butter; sprinkle over potato mixture. Bake uncovered 30 to 40 minutes or until potatoes are tender and topping is golden.

High Altitude (3500-6500 ft): Boil potatoes 8 to 11 minutes. Use 13x9-inch baking dish.

Nutritional Info: 1 Serving: Calories 490 (Calories from Fat 220); Total Fat 25g (Saturated Fat 14g, Trans Fat 1g); Cholesterol 75mg; Sodium 720mg; Total Carbohydrate 47g (Dietary Fiber 4g, Sugars 6g); Protein 19g. % Daily Value: Vitamin A 20%; Vitamin C 10%; Calcium 30%; Iron 10%. Exchanges: 2 Starch, 1 Other Carbohydrate, 2 Lean Meat, 3-1/2 Fat. Carbohydrate Choices: 3.

Betty's Kitchen Tips

Substitution: Use 1 can (14-3/4 oz) red salmon, skinned, for the smoked salmon.

Special Touch: This is a new rendition of scalloped potatoes and ham; it's great to serve at a brunch.

ham and swiss brunch bake

Prep Time: 25 Minutes
Start to Finish: 2 Hours
Servings: 10

- 1 loaf (1 lb) French bread, cut into 1/2-inch slices
- 2 tablespoons Dijon mustard
- 8 oz thinly sliced cooked ham
- 8 oz thinly sliced Swiss cheese
- 4 eggs
- 2 cups milk
- 1/4 cup grated Parmesan cheese
- 1/4 cup Progresso® plain bread crumbs
- 2 tablespoons chopped fresh parsley
- 3 tablespoons butter or margarine, melted

1 In ungreased 13x9-inch (3-quart) baking dish, arrange half of the bread slices, overlapping as needed. Brush bread in dish with mustard. Top evenly with ham and Swiss cheese, overlapping as needed. Top with remaining bread slices, arranging them over first layer of bread slices to make sandwiches.

2 In medium bowl, beat eggs and milk with wire whisk until well blended. Carefully pour over sandwiches. Cover and refrigerate at least 1 hour but no longer than 12 hours.

3 Mix Parmesan cheese, bread crumbs, parsley and butter. Heat oven to 375°F. Uncover casserole. Sprinkle with crumb topping. Bake 30 to 35 minutes or until sandwiches are puffed and golden brown.

High Altitude (3500-6500 ft): Heat oven to 400°F. Reserve crumb topping. Cover and bake 15 minutes. Sprinkle crumb topping over casserole. Bake uncovered 20 minutes longer.

Nutritional Info: 1 Serving: Calories 360 (Calories from Fat 140); Total Fat 16g (Saturated Fat 9g, Trans Fat 0g); Cholesterol 135mg; Sodium 810mg; Total Carbohydrate 32g (Dietary Fiber 1g, Sugars 7g); Protein 22g. % Daily Value: Vitamin A 10%; Vitamin C 0%; Calcium 30%; Iron 15%. Exchanges: 1-1/2 Starch, 1/2 Other Carbohydrate, 2-1/2 Medium-Fat Meat, 1/2 Fat. Carbohydrate Choices: 2.

Betty's Kitchen Tips

Do-Ahead: Prepare this dish the night before. Cover and refrigerate the sandwiches separately from the topping. Add the topping just before baking.

Special Touch: Serve with a colorful selection of fresh fruit.

bananas foster french toast

Prep Time: 20 Minutes
Start to Finish: 9 Hours 10 Minutes
Servings: 8

- -

8	slices cinnamon bread, cut into 1/2-inch cubes (about 8 cups)
8	eggs
1	cup milk

2-1/2	cups real maple syrup
1	teaspoon rum extract
6	ripe bananas, cut into 1/2-inch slices
1	cup chopped pecans

- -

1 Spray bottom of 13x9-inch (3-quart) baking dish with cooking spray. Arrange bread cubes in baking dish. In large bowl, beat eggs, milk and 1/2 cup of the maple syrup with wire whisk. Pour over bread in baking dish. Cover and refrigerate 8 hours or overnight.

2 Heat oven to 350°F. Uncover; bake 35 to 40 minutes or until golden brown along edges. Let stand 7 to 10 minutes before serving.

3 Meanwhile, in medium microwavable bowl, microwave remaining 2 cups maple syrup uncovered on High 1 to 2 minutes, stirring every 30 seconds, until warm. Stir in rum extract.

4 Sprinkle banana slices and pecans evenly over bread; drizzle with warmed syrup mixture. Serve immediately.

High Altitude (3500-6500 ft): No change.

Nutritional Info: 1 Serving: Calories 620 (Calories from Fat 150); Total Fat 17g (Saturated Fat 3g, Trans Fat 0g); Cholesterol 215mg; Sodium 260mg; Total Carbohydrate 105g (Dietary Fiber 4g, Sugars 75g); Protein 11g. % Daily Value: Vitamin A 8%; Vitamin C 6%; Calcium 20%; Iron 20%. Exchanges: 2 Starch, 1 Fruit, 4 Other Carbohydrate, 1/2 High-Fat Meat, 2-1/2 Fat. Carbohydrate Choices: 7.

Betty's Kitchen Tips

Purchasing: Rum extract can be found in the baking section of your local grocery store.
Special Touch: Serve with crisp bacon or sausage.

appetizers
& QUICK BREADS

p. 32

21

35

26

planked salmon platter

Prep Time: 50 Minutes
Start to Finish: 1 Hour 50 Minutes
Servings: 16 (2 tablespoons salmon, 2 bread slices and 1/16 of accompaniments each)

Salmon

1	untreated cedar plank, 12x6 inches
1	salmon fillet, about 1 inch thick (1 lb)
2	tablespoons mayonnaise or salad dressing
2	teaspoons spicy brown mustard
1	teaspoon grated lemon peel

Accompaniments

1/2	cup sour cream
1	teaspoon chopped fresh or 1/2 teaspoon dried dill weed
1	jar (3-1/2 oz) small capers, drained
1/4	cup spicy brown mustard
2	hard-cooked eggs, finely chopped
1	cup thinly sliced cucumber
32	slices cocktail rye bread

1 Soak cedar plank in water for 1 to 2 hours.

2 Heat gas or charcoal grill for indirect cooking (medium heat) as directed by manufacturer. Place salmon, skin side down, on plank. In small bowl, mix mayonnaise, 2 teaspoons mustard and the lemon peel. Brush generously over salmon.

3 Place plank with salmon on unheated side of two-burner gas grill or over drip pan on charcoal grill. (if using one-burner gas grill, cook over low heat). Cover grill; cook 25 to 30 minutes or until salmon flakes easily with fork.

4 Using spatula, remove salmon from plank to platter, or leave salmon on plank and place on wood cutting board or platter.

5 In small bowl, mix sour cream and dill weed. Place remaining accompaniments except bread in individual small bowls. Place sour cream mixture and remaining accompaniments around salmon. Serve salmon and accompaniments with bread.

Broil Directions: Set oven control to broil. Place salmon, skin side down, on rack in broiler pan. (Do not use cedar plank.) Broil with top 6 inches from heat about 15 minutes or until salmon flakes easily with fork.

High Altitude (3500-6500 ft): No change.

Nutritional Info: 1 Serving: Calories 110 (Calories from Fat 50); Total Fat 6g (Saturated Fat 2g, Trans Fat 0g); Cholesterol 50mg; Sodium 420mg; Total Carbohydrate 8g (Dietary Fiber 1g, Sugars 1g); Protein 7g. % Daily Value: Vitamin A 4%; Vitamin C 0%; Calcium 2%; Iron 4%. Exchanges: 1/2 Starch, 1 Lean Meat, 1/2 Fat. Carbohydrate Choices: 1/2.

Betty's Kitchen Tip

• Six-inch-wide cedar planks can be purchased at hardware stores; cut into 1-foot sections.

chocolate chip-pumpkin bread

Prep Time: 15 Minutes
Start to Finish: 3 Hours 10 Minutes
Servings: 2 loaves (16 servings each)

EASY

4	cups Gold Medal® all-purpose flour
2	teaspoons baking soda
1	teaspoon salt
1	teaspoon ground cinnamon
1/2	teaspoon ground nutmeg
2	cups sugar
3/4	cup butter or margarine, softened
4	eggs
1/2	cup water
1	can (15 oz) pumpkin (not pumpkin pie mix)
1	cup plus 2 tablespoons miniature semisweet chocolate chips
2	tablespoons chopped pecans
2	teaspoons sugar

1 Heat oven to 350°F. Grease bottom only of two 8x4-inch loaf pans with shortening; lightly flour (or spray bottoms of pans with cooking spray; do not flour).

2 In medium bowl, stir flour, baking soda, salt, cinnamon and nutmeg until mixed; set aside. In large bowl, beat 2 cups sugar and the butter with electric mixer on medium speed 1 to 2 minutes or until creamy. Add eggs, one at a time, beating well. Beat in water and pumpkin on low speed. Add flour mixture; beat on low speed about 1 minute or until moistened. Stir in 1 cup of the chocolate chips. Spread evenly in pans. Sprinkle tops with remaining 2 tablespoons chocolate chips, the pecans and 2 teaspoons sugar.

3 Bake 1 hour 5 minutes to 1 hour 15 minutes or until toothpick inserted in center comes out clean. Cool in pans 10 minutes; remove to cooling rack. Cool completely, about 1-1/2 hours.

High Altitude (3500-6500 ft): No change.

Nutritional Info: 1 Serving: Calories 200 (Calories from Fat 70); Total Fat 7g (Saturated Fat 4g, Trans Fat 0g); Cholesterol 40mg; Sodium 190mg; Total Carbohydrate 30g (Dietary Fiber 1g, Sugars 16g); Protein 3g. % Daily Value: Vitamin A 45%; Vitamin C 0%; Calcium 0%; Iron 6%. Exchanges: 1 Starch, 1 Other Carbohydrate, 1-1/2 Fat. Carbohydrate Choices: 2.

Betty's Kitchen Tip

• To ensure your loaf has a gently rounded top and no "lipping" at the edges, grease or spray only the bottom of the pans. It's okay if the top of your loaf has a large, lengthwise crack; this is common in quick breads.

fresh raspberry coffee cake

Prep Time: 20 Minutes
Start to Finish: 1 Hour 10 Minutes
Servings: 9

Coffee Cake

1/2	cup butter or margarine, melted
3/4	cup milk
1	teaspoon vanilla
1	egg
2	cups Gold Medal® all-purpose flour
1/2	cup granulated sugar
2	teaspoons baking powder
1/2	teaspoon salt
1	cup fresh raspberries

Glaze

1/2	cup powdered sugar
1	tablespoon butter or margarine, softened
2	to 3 teaspoons water
1/4	teaspoon almond extract

1 Heat oven to 400°F. Spray 9- or 8-inch square pan with baking spray with flour.

2 In medium bowl, beat melted butter, milk, vanilla and egg with spoon. Stir in flour, granulated sugar, baking powder and salt just until flour is moistened. Fold in raspberries. Spread in pan.

3 Bake 25 to 30 minutes or until top is golden brown and toothpick inserted in center comes out clean. Cool 20 minutes.

4 Mix glaze ingredients until thin enough to drizzle. Drizzle over warm coffee cake.

High Altitude (3500-6500 ft): No change.

Nutritional Info: 1 Serving: Calories 300 (Calories from Fat 120); Total Fat 13g (Saturated Fat 8g, Trans Fat 0g); Cholesterol 55mg; Sodium 260mg; Total Carbohydrate 42g (Dietary Fiber 1g, Sugars 19g); Protein 4g. % Daily Value: Vitamin A 8%; Vitamin C 4%; Calcium 6%; Iron 8%. Exchanges: 1 Starch, 2 Other Carbohydrate, 2-1/2 Fat. Carbohydrate Choices: 3.

Betty's Kitchen Tips

Variation: Next time, try making this coffee cake with fresh blackberries instead of raspberries.

Success Hint: This coffee cake is best served warm, but you can microwave a piece for 10 to 15 seconds on High to bring back that fresh-from-the-oven taste.

asian chicken salad lettuce wraps

Prep Time: 15 Minutes
Start to Finish: 15 Minutes
Servings: 24

EASY **QUICK**

- 2 cups finely chopped cooked chicken
- 4 medium green onions, diagonally sliced (1/4 cup)
- 1 can (8 oz) sliced water chestnuts, drained, finely chopped
- 1/2 cup spicy peanut sauce (from 7-oz bottle)
- 1 tablespoon chopped fresh mint leaves
- 1/4 teaspoon crushed red pepper flakes
- 24 small (about 3 inch) Bibb lettuce leaves (about 1-1/2 heads), breaking larger leaves into smaller size
- 1/2 cup chopped salted roasted peanuts

1 In medium bowl, mix all ingredients except lettuce and peanuts.

2 Spoon about 2 tablespoons chicken mixture onto each lettuce leaf. Sprinkle with peanuts.

High Altitude (3500-6500 ft): No change.

Nutritional Info: 1 Serving: Calories 60 (Calories from Fat 35); Total Fat 3.5g (Saturated Fat 1g, Trans Fat 0g); Cholesterol 10mg; Sodium 35mg; Total Carbohydrate 3g (Dietary Fiber 0g, Sugars 0g); Protein 5g. % Daily Value: Vitamin A 4%; Vitamin C 2%; Calcium 0%; Iron 2%. Exchanges: 1/2 Lean Meat, 1/2 Fat. Carbohydrate Choices: 0.

Betty's Kitchen Tips

Variation: Like spicy food? Increase the crushed red pepper flakes to 1/2 teaspoon.

Leftovers: If you have leftover fresh mint leaves, drop a few in a pitcher of iced tea for a refreshing summer drink.

ginger-topped pumpkin bread

Prep Time: 15 Minutes
Start to Finish: 2 Hours 35 Minutes
Servings: 2 loaves (24 servings each)

EASY LOW FAT

Bread

1	can (15 oz) pumpkin (not pumpkin pie mix)
1-2/3	cups granulated sugar
2/3	cup unsweetened applesauce
1/2	cup milk
2	teaspoons vanilla
1	cup fat-free egg product or 2 eggs plus 4 egg whites
3	cups Gold Medal® all-purpose flour
2	teaspoons baking soda
1	teaspoon salt
1	teaspoon ground cinnamon
1/2	teaspoon baking powder
1/2	teaspoon ground cloves

Glaze and Topping

2/3	cup powdered sugar
2	to 3 teaspoons warm water
1/4	teaspoon vanilla
3	tablespoons finely chopped crystallized ginger

1 Move oven rack to low position so tops of pans will be in center of oven. Heat oven to 350°F. Grease bottoms only of 2 (8x4- or 9x5-inch) loaf pans with shortening, or spray with cooking spray.

2 In large bowl, mix pumpkin, granulated sugar, applesauce, milk, vanilla and egg product. Stir in remaining bread ingredients. Pour into pans.

3 Bake 1 hour to 1 hour 10 minutes or until toothpick inserted in center comes out clean. Cool 10 minutes. Loosen sides of loaves from pans; remove to cooling rack. Cool completely, about 1 hour.

4 In small bowl, mix powdered sugar, warm water and 1/4 teaspoon vanilla until thin enough to drizzle. Drizzle over loaves. Sprinkle with ginger.

High Altitude (3500-6500 ft): No change.

Nutritional Info: 1 Serving: Calories 70 (Calories from Fat 0); Total Fat 0g (Saturated Fat 0g, Trans Fat 0g); Cholesterol 0mg; Sodium 120mg; Total Carbohydrate 16g (Dietary Fiber 0g, Sugars 9g); Protein 1g. % Daily Value: Vitamin A 30%; Vitamin C 0%; Calcium 0%; Iron 4%. Exchanges: 1/2 Starch, 1/2 Other Carbohydrate. Carbohydrate Choices: 1.

Betty's Kitchen Tips

Purchasing: You will find crystallized ginger in glass jars or plastic bags with the other baking ingredients at the grocery store.

Health Twist: Applesauce is the ingredient that adds moistness instead of oil in this updated favorite; ginger adds a new look and taste.

dried cherry-almond bread

Prep Time: 30 Minutes
Start to Finish: 3 Hours 15 Minutes
Servings: 1 loaf (24 servings)

1-1/2	cups boiling water
2	bags (5.5 oz each) dried cherries
1	cup packed brown sugar
1/2	cup butter or margarine, softened
2	eggs
1/2	teaspoon almond extract
1-3/4	cups Gold Medal® all-purpose flour

1-1/2	teaspoons baking powder
1/2	teaspoon salt
1-1/2	cups slivered almonds

Glaze

1/2	cup powdered sugar
1/4	teaspoon almond extract
1	to 2 teaspoons milk

1 In medium bowl, pour boiling water over cherries; let stand 20 minutes. Drain. Pat dry with paper towels. Heat oven to 325°F. Spray 9x5-inch loaf pan with baking spray with flour.

2 In large bowl, beat brown sugar and softened butter with electric mixer on medium speed until well mixed. Beat in eggs and 1/2 teaspoon almond extract.

Stir in flour, baking powder and salt just until dry ingredients are moistened. Stir in almonds and cherries. Pour into pan.

3 Bake 1 hour 10 minutes to 1 hour 20 minutes or until toothpick inserted in center comes out clean and top is dark golden brown. Cool 10 minutes on cooling rack. Loosen sides of loaf from pan; remove from pan, and place top side up on cooling rack. Cool completely, about 1 hour.

4 In small bowl, mix glaze ingredients until smooth. Drizzle over cooled bread. Wrap tightly; store at room temperature. Cut loaf into 12 slices; cut each slice in half.

High Altitude (3500-6500 ft): No change.

Nutritional Info: 1 Serving: Calories 240 (Calories from Fat 100); Total Fat 12g (Saturated Fat 5g, Trans Fat 0g); Cholesterol 40mg; Sodium 140mg; Total Carbohydrate 31g (Dietary Fiber 1g, Sugars 21g); Protein 3g. % Daily Value: Vitamin A 6%; Vitamin C 0%; Calcium 6%; Iron 6%. Exchanges: 1 Starch, 1 Other Carbohydrate, 2-1/2 Fat. Carbohydrate Choices: 2.

fresh herb veggie dip

Prep Time: 30 Minutes
Start to Finish: 30 Minutes
Servings: 32 (1 tablespoon dip and 3 crackers each)

QUICK

1	container (8 oz) whipped cream cheese spread
2	tablespoons finely chopped fresh chives
1	tablespoon finely chopped fresh oregano leaves
1	tablespoon finely chopped fresh thyme leaves
1/8	teaspoon ground red pepper (cayenne)

Dash salt

1/2	cup shredded carrot (about 1 small)
1/4	cup sliced green onions (4 medium)
1/4	cup thinly sliced, quartered radishes (2 medium)
96	small baked wheat snack crackers (about 6.6 oz)

1 In medium bowl, mix cream cheese spread, chives, oregano, thyme, red pepper and salt until well blended. Spread in 10-inch circle on 12-inch serving plate.

2 Layer cheese mixture with carrot, onions and radishes. Serve with crackers.

High Altitude (3500-6500 ft): No change.

Nutritional Info: 1 Serving: Calories 60 (Calories from Fat 35); Total Fat 3.5g (Saturated Fat 2g, Trans Fat 0g); Cholesterol 10mg; Sodium 65mg; Total Carbohydrate 4g (Dietary Fiber 0g, Sugars 0g); Protein 1g. % Daily Value: Vitamin A 8%; Vitamin C 0%; Calcium 0%; Iron 0%. Exchanges: 1/2 Starch, 1/2 Fat. Carbohydrate Choices: 0.

Betty's Kitchen Tips

Variation: If you love garlic, add 1 finely chopped garlic clove.

Do-Ahead: Get a jump-start on this appetizer by making the cheese mixture a day ahead—the flavor actually improves. Prepare the fresh vegetables, and store in individual plastic bags in the refrigerator. Assemble the dip up to 2 hours before serving.

almond-mocha muffins

Prep Time: 15 Minutes
Start to Finish: 50 Minutes
Servings: 12 muffins

EASY

2	cups Gold Medal® all-purpose flour
2	tablespoons unsweetened baking cocoa
2-1/2	teaspoons baking powder
1/2	teaspoon salt
1/2	cup packed brown sugar
1	cup milk
1/3	cup vegetable oil

1	tablespoon instant coffee granules or crystals
1	egg
1/2	cup semisweet chocolate chips
1/2	cup chopped roasted almonds

Glaze

1/2	cup semisweet chocolate chips
1/4	teaspoon vegetable oil

1 Heat oven to 400°F. Grease or spray bottoms only of 12 regular-size muffin cups, or place paper baking cup in each muffin cup.

2 In medium bowl, mix flour, cocoa, baking powder and salt; set aside. In large bowl, beat brown sugar, milk, oil, coffee and egg with fork or wire whisk. Stir in flour mixture just until flour is moistened. Stir in chocolate chips and almonds. Divide batter evenly among muffin cups.

3 Bake 18 to 20 minutes or until toothpick inserted in center comes out clean. Immediately remove muffins from pan to cooling rack. Cool 15 minutes.

4 In small microwavable bowl, microwave glaze ingredients uncovered on High about 45 seconds, stirring every 15 seconds, until chips can be stirred smooth. Drizzle over muffins.

High Altitude (3500-6500 ft): No change.

Nutritional Info: 1 Muffin: Calories 300 (Calories from Fat 130); Total Fat 14g (Saturated Fat 4g, Trans Fat 0g); Cholesterol 20mg; Sodium 220mg; Total Carbohydrate 37g (Dietary Fiber 2g, Sugars 18g); Protein 5g. % Daily Value: Vitamin A 0%; Vitamin C 0%; Calcium 10%; Iron 10%. Exchanges: 1-1/2 Starch, 1 Other Carbohydrate, 2-1/2 Fat. Carbohydrate Choices: 2-1/2.

wasabi shrimp cocktail

Prep Time: 20 Minutes
Start to Finish: 20 Minutes
Servings: 12

QUICK LOW FAT

- 12 cooked large (21 to 30 count) deveined peeled shrimp with tails left on (about 1/2 lb)
- 2 tablespoons cream cheese, softened
- 2 teaspoons wasabi paste
- 3 teaspoons chopped fresh cilantro
- 1/4 cup seafood cocktail sauce

1 With sharp knife, cut along back curve of each shrimp, not cutting through to other side. Pat dry with paper towels.

2 In small bowl, mix cream cheese, wasabi paste and 1 teaspoon of the chopped cilantro. Spread each shrimp open; fill with cream cheese mixture and sprinkle lightly with remaining cilantro. Place on serving plate. Serve with cocktail sauce.

High Altitude (3500-6500 ft): No change.

Nutritional Info: 1 Serving: Calories 20 (Calories from Fat 10); Total Fat 1g (Saturated Fat 0.5g, Trans Fat 0g); Cholesterol 15mg; Sodium 85mg; Total Carbohydrate 2g (Dietary Fiber 0g, Sugars 1g); Protein 1g. % Daily Value: Vitamin A 2%; Vitamin C 2%; Calcium 0%; Iron 0%. Exchanges: Free. Carbohydrate Choices: 0.

Betty's Kitchen Tips

Purchasing: Large to extra-large shrimp are a good choice for shrimp cocktail. If one size is on sale at your grocery store, purchase that one. The cream cheese mixture will fill fewer extra-large shrimp.

Success Hint: Look for wasabi paste in tubes in the Asian-foods section of the grocery store. Refrigerate after opening.

easy cranberry-orange scones

Prep Time: 20 Minutes
Start to Finish: 1 Hour
Servings: 8 scones

1	cup Gold Medal® whole wheat flour		1/3	cup cold butter, cut into 8 pieces
1	cup Gold Medal® all-purpose flour		1/3	cup milk
1/4	cup granulated sugar		1/4	cup orange juice
2	teaspoons grated orange peel		1/2	cup sweetened dried cranberries
1-1/2	teaspoons cream of tartar		1/3	cup powdered sugar
3/4	teaspoon baking soda		2	to 3 teaspoons milk
1/4	teaspoon salt			

1 Heat oven to 350°F. In large bowl, mix flours, 1/4 cup granulated sugar, the orange peel, cream of tartar, baking soda and salt. Cut in butter, using pastry blender (or pulling 2 table knives through ingredients in opposite directions), until mixture looks like fine crumbs. Stir in 1/3 cup milk, the orange juice and cranberries just until dry ingredients are moistened.

2 On ungreased cookie sheet, pat dough into 8-inch round. Cut into 8 wedges; do not separate.

3 Bake 20 to 25 minutes or until golden brown. Cool 5 minutes; remove from cookie sheet to cooling rack. Cool 10 minutes.

4 In small bowl, mix powdered sugar and 2 to 3 teaspoons milk until thin enough to drizzle. Drizzle over warm scones. Serve warm or cool.

High Altitude (3500-6500 ft): No change.

Nutritional Info: 1 Scone: Calories 260 (Calories from Fat 80); Total Fat 8g (Saturated Fat 5g, Trans Fat 0g); Cholesterol 20mg; Sodium 250mg; Total Carbohydrate 42g (Dietary Fiber 3g, Sugars 18g); Protein 4g. % Daily Value: Vitamin A 6%; Vitamin C 2%; Calcium 2%; Iron 8%. Exchanges: 1 Starch, 2 Other Carbohydrate, 1-1/2 Fat. Carbohydrate Choices: 3.

Betty's Kitchen Tip

• Use dried blueberries instead of the cranberries if you'd like. You can also substitute grated lemon peel for the orange peel.

tuna salad bruschetta

Prep Time: 20 Minutes
Start to Finish: 1 Hour 20 Minutes
Servings: 24

- 1 can (5 or 6 oz) albacore chunk white tuna in water, well drained
- 1/4 cup thinly sliced green onions (4 medium)
- 1/4 cup finely chopped red bell pepper
- 1/4 cup finely chopped pitted kalamata olives
- 3 tablespoons French vinaigrette or olive oil and vinegar dressing
- 1/2 cup thinly sliced or finely shredded romaine lettuce
- 24 slices (1/4 inch thick) baguette French bread

1 In medium bowl, gently fold together all ingredients except lettuce and bread. Cover; refrigerate at least 1 hour before serving.

2 Just before serving, stir lettuce into tuna mixture. Serve as topping for bread slices.

High Altitude (3500-6500 ft): No change.

Nutritional Info: 1 Serving: Calories 35 (Calories from Fat 10); Total Fat 1g (Saturated Fat 0g, Trans Fat 0g); Cholesterol 0mg; Sodium 105mg; Total Carbohydrate 4g (Dietary Fiber 0g, Sugars 0g); Protein 2g. % Daily Value: Vitamin A 2%; Vitamin C 4%; Calcium 0%; Iron 2%. Exchanges: 1/2 Lean Meat. Carbohydrate Choices: 0.

LOW FAT

Betty's Kitchen Tips

Substitution: Albacore tuna has a very mild flavor and firm texture. You could substitute chunk light tuna, but the flavor will be stronger. For an extra-special appetizer, substitute a can of lump crabmeat.

How-To: Thinly slice lettuce by rolling up a few leaves and slicing across with a sharp knife, or purchase a bag of already shredded lettuce from the produce section of the grocery store.

cranberry-filled sour cream coffee cake with orange glaze

Prep Time: 25 Minutes
Start to Finish: 2 Hours 10 Minutes
Servings: 16

Cranberry Filling
- 2 cups fresh cranberries
- 1/2 cup sugar
- 1 tablespoon grated orange peel

Coffee Cake
- 3 cups Gold Medal® all-purpose flour
- 1-1/2 teaspoons baking powder
- 1-1/2 teaspoons baking soda
- 3/4 teaspoon salt
- 1-1/2 cups granulated sugar
- 3/4 cup butter, softened
- 1-1/2 teaspoons vanilla
- 3 eggs
- 1-1/2 cups sour cream

Orange Glaze
- 3/4 cup powdered sugar
- 2 to 3 teaspoons orange juice

1 Heat oven to 350°F. Grease or spray 12-cup fluted tube cake pan.

2 In food processor, place filling ingredients. Cover; process until finely chopped. Set aside. In large bowl, stir flour, baking powder, baking soda and salt until well mixed; set aside.

3 In another large bowl, beat granulated sugar, butter, vanilla and eggs with electric mixer on medium speed 2 minutes, scraping bowl occasionally. Beat about one-fourth of the flour mixture and sour cream at a time alternately into sugar mixture on low speed until blended.

4 Spread one-half of the batter (about 3 cups) in pan; spoon cranberry filling over batter (do not touch filling to side of pan). Top with remaining batter; spread evenly.

5 Bake 55 to 65 minutes or until toothpick inserted near center comes out clean. Cool 10 minutes in pan on cooling rack. Remove from pan to cooling rack. Cool 20 minutes. In small bowl, mix glaze ingredients until thin enough to drizzle. Drizzle over coffee cake. Serve warm or cool.

High Altitude (3500-6500 ft): No change.

Nutritional Info: 1 Serving: Calories 350 (Calories from Fat 130); Total Fat 14g (Saturated Fat 8g, Trans Fat 0g); Cholesterol 75mg; Sodium 360mg; Total Carbohydrate 51g (Dietary Fiber 1g, Sugars 32g); Protein 4g. % Daily Value: Vitamin A 10%; Vitamin C 2%; Calcium 6%; Iron 8%. Exchanges: 1 Starch, 2-1/2 Other Carbohydrate, 2-1/2 Fat. Carbohydrate Choices: 3-1/2.

muffuletta slices

Prep Time: 15 Minutes
Start to Finish: 15 Minutes
Servings: 18

EASY QUICK

1 baguette French bread (16 oz; about 20 inches long), cut in half horizontally

1/4 cup chives-and-onion cream cheese spread (from 8-oz container)

1 jar (6-1/2 oz) marinated artichoke hearts, well drained, patted dry and finely chopped

1/4 cup basil pesto

1/2 cup roasted red bell peppers (from 12-oz jar), patted dry, cut into 1-1/2-inch strips

1/4 lb thinly sliced salami

Assorted large pitted kalamata and pimiento-stuffed green olives, if desired

1 Remove some of soft bread from center of top half of baguette to make a long, narrow well. If desired, cut off about 1/2 inch of pointed ends of baguette.

2 In small bowl, mix cream cheese spread and artichokes. Generously spread mixture in long, narrow well in top half of baguette. Spread pesto over cream cheese mixture.

3 Place roasted pepper strips on bottom half of baguette. Fold salami slices in half; layer diagonally over peppers, overlapping slices slightly.

4 Place top half of baguette, pesto side down, over salami; press halves together well. Thread olives onto toothpicks or cocktail picks; insert toothpicks through all layers at 1-inch intervals. Cut between toothpicks into 18 slices.

High Altitude (3500-6500 ft): No change.

Nutritional Info: 1 Serving: Calories 140 (Calories from Fat 50); Total Fat 6g (Saturated Fat 2g, Trans Fat 0g); Cholesterol 10mg; Sodium 380mg; Total Carbohydrate 16g (Dietary Fiber 1g, Sugars 3g); Protein 5g. % Daily Value: Vitamin A 4%; Vitamin C 15%; Calcium 2%; Iron 6%. Exchanges: 1 Starch, 1 Fat. Carbohydrate Choices: 1.

Betty's Kitchen Tips

Do-Ahead: This appetizer loaf can be assembled several hours ahead. Wrap it tightly in plastic wrap and refrigerate until you're ready to cut and serve.

Variation: Substitute thinly sliced turkey or other deli meat for the salami, if you like.

brown bread muffins

Prep Time: 10 Minutes
Start to Finish: 30 Minutes
Servings: 12 muffins

1-1/2	cups Gold Medal® all-purpose flour
1/2	cup cornmeal
3/4	cup packed brown sugar
1	teaspoon baking powder
1/2	teaspoon baking soda
1/2	teaspoon salt
1	cup buttermilk
1/4	cup butter or margarine, melted
2	tablespoons molasses
1	egg
1/2	cup currants or raisins

1 Heat oven to 400°F. Place paper baking cup in each of 12 regular-size muffin cups; spray baking cups.

2 In medium bowl, mix flour, cornmeal, brown sugar, baking powder, baking soda and salt; set aside. In large bowl, beat buttermilk, melted butter, molasses and egg. Stir in flour mixture just until flour is moistened. Stir in currants. Divide batter evenly among muffin cups.

3 Bake 17 to 20 minutes or until toothpick inserted in center comes out clean. Immediately remove muffins from pan to cooling rack. Serve warm.

High Altitude (3500-6500 ft): No change.

Nutritional Info: 1 Muffin: Calories 220 (Calories from Fat 45); Total Fat 5g (Saturated Fat 3g, Trans Fat 0g); Cholesterol 30mg; Sodium 250mg; Total Carbohydrate 39g (Dietary Fiber 1g, Sugars 21g); Protein 3g. % Daily Value: Vitamin A 4%; Vitamin C 0%; Calcium 8%; Iron 8%. Exchanges: 1 Starch, 1-1/2 Other Carbohydrate, 1 Fat. Carbohydrate Choices: 2-1/2.

cinnamon-topped zucchini bread

Prep Time: 15 Minutes
Start to Finish: 3 Hours 25 Minutes
Servings: 2 loaves (16 servings each)

EASY

Bread

3	cups shredded zucchini (2 to 3 medium)
1-2/3	cups sugar
2/3	cup vegetable oil
2	teaspoons vanilla
4	eggs
3	cups Gold Medal® whole wheat flour
2	teaspoons baking soda
1	teaspoon salt
1	teaspoon ground cinnamon
1/2	teaspoon baking powder

Topping

3	tablespoons sugar
1/2	teaspoon ground cinnamon
1	tablespoon cold butter

1 Move oven rack to low position so tops of pans will be in center of oven. Heat oven to 350°F. Grease bottoms only of 2 (8x4-inch) loaf pans or 1 (9x5-inch) loaf pan with shortening, or spray with cooking spray.

2 In large bowl, stir zucchini, sugar, oil, vanilla and eggs until well mixed. Stir in remaining bread ingredients; mix well. Pour into pan(s). In small bowl, mix topping ingredients with fork until crumbly. Sprinkle over batter in pan(s).

3 Bake 8-inch loaves 50 to 60 minutes, 9-inch loaf 1 hour 10 minutes to 1 hour 20 minutes, or until toothpick inserted in center comes out clean. Cool in pan(s) on cooling rack 10 minutes.

4 Loosen sides of loaves from pan(s); remove, and place top side up on cooling rack. Cool completely, about 2 hours, before slicing. Wrap tightly and store at room temperature up to 4 days, or refrigerate up to 10 days.

High Altitude (3500-6500 ft): No change.

Nutritional Info: 1 Serving: Calories 140 (Calories from Fat 50); Total Fat 6g (Saturated Fat 1g, Trans Fat 0g); Cholesterol 25mg; Sodium 170mg; Total Carbohydrate 20g (Dietary Fiber 1g, Sugars 12g); Protein 2g. % Daily Value: Vitamin A 0%; Vitamin C 0%; Calcium 0%; Iron 4%. Exchanges: 1/2 Starch, 1 Other Carbohydrate, 1 Fat. Carbohydrate Choices: 1.

Betty's Kitchen Tip

• To reduce the fat, substitute 1/3 cup vegetable oil and 1/3 cup applesauce for the 2/3 cup vegetable oil.

ginger-date scones

Prep Time: 20 Minutes
Start to Finish: 35 Minutes
Servings: 10 scones

- -

2-1/4 cups Gold Medal® all-purpose flour
1/4 cup packed brown sugar
1-1/2 teaspoons baking powder
1/2 teaspoon baking soda
1/4 teaspoon salt
1/2 cup cold butter or margarine, cut into 8 pieces
1 cup buttermilk
1/2 cup chopped dates
1/4 cup candied ginger, chopped
1 tablespoon coarse sugar

- -

1 Heat oven to 425°F. In medium bowl, mix flour, brown sugar, baking powder, baking soda and salt. With pastry blender or pulling 2 table knives in opposite directions, cut in butter until mixture looks like fine crumbs. Stir in buttermilk until dough leaves side of bowl and forms a ball. Stir in dates and ginger.

2 On ungreased cookie sheet, drop dough by about 1/3 cupfuls about 1 inch apart. Sprinkle with coarse sugar.

3 Bake 12 to 15 minutes or until golden brown. Immediately remove from cookie sheet. Serve warm.

High Altitude (3500-6500 ft): No change.

Nutritional Info: 1 Scone: Calories 260 (Calories from Fat 90); Total Fat 10g (Saturated Fat 6g, Trans Fat 0g); Cholesterol 25mg; Sodium 280mg; Total Carbohydrate 38g (Dietary Fiber 1g, Sugars 13g); Protein 4g. % Daily Value: Vitamin A 6%; Vitamin C 0%; Calcium 10%; Iron 8%. Exchanges: 1 Starch, 1-1/2 Other Carbohydrate, 2 Fat. Carbohydrate Choices: 2-1/2.

Betty's Kitchen Tip

• If you don't have dates on hand, you can substitute any variety of raisins.

pumpkin-cranberry muffins

Prep Time: 15 Minutes
Start to Finish: 40 Minutes
Servings: 12 muffins

EASY

2	cups Gold Medal® all-purpose flour	1	cup canned pumpkin (not pumpkin pie filling)
3/4	cup sugar	1/2	cup vegetable oil
3	teaspoons baking powder	2	eggs
1	teaspoon ground cinnamon	1	cup sweetened dried cranberries
1/2	teaspoon ground ginger	1/2	cup chopped pecans
1/4	teaspoon salt		Coarse sugar, if desired

1 Heat oven to 400°F. Grease 12 regular-size muffin cups with shortening, or line with paper baking cups.

2 In large bowl, mix flour, sugar, baking powder, cinnamon, ginger and salt. Stir in pumpkin, oil, eggs, cranberries and pecans just until moistened. Divide batter evenly among muffin cups. Sprinkle coarse sugar evenly over batter in each cup.

3 Bake 20 to 25 minutes or until toothpick inserted in center comes out clean. Remove muffins from pan to cooling rack. Serve warm.

High Altitude (3500-6500 ft): No change.

Nutritional Info: 1 Muffin: Calories 300 (Calories from Fat 120); Total Fat 14g (Saturated Fat 2g, Trans Fat 0g); Cholesterol 35mg; Sodium 180mg; Total Carbohydrate 40g (Dietary Fiber 2g, Sugars 21g); Protein 4g. % Daily Value: Vitamin A 60%; Vitamin C 0%; Calcium 8%; Iron 10%. Exchanges: 1-1/2 Starch, 1 Other Carbohydrate, 2-1/2 Fat. Carbohydrate Choices: 2-1/2.

Betty's Kitchen Tips

Variation: Instead of cranberries, try making these muffins with dried cherries.

Success Hint: Take care not to overmix the batter. Overmixing can result in tough muffins with peaked tops and tunnels inside.

bacon-tomato dip

Prep Time: 15 Minutes
Start to Finish: 15 Minutes
Servings: 12 (2 tablespoons dip and 3 vegetable pieces each)

EASY QUICK

- 1 container (8 oz) reduced-fat sour cream
- 1/4 cup reduced-fat mayonnaise or salad dressing
- 2 tablespoons cooked real bacon pieces (from 2.8-to 3-oz package or jar)
- 1 medium tomato, seeded, diced (3/4 cup)
- 2 medium green onions, sliced (2 tablespoons)

Assorted fresh vegetables (bell pepper strips, broccoli florets, cauliflower florets, cucumber slices and/or radishes)

1 In medium bowl, mix sour cream and mayonnaise. Stir in bacon, tomato and onions.

2 Serve with cut-up fresh vegetables for dipping.

High Altitude (3500-6500 ft): No change.

Nutritional Info: 1 Serving: Calories 50 (Calories from Fat 40); Total Fat 4.5g (Saturated Fat 2g, Trans Fat 0g); Cholesterol 10mg; Sodium 60mg; Total Carbohydrate 2g (Dietary Fiber 0g, Sugars 1g); Protein 1g. % Daily Value: Vitamin A 4%; Vitamin C 4%; Calcium 2%; Iron 0%. Exchanges: 1/2 Vegetable, 1 Fat. Carbohydrate Choices: 0.

Betty's Kitchen Tips

Purchasing: Packages of cooked real bacon pieces are found near the salad dressings in the grocery store. If you prefer, you can cook and crumble bacon yourself.

How-To: To seed the tomato, cut it in half and squeeze gently over the sink to remove seeds and juice. Use your fingers to remove any seeds that remain in the tomato.

glorious morning muffins

Prep Time: 20 Minutes
Start to Finish: 50 Minutes
Servings: 18 muffins

2	eggs
3/4	cup vegetable oil
1/4	cup milk
2	teaspoons vanilla
1	cup Gold Medal® all-purpose flour
1	cup Gold Medal® whole wheat flour
1	cup packed brown sugar
2	teaspoons baking soda

2	teaspoons ground cinnamon
1/2	teaspoon salt
1-1/2	cups shredded carrots (2 to 3 medium)
1	cup shredded peeled apple
1/2	cup coconut
1/2	cup raisins
3/4	cup sliced almonds

1 Heat oven to 350°F. Place paper baking cup in each of 18 regular-size muffin cups, or grease with shortening. In large bowl, beat eggs, oil, milk and vanilla with wire whisk until well blended. Add flours, brown sugar, baking soda, cinnamon and salt; stir just until dry ingredients are moistened. With spoon, stir in carrots, apple, coconut, raisins and 1/2 cup of the almonds.

2 Divide batter among muffin cups, filling each about 3/4 full. Sprinkle remaining 1/4 cup almonds over batter.

3 Bake 20 to 25 minutes or until toothpick inserted in center comes out clean. Cool 5 minutes; remove from muffin cups.

High Altitude (3500-6500 ft): No change.

Nutritional Info: 1 Muffin: Calories 250 (Calories from Fat 110); Total Fat 13g (Saturated Fat 2.5g, Trans Fat 0g); Cholesterol 25mg; Sodium 230mg; Total Carbohydrate 29g (Dietary Fiber 2g, Sugars 17g); Protein 3g. % Daily Value: Vitamin A 30%; Vitamin C 0%; Calcium 4%; Iron 8%. Exchanges: 1 Starch, 1 Other Carbohydrate, 2-1/2 Fat. Carbohydrate Choices: 2.

Betty's Kitchen Tip

• These muffins freeze well. To serve, thaw at room temperature, or heat in microwave to warm.

cozy
MAIN DISHES

p. 49

41

57

58

country french chicken and rice

Prep Time: 25 Minutes
Start to Finish: 3 Hours 25 Minutes
Servings: 8

1/4 cup chopped oil-packed sun-dried tomatoes, drained
2 tablespoons herbes de Provence
2 tablespoons olive oil
2 tablespoons lemon juice
1 tablespoon finely chopped garlic
1 teaspoon salt
8 bone-in chicken thighs, skin and fat removed (about 2 lb)

1-1/2 cups sliced mushrooms
1 cup uncooked regular long-grain white rice
1 medium carrot, shredded (3/4 cup)
2 cups boiling water
1 tablespoon chopped fresh Italian (flat-leaf) parsley
2 teaspoons grated lemon peel

1 In heavy-duty 1-gallon resealable food-storage plastic bag, mix tomatoes, herbes de Provence, oil, lemon juice, garlic and 1/2 teaspoon of the salt. Add chicken thighs and mushrooms; seal bag. Turn to coat thighs and mushrooms in marinade. Refrigerate 2 to 24 hours.

2 Heat oven to 375°F. Spray 13x9-inch (3-quart) baking dish with cooking spray.

3 Place rice, carrot and remaining 1/2 teaspoon salt in baking dish; stir in boiling water. Place chicken thighs, mushrooms and marinade evenly over rice mixture.

4 Cover with foil. Bake 50 to 60 minutes or until liquid is absorbed and juice of chicken is no longer pink when centers of thickest pieces are cut. Sprinkle with parsley and lemon peel.

High Altitude (3500-6500 ft): No change.

Nutritional Info: 1 Serving: Calories 260 (Calories from Fat 90); Total Fat 10g (Saturated Fat 2.5g, Trans Fat 0g); Cholesterol 45mg; Sodium 360mg; Total Carbohydrate 23g (Dietary Fiber 1g, Sugars 1g); Protein 18g. % Daily Value: Vitamin A 40%; Vitamin C 6%; Calcium 4%; Iron 20%. Exchanges: 1-1/2 Starch, 2 Lean Meat, 1/2 Fat. Carbohydrate Choices: 1-1/2.

Betty's Kitchen Tip

• If herbes de Provence is not available, use any combination of dried basil, fennel seed, lavender, marjoram, rosemary, sage, summer savory, tarragon and/or thyme.

roasted tilapia and vegetables

Prep Time: 15 Minutes
Start to Finish: 35 Minutes
Servings: 4

EASY

- 1/2 lb fresh asparagus spears, cut in half
- 2 small zucchini, halved lengthwise, cut into 1/2-inch pieces
- 1 red bell pepper, cut into 1/2-inch strips
- 1 large onion, cut into 1/2-inch wedges, separated
- 2 tablespoons olive oil
- 2 teaspoons Montreal steak seasoning
- 4 tilapia fillets (about 1-1/2 lb)
- 1 tablespoon butter or margarine, melted
- 1/2 teaspoon paprika

1 Heat oven to 450°F. In large bowl, mix asparagus, zucchini, bell pepper, onion and oil. Sprinkle with 1 teaspoon of the steak seasoning; toss to coat. Spread vegetables in ungreased 15x10x1-inch pan. Place on lower oven rack in oven; bake 5 minutes.

2 Meanwhile, spray 13x9-inch (3-quart) glass baking dish with cooking spray. Pat tilapia fillets dry with paper towels. Brush with butter; sprinkle with remaining 1 teaspoon steak seasoning and paprika. Place in baking dish.

3 Place baking dish on middle rack in oven. Bake fish and vegetables 17 to 18 minutes longer or until fish flakes easily with fork and vegetables are tender.

High Altitude (3500-6500 ft): No change.

Nutritional Info: 1 Serving: Calories 290 (Calories from Fat 110); Total Fat 12g (Saturated Fat 3.5g, Trans Fat 0g); Cholesterol 100mg; Sodium 520mg; Total Carbohydrate 11g (Dietary Fiber 3g, Sugars 5g); Protein 35g. % Daily Value: Vitamin A 40%; Vitamin C 45%; Calcium 6%; Iron 10%. Exchanges: 2 Vegetable, 4 Lean Meat, 1/2 Fat. Carbohydrate Choices: 1.

Betty's Kitchen Tip

- Any firm white fish fillets can be used. Baking time will vary depending on the thickness of the fillets.

make-ahead cheeseburger lasagna

Prep Time: 35 Minutes
Start to Finish: 10 Hours 5 Minutes
Servings: 8

1-1/2   lb lean (at least 80%) ground beef
3   tablespoons instant minced onion
1   can (15 oz) tomato sauce
1-1/2   cups water
1/2   cup ketchup
1   tablespoon yellow mustard
1   egg
1   container (15 oz) ricotta cheese

2   cups shredded Cheddar-American cheese blend (8 oz)
12   uncooked lasagna noodles
1   cup shredded Cheddar cheese (4 oz)
1   cup shredded lettuce
1   medium tomato, sliced, if desired
1/2   cup dill pickle slices, if desired

1 Spray 13x9-inch (3-quart) baking dish with cooking spray. In 12-inch nonstick skillet, cook beef and onion over medium-high heat 5 to 7 minutes, stirring frequently, until beef is brown; drain. Stir in tomato sauce, water, ketchup and mustard. Simmer 5 minutes, stirring occasionally.

2 Meanwhile, in medium bowl, beat egg with fork or wire whisk. Stir in ricotta cheese and 2 cups of the cheese blend.

3 Spread 1 cup beef mixture over bottom of baking dish. Top with 4 uncooked noodles. Spread half of the ricotta mixture over noodles; top with 1-1/2 cups beef mixture. Repeat layers once with 4 noodles, remaining ricotta mixture and 1-1/2 cups beef mixture. Top with remaining 4 noodles, beef mixture and 1 cup Cheddar cheese. Cover with foil; refrigerate at least 8 hours or overnight.

4 Heat oven to 350°F. Bake lasagna, covered, 45 minutes. Uncover; bake 25 to 35 minutes longer or until bubbly. Remove from oven. Cover with foil; let stand 5 to 10 minutes before cutting.

5 Just before serving, top with lettuce, tomato and pickles. Serve with additional ketchup if desired.

High Altitude (3500-6500 ft): Use 1-3/4 cups water.

Nutritional Info: 1 Serving: Calories 570 (Calories from Fat 270); Total Fat 29g (Saturated Fat 16g, Trans Fat 1g); Cholesterol 140mg; Sodium 1050mg; Total Carbohydrate 38g (Dietary Fiber 3g, Sugars 9g); Protein 38g. % Daily Value: Vitamin A 25%; Vitamin C 8%; Calcium 40%; Iron 20%. Exchanges: 2 Starch, 1/2 Other Carbohydrate, 4-1/2 Medium-Fat Meat, 1 Fat. Carbohydrate Choices: 2-1/2.

turkey tetrazzini

Prep Time: 25 Minutes
Start to Finish: 1 Hour
Servings: 6

- 1/2 lb uncooked spaghetti, broken into thirds
- 5 tablespoons butter or margarine
- 1/2 cup chopped onion (1 medium)
- 1 bell pepper, chopped
- 1 package (8 oz) fresh button mushrooms, quartered
- 1/3 cup dry sherry
- 2 containers (10 oz each) refrigerated reduced-fat Alfredo pasta sauce
- 1/2 cup plus 2 tablespoons finely shredded Parmesan cheese
- 3 cups cut-up cooked turkey
- 1/2 cup bread crumbs
- 1/2 cup sliced almonds

1 Heat oven to 350°F. Spray 13x9-inch (3-quart) baking dish with cooking spray. Cook and drain spaghetti as directed on package using minimum cook time. In 4-quart Dutch oven or saucepan, melt 3 tablespoons of the butter over medium heat. Cook and stir onion in butter 3 minutes or until onion begins to soften. Stir in bell pepper and mushrooms. Cook and stir 5 to 8 minutes longer or until vegetables are tender.

2 Stir sherry, Alfredo sauce and 1/2 cup of the cheese into mushroom mixture. Cook and stir about 2 minutes or just until hot and ingredients are blended. Stir in turkey and spaghetti. Spoon into baking dish.

3 In small bowl, stir together bread crumbs, remaining 2 tablespoons butter and remaining 2 tablespoons cheese. Sprinkle crumbs and almonds evenly over mushroom mixture. Bake 30 to 35 minutes or until hot and topping is golden brown.

High Altitude (3500-6500 ft): No change.

Nutritional Info: 1 Serving: Calories 660 (Calories from Fat 300); Total Fat 33g (Saturated Fat 16g, Trans Fat 1g); Cholesterol 125mg; Sodium 860mg; Total Carbohydrate 50g (Dietary Fiber 5g, Sugars 7g); Protein 39g. % Daily Value: Vitamin A 30%; Vitamin C 30%; Calcium 35%; Iron 15%. Exchanges: 3 Starch, 1 Vegetable, 4 Lean Meat, 4 Fat. Carbohydrate Choices: 3.

Betty's Kitchen Tips

Substitution: Linguini or fettuccini can be substituted for the spaghetti.
Success Hint: Serve with spinach salad.

philly cheese and ground beef casserole

Prep Time: 20 Minutes
Start to Finish: 1 Hour
Servings: 8

1-1/2	lb lean (at least 80%) ground beef
1	package (8 oz) sliced mushrooms
1	teaspoon salt
1/2	teaspoon pepper
8	slices (1 oz each) provolone cheese
2	tablespoons butter or margarine

2	large onions, halved and thinly sliced into wedges
2	medium red bell peppers, cut into strips
2	cloves garlic, finely chopped
1	can (16.3 oz) Pillsbury® Grands!® Homestyle original biscuits

1 Heat oven to 350°F. Spray 13x9-inch (3-quart) baking dish with cooking spray.

2 In 12-inch skillet, cook beef, mushrooms, salt and pepper over medium-high heat 7 to 9 minutes, stirring frequently, until beef is thoroughly cooked; drain. Place in baking dish. Arrange cheese over beef mixture, overlapping slices if needed.

3 In same skillet, melt butter over medium-high heat. Add onions and bell peppers.

4 Separate dough into 8 biscuits. On lightly floured surface, pat biscuits into 5-inch circles. Arrange the biscuits over the vegetable mixture.

Cook over medium-high heat 3 to 5 minutes, stirring frequently, until peppers are crisp-tender. Stir in garlic; cook 1 to 2 minutes longer. Spoon over cheese in baking dish.

5 Bake 35 to 40 minutes or until biscuits are golden brown on top.

High Altitude (3500-6500 ft): No change.

Nutritional Info: 1 Serving: Calories 490 (Calories from Fat 250); Total Fat 28g (Saturated Fat 13g, Trans Fat 4g); Cholesterol 80mg; Sodium 1200mg; Total Carbohydrate 31g (Dietary Fiber 1g, Sugars 9g); Protein 27g. % Daily Value: Vitamin A 25%; Vitamin C 35%; Calcium 30%; Iron 20%. Exchanges: 1-1/2 Starch, 1-1/2 Vegetable, 2-1/2 Medium-Fat Meat, 3 Fat. Carbohydrate Choices: 2.

Betty's Kitchen Tip

• To easily cut peppers, cut a thin slice off bottom of pepper. Set pepper on cutting board, cut side down. Cut strips of pepper from stem down to board, cutting just the flesh and leaving seeds and core attached to stem.

black bean enchiladas

Prep Time: 20 Minutes
Start to Finish: 55 Minutes
Servings: 10 enchiladas

LOW FAT

- 1 tablespoon vegetable oil
- 1/2 cup chopped onion (1 medium)
- 1 teaspoon ground cumin
- 1 cup Green Giant® Niblets® frozen whole kernel corn, thawed
- 3/4 cup Old El Paso® Thick 'n Chunky medium salsa
- 1 can (15 oz) Progresso® black beans, rinsed and drained
- 2 cups shredded Monterey Jack cheese (8 oz)
- 10 corn tortillas (6 inch)
- 1 can (10 oz) Old El Paso® enchilada sauce

Chopped avocado, black olives, sour cream and cilantro, if desired

1 Heat oven to 350°F. Spray 11x7-inch (2-quart) baking dish with cooking spray. In 10-inch skillet, heat oil over medium heat. Add onion and cumin; cook and stir 4 to 5 minutes or until onion is tender. Stir in corn, salsa, beans and 1 cup of the cheese. Remove from heat.

2 On microwavable plate, stack tortillas and cover with paper towel; microwave on High 1 minute to soften. Place 1/4 cup bean mixture along center of each tortilla. Roll up tightly, and place seam sides down in baking dish; spoon remaining bean mixture on top. Pour enchilada sauce over enchiladas, spreading to coat all tortillas. Sprinkle with remaining 1 cup cheese.

3 Bake covered 25 to 30 minutes or until cheese is melted and sauce is bubbly around the edges. Garnish with the remaining ingredients.

High Altitude (3500-6500 ft): Bake covered 30 minutes; uncover and bake 5 minutes longer.

Nutritional Info: 1 Enchilada: Calories 240 (Calories from Fat 90); Total Fat 10g (Saturated Fat 4.5g, Trans Fat 0g); Cholesterol 20mg; Sodium 390mg; Total Carbohydrate 27g (Dietary Fiber 6g, Sugars 3g); Protein 10g. % Daily Value: Vitamin A 6%; Vitamin C 0%; Calcium 20%; Iron 8%. Exchanges: 1 Starch, 1 Other Carbohydrate, 1 Lean Meat, 1 Fat. Carbohydrate Choices: 2.

Betty's Kitchen Tips

Variation: Vary the spice by using mild, medium or hot salsa, or mild or hot enchilada sauce.

Substitution: Try Hominy Enchiladas by substituting 1 can (15 oz) hominy for the black beans.

beer-cheese mac and sausages

Prep Time: 20 Minutes
Start to Finish: 1 Hour
Servings: 8

1	package (7 oz) elbow macaroni (2 cups)	
3	tablespoons butter	
1/4	cup finely chopped onion	
3	tablespoons Gold Medal® all-purpose flour	
2	cups half-and-half	
1	teaspoon ground mustard	
1/2	teaspoon red pepper sauce	

1/4	teaspoon salt
1	cup beer or non-alcoholic beer
2	cups shredded marble jack cheese (8 oz)
1	package (1 lb) cocktail-size fully cooked smoked sausages
2	cups popped microwave popcorn

1 Heat oven to 350°F. Spray 2-1/2-quart casserole with cooking spray. Cook and drain macaroni as directed on package using minimum cook time. Rinse and return to saucepan.

2 While macaroni is cooking, in 3-quart saucepan, melt butter over medium heat. Cook and stir onion in butter 2 to 3 minutes or until softened. Stir in flour; cook and stir 1 minute. Gradually stir in half-and-half, mustard, pepper sauce and salt; heat until thickened and bubbly, stirring constantly, about 5 minutes. Stir in beer. Remove from heat; let stand 2 to 3 minutes. Stir in cheese until melted. Add sausages to cooked macaroni. Stir in cheese sauce. Spoon mixture into casserole.

3 Bake 30 to 40 minutes or until bubbly and top begins to brown. Top with popcorn just before serving.

High Altitude (3500-6500 ft): Heat oven to 375°F.

Nutritional Info: 1 Serving: Calories 500 (Calories from Fat 310); Total Fat 34g (Saturated Fat 16g, Trans Fat 1g); Cholesterol 80mg; Sodium 1130mg; Total Carbohydrate 30g (Dietary Fiber 1g, Sugars 5g); Protein 16g. % Daily Value: Vitamin A 10%; Vitamin C 0%; Calcium 25%; Iron 10%. Exchanges: 2 Starch, 1-1/2 High-Fat Meat, 4 Fat. Carbohydrate Choices: 2.

Betty's Kitchen Tips

Success Hint: Allow the white sauce to cool a couple of minutes before adding the cheese. This keeps the cheese from separating and becoming grainy.

Serve-With: Serve this perfect football-game casserole with soft pretzels and fresh veggies, such as carrots, celery, pepper strips and cucumber slices.

easy cheesy manicotti

Prep Time: 25 Minutes
Start to Finish: 1 Hour 45 Minutes
Servings: 7 (2 shells each)

- 1 jar (26 oz) chunky-style tomato pasta sauce
- 2 boxes (9 oz each) Green Giant® frozen spinach, thawed, well drained
- 1 container (12 oz) small curd creamed cottage cheese (1-1/2 cups)
- 1/3 cup grated Parmesan cheese
- 1 teaspoon dried oregano leaves, crumbled
- 1/4 teaspoon pepper
- 1 package (8 oz) manicotti shells (14 shells)
- 1/4 cup water
- 2 cups shredded mozzarella cheese (8 oz)

1 Heat oven to 350°F. In ungreased 13x9-inch (3-quart) baking dish, spread about one-third of the pasta sauce.

2 Mix spinach, cottage cheese, Parmesan cheese, oregano and pepper. Fill uncooked manicotti shells with spinach mixture; place on sauce in baking dish.

3 In medium bowl, mix remaining pasta sauce and water. Pour sauce mixture evenly over shells, covering completely. Cover; bake 1 hour. Sprinkle with mozzarella cheese. Cover; bake 15 to 20 minutes longer or until shells are tender.

High Altitude (3500-6500 ft): Heat oven to 375°F. Decrease second bake time to 5 to 10 minutes.

Nutritional Info: 1 Serving: Calories 440 (Calories from Fat 130); Total Fat 15g (Saturated Fat 7g, Trans Fat 0g); Cholesterol 30mg; Sodium 1000mg; Total Carbohydrate 52g (Dietary Fiber 5g, Sugars 13g); Protein 25g. % Daily Value: Vitamin A 130%; Vitamin C 8%; Calcium 45%; Iron 20%. Exchanges: 2 Starch, 1 Other Carbohydrate, 1 Vegetable, 2-1/2 Medium-Fat Meat. Carbohydrate Choices: 3-1/2.

Betty's Kitchen Tips

Do-Ahead: Before baking, cover and refrigerate manicotti up to 24 hours; bake as directed in recipe. Or cover tightly, label and freeze up to 1 month; bake about 2 hours.

Success Hint: Try using a baby spoon to fill the manicotti shells—it works great!

green chile chicken lasagna

Prep Time: 25 Minutes
Start to Finish: 1 Hour 35 Minutes
Servings: 10

- 1   container (15 oz) ricotta cheese
- 1   egg
- 1   cup grated Parmesan cheese
- 2   cups chopped cooked chicken
- 2   cans (10 oz each) Old El Paso® green enchilada sauce
- 2   cans (4 oz each) Old El Paso® chopped green chiles
- 1   package (8 oz) oven ready lasagna (12 noodles)
- 4   cups shredded mozzarella cheese (16 oz)

1 Heat oven to 350°F. In medium bowl, mix ricotta cheese, egg and 1/2 cup of the Parmesan cheese; set aside. In another medium bowl, mix chicken, enchilada sauce and green chiles.

2 In ungreased 13x9-inch (3-quart) baking dish, spread 1 cup of the chicken mixture. Top with 3 uncooked lasagna noodles; press gently into chicken mixture. Spread with 2/3 cup of the ricotta mixture. Sprinkle with 1 cup of the mozzarella cheese. Repeat layers 3 times. Sprinkle with remaining 1/2 cup Parmesan cheese. Cover with foil.

3 Bake 45 minutes. Remove foil; bake 10 to 15 minutes longer or until lasagna is tender, cheese is bubbly and edges are lightly browned. Let stand 10 minutes before serving.

High Altitude (3500-6500 ft): In step 3, remove foil and bake 15 to 20 minutes longer.

Nutritional Info: 1 Serving: Calories 420 (Calories from Fat 180); Total Fat 20g (Saturated Fat 11g, Trans Fat 0g); Cholesterol 90mg; Sodium 880mg; Total Carbohydrate 28g (Dietary Fiber 1g, Sugars 3g); Protein 33g. % Daily Value: Vitamin A 10%; Vitamin C 6%; Calcium 60%; Iron 10%. Exchanges: 1-1/2 Starch, 1/2 Other Carbohydrate, 4 Lean Meat, 1 Fat. Carbohydrate Choices: 2.

Betty's Kitchen Tips

Substitution: Green enchilada sauce is more mild than red enchilada sauce. Red enchilada sauce can be substituted, but the flavor will be spicier.

Do-Ahead: Lasagna can be made the night before, refrigerated and baked the next day. Add a few minutes of bake time.

contemporary tuna-noodle casserole

Prep Time: 20 Minutes
Start to Finish: 50 Minutes
Servings: 6

- 2 cups uncooked fusilli pasta (6 oz)
- 1 jar (16 oz) Alfredo pasta sauce
- 1/3 cup dry white wine or chicken broth
- 1 teaspoon Italian seasoning
- 1 teaspoon grated lemon peel
- 2 cans (5 oz each) solid white albacore tuna in water, drained
- 1 box (9 oz) Green Giant® frozen sugar snap peas, thawed, drained
- 1 jar (4.5 oz) Green Giant® whole mushrooms, drained
- 1/2 cup dry Progresso® plain bread crumbs
- 2 tablespoons butter or margarine, melted

1 Heat oven to 375°F. Spray 2-quart baking dish with cooking spray.

2 Cook and drain pasta as directed on package using minimum cook time. In large bowl, stir Alfredo sauce, wine, Italian seasoning, lemon peel, tuna, peas, mushrooms and pasta. Spoon into baking dish.

3 In small bowl, stir together bread crumbs and butter; sprinkle over pasta.

4 Bake 25 to 30 minutes or until topping is golden brown.

High Altitude (3500-6500 ft): Bake 30 to 35 minutes.

Nutritional Info: 1 Serving: Calories 530 (Calories from Fat 260); Total Fat 29g (Saturated Fat 18g, Trans Fat 1g); Cholesterol 100mg; Sodium 730mg; Total Carbohydrate 41g (Dietary Fiber 3g, Sugars 4g); Protein 24g. % Daily Value: Vitamin A 30%; Vitamin C 8%; Calcium 20%; Iron 20%. Exchanges: 2-1/2 Starch, 2-1/2 Lean Meat, 4 Fat. Carbohydrate Choices: 3.

Betty's Kitchen Tips

Substitution: Land lovers can substitute 2 cups cut-up cooked chicken for the tuna.

Variation: For a retro topping, omit the buttered bread crumbs, and substitute 1/2 cup crushed potato chips.

ham and cheese ziti

Prep Time: 30 Minutes
Start to Finish: 55 Minutes
Servings: 8 (1-1/3 cups each)

- 1 package (16 oz) ziti pasta (5 cups)
- 1/2 cup butter or margarine
- 2 cloves garlic, finely chopped
- 1/2 cup Gold Medal® all-purpose flour
- 1 teaspoon salt
- 4 cups milk

- 1 teaspoon Dijon mustard
- 4 cups shredded Colby cheese (16 oz)
- 8 oz sliced cooked deli ham, cut into thin strips
- 2/3 cup grated Parmesan cheese

1 Heat oven to 350°F. Cook and drain pasta as directed on package using minimum cook time.

2 Meanwhile, in 4-quart saucepan or Dutch oven, melt butter over low heat. Cook garlic in butter 30 seconds, stirring frequently. Stir in flour and salt, using wire whisk. Cook over medium heat, stirring constantly, until mixture is smooth and bubbly.

3 Gradually stir in milk. Heat to boiling, stirring constantly. Boil and stir 1 minute. Stir in mustard and Colby cheese. Cook, stirring occasionally, until cheese is melted. Stir pasta and ham into cheese sauce. Pour pasta mixture into ungreased 13x9-inch baking dish. Sprinkle with Parmesan cheese. Bake 20 to 25 minutes or until bubbly.

High Altitude (3500-6500 ft): Use 4-1/2 cups milk. After stirring in flour and salt in step 2, cook over medium-high heat until smooth and bubbly. Bake 25 to 30 minutes.

Nutritional Info: 1 Serving: Calories 740 (Calories from Fat 340); Total Fat 38g (Saturated Fat 23g, Trans Fat 1g); Cholesterol 120mg; Sodium 1470mg; Total Carbohydrate 62g (Dietary Fiber 3g, Sugars 8g); Protein 37g. % Daily Value: Vitamin A 25%; Vitamin C 0%; Calcium 70%; Iron 20%. Exchanges: 3 Starch, 1 Other Carbohydrate, 4 High-Fat Meat, 1 Fat. Carbohydrate Choices: 4.

Betty's Kitchen Tips

Success Hint: To prevent lumps in the cheese sauce, use a wire whisk to stir in the flour and milk.

Purchasing: Ziti is a pasta that looks a little bit like its cousin, macaroni. Ziti is thicker and longer than macaroni and is more tube-shaped. It's a perfect pasta for chunky sauces, meat dishes and baked casseroles.

taco casserole

Prep Time: 20 Minutes
Start to Finish: 50 Minutes
Servings: 4

- 1 lb lean (at least 80%) ground beef
- 1 can (15 to 16 oz) chili beans in sauce, undrained
- 1 can (8 oz) tomato sauce
- 2 tablespoons Old El Paso® taco sauce, picante sauce or salsa
- 2 to 4 teaspoons chili powder
- 1 teaspoon garlic powder
- 2 cups coarsely broken tortilla chips
- 8 medium green onions, sliced (1/2 cup)
- 1 medium tomato, chopped (3/4 cup)
- 1 cup shredded Cheddar or Monterey Jack cheese (4 oz)

1 Heat oven to 350°F. In 10-inch skillet, cook beef over medium-high heat 5 to 7 minutes, stirring occasionally, until brown; drain. Reduce heat to medium. Stir in beans, tomato sauce, taco sauce, chili powder and garlic powder. Heat to boiling over medium heat, stirring occasionally.

2 In ungreased 1-1/2-quart casserole, place tortilla chips. Top with beef mixture. Sprinkle with onions, tomato and cheese.

3 Bake 20 to 30 minutes or until hot and bubbly. Arrange additional tortilla chips around edge of casserole if desired.

High Altitude (3500-6500 ft): Bake 25 to 30 minutes.

Nutritional Info: 1 Serving: Calories 660 (Calories from Fat 300); Total Fat 33g (Saturated Fat 12g, Trans Fat 1.5g); Cholesterol 100mg; Sodium 1630mg; Total Carbohydrate 53g (Dietary Fiber 8g, Sugars 9g); Protein 36g. % Daily Value: Vitamin A 35%; Vitamin C 15%; Calcium 25%; Iron 40%. Exchanges: 3 Starch, 1/2 Other Carbohydrate, 4 Lean Meat, 4 Fat. Carbohydrate Choices: 3-1/2.

Betty's Kitchen Tips

Success Hint: The tortilla chips at the bottom of the bag are perfect for this casserole because they're already "coarsely broken."

Substitution: Lean ground turkey can be substituted for the ground beef.

italian chicken bracciole

Prep Time: 25 Minutes
Start to Finish: 1 Hour 40 Minutes
Servings: 6

4	slices bacon, chopped
1/2	cup chopped onion (1 medium)
1	clove garlic, chopped
1/4	cup Progresso® Italian-style bread crumbs
1/4	cup grated Parmesan cheese
2	tablespoons chopped fresh rosemary leaves
1	egg

6	boneless skinless chicken thighs
1	tablespoon olive oil
1	tablespoon butter or margarine
1	can (14.5 oz) diced tomatoes with Italian-style herbs, undrained
3	tablespoons tomato paste

1 Heat oven to 350°F. Spray 11x7-inch baking dish with cooking spray. In 12-inch skillet, cook bacon over medium-high heat, stirring frequently, until crisp. Reduce heat to low; add onion and garlic; cook 2 to 3 minutes, stirring occasionally, until soft. Remove from heat; stir in bread crumbs. Stir in cheese, rosemary and egg; mix well.

2 Unfold chicken thighs so inside faces up. Spoon stuffing over thighs, about 2 tablespoons each. Fold over, and secure with toothpicks. In same skillet, heat olive oil and butter. Cook thighs in skillet 2 minutes per side, until brown. Place in baking dish. In medium bowl, mix diced tomatoes and tomato paste. Pour over chicken.

3 Cover with foil. Bake 1 hour to 1 hour 15 minutes or until thermometer inserted in center of chicken stuffing reads 165°F. Serve over cooked spaghetti if desired.

High Altitude (3500-6500 ft): No change.

Nutritional Info: 1 Serving: Calories 250 (Calories from Fat 130); Total Fat 14g (Saturated Fat 5g, Trans Fat 0g); Cholesterol 90mg; Sodium 500mg; Total Carbohydrate 9g (Dietary Fiber 1g, Sugars 4g); Protein 21g. % Daily Value: Vitamin A 8%; Vitamin C 8%; Calcium 10%; Iron 15%. Exchanges: 1/2 Other Carbohydrate, 3 Medium-Fat Meat. Carbohydrate Choices: 1/2.

Betty's Kitchen Tips

Serve-With: To complete the meal, serve with hot cooked pasta and a green salad.

Success Hint: Italian cooks use small amounts of tomato paste to boost tomato flavor and thicken tomato mixtures; they would rarely use an entire 6-oz can. Purchase tomato paste in a tube that can be refrigerated, or spoon out dollops of leftover tomato paste from a can, and freeze them. Then place in a freezer bag to use in future recipes.

salmon paella bake

Prep Time: 15 Minutes
Start to Finish: 1 Hour
Servings: 6

EASY

- 1-1/2 cups uncooked Arborio rice
- 1 medium onion, chopped (1/2 cup)
- 1 large red bell pepper, chopped (about 1-3/4 cups)
- 1 teaspoon grated lemon peel
- 3/4 teaspoon salt
- 1/2 teaspoon crushed saffron threads
- 4 cups chicken broth
- 1/2 lb smoked turkey kielbasa sausage, cut into 3/4-inch slices
- 1 salmon fillet (1-1/2 lb), skin removed and cut into 6 pieces
- 1 tablespoon vegetable oil
- 2 tablespoons chopped fresh Italian (flat-leaf) parsley

1 Heat oven to 350°F. Spray 13x9-inch (3-quart) baking dish with cooking spray. Place rice, onion, bell pepper, lemon peel, 1/2 teaspoon of the salt and the saffron in baking dish.

2 Heat chicken broth to boiling. Stir broth into rice mixture. Arrange kielbasa slices over rice. Cover with foil. Bake 20 minutes.

3 Arrange salmon over rice; brush fillets with vegetable oil. Sprinkle with remaining 1/4 teaspoon salt. Bake uncovered 20 to 25 minutes longer or until fish flakes easily with fork, rice is tender and broth is absorbed. Sprinkle salmon with parsley.

High Altitude (3500-6500 ft): Increase chicken broth to 4-1/2 cups and bake time in step 3 to 23 to 28 minutes.

Nutritional Info: 1 Serving: Calories 450 (Calories from Fat 120); Total Fat 14g (Saturated Fat 3.5g, Trans Fat 0g); Cholesterol 95mg; Sodium 1430mg; Total Carbohydrate 44g (Dietary Fiber 1g, Sugars 2g); Protein 37g. % Daily Value: Vitamin A 20%; Vitamin C 35%; Calcium 4%; Iron 20%. Exchanges: 3 Starch, 4 Lean Meat. Carbohydrate Choices: 3.

Betty's Kitchen Tips

Purchasing: When shopping for the fish, look for a salmon fillet with uniform thickness so fish cooks evenly. Ask the butcher to remove the skin.

Variation: For a kick of spice, add a chopped jalapeño chile with the rice, and substitute chopped fresh cilantro for the parsley.

layered mexican casserole

Prep Time: 20 Minutes
Start to Finish: 1 Hour
Servings: 6

1	lb lean (at least 80%) ground beef
1	jar (16 oz) Old El Paso® Thick 'n Chunky salsa
8	corn tortillas (6 inch)
1	can (16 oz) Old El Paso® refried beans

1-1/2	cups shredded Mexican cheese blend (6 oz)
1	can (15 oz) Spanish rice
1	cup coarsely crushed tortilla chips

---

1 Heat oven to 350°F. Spray 11x7-inch (2-quart) baking dish with cooking spray. In 10-inch skillet, cook beef over medium-high heat 5 to 7 minutes, stirring frequently, until thoroughly cooked; drain. Stir in 1 cup of the salsa; heat about 2 minutes or until hot.

2 Line baking dish with 4 tortillas, overlapping to fit. In medium bowl, stir together refried beans and remaining salsa; spoon over tortillas, and spread evenly. Top with half of the meat mixture and 3/4 cup of the cheese. Layer 4 more tortillas over cheese. Spoon and spread

Spanish rice over tortillas. Top with remaining meat mixture and cheese. Top with tortilla chips.

3 Bake 30 to 40 minutes or until hot in center and bubbling along sides.

High Altitude (3500-6500 ft): Use 13x9-inch baking dish. Bake 37 to 42 minutes.

Nutritional Info: 1 Serving: Calories 470 (Calories from Fat 180); Total Fat 20g (Saturated Fat 9g, Trans Fat 1g); Cholesterol 80mg; Sodium 1150mg; Total Carbohydrate 48g (Dietary Fiber 7g, Sugars 6g); Protein 26g. % Daily Value: Vitamin A 20%; Vitamin C 10%; Calcium 30%; Iron 25%. Exchanges: 2-1/2 Starch, 1/2 Other Carbohydrate, 2-1/2 Medium-Fat Meat, 1 Fat. Carbohydrate Choices: 3.

Betty's Kitchen Tips

Purchasing: Look for cans of Spanish rice in the section with Mexican/Hispanic items. If canned Spanish rice is not available, cook an envelope of Spanish rice mix and use about 1-3/4 cups of the rice.

Serve-With: Serve this hearty Tex-Mex casserole with your favorite taco toppers—shredded lettuce, chopped tomato or avocado, sour cream or taco sauce.

provençal roast chicken

Prep Time: 15 Minutes
Start to Finish: 2 Hours 15 Minutes
Servings: 6

EASY LOW FAT

- 1 whole chicken (3 to 3-1/2 lb)
- 1 lemon
- 1 teaspoon olive oil
- 1 tablespoon dried herbes de Provence
- 1/4 teaspoon pepper
- 8 new potatoes (1-1/2 lb), cut into fourths
- 2 medium zucchini, cut into 1-1/2-inch pieces
- 1 can (14-1/2 oz) diced tomatoes with basil, garlic and oregano, drained
- 1/2 cup chopped pitted kalamata olives

1 Heat oven to 400°F. Place chicken, breast side up, in ungreased shallow roasting pan.

2 Grate peel from lemon; squeeze juice. In small bowl, mix lemon peel, lemon juice and oil. Drizzle half of lemon mixture over chicken; pat herbes de Provence and pepper on skin of chicken. Place squeezed lemon halves inside chicken cavity.

3 In large bowl, toss potatoes, zucchini, tomatoes, olives and remaining lemon mixture. Arrange vegetables around chicken in roasting pan. Insert ovenproof meat thermometer in chicken so tip is in thickest part of inside thigh and does not touch bone.

4 Bake 1 hour 45 minutes to 2 hours or until thermometer reads 180°F, legs move easily when lifted or twisted and vegetables are tender.

High Altitude (3500-6500 ft): No change.

Nutritional Info: 1 Serving: Calories 320 (Calories from Fat 80); Total Fat 9g (Saturated Fat 2.5g, Trans Fat 0g); Cholesterol 85mg; Sodium 290mg; Total Carbohydrate 26g (Dietary Fiber 4g, Sugars 4g); Protein 31g. % Daily Value: Vitamin A 6%; Vitamin C 25%; Calcium 8%; Iron 25%. Exchanges: 1-1/2 Starch, 1 Vegetable, 3 Lean Meat. Carbohydrate Choices: 2.

Betty's Kitchen Tips

How-To: The peel, or zest, of citrus fruits comes from the outermost layer of skin. It contains pungent, aromatic oils that add intense flavor to foods. Remove the colored outer peel (not the white) by using a grater, paring knife or vegetable peeler.

Did You Know? Herbes de Provence combines favorite herbs from the Provence region in southern France. It commonly contains basil, fennel seed, lavender, marjoram, rosemary, sage, summer savory and thyme.

mom's macaroni and cheese

Prep Time: 10 Minutes
Start to Finish: 40 Minutes
Servings: 5

EASY

1-1/2	cups uncooked elbow macaroni (5 oz)
2	tablespoons butter or margarine
1	small onion, chopped (1/4 cup)
1/2	teaspoon salt
1/4	teaspoon pepper

1/4	cup Gold Medal® all-purpose flour
1-3/4	cups milk
6	oz American cheese loaf, cut into 1/2-inch cubes

1 Heat oven to 375°F. Cook and drain macaroni as directed on package using minimum cook time.

2 Meanwhile, in 2-quart saucepan, melt butter over medium heat. Cook onion, salt and pepper in butter, stirring occasionally, until onion is crisp-tender.

3 In small bowl, mix flour and milk until smooth; stir into onion mixture. Heat to boiling, stirring constantly. Boil and stir 1 minute; remove from heat. Stir in cheese until melted. Stir in macaroni. Into ungreased 1-1/2-quart casserole, spoon macaroni mixture.

4 Bake about 30 minutes or until bubbly and light brown.

High Altitude (3500-6500 ft): Increase milk to 2-1/4 cups. In step 3, boil and stir 2 minutes; do not remove from heat. Stir in cheese, and boil 1 minute longer. Remove from heat, and stir until cheese is melted.

Nutritional Info: 1 Serving: Calories 410 (Calories from Fat 160); Total Fat 18g (Saturated Fat 11g, Trans Fat 0.5g); Cholesterol 50mg; Sodium 1030mg; Total Carbohydrate 44g (Dietary Fiber 2g, Sugars 6g); Protein 17g. % Daily Value: Vitamin A 15%; Vitamin C 0%; Calcium 30%; Iron 10%. Exchanges: 2 Starch, 1 Other Carbohydrate, 1-1/2 High-Fat Meat, 1 Fat. Carbohydrate Choices: 3.

Betty's Kitchen Tips

Variation: For a spicy change, use 6 oz from a loaf of Mexican prepared cheese product with jalapeño peppers instead of the American cheese.

Success Hint: Use American cheese in this recipe because it melts better than natural Cheddar and won't curdle during cooking.

everyday cassoulet

Prep Time: 20 Minutes
Start to Finish: 2 Hours 20 Minutes
Servings: 6

4	strips bacon, chopped
1/2	lb bulk pork sausage
1/2	lb boneless pork tenderloin, cubed
1/3	cup diced onion
2	cloves garlic, finely chopped
2	cans (15 oz each) cannellini beans, drained
1	can (14.5 oz) diced tomatoes, undrained
1/2	cup chicken broth
1/4	cup white wine or chicken broth
1	teaspoon dried sage leaves
1	teaspoon dried thyme leaves
1/4	teaspoon pepper
1	dried bay leaf

LOW FAT

1 Heat oven to 350°F. In 12-inch skillet, cook bacon over medium-high heat, stirring occasionally, until crisp. Remove from skillet. Add sausage, cubed pork, onion and garlic to skillet. Cook until pork is browned, stirring occasionally. Stir in bacon and remaining ingredients. Pour into ungreased 2-1/2-quart casserole.

2 Cover casserole. Bake 1 hour 45 minutes. Uncover; bake 15 minutes longer or until pork is fork tender and flavors are blended. Remove bay leaf; spoon into decorative soup bowls to serve.

High Altitude (3500-6500 ft): No change.

Nutritional Info: 1 Serving: Calories 330 (Calories from Fat 80); Total Fat 9g (Saturated Fat 3g, Trans Fat 0g); Cholesterol 45mg; Sodium 820mg; Total Carbohydrate 34g (Dietary Fiber 8g, Sugars 3g); Protein 26g. % Daily Value: Vitamin A 2%; Vitamin C 6%; Calcium 15%; Iron 35%. Exchanges: 2 Starch, 3 Lean Meat. Carbohydrate Choices: 2.

Betty's Kitchen Tips

Substitution: You can substitute canned great northern beans for the cannellini beans, if you prefer.

Serve-With: Serve with toasted French bread slices on the side.

home-style chicken dinner

Prep Time: 30 Minutes
Start to Finish: 1 Hour 20 Minutes
Servings: 4

- 2 teaspoons dried basil leaves
- 1 teaspoon seasoned salt
- 1 teaspoon garlic pepper blend
- 2 tablespoons olive oil
- 3 to 3-1/2 lb cut-up broiler fryer chicken, skin removed if desired
- 6 small unpeeled red potatoes, cut into fourths (2 cups)

- 2 medium dark-orange sweet potatoes, peeled, cut into 1-inch pieces (3 cups)
- 1 medium green bell pepper, cut into 1-inch pieces (1 cup)
- 3 plum (Roma) tomatoes, cut into fourths

1 Heat oven to 400°F. Spray 13x9-inch (3-quart) baking dish with cooking spray. In large bowl, mix basil, seasoned salt, garlic pepper blend and oil. Brush about half of the mixture on chicken. Add remaining ingredients to bowl; toss to coat.

2 Place vegetables in baking dish. Place chicken on vegetables. Brush with any remaining oil mixture.

3 Bake 45 to 50 minutes or until vegetables are tender and juice of chicken is no longer pink when centers of thickest pieces are cut. Serve with pan juices.

High Altitude (3500-6500 ft): No change.

Nutritional Info: 1 Serving: Calories 580 (Calories from Fat 260); Total Fat 29g (Saturated Fat 7g, Trans Fat 0.5g); Cholesterol 140mg; Sodium 510mg; Total Carbohydrate 33g (Dietary Fiber 5g, Sugars 8g); Protein 46g. % Daily Value: Vitamin A 310%; Vitamin C 45%; Calcium 8%; Iron 25%. Exchanges: 1-1/2 Starch, 1/2 Other Carbohydrate, 6 Medium-Fat Meat. Carbohydrate Choices: 2.

Betty's Kitchen Tips

Purchasing: Look for sweet potatoes that are dark orange or red in color to give this dish wonderful color, texture and flavor. Light-colored varieties tend to be mealy.

Substitution: You can use 1/2 teaspoon each garlic powder and coarse pepper instead of the garlic pepper blend.

grilled
ENTREES

p. 75

65

87

83

kielbasa, caramelized onion and basil pizzas

Prep Time: 1 Hour 20 Minutes
Start to Finish: 1 Hour 20 Minutes
Servings: 8 individual pizzas

1 tablespoon olive or vegetable oil
1 medium red onion, thinly sliced
(about 1-1/2 cups)
Olive oil cooking spray
2 cans (13.8 oz each) Pillsbury® refrigerated
classic pizza crust

1 jar (14 oz) pizza sauce
2 cups (about 8 oz) thinly sliced cooked
kielbasa sausage (from 16-oz package)
2 cups shredded mozzarella cheese (8 oz)
1 cup fresh basil leaves

1 In 10-inch skillet, heat oil over medium heat. Add onion; cook 10 minutes, stirring occasionally. Reduce heat to medium-low; cook 5 to 10 minutes longer, stirring frequently, until onions are very tender and golden. Remove from heat; set aside.

2 Heat gas or charcoal grill for indirect cooking as directed by manufacturer. Spray 2 large cookie sheets with cooking spray. Unroll both cans of dough; cut each rectangle of dough into 4 equal rectangles. Spray both sides of each rectangle with cooking spray; place on cookie sheets.

3 Place 2 or 3 dough rectangles at a time directly on grill rack on unheated side

of two-burner gas grill or over drip pan on charcoal grill. (If using one-burner gas grill, cook over low heat.) Cover grill; cook 5 to 7 minutes or until edges of dough look dry (check occasionally to make sure bottoms of crusts are cooking evenly; rotate crusts if necessary). Cook about 2 minutes longer or until bottoms of crusts are golden and have grill marks. Using large pancake turner, remove crusts from grill to cookie sheet. Repeat with remaining dough rectangles.

4 Turn cooked crusts over so cooked sides are up; spread evenly with pizza sauce. Top each with sausage, onions and cheese.

5 Heat oven to 200°F. Return 4 pizzas at a time to grill rack over indirect heat. Cover grill; cook about 5 minutes or until bottoms are golden brown and cheese is melted. Remove cooked pizzas from grill to cookie sheet; place in oven to keep warm while cooking remaining pizzas. Sprinkle basil over pizzas.

High Altitude (3500-6500 ft): No change.

Nutritional Info: 1 Individual Pizza: Calories 500 (Calories from Fat 200); Total Fat 22g (Saturated Fat 9g, Trans Fat 0g); Cholesterol 40mg; Sodium 1290mg; Total Carbohydrate 55g (Dietary Fiber 3g, Sugars 11g); Protein 21g. % Daily Value: Vitamin A 15%; Vitamin C 6%; Calcium 30%; Iron 20%. Exchanges: 1 Starch, 2-1/2 Other Carbohydrate, 2-1/2 High-Fat Meat, 1/2 Fat. Carbohydrate Choices: 3-1/2.

taco burgers

Prep Time: 30 Minutes
Start to Finish: 30 Minutes
Servings: 4 sandwiches

QUICK

- 1   lb lean (at least 80%) ground beef
- 1   package (1 oz) Old El Paso® taco seasoning mix
- 4   slices (1 oz each) Monterey Jack cheese
- 4   burger buns, split
- 1   avocado, pitted, peeled and sliced
- 1/4   cup Old El Paso® Thick 'n Chunky salsa
- 1   jalapeño chile, chopped, if desired

1 Heat gas or charcoal grill. In medium bowl, mix beef and taco seasoning mix. Shape mixture into 4 patties, about 3/4 inch thick.

2 Place patties on grill over medium heat. Cover grill; cook 13 to 15 minutes, turning once, until meat thermometer inserted in center of patties reads 160°F. Top each patty with cheese slice. Cook 1 to 2 minutes longer or until cheese begins to melt. Serve in buns with avocado and salsa. Top with chopped chile.

High Altitude (3500-6500 ft): No change.

Nutritional Info: 1 Sandwich: Calories 500 (Calories from Fat 260); Total Fat 28g (Saturated Fat 11g, Trans Fat 1.5g); Cholesterol 95mg; Sodium 1210mg; Total Carbohydrate 29g (Dietary Fiber 3g, Sugars 4g); Protein 31g. % Daily Value: Vitamin A 10%; Vitamin C 2%; Calcium 30%; Iron 20%. Exchanges: 2 Starch, 3-1/2 Medium-Fat Meat, 1-1/2 Fat. Carbohydrate Choices: 2.

Betty's Kitchen Tips

Substitutions: This recipe calls for ground beef, but feel free to use ground turkey instead. You can also use pepper Jack for the cheese.

Serve-With: Favorite taco toppings such as sour cream, shredded lettuce and chopped tomatoes can be served, too.

"philly" new york strip steaks

Prep Time: 25 Minutes
Start to Finish: 25 Minutes
Servings: 4

QUICK

- 4 boneless beef New York strip steaks or top loin strip steaks, 3/4 to 1 inch thick (about 2 lb)
- 4 teaspoons Montreal steak grill seasoning
- 1 medium green bell pepper, cut into 1/2-inch strips

- 1 medium red bell pepper, cut into 1/2-inch strips
- 1 large onion, cut into 1/2-inch wedges
- 2 teaspoons olive or vegetable oil
- 4 slices (3/4 oz each) Muenster cheese

1 Heat gas or charcoal grill. Sprinkle beef steaks with 3 teaspoons of the grill seasoning. In large bowl, mix bell peppers and onion with oil and remaining 1 teaspoon grill seasoning. Spoon vegetables into grill basket (grill "wok").

2 Place steaks and grill basket on grill over medium heat. Cover grill; cook 8 to 10 minutes, turning steaks once and stirring vegetables 2 or 3 times, until beef is desired doneness and vegetables are crisp-tender. Place cheese on steaks. Cover grill; cook about 1 minute longer or until cheese is melted.

3 Place each steak on serving plate. Spoon vegetables over steaks.

High Altitude (3500-6500): No change.

Nutritional Info: 1 Serving: Calories 470 (Calories from Fat 160); Total Fat 18g (Saturated Fat 7g, Trans Fat 0.5g); Cholesterol 180mg; Sodium 900mg; Total Carbohydrate 7g (Dietary Fiber 2g, Sugars 4g); Protein 70g. % Daily Value: Vitamin A 25%; Vitamin C 50%; Calcium 15%; Iron 35%. Exchanges: 1 Low-Fat Milk, 1-1/2 Vegetable, 4 Medium-Fat Meat. Carbohydrate Choices: 1/2.

Betty's Kitchen Tips

Success Hint: Use your favorite meltable cheese on these yummy cheese steaks. Try Swiss, provolone or even blue cheese for a tangy flavor.

Purchasing: Strip steaks weigh on average about 1/2 pound. For light eaters, you can plan on dividing one steak between two people.

pork chops with maple-apple glaze

Prep Time: 20 Minutes
Start to Finish: 20 Minutes
Servings: 4

QUICK LOW FAT

- 1/4   cup real maple syrup
- 1/4   cup apple butter
- 1/2   teaspoon ground mustard
- 4   bone-in pork loin chops (1/2 to 3/4 inch thick), trimmed of fat
- 1/2   teaspoon garlic-pepper blend
- 1/4   teaspoon salt

1 Heat gas or charcoal grill. In 1-quart saucepan, mix syrup, apple butter and mustard. Cook over low heat about 1 minute, stirring occasionally, until well blended.

2 Sprinkle pork with garlic-pepper blend and salt; place on grill over medium heat. Brush with maple mixture. Cover grill; cook 10 to 12 minutes, turning and brushing with maple mixture 2 or 3 times, until pork is no longer pink and meat thermometer inserted in center reads 160°F. Discard any remaining maple mixture.

High Altitude (3500-6500 ft): No change.

Nutritional Info: 1 Serving: Calories 260 (Calories from Fat 70); Total Fat 8g (Saturated Fat 3g, Trans Fat 0g); Cholesterol 65mg; Sodium 190mg; Total Carbohydrate 23g (Dietary Fiber 0g, Sugars 20g); Protein 23g. % Daily Value: Vitamin A 0%; Vitamin C 0%; Calcium 2%; Iron 6%. Exchanges: 1 Starch, 1/2 Other Carbohydrate, 2-1/2 Lean Meat. Carbohydrate Choices: 1-1/2.

Betty's Kitchen Tips

Substitution: You can use maple-flavored syrup instead of the real maple syrup.

Serve-With: Serve the pork with Dilled Carrots and Pea Pods on p. 145.

pork tenderloin with raspberry-chipotle glaze

Prep Time: 15 Minutes
Start to Finish: 15 Minutes
Servings: 4

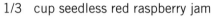

EASY QUICK LOW FAT

1 pork tenderloin (about 1 lb)	1/3 cup seedless red raspberry jam
2 teaspoons olive or vegetable oil	1 to 2 teaspoons finely chopped chipotle chiles and adobo sauce (from 7-oz can)
1/2 teaspoon salt	
1/2 teaspoon chili powder	1 teaspoon water
1/4 teaspoon pepper	

1 Heat closed medium-size contact grill for 5 minutes. Position drip tray to catch drippings.

2 Meanwhile, cut pork in half lengthwise, then cut crosswise to make 4 equal pieces. Brush all sides with oil; sprinkle with salt, chili powder and pepper.

3 When grill is heated, place pork on grill. Close grill; cook 7 to 9 minutes or until no longer pink in center.

4 Meanwhile, in small microwavable bowl, mix jam, chiles and water. Microwave uncovered on High 20 to 30 seconds or until jam is melted and mixture is warm; stir well. To serve, drizzle raspberry mixture over pork.

High Altitude (3500-6500 ft): No change.

Nutritional Info: 1 Serving: Calories 260 (Calories from Fat 80); Total Fat 9g (Saturated Fat 2.5g, Trans Fat 0g); Cholesterol 50mg; Sodium 410mg; Total Carbohydrate 22g (Dietary Fiber 1g, Sugars 15g); Protein 23g. % Daily Value: Vitamin A 6%; Vitamin C 30%; Calcium 0%; Iron 6%. Exchanges: 1-1/2 Other Carbohydrate, 3 Lean Meat. Carbohydrate Choices: 1-1/2.

Betty's Kitchen Tips

Storage: Seal remaining chipotle chiles in a freezer bag, and freeze for later use.

Success Hint: To fit these longer pieces of meat on the grill, place 3 pieces crosswise and the last piece lengthwise beside them.

Did You Know? One end of a tenderloin is usually thinner than the other end. Make those pieces a little larger than the thicker end, and they will be about the same weight.

chicken with oregano-peach sauce

Prep Time: 35 Minutes
Start to Finish: 35 Minutes
Servings: 4

LOW FAT

- 1/2 cup peach preserves
- 1/4 cup raspberry vinegar
- 2 tablespoons chopped fresh oregano leaves
- 4 boneless skinless chicken breasts (about 1-1/4 lb)
- 1/2 teaspoon garlic-pepper blend
- 1/2 teaspoon seasoned salt

1 Heat gas or charcoal grill. In 1-quart saucepan, heat preserves and vinegar to boiling, stirring constantly, until preserves are melted. Spoon about 1/4 cup mixture into small bowl or custard cup for brushing on chicken. Stir oregano into remaining mixture and reserve to serve with chicken.

2 Sprinkle chicken with garlic-pepper blend and seasoned salt; place on grill over medium heat. Cover grill; cook 15 to 20 minutes, turning once and brushing with preserves mixture during last 10 minutes of grilling, until juice of chicken is clear when center of thickest part is cut (170°F). Discard any remaining preserves mixture brushed on chicken. Serve chicken with reserved preserves mixture with oregano.

High Altitude (3500-6500 ft): No change.

Nutritional Info: 1 Serving: Calories 230 (Calories from Fat 60); Total Fat 7g (Saturated Fat 1g, Trans Fat 0g); Cholesterol 25mg; Sodium 240mg; Total Carbohydrate 34g (Dietary Fiber 1g, Sugars 24g); Protein 8g. % Daily Value: Vitamin A 4%; Vitamin C 4%; Calcium 6%; Iron 10%. Exchanges: 2-1/2 Starch, 1 Fat. Carbohydrate Choices: 2.

Betty's Kitchen Tip

• When grilling, use long-handled tongs and wear oven mitts to protect yourself from burns.

smoky chicken breasts with alabama white barbecue sauce

Prep Time: 20 Minutes
Start to Finish: 20 Minutes
Servings: 4

QUICK

4	boneless skinless chicken breasts (about 1-1/4 lb)
1	tablespoon olive or vegetable oil
2	teaspoons Montreal chicken grill seasoning
1	tablespoon packed brown sugar
1/2	teaspoon chipotle chili pepper powder

1/3	cup mayonnaise or salad dressing
2	tablespoons lemon juice
2	teaspoons sugar
2	teaspoons cider vinegar
1/4	teaspoon pepper

1 Heat gas or charcoal grill. Between pieces of plastic wrap or waxed paper, place each chicken breast smooth side down; gently pound with flat side of meat mallet or rolling pin until about 1/4 inch thick. Brush all sides of chicken with oil. In small bowl, mix grill seasoning, brown sugar and chili pepper powder; sprinkle on both sides of chicken.

2 Place chicken on grill over medium heat. Cover grill; cook 5 to 6 minutes, turning once, until chicken is no longer pink in center.

3 Meanwhile, in small bowl, beat remaining ingredients with wire whisk until blended. Drizzle mayonnaise mixture over chicken.

High Altitude (3500-6500 ft): No change.

Nutritional Info: 1 Serving: Calories 360 (Calories from Fat 200); Total Fat 23g (Saturated Fat 4g, Trans Fat 0g); Cholesterol 95mg; Sodium 190mg; Total Carbohydrate 7g (Dietary Fiber 0g, Sugars 6g); Protein 32g. % Daily Value: Vitamin A 4%; Vitamin C 0%; Calcium 2%; Iron 8%. Exchanges: 1/2 Other Carbohydrate, 4-1/2 Lean Meat, 1-1/2 Fat. Carbohydrate Choices: 1/2.

Betty's Kitchen Tips

Did You Know? White barbecue sauce is popular in northern Alabama. It starts with a base of mayonnaise instead of tomato or vinegar.

Success Hint: Chipotle chili pepper powder has a distinct "bite" and smoky flavor. Use more or less to your taste. You can also substitute regular chili powder, but it won't have the slight smoky flavor.

ham and potatoes au gratin

Prep Time: 40 Minutes
Start to Finish: 40 Minutes
Servings: 4 (1-1/2 cups each)

- -

1-3/4	cups cubed (3/4 inch) cooked ham (3/4 lb)
3	medium baking potatoes, peeled, cut in half lengthwise, then cut into 1/8-inch wedges (about 3 cups)
1-1/3	cups Alfredo pasta sauce (from 16-oz jar)
1	cup shredded Swiss cheese (4 oz)
2	tablespoons chopped fresh chives, if desired

- -

1 Heat gas or charcoal grill. Cut a 20x18-inch sheet of heavy-duty foil; spray with cooking spray. Place ham on center of sheet. Top with potatoes, pasta sauce and cheese.

2 Bring up 2 sides of foil over ham mixture so edges meet. Seal edges, making tight 1/2-inch fold; fold again, allowing space for heat circulation and expansion. Fold other sides to seal.

3 Place packet on grill over low heat. Cover grill; cook 20 to 25 minutes, rotating packet 1/2 turn after 10 minutes, until potatoes are tender.

4 To serve, cut large X across top of packet; carefully fold back foil to allow steam to escape. Sprinkle with chives.

High Altitude (3500-6500 ft): No change.

Nutritional Info: 1 Serving: Calories 600 (Calories from Fat 380); Total Fat 42g (Saturated Fat 24g, Trans Fat 1g); Cholesterol 140mg; Sodium 920mg; Total Carbohydrate 27g (Dietary Fiber 2g, Sugars 2g); Protein 28g. % Daily Value: Vitamin A 20%; Vitamin C 8%; Calcium 40%; Iron 10%. Exchanges: 2 Starch, 4 Very Lean Meat, 6-1/2 Fat. Carbohydrate Choices: 2.

Betty's Kitchen Tips

Success Hint: To double the recipe, double the ingredients and divide them between two foil packets.

Substitution: Shredded Parmesan cheese can be substituted for the Swiss cheese.

caribbean pork with pineapple salsa

Prep Time: 20 Minutes
Start to Finish: 9 Hours
Servings: 6 (6 oz pork and 1/3 cup salsa each)

LOW FAT

Marinade

- 2 tablespoons packed brown sugar
- 2 teaspoons ground cinnamon
- 2 teaspoons ground allspice
- 1 teaspoon crushed red pepper flakes
- 1 cup orange juice
- 3 tablespoons fresh lime juice
- 3 large cloves garlic, finely chopped (1-1/2 teaspoons)

Pork

- 3 pork tenderloins (3/4 lb each), trimmed of fat

Salsa

- 2 cups chopped fresh pineapple
- 1/4 cup chopped red bell pepper
- 1/4 cup chopped fresh cilantro
- 1 tablespoon packed brown sugar
- 1 tablespoon fresh lime juice
- 2 teaspoons ground cumin
- 3 jalapeño chiles, seeded, chopped (about 3 tablespoons)
- 1 tablespoon olive oil

1 In large resealable food-storage plastic bag, mix marinade ingredients. Place pork tenderloins in bag; seal bag and turn to coat. Refrigerate at least 8 hours or overnight to marinate, turning bag over once or twice.

2 Heat gas or charcoal grill for indirect cooking as directed by manufacturer. Remove pork from marinade; discard marinade. Before cooking with indirect heat, place pork on grill directly over medium heat. Cover grill; cook 5 minutes. Turn pork; cook 5 minutes on other side.

3 To cook with indirect heat, move partially cooked pork to unheated side of two-burner gas grill or over drip pan on charcoal grill. (If using one-burner gas grill, cook over low heat.) Cover grill; cook 25 to 30 minutes longer or until pork has slight blush of pink in center and meat thermometer inserted in center reads 160°F.

4 Meanwhile, in medium bowl, mix all salsa ingredients except oil. Stir in oil.

5 Place pork on cutting board; let stand 5 minutes. Cut diagonally into slices; serve with salsa.

High Altitude (3500-6500): No change.

Nutritional Info: 1 Serving: Calories 310 (Calories from Fat 80); Total Fat 9g (Saturated Fat 2.5g, Trans Fat 0g); Cholesterol 70mg; Sodium 85mg; Total Carbohydrate 21g (Dietary Fiber 2g, Sugars 16g); Protein 34g. % Daily Value: Vitamin A 10%; Vitamin C 45%; Calcium 4%; Iron 10%. Exchanges: 1-1/2 Starch, 3-1/2 Lean Meat. Carbohydrate Choices: 1-1/2.

Betty's Kitchen Tips

Do-Ahead: The salsa can be made a day ahead, covered and refrigerated.

Time-Saver: Any type of purchased fruit salsa can be used, such as peach, pineapple or mango. Using a purchased fruit salsa cuts the time on this recipe.

korean steak

Prep Time: 40 Minutes
Start to Finish: 2 Hours 40 Minutes
Servings: 6

1/2 cup reduced-sodium soy sauce
1/2 cup rice vinegar
1 tablespoon finely chopped gingerroot
1 tablespoon Dijon mustard

6 medium green onions, sliced (6 tablespoons)
4 cloves garlic, crushed
1 boneless beef sirloin steak, 1-1/2 inches thick (2-1/4 lb)

1 In a large resealable food-storage plastic bag, mix all ingredients except beef.

2 Score beef crosswise by making cuts 1/2 inch apart and 1/4 inch deep (beef will absorb more of the marinade and cook more evenly). Place beef in bag; seal bag and turn to coat. Refrigerate 2 hours to marinate, turning bag once after 1 hour.

3 Heat gas or charcoal grill. Remove beef from marinade; reserve marinade in 1-quart saucepan. Pat beef dry with paper towel. Place beef on grill over medium heat. Cover grill; cook 10 minutes. Turn beef; cover grill and cook 10 to 15 minutes longer for medium-rare (145°F). Cook 2 minutes longer for medium (160°F).

4 Meanwhile, heat reserved marinade to boiling over medium-high heat; boil 3 minutes, stirring frequently. Remove and discard garlic.

5 To serve, cut beef into slices; spoon sauce over beef.

High Altitude (3500-6500 ft): No change.

Nutritional Info: 1 Serving: Calories 310 (Calories from Fat 170); Total Fat 19g (Saturated Fat 7g, Trans Fat 1g); Cholesterol 90mg; Sodium 850mg; Total Carbohydrate 4g (Dietary Fiber 0g, Sugars 2g); Protein 30g. % Daily Value: Vitamin A 4%; Vitamin C 4%; Calcium 4%; Iron 25%. Exchanges: 4-1/2 Lean Meat, 1 Fat. Carbohydrate Choices: 0.

Betty's Kitchen Tips

Time Saver: A quick way to peel fresh gingerroot is to scrape the skin off with the edge of a teaspoon.

Success Hint: Any type of quick-cooking steak, such as strip or skirt, can be used.

blackberry-glazed salmon

Prep Time: 20 Minutes
Start to Finish: 20 Minutes
Servings: 6

QUICK LOW FAT

- 1/2 cup seedless blackberry jam
- 3 tablespoons red wine vinegar
- 1 salmon fillet (2-1/4 lb), thawed if frozen, cut into 6 (6-oz) pieces

Olive oil cooking spray

- 1 tablespoon lemon-pepper seasoning salt
- 1 cup fresh blackberries

1 Heat gas or charcoal grill. In 1-quart saucepan, cook jam and vinegar over medium heat 2 to 3 minutes, stirring constantly, until jam is melted. Remove from heat; set aside.

2 Spray both sides of salmon pieces with cooking spray. Rub lemon-pepper seasoning salt over both sides of salmon. Place large sheet of heavy-duty foil on grill rack over medium heat. Place salmon, skin sides down, on foil. Cover grill; cook 8 to 10 minutes or until fish flakes easily with fork. Remove from heat.

3 Serve salmon topped with blackberry glaze and berries.

High Altitude (3500-6500 ft): No change.

Nutritional Info: 1 Serving: Calories 300 (Calories from Fat 90); Total Fat 10g (Saturated Fat 2.5g, Trans Fat 0g); Cholesterol 100mg; Sodium 480mg; Total Carbohydrate 21g (Dietary Fiber 1g, Sugars 14g); Protein 32g. % Daily Value: Vitamin A 4%; Vitamin C 8%; Calcium 4%; Iron 8%. Exchanges: 1 Other Carbohydrate, 4-1/2 Lean Meat. Carbohydrate Choices: 1-1/2.

Betty's Kitchen Tips

Do-Ahead: The glaze can be made ahead and gently rewarmed to serve over the grilled salmon.

Did You Know? Salmon is one of the top food sources of the heart-healthy omega-3 fatty acids.

ribs with cherry cola barbecue sauce

Prep Time: 30 Minutes
Start to Finish: 2 Hours
Servings: 6

Ribs

5	to 6 lb pork baby back ribs
1	teaspoon seasoned salt
1	teaspoon garlic-pepper blend
1/2	teaspoon ground ginger

Sauce

1	cup barbecue sauce
1	can (12 oz) cherry cola carbonated beverage
1/4	cup cherry preserves
1/2	teaspoon ground mustard
1 to 2	teaspoons buffalo wing hot sauce or other hot sauce

1 Heat oven to 350°F. Cut ribs into serving-size sections. Rub ribs with seasoned salt, garlic-pepper blend and ginger. Place ribs in ungreased 15x10x1-inch pan, overlapping slightly. Bake uncovered about 1 hour 30 minutes or until tender.

2 Meanwhile, in 2-quart saucepan, mix sauce ingredients. Heat to boiling. Reduce heat to medium-low; simmer uncovered 30 to 40 minutes, stirring occasionally, until flavors are blended and barbecue sauce is slightly thickened.

3 Heat gas or charcoal grill. Place ribs on grill over medium heat. Cover grill; cook 10 to 15 minutes, turning and brushing occasionally with sauce to glaze.

4 Heat remaining sauce to boiling; boil and stir 1 minute. Serve sauce with ribs.

High Altitude (3500-6500 ft): No change.

Nutritional Info: 1 Serving: Calories 980 (Calories from Fat 600); Total Fat 66g (Saturated Fat 24g, Trans Fat 0g); Cholesterol 265mg; Sodium 1650mg; Total Carbohydrate 33g (Dietary Fiber 0g, Sugars 27g); Protein 64g. % Daily Value: Vitamin A 2%; Vitamin C 4%; Calcium 15%; Iron 30%. Exchanges: 2 Other Carbohydrate, 9 Medium-Fat Meat, 4 Fat. Carbohydrate Choices: 2.

Betty's Kitchen Tips

Time-Saver: Precooking the ribs in the oven shortens the grilling time, helps tenderize the meat and removes some of the fat.

Substitution: You can use regular cola instead of the cherry cola, if you like.

ham steak with mustard sauce

Prep Time: 15 Minutes
Start to Finish: 15 Minutes
Servings: 4

EASY **QUICK**

- 1   tablespoon Dijon mustard
- 1   tablespoon honey
- 1   tablespoon apricot preserves
- 1   slice (1-lb) cooked ham
      (1/2 inch thick)

1 Heat gas or charcoal grill. In small bowl, mix mustard, honey and preserves; set aside.

2 Place ham on grill over medium-high heat. Cover grill; cook 4 minutes. Turn ham; brush with about 1/2 of mustard mixture. Cover grill; cook 4 minutes. Turn ham again; brush with remaining mustard mixture. Cover grill; cook about 2 minutes longer or until ham is thoroughly heated.

High Altitude (3500-6500 ft): No change.

Nutritional Info: 1 Serving: Calories 240 (Calories from Fat 130); Total Fat 15g (Saturated Fat 5g, Trans Fat 0g); Cholesterol 60mg; Sodium 980mg; Total Carbohydrate 8g (Dietary Fiber 0g, Sugars 7g); Protein 19g. % Daily Value: Vitamin A 0%; Vitamin C 0%; Calcium 0%; Iron 8%. Exchanges: 1/2 Other Carbohydrate, 2-1/2 Lean Meat, 1-1/2 Fat. Carbohydrate Choices: 1/2.

Betty's Kitchen Tips

Purchasing: Ham steak, sometimes labeled "ham slice," is a center-cut piece of ham that's usually fairly lean. Look for it with the other ham in the meat department.

Serve-With: Add a crisp salad and fresh steamed veggies to complete the meal. Try Caprese Salad with Greens on p. 173.

lemon salmon

Prep Time: 30 Minutes
Start to Finish: 30 Minutes
Servings: 4

1-1/2 lb salmon fillets, skin removed, cut into 4 serving pieces
2 tablespoons vegetable oil
1/2 teaspoon salt

1/2 teaspoon pepper
1 medium lemon, cut into 1/8-inch slices (about 12)
2 tablespoons finely chopped fresh parsley

1 Heat gas or charcoal grill. Cut 4 (18x12-inch) sheets of heavy-duty foil. Place salmon piece on center of each sheet. Brush 1/2 tablespoon oil over both sides of each salmon piece. Sprinkle each piece with 1/8 teaspoon salt and 1/8 teaspoon pepper. Place about 3 lemon slices flat or overlapping on each piece.

2 Bring up 2 sides of foil over salmon so edges meet. Seal edges, making tight 1/2-inch fold; fold again, allowing space for heat circulation and expansion. Fold other sides to seal.

3 Place packets on grill over medium-low heat. Cover grill; cook 13 to 16 minutes, rotating packets 1/2 turn after about 7 minutes, until salmon flakes easily with fork.

4 To serve, cut large X across top of each packet; carefully fold back foil to allow steam to escape. Sprinkle with parsley.

High Altitude (3500-6500 ft): No change.

Nutritional Info: 1 Serving: Calories 310 (Calories from Fat 150); Total Fat 17g (Saturated Fat 4g, Trans Fat 0g); Cholesterol 110mg; Sodium 400mg; Total Carbohydrate 3g (Dietary Fiber 1g, Sugars 0g); Protein 36g. % Daily Value: Vitamin A 6%; Vitamin C 15%; Calcium 4%; Iron 8%. Exchanges: 1/2 Fruit, 5-1/2 Very Lean Meat, 2 Fat. Carbohydrate Choices: 0.

Betty's Kitchen Tip

• To store fresh herbs, wrap in slightly damp paper towels, place inside a resealable food-storage plastic bag and refrigerate.

buffalo chicken kabobs

Prep Time: 40 Minutes
Start to Finish: 40 Minutes
Servings: 4

- 1 lb boneless skinless chicken breasts, cut into 24 cubes
- 24 (about 1-1/2 cups) refrigerated new potato wedges (from 1-lb 4-oz bag)
- 24 pieces (about 1 inch) celery
- 2 tablespoons olive or vegetable oil
- 1 teaspoon red pepper sauce
- 1/2 teaspoon black and red pepper blend
- 1/2 teaspoon seasoned salt
- 6 cups torn romaine lettuce
- 1/2 cup shredded carrot
- 1/2 cup blue cheese dressing

1 Heat gas or charcoal grill. On each of 8 (8- to 10-inch) metal skewers, thread chicken, potatoes and celery alternately, leaving 1/4-inch space between each piece. Mix oil and pepper sauce; brush over chicken and vegetables. Sprinkle with pepper blend and seasoned salt.

2 Place kabobs on grill over medium heat. Cover grill; cook 15 to 20 minutes, turning occasionally, until chicken is no longer pink in center and potatoes are tender.

3 On 4 individual serving plates, arrange lettuce and carrot. Top each with 2 kabobs. Serve with dressing.

High Altitude (3500-6500 ft): No change.

Nutritional Info: 1 Serving: Calories 440 (Calories from Fat 240); Total Fat 27g (Saturated Fat 4.5g, Trans Fat 0g); Cholesterol 75mg; Sodium 780mg; Total Carbohydrate 21g (Dietary Fiber 7g, Sugars 8g); Protein 28g. % Daily Value: Vitamin A 150%; Vitamin C 25%; Calcium 15%; Iron 15%. Exchanges: 1/2 Starch, 1/2 Other Carbohydrate, 1 Vegetable, 3-1/2 Lean Meat, 3-1/2 Fat. Carbohydrate Choices: 1-1/2.

Betty's Kitchen Tip

- For kabobs, always cut the meat and vegetables the size specified in the recipe to ensure the pieces cook evenly and are done at the same time.

garlic, lemon and pepper butterflied chicken

Prep Time: 50 Minutes
Start to Finish: 9 Hours 5 Minutes
Servings: 4

1	whole chicken (3 to 3-1/2 lb)	2	teaspoons cracked black pepper
1/4	cup fresh lemon juice	6	cloves garlic, crushed
1/4	cup olive or vegetable oil	1	teaspoon salt

1 Place chicken, breast side down, on cutting board. With kitchen scissors (or sharp knife), cut along one side of backbone from neck to tail, then cut along other side of backbone and remove bone.

2 Turn chicken breast side up, and place flat with legs and wings to the sides. Press down on breast bone with palm of hand to flatten chicken.

3 In large resealable food-storage plastic bag, mix remaining ingredients. Place chicken, breast side down, in bag; seal bag and turn to coat. Refrigerate 8 hours or overnight to marinate, turning once or twice.

4 Heat gas or charcoal grill on high heat at least 15 minutes before adding chicken.

5 Remove chicken from marinade; discard marinade. Reduce grill heat to medium. Place chicken, breast side up, on grill. Cover grill; cook 20 minutes. Turn chicken, breast side down. Cover grill; cook 10 to 15 minutes longer or until brown and juice of chicken is clear when thickest piece is cut to bone (170°F for breasts; 180°F for thighs and drumsticks). Cut chicken into 4 quarters to serve.

High Altitude (3500-6500 ft): No change.

Nutritional Info: 1 Serving: Calories 480 (Calories from Fat 300); Total Fat 34g (Saturated Fat 8g, Trans Fat 0.5g); Cholesterol 130mg; Sodium 720mg; Total Carbohydrate 3g (Dietary Fiber 0g, Sugars 0g); Protein 41g. % Daily Value: Vitamin A 4%; Vitamin C 4%; Calcium 4%; Iron 15%. Exchanges: 5-1/2 Lean Meat, 3-1/2 Fat. Carbohydrate Choices: 0.

Betty's Kitchen Tips

Purchasing: Cracked black pepper can be found in the spice section of the supermarket. Coarse ground black pepper can be substituted.

Success Hint: You'll need 2 medium lemons to get 1/4 cup juice.

seafood jambalaya packets

Prep Time: 30 Minutes
Start to Finish: 45 Minutes
Servings: 6

LOW FAT

● ●

1-1/2	cups uncooked regular long-grain white rice
3	cups water
1	lb uncooked deveined peeled large shrimp, thawed if frozen, tail shells removed
1	lb sea scallops, thawed if frozen
1	can (14.5 oz) diced tomatoes with garlic and onions, undrained
1	medium green bell pepper, chopped (1 cup)
1	medium onion, chopped (1/2 cup)
3	to 4 teaspoons Cajun seasoning

● ●

1 Heat gas or charcoal grill. Cut 6 (18x12-inch) sheets of heavy-duty foil. Cook rice in water as directed on package. In large bowl, mix cooked rice and remaining ingredients. Place 1/6 of mixture (dividing shrimp and scallops evenly) on center of each sheet.

2 Bring up 2 sides of foil over shrimp mixture so edges meet. Seal edges, making tight 1/2-inch fold; fold again, allowing space for heat circulation and expansion. Fold other sides to seal.

3 Place packets on grill over low heat. Cover grill; cook 12 to 15 minutes, rotating packets 1/2 turn after 6 minutes, until shrimp are pink.

4 To serve, cut large X across top of each packet; carefully fold back foil to allow steam to escape.

High Altitude (3500-6500 ft): No change.

Nutritional Info: 1 Serving: Calories 300 (Calories from Fat 15); Total Fat 2g (Saturated Fat 0g, Trans Fat 0g); Cholesterol 130mg; Sodium 330mg; Total Carbohydrate 45g (Dietary Fiber 2g, Sugars 3g); Protein 25g. % Daily Value: Vitamin A 6%; Vitamin C 20%; Calcium 10%; Iron 30%. Exchanges: 2-1/2 Starch, 1/2 Fruit, 2 Very Lean Meat. Carbohydrate Choices: 3.

Betty's Kitchen Tips

Variation: To pump up the heat even more, add 1 teaspoon red pepper sauce.

Success Hint: You can spoon the jambalaya from the foil packets onto plates, or eat right from the packets.

shrimp fajitas

Prep Time: 30 Minutes
Start to Finish: 50 Minutes
Servings: 6

Marinade

- 1 tablespoon lime juice
- 1 tablespoon olive or vegetable oil
- 1 teaspoon salt
- 1 teaspoon chili powder
- 1 teaspoon ground cumin
- 2 medium cloves garlic, crushed

Pinch ground red pepper (cayenne)

Fajitas

- 2 lb uncooked deveined peeled medium shrimp, thawed if frozen, tail shells removed
- 2 medium red bell peppers, cut into strips (about 2 cups)
- 1 medium red onion, sliced (about 2 cups)

Olive oil cooking spray

- 6 Old El Paso® flour tortillas for burritos (8 inch; from 11-oz package)
- 1-1/2 cups refrigerated guacamole (from 14-oz package)

1 Heat gas or charcoal grill. In 1-gallon resealable food-storage plastic bag, mix marinade ingredients until well blended. Add shrimp; toss to coat. Cover; refrigerate 20 minutes to marinate, turning once. Meanwhile, in medium bowl, place bell peppers and onion; spray with cooking spray. Place vegetables in grill basket (grill "wok"). Wrap tortillas in foil; set aside.

2 Place basket on grill rack over medium heat. Cover grill; cook 10 minutes, turning vegetables once.

3 Drain shrimp; discard marinade. Add shrimp to grill basket. Cover grill; cook 5 to 7 minutes longer, turning shrimp and vegetables once, until shrimp are pink. Place wrapped tortillas on grill. Cook 2 minutes, turning once, until warm.

4 On serving platter, place shrimp and vegetables; cover to keep warm. Place warmed tortillas on plate; place guacamole in serving bowl. For each serving, top tortilla with shrimp, vegetables and guacamole; fold tortilla over filling.

High Altitude (3500-6500 ft): No change.

Nutritional Info: 1 Serving: Calories 320 (Calories from Fat 110); Total Fat 12g (Saturated Fat 2.5g, Trans Fat 1g); Cholesterol 175mg; Sodium 1140mg; Total Carbohydrate 29g (Dietary Fiber 3g, Sugars 4g); Protein 23g. % Daily Value: Vitamin A 35%; Vitamin C 60%; Calcium 10%; Iron 25%. Exchanges: 2 Starch, 2-1/2 Lean Meat, 1/2 Fat. Carbohydrate Choices: 2.

Betty's Kitchen Tips

Success Hint: Do not marinate the shrimp longer than 20 minutes or they will start to cook in the marinade.

Purchasing: Look for prepared guacamole in the refrigerated section of your supermarket.

chicken kabobs with thai peanut sauce

Prep Time: 25 Minutes
Start to Finish: 25 Minutes
Servings: 6

QUICK

Sauce

1/2	cup creamy peanut butter
1/2	cup reduced-sodium soy sauce
1/4	cup rice vinegar
1/3	cup sugar
1/4	teaspoon red pepper sauce

Kabobs

6	boneless skinless chicken breasts (2 lb), each cut lengthwise into 4 strips
1	large red bell pepper, cut into 24 pieces

Cooking spray

1 Heat gas or charcoal grill. In 2-quart saucepan, mix peanut butter, soy sauce and vinegar until smooth. Stir in sugar and pepper sauce. Cook over medium-high heat about 2 minutes, stirring constantly, until thickened. Place 3/4 cup sauce in small serving bowl to use as dipping sauce.

2 On each of 6 (12-inch) metal skewers, thread 4 chicken strips and 4 bell pepper pieces alternately, leaving about 1/4-inch space between each piece. Brush chicken and bell pepper with some of the remaining sauce.

3 Spray kabobs with cooking spray to prevent sticking. Place kabobs on grill over medium heat. Cover grill; cook 5 minutes. Turn kabobs and brush with sauce; cook 2 to 3 minutes longer or until chicken is no longer pink in center. Discard any remaining sauce used for brushing kabobs during grilling. Serve kabobs with reserved sauce for dipping.

High Altitude (3500-6500): No change.

Nutritional Info: 1 Serving: Calories 400 (Calories from Fat 160); Total Fat 17g (Saturated Fat 4g, Trans Fat 0g); Cholesterol 95mg; Sodium 900mg; Total Carbohydrate 19g (Dietary Fiber 2g, Sugars 15g); Protein 41g. % Daily Value: Vitamin A 20%; Vitamin C 30%; Calcium 4%; Iron 10%. Exchanges: 1 Other Carbohydrate, 6 Lean Meat. Carbohydrate Choices: 1.

Betty's Kitchen Tips

Substitution: White vinegar diluted with a little water can be used instead of the rice vinegar.

Success Hint: Make the sauce ahead and gently reheat when needed. Or use purchased peanut sauce; for best results, choose a thick peanut sauce.

unsloppy joe burgers

Prep Time: 15 Minutes
Start to Finish: 15 Minutes
Servings: 4 sandwiches

EASY QUICK

- 1 lb extra-lean (at least 90%) ground beef
- 2 tablespoons dried minced onion
- 1 tablespoon packed brown sugar
- 1 tablespoon cider vinegar
- 1 tablespoon Worcestershire sauce
- 1/2 cup ketchup
- 4 sandwich buns, split

Leaf lettuce, if desired

Tomato slices, if desired

1 Heat closed medium-size contact grill for 5 minutes. Position drip tray to catch drippings.

2 Meanwhile, in large bowl, mix beef, onion, brown sugar, vinegar, Worcestershire sauce and 1/4 cup of the ketchup. Shape the mixture into 4 patties, about 1/2 inch thick.

3 When grill is heated, place the patties on grill. Close grill; cook 4 to 7 minutes or until thoroughly cooked and no longer pink in center.

4 Serve burgers in buns with lettuce, tomato and remaining ketchup.

High Altitude (3500-6500 ft): No change.

Nutritional Info: 1 Sandwich: Calories 350 (Calories from Fat 100); Total Fat 11g (Saturated Fat 4g, Trans Fat 1g); Cholesterol 70mg; Sodium 630mg; Total Carbohydrate 35g (Dietary Fiber 1g, Sugars 15g); Protein 26g. % Daily Value: Vitamin A 6%; Vitamin C 6%; Calcium 8%; Iron 25%. Exchanges: 2 Starch, 1/2 Other Carbohydrate, 3 Lean Meat. Carbohydrate Choices: 2.

Betty's Kitchen Tip

- For toasted buns, remove cooked burgers from grill; wipe grill plates with paper towel. Place 2 buns, cut sides down, on grill. Close grill; cook 1 minute. Repeat with remaining buns.

greek chicken salad

Prep Time: 20 Minutes
Start to Finish: 20 Minutes
Servings: 4

1-1/4 lb uncooked chicken breast tenders (not breaded)
2 teaspoons olive or vegetable oil
2 teaspoons Greek seasoning
1 bag (10 oz) washed fresh baby spinach leaves

1 medium cucumber, peeled, seeded and diced
1 cup halved grape or cherry tomatoes
1/4 cup halved pitted kalamata olives
2/3 cup vinaigrette dressing
1/4 cup crumbled feta cheese

1 Heat gas or charcoal grill. Toss the chicken tenders with oil; sprinkle with Greek seasoning.

2 Place chicken on grill over medium heat. Cover grill; cook 5 to 6 minutes, turning once, until no longer pink in center.

3 Meanwhile, in large bowl, toss spinach, cucumber, tomatoes and olives with dressing. Spoon onto 4 serving plates; serve with chicken tenders. Sprinkle with cheese.

High Altitude (3500-6500 ft): No change.

Nutritional Info: 1 Serving: Calories 390 (Calories from Fat 190); Total Fat 22g (Saturated Fat 4g, Trans Fat 0g); Cholesterol 95mg; Sodium 1020mg; Total Carbohydrate 12g (Dietary Fiber 3g, Sugars 8g); Protein 36g. % Daily Value: Vitamin A 120%; Vitamin C 25%; Calcium 15%; Iron 15%. Exchanges: 1/2 Other Carbohydrate; 1-1/2 Vegetable, 3-1/2 Lean Meat, 2 Fat. Carbohydrate Choices: 1.

Betty's Kitchen Tips

Success Hint: If chicken tenders are not available, cut boneless skinless chicken breasts lengthwise into thin strips.

Purchasing: Almost any savory vinaigrette, or oil-and-vinegar dressing, would work with this recipe. Several brands of plain vinaigrettes are available, plus varieties with balsamic vinegar and various herbs.

cheesy mini meat loaves

Prep Time: 20 Minutes
Start to Finish: 20 Minutes
Servings: 4

QUICK

1	lb extra-lean (at least 90%) ground beef
1/4	cup Progresso® plain bread crumbs
3	tablespoons ketchup
1	teaspoon onion salt
1/2	teaspoon pepper
1	egg
1/2	cup shredded Cheddar cheese (2 oz)
4	slices center-cut bacon (about 3-1/2 oz), cut crosswise in half

1 Heat closed medium-size contact grill for 5 minutes. Position the drip tray to catch drippings.

2 Meanwhile, in a large bowl, mix all ingredients except bacon. On work surface, pat mixture into 7-inch square. Cut into 4 (3-1/2-inch) squares.

3 When grill is heated, place beef squares on grill. Top each square with 2 half-slices bacon. Close grill; cook 6 to 10 minutes or until squares are thoroughly cooked and no longer pink in center and bacon is browned.

High Altitude (3500-6500 ft): No change.

Nutritional Info: 1 Serving: Calories 320 (Calories from Fat 160); Total Fat 18g (Saturated Fat 8g, Trans Fat 0.5g); Cholesterol 140mg; Sodium 880mg; Total Carbohydrate 9g (Dietary Fiber 0g, Sugars 4g); Protein 30g. % Daily Value: Vitamin A 6%; Vitamin C 0%; Calcium 10%; Iron 15%. Exchanges: 1/2 Starch, 3-1/2 Medium-Fat Meat. Carbohydrate Choices: 1/2.

Betty's Kitchen Tips

Variation: Use Italian-style bread crumbs for a different flavor. You could also use pizza or spaghetti sauce for the ketchup.

Substitution: Center-cut bacon has had the fatty ends cut off. You can use slices of regular bacon—just trim about 3/4 inch off of each end. The half-strips should just cover the surface of each beef square.

jerk shrimp kabobs

Prep Time: 35 Minutes
Start to Finish: 35 Minutes
Servings: 4 kabobs

2	tablespoons olive or vegetable oil
2	teaspoons Caribbean jerk seasoning (dry)
1/4	teaspoon salt
1-1/2	lb uncooked deveined peeled large shrimp (21 to 30 count) or extra-large shrimp (16 to 20 count), thawed if frozen, tail shells removed
16	chunks (about 1 inch) fresh pineapple
1	red bell pepper, cut into 16 pieces
1/4	cup pineapple preserves
2	tablespoons lime juice

1 Heat gas or charcoal grill. In large bowl, mix oil, jerk seasoning and salt. Add shrimp, pineapple and bell pepper; toss to coat.

2 On each of 4 (12- to 15-inch) metal skewers, thread shrimp, pineapple and bell pepper alternately, leaving 1/4-inch space between each piece. In small bowl, mix preserves and lime juice; set aside.

3 Place kabobs on grill over medium heat. Cover grill; cook 4 minutes. Turn kabobs; brush with preserves mixture. Cover grill; cook 4 to 8 minutes longer or until the shrimp are pink. Discard any remaining preserves mixture.

High Altitude (3500-6500 ft): No change.

Nutritional Info: 1 Kabob: Calories 250 (Calories from Fat 70); Total Fat 8g (Saturated Fat 1.5g, Trans Fat 0g); Cholesterol 240mg; Sodium 440mg; Total Carbohydrate 16g (Dietary Fiber 1g, Sugars 11g); Protein 26g. % Daily Value: Vitamin A 25%; Vitamin C 35%; Calcium 6%; Iron 25%. Exchanges: 1 Other Carbohydrate, 3-1/2 Lean Meat. Carbohydrate Choices: 1.

Betty's Kitchen Tips

How-To: To devein the shrimp, use the point of a sharp knife to cut a slit along the back curve of the shrimp. Pull out the dark vein, and rinse the shrimp under cold water.

Serve-With: Continue the Caribbean theme by serving the kabobs on a bed of cooked white rice along with fresh fruit and a black bean salad from the deli.

Did You Know? Although the ingredients in Caribbean jerk seasoning vary, they're usually a blend of chiles, thyme, sweet spices, garlic and onions. Traditionally, jerk seasoning is used to flavor grilled meats.

tuna steaks with green onions and orange butter

Prep Time: 20 Minutes
Start to Finish: 20 Minutes
Servings: 4

QUICK

- 1/4   cup butter, softened
- 1   tablespoon finely chopped green onion (1 medium)
- 1   teaspoon grated orange peel
- 4   teaspoons extra-virgin olive oil
- 1/2   teaspoon celery salt
- 1/2   teaspoon cracked black pepper
- 4   tuna steaks, 1 inch thick (about 1-1/4 lb)
- 4   green onions, trimmed

1 Heat gas or charcoal grill. In small bowl, mix butter, 1 tablespoon chopped green onion and the orange peel; set aside.

2 In another small bowl, mix oil, celery salt and pepper. Brush oil mixture on both sides of tuna steaks and over whole green onions.

3 Place tuna on grill over medium heat. Cover grill; cook 8 to 10 minutes, turning once, until tuna flakes easily with fork and is slightly pink in center. Add onions to grill during last 5 minutes of grilling; turn occasionally. Cover tuna and let stand 5 minutes before serving. Serve tuna and onions with dollops of orange butter.

High Altitude (3500-6500 ft): No change.

Nutritional Info: 1 Serving: Calories 330 (Calories from Fat 210); Total Fat 23g (Saturated Fat 10g, Trans Fat 0g); Cholesterol 115mg; Sodium 350mg; Total Carbohydrate 2g (Dietary Fiber 0g, Sugars 0g); Protein 27g. % Daily Value: Vitamin A 15%; Vitamin C 6%; Calcium 4%; Iron 8%. Exchanges: 4 Lean Meat, 2 Fat. Carbohydrate Choices: 0.

Betty's Kitchen Tips

Substitution: Celery salt adds a nice flavor to the tuna, but plain salt can be substituted.

Success Hint: If you have leftover cooked tuna, flake it and use in your favorite tuna salad recipe. Delicious!

cuban pork pressed sandwiches

Prep Time: 30 Minutes
Start to Finish: 30 Minutes
Servings: 4 sandwiches

QUICK

- 1/2 lb pork tenderloin, cut crosswise into 4 slices
- 3 tablespoons olive oil-and-vinegar dressing
- 2 teaspoons grated lime peel
- 1 teaspoon dried oregano leaves
- 4 slices (1 oz each) provolone cheese (from deli)

- 4 soft kaiser rolls, split
- 8 thin slices (1 oz each) baked ham (from deli)
- 3 tablespoons yellow mustard
- 3 tablespoons dill pickle relish

1 Between pieces of plastic wrap, gently pound pork with flat side of meat mallet until very thin. Place in glass baking dish. In small bowl, mix dressing, lime peel and oregano. Spread over pork; turn pork to coat. Let stand while heating contact grill.

2 Heat closed medium-size contact grill for 5 minutes. Position drip tray to catch drippings. Place pork on grill. Close grill; cook 5 to 6 minutes or until no longer pink in center. Meanwhile, place cheese on cut sides of roll bottoms; top with ham, pleating to fit. Spread mustard and pickle

relish on cut sides of bun tops. Place grilled pork on ham; place roll tops, relish sides down, on pork. Press down firmly on tops of sandwiches (sandwiches are thick).

3 Carefully wipe off grill plates; spray with cooking spray. Place sandwiches on grill. Carefully close grill so tops of rolls don't slip off sandwiches. Gently press top of grill until sandwiches are compressed. Cook 3 to 4 minutes or until rolls are toasted and cheese is melted.

High Altitude (3500-6500 ft): No change.

Nutritional Info: 1 Sandwich: Calories 430 (Calories from Fat 170); Total Fat 19g (Saturated Fat 7g, Trans Fat 1g); Cholesterol 75mg; Sodium 1740mg; Total Carbohydrate 31g (Dietary Fiber 2g, Sugars 3g); Protein 35g. % Daily Value: Vitamin A 6%; Vitamin C 0%; Calcium 30%; Iron 20%. Exchanges: 2 Starch, 4 Lean Meat, 1 Fat. Carbohydrate Choices: 2.

Betty's Kitchen Tips

Variation: Large Cuban rolls or sandwich buns would also work for this recipe.

Substitution: Mustard and dill pickles are traditional in Cuban pork sandwiches. If you don't like either, you could substitute mayonnaise and sweet pickle relish, or omit the relish.

sour cream and onion burgers

Prep Time: 25 Minutes
Start to Finish: 25 Minutes
Servings: 8 sandwiches

QUICK

2	lb lean (at least 80%) ground beef
1	package (1 oz) onion soup mix
1	cup sour cream
1/2	cup Progresso® plain bread crumbs
1/8	teaspoon pepper
1	round focaccia bread (about 10 inches in diameter), cut horizontally in half, then cut into 8 wedges

Leaf lettuce, if desired

1 Heat gas or charcoal grill. In large bowl, mix all ingredients except focaccia and lettuce. Shape mixture into 8 patties, about 1/2 inch thick.

2 Place patties on grill over medium heat. Cover grill; cook 10 to 15 minutes, turning once, until meat thermometer inserted in center of patties reads 160°F. Serve with lettuce on focaccia.

High Altitude (3500-6500 ft): No change.

Nutritional Info: 1 Sandwich: Calories 400 (Calories from Fat 190); Total Fat 21g (Saturated Fat 9g, Trans Fat 1g); Cholesterol 90mg; Sodium 620mg; Total Carbohydrate 27g (Dietary Fiber 1g, Sugars 5g); Protein 25g. % Daily Value: Vitamin A 4%; Vitamin C 0%; Calcium 15%; Iron 20%. Exchanges: 1-1/2 Starch, 3 Medium-Fat Meat, 1 Fat. Carbohydrate Choices: 2.

Betty's Kitchen Tips

Variation: Try sprinkling burgers with canned French-fried onions for fun, flavor and crunch!

Time-Saver: Save time on cleanup—serve dinner on disposable plates. Spend the extra time chatting with your kids about their school day.

flank steak with smoky honey mustard sauce

Prep Time: 30 Minutes
Start to Finish: 30 Minutes
Servings: 6

QUICK

Sauce

1/4	cup honey mustard dressing
1	tablespoon frozen (thawed) orange juice concentrate
1	tablespoon water
1	small clove garlic, finely chopped
1	chipotle chile in adobo sauce (from 7-oz can), finely chopped

Steak

1	beef flank steak (about 1-1/2 lb)
6	Old El Paso® flour tortillas for burritos (8 inch; from 11-oz package)

1 Heat gas or charcoal grill. In small bowl, mix sauce ingredients; reserve 2 tablespoons. Make cuts about 1/2 inch apart and 1/8 inch deep in diamond pattern in both sides of beef. Brush reserved sauce on both sides of beef.

2 Place beef on grill over medium heat. Cover grill; cook 17 to 20 minutes, turning once, until desired doneness. Cut beef across grain into thin slices. Serve with remaining sauce and tortillas.

High Altitude (3500-6500): No change.

Nutritional Info: 1 Serving: Calories 360 (Calories from Fat 140); Total Fat 16g (Saturated Fat 4.5g, Trans Fat 1.5g); Cholesterol 55mg; Sodium 460mg; Total Carbohydrate 22g (Dietary Fiber 0g, Sugars 2g); Protein 31g. % Daily Value: Vitamin A 0%; Vitamin C 4%; Calcium 6%; Iron 20%. Exchanges: 1-1/2 Starch, 4 Lean Meat, 1/2 Fat. Carbohydrate Choices: 1-1/2.

Betty's Kitchen Tips

Variation: To make this dish more like fajitas, add ingredients such as chopped tomatoes, shredded lettuce, diced avocado, shredded cheese, sliced olives, sliced green onions and diced bell pepper to the menu.

Did You Know? Flank steak is a long, thin piece of boneless beef cut from the lower hindquarters. Flank steak is known to be a less-tender cut and should be very thinly sliced across the grain for serving. It is typically used for fajitas or London broil.

MEAL-IN-ONE CASSEROLES

p. 98

103

111

95

buffalo chicken and potatoes

Prep Time: 10 Minutes
Start to Finish: 1 Hour 5 Minutes
Servings: 6 (1-3/4 cups each)

EASY

1-1/4   lb boneless skinless chicken breasts, cut into 1-inch strips
1/3   cup buffalo wing sauce
6   cups frozen (thawed) southern-style hash brown potatoes
1   cup ranch or blue cheese dressing

1/2   cup shredded Cheddar cheese (2 oz)
1   can (10 oz) condensed cream of celery soup
1/2   cup corn flake crumbs
2   tablespoons butter or margarine, melted
1/4   cup chopped green onions (3 to 4 medium)

1   Heat oven to 350°F. Spray 13x9-inch (3-quart) baking dish with cooking spray.

2   In medium bowl, stir together chicken strips and wing sauce.

3   In large bowl, stir together potatoes, dressing, cheese and soup. Spoon into baking dish. Place chicken strips in single layer over potato mixture.

4   In small bowl, stir together crumbs and butter. Sprinkle in baking dish.

5   Cover with foil. Bake 30 minutes; uncover and bake 20 to 25 minutes longer or until potatoes are tender and juice of chicken is no longer pink when centers of thickest pieces are cut. Sprinkle with green onions.

High Altitude (3500-6500 ft): Heat oven to 375°F. In step 3, stir 1/4 cup water in with the potatoes.

Nutritional Info: 1 Serving: Calories 620 (Calories from Fat 300); Total Fat 33g (Saturated Fat 9g, Trans Fat 0g); Cholesterol 90mg; Sodium 1240mg; Total Carbohydrate 51g (Dietary Fiber 5g, Sugars 5g); Protein 28g. % Daily Value: Vitamin A 20%; Vitamin C 15%; Calcium 10%; Iron 15%. Exchanges: 2-1/2 Starch, 1 Other Carbohydrate, 3 Lean Meat, 4-1/2 Fat. Carbohydrate Choices: 3-1/2.

Betty's Kitchen Tips

Substitution: For authentic flavor, go with red hot buffalo wing sauce. Other flavors to try include teriyaki, sweet and sour or barbecue.

Variation: For a cheesy hash brown side dish, omit the chicken and wing sauce. Serve casserole with barbecued chicken or baked ham.

Time-Saver: Try using precut chicken tenders to make prep time shorter.

Serve-With: Serve casserole with additional blue cheese dressing.

german pork & cabbage casserole

Prep Time: 20 Minutes
Start to Finish: 1 Hour 5 Minutes
Servings: 6 (1 rib and 1 cup vegetable mixture each)

- 3 slices bacon
- 6 country-style pork ribs
- 1/2 teaspoon salt
- 1/4 teaspoon pepper
- 5 cups coleslaw mix (from 16-oz bag)
- 1 cup chopped onion (1 large)
- 1 can (8 oz) sauerkraut, drained
- 1 apple, chopped
- 1 cup julienne (matchstick-cut) carrots
- 3/4 cup apple cider
- 1 teaspoon caraway seed

Nutritional Info: 1 Serving: Calories 280 (Calories from Fat 120); Total Fat 13g (Saturated Fat 4.5g, Trans Fat 0g); Cholesterol 60mg; Sodium 610mg; Total Carbohydrate 18g (Dietary Fiber 4g, Sugars 11g); Protein 21g. % Daily Value: Vitamin A 100%; Vitamin C 25%; Calcium 6%; Iron 10%. Exchanges: 1/2 Other Carbohydrate, 2 Vegetable, 2-1/2 Medium-Fat Meat. Carbohydrate Choices: 1.

1 Heat oven to 350°F. Spray 13x9-inch (3-quart) baking dish with cooking spray. In 12-inch nonstick skillet, cook bacon until crisp; remove from skillet and crumble into small bowl. Season ribs with salt and pepper. In same skillet, cook ribs in bacon drippings over high heat 3 to 4 minutes, turning once, until brown. Place in baking dish, reserving fat in skillet.

2 In same skillet, place coleslaw mix and onion; cook over medium heat about 3 minutes, stirring occasionally, until softened and wilted. Remove from heat. Add bacon, sauerkraut, apple, carrots, apple cider and caraway seed; mix well. Spoon into baking dish on top of pork.

3 Cover with foil. Bake 30 to 45 minutes or until pork is no longer pink and meat thermometer inserted in center reads 160°F.

High Altitude (3500-6500 ft): In step 3, cover and bake 40 to 45 minutes.

Betty's Kitchen Tips

Substitution: Ribs can be bone-in or boneless. One boneless rib usually supplies enough meat for one serving.

Success Hint: If you prefer, you can slice your own cabbage instead of using the bag of coleslaw mix. Slice the cabbage very finely. Look for matchstick-cut carrots in the produce section of the grocery store.

chicken paprika shepherd's pie

Prep Time: 20 Minutes
Start to Finish: 55 Minutes
Servings: 4

1 pouch Betty Crocker® roasted garlic mashed potatoes (from 7.2-oz box)	1/2 cup chopped onion (1 medium)
1 cup hot water	1-1/2 cups Green Giant® Valley Fresh Steamers™ frozen mixed vegetables
1/2 cup milk	1 jar (12 oz) home-style chicken gravy
3 tablespoons butter or margarine	2-1/4 teaspoons paprika
1 lb boneless skinless chicken breasts, cut into 1/2-inch pieces	1/2 cup sour cream

1. Heat oven to 350°F. Spray 2-quart shallow casserole or 8-inch square baking dish with cooking spray. Make mashed potatoes as directed on box for 4 servings—except use 1 cup hot water, 1/2 cup milk and 2 tablespoons of the butter.

2. Meanwhile, in 12-inch nonstick skillet, melt remaining 1 tablespoon butter over medium-high heat. Cook chicken and onion in butter 4 to 6 minutes, stirring frequently, until chicken is no longer pink in center. Stir in vegetables, gravy and 2 teaspoons of the paprika. Cover; cook over medium-low heat 5 minutes, stirring frequently to prevent sticking.

3. Stir in sour cream. Spoon into casserole. Spoon or pipe potatoes in 8 mounds around edge of casserole. Sprinkle potatoes with remaining 1/4 teaspoon paprika. Bake 25 to 35 minutes or until mixture bubbles around edge of casserole.

High Altitude (3500-6500 ft): No change.

Nutritional Info: 1 Serving: Calories 500 (Calories from Fat 220); Total Fat 24g (Saturated Fat 12g, Trans Fat 0.5g); Cholesterol 115mg; Sodium 940mg; Total Carbohydrate 37g (Dietary Fiber 5g, Sugars 7g); Protein 33g. % Daily Value: Vitamin A 80%; Vitamin C 4%; Calcium 10%; Iron 15%. Exchanges: 1-1/2 Starch, 1/2 Other Carbohydrate, 1 Vegetable, 4 Lean Meat, 2 Fat. Carbohydrate Choices: 2-1/2.

Betty's Kitchen Tip

• To add a slightly smoky flavor to the casserole, add about 1/4 lb sliced smoked kielbasa sausage when you stir in the vegetables.

loaded baked potato casserole

Prep Time: 15 Minutes
Start to Finish: 1 Hour
Servings: 8

EASY

- 1 package (30 oz) frozen extra-spicy and crispy potato wedges
- 2 cups chopped fully cooked ham (12 oz)
- 8 slices bacon, crisply cooked and crumbled
- 1 medium red bell pepper, chopped
- 1 cup chopped green onions (10 medium)
- 1 jar (15 oz) cheese dip
- 1/2 cup sour cream

1 Heat oven to 375°F. Spray 13x9-inch (3-quart) baking dish with cooking spray.

2 Arrange potato wedges in baking dish; bake 10 to 15 minutes or until thawed and beginning to brown. Top with half each of the ham, bacon, bell pepper and green onions. Spread cheese dip on top. Sprinkle with remaining ham, bacon and bell pepper.

3 Bake 20 to 30 minutes or until cheese dip is melted and potatoes are tender. Top with dollops of sour cream and remaining green onions.

High Altitude (3500-6500 ft): No change.

Nutritional Info: 1 Serving: Calories 300 (Calories from Fat 150); Total Fat 17g (Saturated Fat 8g, Trans Fat 0.5g); Cholesterol 60mg; Sodium 1270mg; Total Carbohydrate 18g (Dietary Fiber 3g, Sugars 6g); Protein 20g. % Daily Value: Vitamin A 20%; Vitamin C 25%; Calcium 15%; Iron 10%. Exchanges: 1/2 Starch, 1/2 Other Carbohydrate, 2-1/2 Medium-Fat Meat, 1 Fat. Carbohydrate Choices: 1.

Betty's Kitchen Tips

Variation: For a loaded side dish, omit the ham. Serve with steaks or chops.

Substitution: For a flavor twist, substitute grilled chicken strips for the ham.

potato-topped meat loaf casserole

Prep Time: 20 Minutes
Start to Finish: 55 Minutes
Servings: 6

Meat Loaf

1	lb extra-lean (at least 90%) ground beef
3	tablespoons Progresso® plain bread crumbs
3	tablespoons steak sauce
1	tablespoon instant minced onion
1/2	teaspoon salt
1/4	teaspoon pepper
1	egg

Filling

1-3/4	cups water
1/2	cup milk
2	tablespoons butter or margarine
1/4	teaspoon salt
2	cups Betty Crocker® Potato Buds® mashed potatoes (dry)
1	egg
1-1/2	cups Green Giant® Valley Fresh Steamers™ frozen chopped broccoli, thawed
1/2	cup shredded sharp Cheddar cheese (2 oz)

1 Heat oven to 350°F. Spray 8-inch square (2-quart) baking dish with cooking spray. In medium bowl, mix first 7 ingredients. Press in bottom and up sides of baking dish to within 1/2 inch of top.

2 In 2-quart saucepan, heat water, milk, butter and 1/4 teaspoon salt to boiling. Remove from heat; stir in potatoes. Let stand 30 seconds. Stir in egg. Stir in broccoli and cheese. Spoon over meat shell.

3 Bake 25 to 30 minutes or until meat loaf is thoroughly cooked and meat thermometer inserted in center of meat reads 170°F. Let stand 5 minutes; drain liquid along edges.

High Altitude (3500-6500 ft): In step 3, bake 30 to 35 minutes.

Nutritional Info: 1 Serving: Calories 330 (Calories from Fat 140); Total Fat 15g (Saturated Fat 8g, Trans Fat 0.5g); Cholesterol 140mg; Sodium 610mg; Total Carbohydrate 26g (Dietary Fiber 2g, Sugars 4g); Protein 23g. % Daily Value: Vitamin A 15%; Vitamin C 15%; Calcium 10%; Iron 15%. Exchanges: 1-1/2 Starch, 2-1/2 Medium-Fat Meat, 1/2 Fat. Carbohydrate Choices: 2.

Betty's Kitchen Tips

Variation: You can use 1-1/2 cups of your favorite vegetable in this recipe. Try frozen mixed vegetables, frozen peas or green beans.

Time-Saver: Use cheese-flavored potatoes and omit the shredded cheese or purchase refrigerated mashed potatoes for this recipe.

Substitution: Substitute your favorite meat (ground chicken, turkey or pork).

tuna and broccoli bake

Prep Time: 10 Minutes
Start to Finish: 55 Minutes
Servings: 6

EASY

- 2 cups fresh broccoli florets
- 2 cans (5 oz each) tuna in water, drained
- 2 cups shredded Cheddar cheese (8 oz)
- 3/4 cup Original Bisquick® mix
- 3/4 cup sour cream
- 3/4 cup milk
- 3 eggs

1. Heat oven to 350°F. Spray 8-inch square (2-quart) baking dish with cooking spray.

2. Sprinkle broccoli, tuna and 1-1/2 cups of the cheese in baking dish.

3. In large bowl, stir Bisquick mix, sour cream, milk and eggs with wire whisk or fork until blended. Pour into baking dish.

4. Bake 30 to 40 minutes or until knife inserted in center comes out clean. Sprinkle with remaining 1/2 cup cheese. Let stand 5 minutes before serving.

High Altitude (3500-6500 ft): In step 4, bake 40 to 50 minutes.

Nutritional Info: 1 Serving: Calories 380 (Calories from Fat 210); Total Fat 24g (Saturated Fat 13g, Trans Fat 1g); Cholesterol 180mg; Sodium 610mg; Total Carbohydrate 15g (Dietary Fiber 1g, Sugars 4g); Protein 26g. % Daily Value: Vitamin A 20%; Vitamin C 25%; Calcium 30%; Iron 10%. Exchanges: 1 Starch, 3 Medium-Fat Meat, 1-1/2 Fat. Carbohydrate Choices: 1.

Betty's Kitchen Tip

- If your family isn't fond of tuna, canned chicken or cubed cooked chicken can be used.

minestrone casserole

Prep Time: 25 Minutes
Start to Finish: 1 Hour 15 Minutes
Servings: 6

- 2 cups uncooked mini lasagna (mafalda) noodles (4 oz)
- 3 tablespoons olive oil
- 1 cup chopped onion (1 large)
- 1 cup sliced carrots, (2 medium)
- 2 medium stalks celery, sliced (1 cup)
- 1 medium green bell pepper, chopped
- 1 medium zucchini or summer squash, quartered lengthwise and sliced

- 2 cloves garlic, chopped
- 2 cans (15 oz each) red kidney beans, drained, rinsed
- 1 can (15 oz) diced tomatoes with Italian herbs, undrained
- 1/2 cup finely shredded Parmesan cheese
- 1 teaspoon salt
- 1/4 teaspoon pepper
- 1/4 cup refrigerated basil pesto

---

1 Heat oven to 350°F. Cook and drain pasta as directed on package using minimum cook time.

2 Meanwhile, in 10-inch skillet, heat oil over medium heat. Add onion, carrots, celery and bell pepper; cover and cook 5 to 8 minutes, stirring occasionally, until carrots are just tender. Uncover; stir in zucchini and garlic. Cook and stir 1 minute longer.

3 Place pasta in ungreased 2-1/2-quart casserole. Stir in carrot mixture, beans, tomatoes, 1/4 cup of the cheese, salt, pepper and pesto. Cover casserole. Bake 40 to 50 minutes or until hot in center. Top each serving with remaining cheese.

High Altitude (3500-6500 ft): No change.

Nutritional Info: 1 Serving: Calories 440 (Calories from Fat 140); Total Fat 16g (Saturated Fat 4g, Trans Fat 0g); Cholesterol 10mg; Sodium 840mg; Total Carbohydrate 54g (Dietary Fiber 11g, Sugars 7g); Protein 19g. % Daily Value: Vitamin A 80%; Vitamin C 30%; Calcium 25%; Iron 25%. Exchanges: 3 Starch, 2 Vegetable, 1 Lean Meat, 2 Fat. Carbohydrate Choices: 3-1/2.

Betty's Kitchen Tips

Variation: Add 1/2 lb bulk Italian sausage, crumbled, cooked and drained, with the beans.

Success Hint: Minestrone is a classic dish that uses what the cook has on hand. Consider using up odds and ends of pasta packages instead of the mini lasagna noodles. Just make sure that they cook about the same length of time.

cheesy tater-topped chicken casserole

Prep Time: 10 Minutes
Start to Finish: 1 Hour 5 Minutes
Servings: 6 (1-1/3 cups each) **EASY**

- 1 bag (24 oz) Green Giant® frozen broccoli, carrots, cauliflower & cheese-flavored sauce
- 2 cups diced cooked chicken
- 4 medium green onions, chopped (1/4 cup)
- 4 cups frozen potato nuggets (from 2-lb bag)
- 1/2 cup finely shredded Cheddar cheese (2 oz)

1 Heat oven to 375°F. In ungreased 11x7-inch (2-quart) baking dish, place broccoli, carrots, cauliflower and cheese sauce. Microwave uncovered on High 3 to 5 minutes, stirring once, until thawed. Stir well until cheese sauce is melted.

2 Stir chicken and 3 tablespoons of the onions into vegetable-cheese mixture. Top with frozen potato nuggets.

3 Bake 40 to 45 minutes or until bubbly around edges and potato nuggets are golden brown. Sprinkle with cheese and remaining 1 tablespoon onion. Bake 5 to 10 minutes longer or until cheese is melted.

High Altitude (3500-6500 ft): No change.

Nutritional Info: 1 Serving: Calories 540 (Calories from Fat 220); Total Fat 24g (Saturated Fat 7g, Trans Fat 8g); Cholesterol 50mg; Sodium 1150mg; Total Carbohydrate 59g (Dietary Fiber 5g, Sugars 2g); Protein 20g. % Daily Value: Vitamin A 8%; Vitamin C 15%; Calcium 10%; Iron 10%. Exchanges: 3 Starch, 1/2 Other Carbohydrate, 1 Vegetable, 1 Medium-Fat Meat, 3-1/2 Fat. Carbohydrate Choices: 4.

Betty's Kitchen Tip

• Try this recipe with diced cooked turkey instead of the chicken and mozzarella cheese in place of the Cheddar.

cheesy chicken pot pie

Prep Time: 20 Minutes
Start to Finish: 1 Hour 10 Minutes
Servings: 4

1	tablespoon vegetable oil
1/2	cup chopped onion (1 medium)
1/2	cup chopped celery (1 medium stalk)
1	cup thinly sliced carrots (2 medium)
1	cup Green Giant® Valley Fresh Steamers™ frozen cut green beans, thawed
2	cups chopped cooked chicken

1	can (10-3/4 oz) condensed cream of chicken soup
1	can (10-1/2 oz) chicken gravy
1/2	teaspoon dried sage leaves
1	cup finely shredded sharp Cheddar cheese (4 oz)
1	Pillsbury® refrigerated pie crust (from 15-oz box), softened as directed on box

1. Heat oven to 375°F. In 10-inch skillet, heat oil over medium-high heat. Add onion and celery. Cook 3 to 5 minutes, stirring occasionally, until crisp-tender. Stir in carrots, green beans, chicken, soup, gravy and sage. Cook until bubbly. Stir in 3/4 cup of the cheese. Spoon into ungreased deep 2-quart casserole.

2. Place pie crust over hot chicken mixture. Fold over edges to fit inside casserole. Cut small slits in surface of crust with paring knife.

3. Bake 40 minutes. Sprinkle remaining 1/4 cup cheese over crust; bake 5 to 6 minutes longer or until crust is deep golden brown and cheese is melted.

High Altitude (3500-6500 ft): In step 3, bake 45 minutes. Continue as directed.

Nutritional Info: 1 Serving: Calories 670 (Calories from Fat 370); Total Fat 41g (Saturated Fat 15g, Trans Fat 0.5g); Cholesterol 105mg; Sodium 1460mg; Total Carbohydrate 44g (Dietary Fiber 3g, Sugars 4g); Protein 31g. % Daily Value: Vitamin A 120%; Vitamin C 4%; Calcium 20%; Iron 10%. Exchanges: 1-1/2 Starch, 1 Other Carbohydrate, 1 Vegetable, 3-1/2 Medium-Fat Meat, 4-1/2 Fat. Carbohydrate Choices: 3.

Betty's Kitchen Tips

Special Touch: Use small canapé cutters to cut out fun shapes in the crust.

How-To: If you have a food processor, use the slicing blade to slice the carrots. Use the metal blade, and pulse on and off to chop the onion and celery.

easy ravioli bake

Prep Time: 10 Minutes
Start to Finish: 1 Hour 20 Minutes
Servings: 8

- 1   jar (26 to 28 oz) tomato pasta sauce (any variety)
- 1   package (25 to 27-1/2 oz) frozen cheese-filled ravioli
- 2   cups shredded mozzarella cheese (8 oz)
- 2   tablespoons grated Parmesan cheese

1 Heat oven to 350°F. Spray bottom and sides of 13x9-inch (3-quart) baking dish with cooking spray.

2 Spread 3/4 cup of the pasta sauce in baking dish. Arrange half of the frozen ravioli in single layer over sauce; top with half of the remaining pasta sauce and 1 cup of the mozzarella cheese. Repeat layers once, starting with ravioli. Sprinkle with Parmesan cheese.

3 Cover with foil. Bake 40 minutes. Remove foil; bake 15 to 20 minutes longer or until bubbly and hot in center. Let stand 10 minutes before cutting.

High Altitude (3500-6500 ft): In step 3, increase first bake time to 50 minutes.

Nutritional Info: 1 Serving: Calories 290 (Calories from Fat 90); Total Fat 10g (Saturated Fat 6g, Trans Fat 0g); Cholesterol 30mg; Sodium 920mg; Total Carbohydrate 36g (Dietary Fiber 2g, Sugars 6g); Protein 14g. % Daily Value: Vitamin A 10%; Vitamin C 6%; Calcium 30%; Iron 10%. Exchanges: 1-1/2 Starch, 1 Other Carbohydrate, 1-1/2 Medium-Fat Meat. Carbohydrate Choices: 2-1/2.

EASY LOW FAT

Betty's Kitchen Tips

Variation: Add one of the following on the first layer of ravioli: 1 cup sliced mushrooms, 1 box (9 oz) Green Giant® frozen spinach, thawed and squeezed to drain, or 1-1/2 oz sliced pepperoni.

Substitution: Do you have meat lovers in your family? Any meat-filled ravioli can be used instead of the cheese-filled variety.

Make-Ahead: To make this super-easy recipe in advance, layer the ingredients in the baking dish, cover tightly with foil, and refrigerate up to 24 hours. Bake as directed.

jerk chicken casserole

Prep Time: 15 Minutes
Start to Finish: 1 Hour
Servings: 6

EASY LOW FAT

1-1/4	teaspoons salt
1/2	teaspoon pumpkin pie spice
3/4	teaspoon ground allspice
3/4	teaspoon dried thyme leaves
1/4	teaspoon ground red pepper (cayenne)
6	boneless skinless chicken thighs
1	tablespoon vegetable oil

1	can (15 oz) Progresso® black beans, drained, rinsed
1	large sweet potato (1 lb), peeled, cubed (3 cups)
1/4	cup honey
1/4	cup lime juice
2	teaspoons cornstarch
2	tablespoons sliced green onions (2 medium)

1 Heat oven to 375°F. Spray 8-inch square (2-quart) baking dish with cooking spray. In small bowl, mix salt, pumpkin pie spice, allspice, thyme and red pepper. Rub mixture on all sides of chicken. In 12-inch nonstick skillet, heat oil over medium-high heat. Cook chicken in oil 2 to 3 minutes per side, until brown.

2 In baking dish, layer beans and sweet potato. Top with browned chicken. In small bowl, mix honey, lime juice and cornstarch; add to skillet. Heat to boiling, stirring constantly. Pour over chicken in baking dish.

3 Bake 35 to 45 minutes or until juice of chicken is clear when center of thickest part is cut (180°F) and sweet potatoes are fork tender. Sprinkle with green onions.

High Altitude (3500-6500 ft): No change.

Nutritional Info: 1 Serving: Calories 320 (Calories from Fat 70); Total Fat 8g (Saturated Fat 2g, Trans Fat 0g); Cholesterol 45mg; Sodium 550mg; Total Carbohydrate 41g (Dietary Fiber 8g, Sugars 16g); Protein 20g. % Daily Value: Vitamin A 210%; Vitamin C 10%; Calcium 8%; Iron 20%. Exchanges: 1-1/2 Starch, 1 Other Carbohydrate, 2 Lean Meat, 1/2 Fat. Carbohydrate Choices: 3.

Betty's Kitchen Tips

Variation: Use a dry jerk seasoning or rub to save time. This recipe yields a mild jerk seasoning rub; an authentic jerk rub will be spicier.

Substitution: You can substitute 1/4 teaspoon ground cinnamon, 1/8 teaspoon ground ginger and 1/8 teaspoon ground nutmeg for the pumpkin pie spice.

wild rice and turkey casserole

Prep Time: 10 Minutes
Start to Finish: 1 Hour 15 Minutes
Servings: 6

2	cups cut-up cooked turkey or chicken
2-1/4	cups boiling water
1/3	cup fat-free (skim) milk
4	medium green onions, sliced (1/4 cup)
1	can (10-3/4 oz) condensed 98% fat-free cream of mushroom soup
1	package (6 oz) original-flavor long-grain and wild rice mix

1 Heat oven to 350°F. In ungreased 2-quart casserole dish, mix all ingredients, including seasoning packet from rice mix.

2 Cover casserole. Bake 45 to 50 minutes or until rice is tender. Uncover; bake 10 to 15 minutes longer or until liquid is absorbed. If desired, sprinkle with additional green onion.

High Altitude (3500-6500 ft): No change.

Nutritional Info: 1 Serving: Calories 180 (Calories from Fat 70); Total Fat 8g (Saturated Fat 2g, Trans Fat 0g); Cholesterol 40mg; Sodium 600mg; Total Carbohydrate 13g (Dietary Fiber 0g, Sugars 2g); Protein 14g. % Daily Value: Vitamin A 4%; Vitamin C 0%; Calcium 4%; Iron 6%. Exchanges: 1 Starch, 1-1/2 Lean Meat, 1/2 Fat. Carbohydrate Choices: 1.

EASY LOW FAT

Betty's Kitchen Tips

Substitution: If you don't have cream of mushroom soup available, you can also use cream of chicken or cream of celery.

Serve-With: This super-easy casserole is low in fat and cholesterol. Serve with whole wheat rolls and fresh green beans for a well-rounded meal.

beef pot pie with potato biscuit crust

Prep Time: 20 Minutes
Start to Finish: 55 Minutes
Servings: 6

1/2   lb deli roast beef, cubed (1-1/2 cups)
2   cups Green Giant® Valley Fresh Steamers™ frozen mixed vegetables
1   medium onion, chopped (1/2 cup)
1   jar (12 oz) beef gravy

2/3   cup Betty Crocker® Potato Buds® mashed potatoes (dry)
2/3   cup hot water
1-1/2   cups Original Bisquick® mix
3   tablespoons milk
1   tablespoon freeze-dried chives

1   Heat oven to 375°F. In 2-quart saucepan, heat beef, frozen vegetables, onion and gravy to boiling over medium heat, stirring frequently. Boil and stir 1 minute. Keep warm.

2   In medium bowl, stir potatoes and hot water until well mixed; let stand until water is absorbed. Stir in Bisquick mix, milk and chives until dough forms. Place dough on surface sprinkled with Bisquick mix; gently roll in Bisquick mix to coat. Shape into a ball; knead 10 times. Pat into 11x7-inch rectangle. Fold dough into thirds.

3   Pour beef mixture into ungreased 11x7-inch (2-quart) glass baking dish. Carefully unfold dough onto beef mixture.

4   Bake 30 to 35 minutes or until crust is golden brown.

High Altitude (3500-6500 ft): Bake 35 to 40 minutes.

Nutritional Info: 1 Serving: Calories 310 (Calories from Fat 90); Total Fat 11g (Saturated Fat 4g, Trans Fat 1.5g); Cholesterol 25mg; Sodium 740mg; Total Carbohydrate 38g (Dietary Fiber 4g, Sugars 4g); Protein 15g. % Daily Value: Vitamin A 50%; Vitamin C 2%; Calcium 6%; Iron 15%. Exchanges: 2 Starch, 1 Vegetable, 1 Lean Meat, 1-1/2 Fat. Carbohydrate Choices: 2-1/2.

Betty's Kitchen Tips

Variation: For Chicken Pot Pie with Potato Biscuit Crust, use rotisserie chicken from the deli and chicken gravy in place of the beef and beef gravy.

Success Hint: It's important that the beef mixture is hot when the crust is placed on top. The heat from below helps cook the topping.

baked chicken panzanella

Prep Time: 10 Minutes
Start to Finish: 40 Minutes
Servings: 6 (1-1/2 cups each)

EASY

- 2 cups chopped cooked chicken
- 1 can (14.5 oz) diced tomatoes with garlic, onion and oregano, drained
- 1/4 cup sliced green onions (4 medium)
- 1 package (5 oz) Italian-seasoned croutons
- 1/4 cup Italian dressing
- 3/4 cup shredded Parmesan cheese
- 1/4 cup sliced fresh basil leaves

1 Heat oven to 350°F. In ungreased 11x7-inch (2-quart) baking dish, layer chicken, tomatoes, green onions and croutons. Drizzle with Italian dressing.

2 Cover with foil. Bake 20 minutes. Uncover; top with cheese. Bake about 10 minutes longer or until hot and cheese is melted. Sprinkle with basil.

High Altitude (3500-6500 ft): No change.

Nutritional Info: 1 Serving: Calories 290 (Calories from Fat 130); Total Fat 14g (Saturated Fat 4.5g, Trans Fat 1.5g); Cholesterol 50mg; Sodium 830mg; Total Carbohydrate 20g (Dietary Fiber 2g, Sugars 4g); Protein 21g. % Daily Value: Vitamin A 6%; Vitamin C 6%; Calcium 20%; Iron 10%. Exchanges: 1 Starch, 1/2 Other Carbohydrate, 2-1/2 Medium-Fat Meat. Carbohydrate Choices: 1.

Betty's Kitchen Tips

Variations: Any cooked chicken will work in this recipe. Use rotisserie chicken or refrigerated cubed cooked chicken. Or use leftover grilled chicken, which would give a slightly smoky flavor to the casserole.

Did You Know? This casserole is a hot version of the Italian bread salad panzanella.

turkey-biscuit pot pie

Prep Time: 25 Minutes
Start to Finish: 55 Minutes
Servings: 6 (1 cup each)

Filling

2-1/2	cups baby-cut carrots (12 oz)
2	cups cut-up fresh broccoli
3	tablespoons butter or margarine
1/2	cup chopped onion (1 medium)
3	tablespoons Gold Medal® all-purpose flour
2	cups chicken broth

1	teaspoon dried sage leaves
2	cups cubed cooked turkey

Biscuits

4	slices bacon
1	cup Original Bisquick® mix
1/2	cup milk
1/2	cup shredded Cheddar cheese (2 oz)

1 Heat oven to 400°F. In 2-quart saucepan, heat 1 cup water to boiling. Add carrots and broccoli; cook about 4 minutes or until carrots and broccoli are crisp-tender. Drain mixture.

2 Meanwhile, in 3-quart saucepan, melt butter over medium heat. Add onion; cook about 2 minutes, stirring occasionally, until tender. Beat in flour with wire whisk.

Gradually beat in broth and sage. Reduce heat to medium-low; cook about 5 minutes, stirring occasionally, until sauce thickens. Stir carrots, broccoli and turkey into sauce. Spoon turkey mixture into ungreased 2-quart casserole.

3 Place bacon on microwavable plate; cover with microwavable paper towel. Microwave on High 4 to 6 minutes or until crisp. Crumble bacon; place in medium bowl. Add remaining biscuit ingredients; stir just until blended. Spoon biscuit batter around edge of turkey mixture.

4 Bake 25 to 30 minutes or until biscuit crust is golden brown.

High Altitude (3500-6500 ft): No change.

Nutritional Info: 1 Serving: Calories 360 (Calories from Fat 160); Total Fat 18g (Saturated Fat 8g, Trans Fat 1g); Cholesterol 75mg; Sodium 900mg; Total Carbohydrate 26g (Dietary Fiber 3g, Sugars 5g); Protein 23g. % Daily Value: Vitamin A 170%; Vitamin C 25%; Calcium 15%; Iron 10%. Exchanges: 1-1/2 Starch, 1 Vegetable, 2-1/2 Lean Meat, 2 Fat. Carbohydrate Choices: 2.

Betty's Kitchen Tip

• You can find fresh sage year-round in the produce section of supermarkets.

swiss steak casserole

Prep Time: 20 Minutes
Start to Finish: 2 Hours 5 Minutes
Servings: 6 (1 cup each)

LOW FAT

3	tablespoons Gold Medal® all-purpose flour
1	teaspoon salt
1	teaspoon paprika
1/2	teaspoon pepper
1	lb boneless beef round steak, cut into 3/4-inch cubes
2	tablespoons vegetable oil
2	cups sliced mushrooms
1	cup frozen pearl onions
1	clove garlic, finely chopped
4	cups sliced carrots (8 medium)
1	can (14.5 oz) stewed tomatoes, undrained

1 Heat oven to 350°F. In medium bowl, mix flour, salt, paprika and pepper. Add steak; toss to coat. In 12-inch skillet, heat 1 tablespoon of the oil over medium-high heat. Add steak, reserving remaining flour mixture; brown steak on all sides. Spoon into ungreased 2-1/2-quart casserole.

2 To same skillet, add remaining 1 tablespoon oil, the mushrooms, onions and garlic. Cook 2 to 3 minutes, stirring constantly, until browned; add to casserole. Add carrots, tomatoes and reserved flour mixture; mix well.

3 Cover casserole. Bake 1 hour 30 minutes to 1 hour 45 minutes or until meat and vegetables are fork-tender.

High Altitude (3500-6500 ft): No change.

Nutritional Info: 1 Serving: Calories 250 (Calories from Fat 70); Total Fat 8g (Saturated Fat 2g, Trans Fat 0g); Cholesterol 55mg; Sodium 680mg; Total Carbohydrate 20g (Dietary Fiber 4g, Sugars 9g); Protein 25g. % Daily Value: Vitamin A 280%; Vitamin C 10%; Calcium 6%; Iron 20%. Exchanges: 1/2 Other Carbohydrate, 2 Vegetable, 3 Lean Meat. Carbohydrate Choices: 1.

Betty's Kitchen Tips

Time-Saver: Take some help from the grocery store. Look for packages of sliced carrots and mushrooms in the produce section to save time.

Serve-With: Serve this saucy meat and vegetable mixture with mashed potatoes or hot cooked rice.

alfredo chicken pot puff pies

Prep Time: 20 Minutes
Start to Finish: 55 Minutes
Servings: 4

1 sheet frozen puff pastry (from 17.3-oz package), thawed as directed on package
1 tablespoon butter or margarine
2 tablespoons finely chopped shallots
2 cups chopped cooked chicken

2 cups frozen peas and carrots
1 jar (16 oz) Alfredo pasta sauce
1 teaspoon dried thyme leaves
1 egg

1 Heat oven to 400°F. Lightly spray 4 (10-oz) custard cups or ramekins with cooking spray. On lightly floured surface, roll puff pastry to 13-inch square. Cut into 4 squares. Lightly press 1 square in bottom and up sides of each custard cup, letting corners hang over sides.

2 In 10-inch skillet, melt butter over medium heat. Add shallots. Cook about 3 minutes, stirring occasionally, until shallots are softened. Add chicken, frozen peas and carrots, and Alfredo sauce. Cook 3 to 4 minutes longer, stirring occasionally, until peas are thawed and mixture is hot. Sprinkle with thyme leaves; stir well.

3 Spoon mixture into pastry-lined custard cups. Fold corners over filling, pinching to almost close tops. In small bowl, beat egg with fork or wire whisk; brush pastry tops with egg.

4 Bake 25 to 30 minutes or until pastry is deep golden brown. Let stand 5 minutes. Serve in cups or remove to individual serving plates.

High Altitude (3500-6500 ft): In step 4, bake 30 to 35 minutes.

Nutritional Info: 1 Serving: Calories 730 (Calories from Fat 450); Total Fat 50g (Saturated Fat 21g, Trans Fat 2.5g); Cholesterol 285mg; Sodium 1070mg; Total Carbohydrate 42g (Dietary Fiber 3g, Sugars 6g); Protein 28g. % Daily Value: Vitamin A 140%; Vitamin C 6%; Calcium 15%; Iron 25%. Exchanges: 1-1/2 Starch, 1 Other Carbohydrate, 1 Vegetable, 3 Lean Meat, 8 Fat. Carbohydrate Choices: 3.

Betty's Kitchen Tip

• Look for the puff pastry in the dessert section of the frozen food aisle in the grocery store.

cheesy gnocchi florentine

Prep Time: 20 Minutes
Start to Finish: 50 Minutes
Servings: 4

- 1   box (9 oz) Green Giant® frozen spinach
- 1   tablespoon butter or margarine
- 1/4   cup chopped onion
- 1   tablespoon Gold Medal® all-purpose flour
- 1-1/4   cups half-and-half or milk
- 1   package (16 oz) shelf-stable gnocchi
- 1   cup shredded Gruyère cheese (4 oz)
- 1/2   cup shredded Muenster cheese (2 oz)
- 1/8   teaspoon ground nutmeg
- 1   large plum (Roma) tomato, thinly sliced
- 1   teaspoon olive oil

1   Heat oven to 350°F. Spray 1-1/2-quart casserole with cooking spray. Cook spinach as directed on package; drain in colander or large strainer. Press to remove excess moisture. Set aside.

2   Meanwhile, in 2-quart saucepan, melt butter. Add onion; cook 2 to 3 minutes, stirring frequently, until tender. Stir in flour. Gradually stir in half-and-half. Stir in gnocchi; heat to boiling. Remove from heat. Stir in cheeses and nutmeg.

3   Spoon about 2 cups of the gnocchi mixture into casserole. Top with spinach, then remaining gnocchi mixture. Top with tomato slices; brush with olive oil.

4   Bake about 30 minutes or until bubbly and browned on top and gnocchi is tender.

High Altitude (3500-6500 ft): No change.

Nutritional Info: 1 Serving: Calories 550 (Calories from Fat 360); Total Fat 40g (Saturated Fat 21g, Trans Fat 3g); Cholesterol 160mg; Sodium 580mg; Total Carbohydrate 19g (Dietary Fiber 2g, Sugars 6g); Protein 27g. % Daily Value: Vitamin A 130%; Vitamin C 6%; Calcium 80%; Iron 10%. Exchanges: 1 Starch, 3-1/2 Medium-Fat Meat, 4-1/2 Fat. Carbohydrate Choices: 1.

Betty's Kitchen Tips

Success Hint: Use sturdy paper towels or clean kitchen towels to wring as much moisture out of the spinach as possible.

Substitution: Three cups frozen gnocchi from a 16-oz bag can be substituted for the shelf-stable variety. Follow directions above.

Variation: Swiss cheese can be used instead of Gruyère cheese.

seven-layer rigatoni

Prep Time: 10 Minutes
Start to Finish: 50 Minutes
Servings: 8

EASY

3 cups uncooked rigatoni pasta (9 oz)
1 lb bulk Italian sausage
1 can (28 oz) crushed tomatoes, undrained
3 cloves garlic, finely chopped
3 tablespoons chopped fresh or 1 tablespoon dried basil leaves

1 package (8 oz) sliced fresh mushrooms (3 cups)
1 jar (7 oz) roasted red bell peppers, drained and chopped
1 cup shredded Parmesan cheese
2-1/2 cups shredded mozzarella cheese (10 oz)

1 Heat oven to 375°F. Spray 13x9-inch (3-quart) baking dish with cooking spray. Cook and drain pasta as directed on package using minimum cook time.

2 While pasta is cooking, in 10-inch skillet, cook sausage over medium heat 5 to 7 minutes, stirring occasionally, until no longer pink; drain. In small bowl, mix tomatoes, garlic and basil.

3 Layer half each of the pasta, sausage, mushrooms, bell peppers, Parmesan cheese, tomato mixture and mozzarella cheese; repeat layers.

4 Bake 35 to 40 minutes or until hot and cheese is golden brown.

High Altitude (3500-6500 ft): Spray one side of piece of foil with cooking spray; cover baking dish with foil, sprayed side down. Bake 45 minutes. Uncover, and bake 10 to 15 minutes longer.

Nutritional Info: 1 Serving: Calories 520 (Calories from Fat 210); Total Fat 23g (Saturated Fat 11g, Trans Fat 0g); Cholesterol 50mg; Sodium 1220mg; Total Carbohydrate 46g (Dietary Fiber 3g, Sugars 6g); Protein 30g. % Daily Value: Vitamin A 30%; Vitamin C 35%; Calcium 50%; Iron 20%. Exchanges: 2 Starch, 1/2 Other Carbohydrate, 1 Vegetable, 3 High-Fat Meat. Carbohydrate Choices: 3.

 Kitchen Tips

Time-Saver: Save time by using the new precooked sausage crumbles available in the meat department at your supermarket.

Variation: You can slash the fat in this family-favorite casserole by using 3/4 lb bulk turkey Italian sausage and reduced-fat mozzarella cheese.

swiss chicken casserole

Prep Time: 15 Minutes
Start to Finish: 1 Hour 5 Minutes
Servings: 8

EASY LOW FAT

4	cups boiling water
2	boxes (6 oz each) sun-dried tomato Florentine long grain and wild rice mix
4	large boneless skinless chicken breasts
8	slices thick-sliced fully cooked deli ham (about 10 oz)
1/4	cup diced red bell pepper
4	slices (1 oz each) Swiss cheese, cut in half

1 Heat oven to 350°F. Spray 13x9-inch (3-quart) baking dish with cooking spray.

2 Stir boiling water, rice and rice seasoning mixes in baking dish.

3 Cut chicken breasts in half lengthwise; wrap ham slice around each chicken piece. Stir bell pepper into rice. Place wrapped chicken over rice. Cover with foil. Bake 40 to 45 minutes; uncover and bake about 10 minutes longer or until liquid is absorbed and juice of chicken is clear when thickest part is cut.

4 Top each chicken breast with cheese. Bake uncovered 3 to 4 minutes or until cheese is melted.

High Altitude (3500-6500 ft): No change.

Nutritional Info: 1 Serving: Calories 240 (Calories from Fat 80); Total Fat 8g (Saturated Fat 4g, Trans Fat 0g); Cholesterol 75mg; Sodium 660mg; Total Carbohydrate 13g (Dietary Fiber 0g, Sugars 0g); Protein 28g. % Daily Value: Vitamin A 6%; Vitamin C 4%; Calcium 15%; Iron 8%. Exchanges: 1 Starch, 3-1/2 Very Lean Meat, 1 Fat. Carbohydrate Choices: 1.

Betty's Kitchen Tips

Variation: Use other varieties of rice mixtures, such as chicken or mushroom.

Serve-With: For a complete dinner, serve with steamed whole green beans.

greek spanakopita pie

Prep Time: 35 Minutes
Start to Finish: 1 Hour 30 Minutes
Servings: 8

- 1   lb lean ground beef
- 1   cup chopped onion (1 large)
- 1   box (9 oz) Green Giant® frozen spinach, thawed and squeezed dry
- 1/4 cup chopped fresh Italian (flat-leaf) parsley
- 1/2 teaspoon salt
- 1/4 teaspoon pepper
- 1   can (15 oz) diced tomatoes with Italian-style herbs, undrained
- 12   sheets frozen phyllo (filo) (14x9 inch), thawed
- 6   tablespoons butter or margarine, melted
- 1/4 cup Progresso® Italian-style bread crumbs
- 1   cup crumbled feta cheese (4 oz)

1 Heat oven to 350°F. Spray 9-inch pie plate with cooking spray.

2 In 10-inch skillet, cook beef and onion over medium-high heat, stirring frequently; drain. Stir in spinach, parsley, salt, pepper, and all but 1/2 cup of the tomatoes. Cook and stir until hot; set aside.

3 Cover phyllo sheets with damp paper towel. Arrange sheets, layering 3 at a time, in an "x" shape and then in a "+" shape to create a spoke pattern on work surface, brushing each with butter and sprinkling with 1 teaspoon of the bread crumbs as it is added. Transfer all layers of phyllo to pie plate, gently easing dough down sides of pie plate and allowing excess dough to hang over edge. Place beef mixture in pie plate; top with feta cheese. Fold overhanging phyllo up and over filling, leaving 2- to 3-inch center of filling uncovered. Spoon remaining 1/2 cup tomatoes in center. Brush phyllo with butter.

4 Bake 40 to 50 minutes or until golden brown. Let stand 5 minutes before serving.

High Altitude (3500-6500 ft): Bake pie 45 to 55 minutes.

Nutritional Info: 1 Serving: Calories 400 (Calories from Fat 220); Total Fat 25g (Saturated Fat 13g, Trans Fat 1.5g); Cholesterol 95mg; Sodium 810mg; Total Carbohydrate 24g (Dietary Fiber 3g, Sugars 4g); Protein 20g. % Daily Value: Vitamin A 80%; Vitamin C 10%; Calcium 20%; Iron 20%. Exchanges: 1 Starch, 1 Vegetable, 2 Medium-Fat Meat, 3 Fat. Carbohydrate Choices: 1-1/2.

Betty's Kitchen Tips

Variation: For a more authentic flavor, substitute ground lamb for the ground beef.

Serve-With: Serve this pie with a Greek salad and retsina, an up-and-coming wine from the Nemea region of Greece.

country chicken and pasta bake

Prep Time: 10 Minutes
Start to Finish: 40 Minutes
Servings: 6

EASY

2	cups uncooked radiatore (nuggets) pasta (6 oz)
3	cups cubed cooked chicken
2	jars (12 oz each) chicken gravy
1	bag (1 lb) frozen broccoli, carrots and cauliflower
1/4	teaspoon dried thyme leaves
1/4	teaspoon salt
1/2	cup herb-seasoned stuffing crumbs
2	tablespoons butter or margarine, melted

1 Heat oven to 375°F. Cook and drain pasta as directed on package using minimum cook time.

2 In ungreased 2-1/2-quart casserole, mix pasta and remaining ingredients except stuffing and butter.

3 Cover casserole; bake 20 minutes. Uncover and stir casserole. In small bowl, mix stuffing and butter; sprinkle on top. Bake uncovered about 10 minutes longer or until hot and topping is brown.

High Altitude (3500-6500 ft): Defrost vegetables. Increase first bake time in step 3 to 40 minutes.

Nutritional Info: 1 Serving: Calories 410 (Calories from Fat 150); Total Fat 16g (Saturated Fat 6g, Trans Fat 0g); Cholesterol 75mg; Sodium 1030mg; Total Carbohydrate 38g (Dietary Fiber 4g, Sugars 3g); Protein 28g. % Daily Value: Vitamin A 35%; Vitamin C 20%; Calcium 6%; Iron 15%. Exchanges: 2 Starch, 1 Vegetable, 3 Medium-Fat Meat. Carbohydrate Choices: 2-1/2.

Betty's Kitchen Tips

Variation: Any frozen vegetable mixture can be used, and with so many choices now available, we know you're likely to keep your favorites on hand.

Success Hint: When cooking pasta to be used in a casserole, cook only the minimum amount of time listed on the package because the pasta will continue to cook and absorb liquid while baking.

baked vegetable risotto

Prep Time: 15 Minutes
Start to Finish: 45 Minutes
Servings: 4

EASY

2 tablespoons extra-virgin olive oil
2 tablespoons finely chopped onion
2 cloves garlic, finely chopped
1 package (8 oz) crimini mushrooms, quartered
2 teaspoons chopped fresh rosemary leaves
1 cup uncooked Arborio rice

1 can (14 oz) chicken or vegetable broth
1/2 cup white wine or water
1-1/2 cups Green Giant® Valley Fresh Steamers™ frozen cut green beans, thawed and drained
1/2 cup roasted red bell peppers (from a jar), cut into strips
1 cup grated Parmesan cheese

1 Heat oven to 400°F. Spray 2-1/2-quart casserole with cooking spray. In 12-inch nonstick skillet, heat olive oil over medium heat. Add onion, garlic, mushrooms and rosemary. Cook 3 to 5 minutes over medium heat, stirring frequently, until mushrooms start to soften.

2 Add rice. Cook 2 minutes, stirring constantly. Add broth and wine; heat to boiling. Remove from heat; pour into casserole.

3 Cover casserole. Bake 15 minutes. Stir in green beans, roasted peppers and 1/2 cup of the cheese. Cover; bake 10 to 15 minutes longer or until liquid is absorbed and rice is tender. Stir in remaining 1/2 cup cheese.

High Altitude (3500-6500 ft): Increase white wine or water to 3/4 cup.

Nutritional Info: 1 Serving: Calories 410 (Calories from Fat 140); Total Fat 15g (Saturated Fat 6g, Trans Fat 0g); Cholesterol 20mg; Sodium 880mg; Total Carbohydrate 48g (Dietary Fiber 2g, Sugars 4g); Protein 18g. % Daily Value: Vitamin A 25%; Vitamin C 25%; Calcium 40%; Iron 15%. Exchanges: 3 Starch, 1 Vegetable, 1 High-Fat Meat, 1 Fat. Carbohydrate Choices: 3.

Betty's Kitchen Tips

Variation: If your family prefers, you could add a cup of chopped cooked ham or chicken to this meatless dish. Add it when you add the rice to the skillet.

Substitution: Crimini mushrooms add a meaty flavor to a meatless main dish. Quartered button mushrooms can be substituted if you prefer.

chicken artichoke casserole

Prep Time: 15 Minutes
Start to Finish: 50 Minutes
Servings: 6 (1-1/3 cups each)

EASY

1	tablespoon olive oil
1	cup chopped red bell pepper
1/4	cup sliced green onions (4 medium)
3	cups chopped cooked chicken
1	can (14 oz) artichoke hearts in water, drained, chopped
1	container (10 oz) refrigerated reduced-fat Alfredo pasta sauce
1	cup shredded Asiago cheese (4 oz)
1/2	cup reduced-fat mayonnaise
1-1/2	cups Romano cheese croutons (from 5-oz bag), coarsely crushed

1 Heat oven to 350°F. Spray 11x7-inch (2-quart) baking dish with cooking spray. In 6-inch skillet, heat olive oil over medium heat. Add bell pepper and green onions; cook 2 to 3 minutes, stirring occasionally, until bell pepper and onions start to soften. In large bowl, mix bell pepper mixture and all remaining ingredients except croutons. Spoon into baking dish. Top with croutons.

2 Bake 30 to 35 minutes or until hot and bubbly. If desired, sprinkle with additional sliced green onions.

High Altitude (3500-6500 ft): In step 2, bake 37 to 42 minutes.

Nutritional Info: 1 Serving: Calories 460 (Calories from Fat 250); Total Fat 28g (Saturated Fat 11g, Trans Fat 1g); Cholesterol 105mg; Sodium 890mg; Total Carbohydrate 20g (Dietary Fiber 4g, Sugars 5g); Protein 30g. % Daily Value: Vitamin A 30%; Vitamin C 30%; Calcium 30%; Iron 10%. Exchanges: 1 Starch, 1 Vegetable, 3-1/2 Medium-Fat Meat, 2 Fat. Carbohydrate Choices: 1.

Betty's Kitchen Tips

Substitution: If refrigerated Alfredo sauce is not available, use about 1 cup of Alfredo sauce from a jar.

Purchasing: Use regular canned artichoke hearts for this recipe, not the marinated ones. Artichoke hearts are available in several sizes. Choose the least expensive, as they are chopped in this recipe.

sausage and pizza bake

Prep Time: 15 Minutes
Start to Finish: 50 Minutes
Servings: 6

EASY

- 3 cups uncooked rotini pasta (9 oz)
- 1 lb bulk Italian sausage
- 1 medium onion, chopped (1/2 cup)
- 1 small bell pepper, chopped (1/2 cup)
- 1/4 cup water

- 4 oz sliced Canadian bacon, cut into fourths
- 1 jar or can (14 or 15 oz) pizza sauce
- 1 can (4 oz) sliced mushrooms, drained
- 3/4 cup shredded pizza cheese blend (3 oz)

1 Heat oven to 350°F. Spray 3-quart casserole with cooking spray. In 3-quart saucepan, cook and drain pasta as directed on package using minimum cook time. Return pasta to saucepan.

2 While pasta is cooking, cook sausage and onion in 10-inch skillet over medium heat 6 to 8 minutes, stirring occasionally, until sausage is no longer pink; drain. Stir sausage mixture, bell pepper, water, bacon, pizza sauce and mushrooms into

pasta. Spoon pasta mixture into casserole. Sprinkle with cheese.

3 Cover casserole. Bake 30 to 35 minutes or until hot and cheese is melted.

High Altitude (3500-6500 ft): Heat oven to 375°F. Use 3/4 cup water. Bake 35 to 40 minutes.

Nutritional Info: 1 Serving: Calories 570 (Calories from Fat 200); Total Fat 23g (Saturated Fat 9g, Trans Fat 0g); Cholesterol 50mg; Sodium 1420mg; Total Carbohydrate 62g (Dietary Fiber 5g, Sugars 8g); Protein 29g. % Daily Value: Vitamin A 20%; Vitamin C 20%; Calcium 15%; Iron 20%. Exchanges: 3 Starch, 1 Other Carbohydrate, 3 Medium-Fat Meat, 1 Fat. Carbohydrate Choices: 4.

Betty's Kitchen Tips

Variation: Pizza cheese is a blend of mozzarella and Cheddar cheeses. If unavailable, use equal parts of mozzarella and Cheddar.

Success Hint: Be sure to thoroughly drain the cooked pasta—a few hard shakes of the colander after the water drains will help. Excess water clinging to the pasta will dilute the sauce.

Special Touch: Do you like Pavarotti? Ellington? Vivaldi? Not sure? Choose a night of the week to accompany dinner with some new tunes. Investigate a style of music you'd like to know better. Borrow CDs from the library or dust off forgotten selections from your own collection.

speedy
SKILLET MEALS

p. 122

119

129

125

easy beef taco skillet

Prep Time: 10 Minutes
Start to Finish: 35 Minutes
Servings: 5

EASY

1   lb lean (at least 80%) ground beef
3   cups hot water
1   box Hamburger Helper® crunchy taco
1   can (15 oz) spicy chili beans in sauce, undrained

1/3   cup milk
1   cup shredded lettuce
1   large tomato, chopped (1 cup)

1 In 10-inch skillet, cook beef over medium-high heat 5 to 7 minutes, stirring occasionally, until thoroughly cooked; drain.

2 Stir in hot water, sauce mix (from Hamburger Helper box) and beans. Heat to boiling, stirring occasionally. Stir in uncooked rice (from Hamburger Helper box).

3 Reduce heat; cover and simmer about 25 minutes, stirring occasionally, until rice is tender (sauce will thicken as it stands). Meanwhile, in small bowl, stir milk and topping mix (from Hamburger Helper box) 30 seconds; set aside.

4 Remove beef mixture from heat. Top each serving with cheese topping, lettuce, tomato and corn chips (from Hamburger Helper box).

High Altitude (3500-6500 ft): No change.

Nutritional Info: 1 Serving: Calories 410 (Calories from Fat 130); Total Fat 14g (Saturated Fat 4.5g, Trans Fat 0.5g); Cholesterol 60mg; Sodium 1460mg; Total Carbohydrate 47g (Dietary Fiber 5g, Sugars 5g); Protein 23g. % Daily Value: Vitamin A 10%; Vitamin C 6%; Calcium 10%; Iron 25%. Exchanges: 2 Starch, 1 Other Carbohydrate, 2-1/2 Lean Meat, 1 Fat. Carbohydrate Choices: 3.

Betty's Kitchen Tip

• A dollop of sour cream or guacamole will really top off this dish!

tuna-noodle skillet supper

Prep Time: 10 Minutes
Start to Finish: 25 Minutes
Servings: 6

EASY QUICK

- 1   tablespoon canola or vegetable oil
- 1   large onion, coarsely chopped (1 cup)
- 4   cups water
- 4   cups uncooked medium egg noodles (8 oz)
- 1   package (8 oz) sliced fresh mushrooms (about 3 cups)
- 2   cans (5 oz each) solid white tuna in water, drained
- 1   jar (16 oz) Alfredo pasta sauce
- 1   cup seasoned croutons, coarsely crushed

1   In 12-inch nonstick skillet, heat oil over medium-high heat. Add onion; cook 2 to 3 minutes, stirring frequently, until softened.

2   Stir in water and noodles. Cover; heat to boiling. Boil 4 minutes.

3   Stir in mushrooms, tuna and pasta sauce (sauce will be thin). Reduce heat to medium; simmer uncovered 4 to 6 minutes or until mushrooms are tender, sauce has slightly thickened and noodles are tender.

4   Remove from heat; let stand 5 minutes. Just before serving, top with croutons.

High Altitude (3500-6500 ft): No change.

Nutritional Info: 1 Serving: Calories 520 (Calories from Fat 270); Total Fat 30g (Saturated Fat 16g, Trans Fat 1g); Cholesterol 120mg; Sodium 540mg; Total Carbohydrate 38g (Dietary Fiber 2g, Sugars 3g); Protein 24g. % Daily Value: Vitamin A 15%; Vitamin C 2%; Calcium 20%; Iron 15%. Exchanges: 1-1/2 Starch, 1 Fruit, 3 Lean Meat, 4 Fat. Carbohydrate Choices: 2-1/2.

Betty's Kitchen Tips

Substitution: If your family doesn't like tuna, make this recipe with two 5-oz cans of chunk chicken breast instead.

Time-Saver: Buy frozen chopped onions, which can be found near the frozen breaded onion rings, to save time.

calico chicken and potatoes skillet

Prep Time: 25 Minutes
Start to Finish: 30 Minutes
Servings: 4 (1-1/4 cups each)

QUICK

- 3 slices bacon, chopped
- 1 small red bell pepper, chopped (1/2 cup)
- 1 bag (1 lb 4 oz) refrigerated cooked diced potatoes with onions
- 1 teaspoon seasoned salt

- 2 cups chopped deli rotisserie chicken (from 2- to 2-1/2-lb chicken)
- 1 cup shredded Cheddar cheese (4 oz)
- 2 medium green onions, chopped (2 tablespoons)

1 In 12-inch nonstick skillet, cook bacon over medium heat 3 to 4 minutes, stirring occasionally, until crisp. Remove bacon with slotted spoon, reserving drippings in skillet. Drain bacon on paper towels.

2 Stir bell pepper, potatoes and seasoned salt into drippings. Cover; cook over medium heat 14 to 16 minutes, stirring occasionally, until the potatoes are golden brown.

3 Stir in chicken. Cover; cook 2 to 3 minutes or until hot. Top with cheese, bacon and green onions. Cover; cook 1 to 2 minutes or until cheese is melted.

High Altitude (3500-6500 ft): No change.

Nutritional Info: 1 Serving: Calories 490 (Calories from Fat 230); Total Fat 25g (Saturated Fat 10g, Trans Fat 0g); Cholesterol 95mg; Sodium 1130mg; Total Carbohydrate 34g (Dietary Fiber 4g, Sugars 4g); Protein 32g. % Daily Value: Vitamin A 20%; Vitamin C 40%; Calcium 20%; Iron 10%. Exchanges: 2 Starch, 3 Lean Meat, 1/2 Medium-Fat Meat, 2 Fat. Carbohydrate Choices: 2.

Betty's Kitchen Tips

Serve-With: Add fresh fruit and sweet rolls for the perfect weekend brunch.

Success Hint: If you have bacon that is already cooked, use about 1 tablespoon butter or margarine for cooking the potato mixture.

simple teriyaki steak dinner

Prep Time: 20 Minutes
Start to Finish: 20 Minutes
Servings: 4

QUICK

1	tablespoon butter or margarine
1	medium bell pepper (any color), coarsely chopped (1 cup)
1-1/2	cups sliced fresh mushrooms (about 5 oz)
4	boneless beef top loin steaks (New York, Kansas City or strip steaks), about 3/4 inch thick (6 oz each)
1/2	teaspoon garlic salt
1/4	teaspoon coarse ground black pepper
1/4	cup teriyaki baste and glaze (from 12-oz bottle)
2	tablespoons water

1 In 12-inch nonstick skillet, melt butter over medium-high heat. Add bell pepper; cook 2 minutes, stirring frequently. Stir in mushrooms. Cook 2 to 3 minutes, stirring frequently, until vegetables are tender. Remove vegetables from skillet; cover to keep warm.

2 Sprinkle beef steaks with garlic salt and pepper. In same skillet, cook steaks over medium heat 6 to 8 minutes, turning once or twice, until desired doneness.

3 Return vegetables to skillet. Stir teriyaki glaze and water into vegetable mixture; spoon over steaks. Cook about 1 minute, stirring vegetables occasionally, until thoroughly heated.

High Altitude (3500-6500 ft): No change.

Nutritional Info: 1 Serving: Calories 370 (Calories from Fat 210); Total Fat 23g (Saturated Fat 9g, Trans Fat 1g); Cholesterol 105mg; Sodium 1040mg; Total Carbohydrate 6g (Dietary Fiber 1g, Sugars 3g); Protein 34g. % Daily Value: Vitamin A 4%; Vitamin C 25%; Calcium 2%; Iron 25%. Exchanges: 1/2 Other Carbohydrate, 1/2 Vegetable, 3-1/2 Medium-Fat Meat, 1 Fat. Carbohydrate Choices: 1/2.

Betty's Kitchen Tip

• Mix up some Betty Crocker® roasted garlic mashed potatoes to serve with the steaks. See page 142 for a do-ahead version of garlic mashed potatoes.

beefy italian ramen skillet

Prep Time: 30 Minutes
Start to Finish: 35 Minutes
Servings: 4

2   packages (3 oz each) beef-flavor ramen noodle soup mix
1   lb lean (at least 80%) ground beef
24 slices pepperoni (1 to 1-1/4 inches in diameter)
1   can (14.5 oz) diced tomatoes with basil, garlic and oregano, undrained

1   cup water
1   small green bell pepper, cut into 1/2-inch pieces (1/2 cup)
1   cup shredded mozzarella cheese (4 oz)

1   Break blocks of noodles in half (reserve one seasoning packet; discard second packet). Set aside.

2   In 10-inch skillet, cook beef and pepperoni over medium-high heat 5 to 7 minutes, stirring occasionally, until beef is thoroughly cooked; drain.

3   Stir in tomatoes, water and reserved seasoning packet. Heat to boiling. Stir in noodles and bell pepper. Cook 3 to 5 minutes, stirring occasionally, until noodles are tender. Remove skillet from heat.

4   Sprinkle cheese around edge of noodle mixture. Cover; let stand about 5 minutes or until cheese is melted.

High Altitude (3500-6500 ft): No change.

Nutritional Info: 1 Serving: Calories 570 (Calories from Fat 310); Total Fat 34g (Saturated Fat 14g, Trans Fat 2g); Cholesterol 120mg; Sodium 960mg; Total Carbohydrate 27g (Dietary Fiber 2g, Sugars 4g); Protein 39g. % Daily Value: Vitamin A 8%; Vitamin C 20%; Calcium 25%; Iron 25%. Exchanges: 2 Starch, 1 Vegetable, 3-1/2 Medium-Fat Meat, 2 Fat. Carbohydrate Choices: 2.

Betty's Kitchen Tip

• By using only one of the two seasoning packets, you'll reduce the amount of sodium in the recipe.

thai tilapia with peanut sauce

Prep Time: 15 Minutes
Start to Finish: 20 Minutes
Servings: 4

EASY QUICK

- 2 teaspoons canola or vegetable oil
- 1 bag (1 lb) frozen stir-fry vegetables (about 4-1/2 cups)
- 1 tablespoon canola or vegetable oil
- 4 tilapia fillets, about 1/2 inch thick (about 1-1/4 lb)
- 4 tablespoons peanut sauce

1 In 12-inch nonstick skillet, heat 2 teaspoons oil over high heat. Add frozen vegetables; cook 4 to 5 minutes, stirring frequently, until crisp-tender. Divide vegetables among 4 dinner plates; cover to keep warm.

2 Add 1 tablespoon oil to same skillet; reduce heat to medium-high. Add fish fillets; cook 3 minutes. Turn fish; spoon and spread 1 tablespoon peanut sauce over each fillet to cover. Cook 2 to 4 minutes longer or until fish flakes easily with fork. Serve fish with vegetables.

High Altitude (3500-6500 ft): No change.

Nutritional Info: 1 Serving: Calories 260 (Calories from Fat 100); Total Fat 11g (Saturated Fat 1.5g, Trans Fat 0g); Cholesterol 75mg; Sodium 160mg; Total Carbohydrate 9g (Dietary Fiber 3g, Sugars 3g); Protein 31g. % Daily Value: Vitamin A 20%; Vitamin C 30%; Calcium 6%; Iron 10%. Exchanges: 1/2 Fruit, 4-1/2 Very Lean Meat, 1-1/2 Fat. Carbohydrate Choices: 1/2.

Betty's Kitchen Tips

Success Hint: If your peanut sauce is too spicy, use 3 tablespoons of the sauce and mix it with 1 tablespoon honey to tone down the spiciness. Any type of fish can be used.

Variation: Several types of stir-fry vegetables are on the market; pick your favorite mixture.

mediterranean chicken and orzo

Prep Time: 40 Minutes
Start to Finish: 40 Minutes
Servings: 4

LOW FAT

- 1 tablespoon olive or vegetable oil
- 4 boneless skinless chicken breasts (about 1-1/4 lb)
- 2 cloves garlic, finely chopped
- 1-1/3 cups uncooked orzo or rosamarina pasta (8 oz)
- 1-3/4 cups Progresso® chicken broth (from 32-oz carton)
- 1/2 cup water
- 3 plum (Roma) tomatoes, cut into quarters, sliced (1-1/2 cups)

- 2 medium zucchini, cut lengthwise into quarters, then cut crosswise into slices (1-1/2 cups)
- 1 medium green bell pepper, chopped (1 cup)
- 1 tablespoon chopped fresh or 1 teaspoon dried rosemary leaves
- 1/2 teaspoon salt
- 1/4 cup crumbled feta cheese (1 oz)

Sliced ripe olives, if desired

1 In 10-inch skillet, heat oil over medium-high heat. Add chicken; cook about 10 minutes, turning once, until brown. Remove chicken from skillet; keep warm.

2 In same skillet, mix garlic, pasta, broth and water. Heat to boiling. Reduce heat; cover and simmer about 8 minutes, stirring occasionally, until most of liquid is absorbed.

3 Stir in remaining ingredients except cheese and olives. Add chicken. Heat to boiling. Reduce heat; cover and simmer about 5 minutes, stirring once, until bell pepper is crisp-tender, pasta is tender and chicken is no longer pink in center. Sprinkle with feta cheese and olives.

High Altitude (3500-6500 ft): No change.

Nutritional Info: 1 Serving: Calories 420 (Calories from Fat 80); Total Fat 9g (Saturated Fat 2g, Trans Fat 0g); Cholesterol 80mg; Sodium 920mg; Total Carbohydrate 44g (Dietary Fiber 4g, Sugars 5g); Protein 40g. % Daily Value: Vitamin A 15%; Vitamin C 40%; Calcium 4%; Iron 20%. Exchanges: 2 Starch, 2 Vegetable, 4 Lean Meat. Carbohydrate Choices: 3.

Betty's Kitchen Tips

Serve-With: Complete this meal with warmed purchased focaccia bread and fresh pears or clusters of red grapes.

Variation: If your family prefers, sprinkle Parmesan cheese over this skillet instead of using feta cheese, and omit the olives.

pizza joes

Prep Time: 25 Minutes
Start to Finish: 25 Minutes
Servings: 8 sandwiches

- 1 lb extra-lean (at least 90%) ground beef
- 1 large onion, coarsely chopped (1 cup)
- 1 medium green bell pepper, coarsely chopped (about 1 cup)
- 2 cups pizza sauce (from two 15-oz jars or cans)
- 8 burger buns, split, toasted
- 1 cup shredded mozzarella cheese (4 oz)

1 Heat 12-inch nonstick skillet over medium-high heat. Add beef, onion and bell pepper; cook 7 to 9 minutes, stirring occasionally, until beef is thoroughly cooked.

2 Stir in pizza sauce. Reduce heat to medium; simmer uncovered about 5 minutes or until thoroughly heated.

3 Fill buns with the beef mixture and the shredded cheese.

High Altitude (3500-6500 ft): No change.

Nutritional Info: 1 Sandwich: Calories 290 (Calories from Fat 90); Total Fat 10g (Saturated Fat 4.5g, Trans Fat 0.5g); Cholesterol 45mg; Sodium 420mg; Total Carbohydrate 30g (Dietary Fiber 3g, Sugars 7g); Protein 20g. % Daily Value: Vitamin A 10%; Vitamin C 15%; Calcium 20%; Iron 20%. Exchanges: 2 Starch, 1 Vegetable, 1 Lean Meat, 1 Fat. Carbohydrate Choices: 2.

LOW FAT

Betty's Kitchen Tips

Substitution: To save time, you can substitute 2 cups frozen diced onion and green bell pepper or look for chopped fresh vegetables in the produce department.

Variation: Bulk Italian pork sausage can be used in place of the ground beef. You'll want to drain it before adding the pizza sauce.

How-To: Coarsely chop the onion and bell pepper in a food processor fitted with a chopping blade.

cheesy mexican mushroom skillet

Prep Time: 20 Minutes
Start to Finish: 25 Minutes
Servings: 4

1-1/2 teaspoons olive or vegetable oil

4 oz uncooked vermicelli, broken into 1-inch pieces

1 medium onion, sliced (about 1 cup)

1 package (8 oz) sliced fresh mushrooms (about 3 cups)

1 can (14.5 oz) diced tomatoes, undrained

2 medium jalapeño chiles, seeded, finely chopped

1/2 cup water

2 teaspoons ground cumin

1/2 teaspoon salt

1 cup shredded Monterey Jack cheese (4 oz)

1 In 12-inch nonstick skillet, heat oil over high heat. Add vermicelli; cook about 2 minutes, stirring frequently, until golden brown.

2 Reduce heat to medium. Stir in onion and mushrooms. Cook 2 minutes, stirring occasionally.

3 Stir in tomatoes, chiles, water, cumin and salt. Reduce heat to medium-low; cover and cook 10 minutes, stirring occasionally.

4 Remove from heat. Sprinkle with cheese. Cover; let stand about 2 minutes to melt cheese.

High Altitude (3500-6500 ft): No change.

Nutritional Info: 1 Serving: Calories 300 (Calories from Fat 110); Total Fat 12g (Saturated Fat 6g, Trans Fat 0g); Cholesterol 25mg; Sodium 600mg; Total Carbohydrate 35g (Dietary Fiber 4g, Sugars 6g); Protein 14g. % Daily Value: Vitamin A 10%; Vitamin C 15%; Calcium 25%; Iron 20%. Exchanges: 2 Starch, 1-1/2 Vegetable, 1/2 High-Fat Meat, 1 Fat. Carbohydrate Choices: 2.

Betty's Kitchen Tips

Success Hint: Wear clean rubber gloves when chopping jalapeños, and do not touch your skin or eyes. When finished, wash the gloves in soap and water.

How-To: Slice onion in a food processor fitted with a slicing blade.

pork and beans

Prep Time: 15 Minutes
Start to Finish: 20 Minutes
Servings: 4

EASY QUICK

1	cup barbecue sauce
2	tablespoons white vinegar
2	tablespoons packed brown sugar
1	can (15 oz) navy beans, drained
2	tablespoons canola or vegetable oil
1/2	teaspoon salt
1/4	teaspoon pepper
4	boneless center-cut pork chops, about 1/2 inch thick (about 1-1/2 lb)

1 In medium bowl, mix barbecue sauce, vinegar, brown sugar and beans; set aside.

2 In 12-inch nonstick skillet, heat oil over medium-high heat. Sprinkle salt and pepper over pork; place in skillet. Cook about 6 minutes, turning once, until both sides are browned.

3 Reduce heat to medium. Stir in bean mixture. Cook 3 to 5 minutes or until pork is no longer pink in center.

High Altitude (3500-6500 ft): No change.

Nutritional Info: 1 Serving: Calories 650 (Calories from Fat 240); Total Fat 26g (Saturated Fat 7g, Trans Fat 0g); Cholesterol 100mg; Sodium 1430mg; Total Carbohydrate 61g (Dietary Fiber 11g, Sugars 27g); Protein 42g. % Daily Value: Vitamin A 2%; Vitamin C 2%; Calcium 10%; Iron 25%. Exchanges: 3-1/2 Starch, 1 Vegetable, 2-1/2 Very Lean Meat, 1-1/2 Lean Meat, 4 Fat. Carbohydrate Choices: 4.

Betty's Kitchen Tips

Serve-With: Pick up a bagged, ready-to-eat salad and your favorite dressing to go with this meal.

Purchasing: Any type of barbecue sauce can be used.

dijon chicken

Prep Time: 30 Minutes
Start to Finish: 30 Minutes
Servings: 4

QUICK

1/2   cup whipping cream
1/4   cup Dijon mustard
1/2   teaspoon salt
1   tablespoon olive or vegetable oil
2   cans (15 oz each) whole potatoes, drained, halved lengthwise

1-1/4   lb boneless skinless chicken thighs, cut into bite-size pieces
2   medium red bell peppers, cut into strips (about 2 cups)
2   cups Green Giant® Valley Fresh Steamers™ frozen baby sweet peas

1 In small bowl, mix whipping cream, mustard and salt; set aside.

2 In 12-inch nonstick skillet, heat the oil over medium-high heat. Add the potatoes and chicken; cook 5 minutes, stirring frequently.

3 Stir in bell peppers and peas. Increase heat to high; cook about 5 minutes, stirring frequently, until chicken is no longer pink in center.

4 Stir in mustard mixture. Cook 1 minute, stirring constantly.

High Altitude (3500-6500 ft): No change.

Nutritional Info: 1 Serving: Calories 530 (Calories from Fat 210); Total Fat 23g (Saturated Fat 10g, Trans Fat 0.5g); Cholesterol 120mg; Sodium 1270mg; Total Carbohydrate 43g (Dietary Fiber 9g, Sugars 7g); Protein 37g. % Daily Value: Vitamin A 70%; Vitamin C 80%; Calcium 10%; Iron 35%. Exchanges: 2 Starch, 2 Vegetable, 4 Very Lean Meat, 4 Fat. Carbohydrate Choices: 3.

Betty's Kitchen Tips

Time-Saver: To cut preparation time, purchase chicken breasts already cut into strips for stir-frying.

Substitution: Boneless skinless chicken breasts can be used instead of chicken thighs.

sweet-and-sour shrimp

Prep Time: 20 Minutes
Start to Finish: 20 Minutes
Servings: 6

QUICK LOW FAT

- 2   packages (8.8 oz each) microwavable long-grain white rice
- 1   tablespoon canola or vegetable oil
- 1   medium onion, cut into 1/2-inch chunks
- 2   medium green bell peppers, cut into 1-inch pieces (about 2 cups)
- 1-1/2   lb uncooked deveined peeled medium shrimp, thawed if frozen, tail shells removed
- 1   can (20 oz) pineapple chunks in juice, drained
- 1-1/2   cups sweet-and-sour sauce

1 Cook rice in microwave as directed on package. Place in bowl; cover to keep warm.

2 In 12-inch skillet, heat oil over high heat. Add onion; cook 1 minute, stirring frequently. Add bell peppers; cook 3 minutes, stirring frequently.

3 Stir in shrimp and pineapple. Cook 3 minutes, stirring frequently. Reduce heat; stir in sweet-and-sour sauce. Cook 1 to 2 minutes, stirring constantly, until shrimp are pink. Serve shrimp mixture over rice.

High Altitude (3500-6500 ft): No change.

Nutritional Info: 1 Serving: Calories 440 (Calories from Fat 60); Total Fat 6g (Saturated Fat 0.5g, Trans Fat 0g); Cholesterol 160mg; Sodium 450mg; Total Carbohydrate 74g (Dietary Fiber 3g, Sugars 40g); Protein 21g. % Daily Value: Vitamin A 8%; Vitamin C 40%; Calcium 8%; Iron 20%. Exchanges: 4 Starch, 1 Fruit, 1-1/2 Very Lean Meat. Carbohydrate Choices: 5.

Betty's Kitchen Tips

Success Hint: Place prepped ingredients on a plate or cutting board in order of use. You won't have to look at the recipe to see what to add next.

Purchasing: Buy fresh-from-the-garden produce at the farmers' market. Keep a cooler in your car to keep items fresh if you're not going straight home.

parmesan chicken

Prep Time: 20 Minutes
Start to Finish: 25 Minutes
Servings: 4

1 tablespoon canola or vegetable oil	1 bag (12 oz) Green Giant® Valley Fresh Steamers™ frozen cut green beans, thawed
2 cloves garlic, finely chopped	2 cups cubed cooked chicken
2 cups marinara sauce	1/2 cup grated Parmesan cheese
2 cups water	
1 package (9 oz) refrigerated fettuccine	

1 In 12-inch skillet, heat oil over medium heat. Add garlic; cook about 30 seconds, stirring occasionally, until softened. Stir in marinara sauce and water. Cover; heat to boiling over medium heat.

2 Add fettuccine and green beans; stir to separate fettuccine. Return to boiling; cover and boil 3 to 5 minutes or until beans are tender.

3 Stir in chicken. Cook 3 to 4 minutes, stirring occasionally, until chicken is heated.

4 Remove from heat. Sprinkle with cheese. Cover; let stand 2 minutes to melt cheese.

High Altitude (3500-6500 ft): No change.

Nutritional Info: 1 Serving: Calories 590 (Calories from Fat 160); Total Fat 18g (Saturated Fat 4.5g, Trans Fat 0g); Cholesterol 115mg; Sodium 1090mg; Total Carbohydrate 71g (Dietary Fiber 6g, Sugars 15g); Protein 36g. % Daily Value: Vitamin A 20%; Vitamin C 10%; Calcium 25%; Iron 30%. Exchanges: 3-1/2 Starch, 2-1/2 Vegetable, 3 Very Lean Meat, 2-1/2 Fat. Carbohydrate Choices: 5.

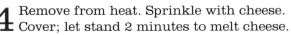

Betty's Kitchen Tip

• If using dried fettuccine, boil it in the sauce 8 minutes before adding the chicken.

potato, broccoli and sausage skillet

Prep Time: 25 Minutes
Start to Finish: 35 Minutes
Servings: 6 (1-1/2 cups each)

2	cups water
2/3	cup milk
2	tablespoons butter or margarine
1	box (4.9 oz) Betty Crocker® scalloped potatoes
2	cups sliced fully cooked reduced-fat Polska-kielbasa sausage (from 1-lb ring)
1/2	cup Old El Paso® Thick 'n Chunky salsa
2	cups Green Giant® Valley Fresh Steamers™ frozen broccoli florets

1 In 12-inch skillet or 3-quart saucepan, heat water, milk and butter to boiling. Stir in potatoes and sauce mix. Add sausage and salsa; stir until well mixed. Reduce heat; cover and simmer 15 minutes, stirring occasionally.

2 Stir in frozen broccoli. Cover; cook 8 minutes longer or until potatoes and broccoli are tender (sauce will thicken as it stands).

High Altitude (3500-6500 ft): No change.

Nutritional Info: 1 Serving: Calories 290 (Calories from Fat 160); Total Fat 18g (Saturated Fat 8g, Trans Fat 1g); Cholesterol 40mg; Sodium 1210mg; Total Carbohydrate 23g (Dietary Fiber 2g, Sugars 5g); Protein 9g. % Daily Value: Vitamin A 15%; Vitamin C 15%; Calcium 6%; Iron 4%. Exchanges: 1 Starch, 1/2 Other Carbohydrate, 1/2 Vegetable, 1 Medium-Fat Meat, 1-1/2 Fat. Carbohydrate Choices: 1-1/2.

Betty's Kitchen Tips

Variation: Substitute your favorite veggie from the garden for the broccoli.

Serve-With: Enjoy the meal with cubed fresh cantaloupe.

asparagus and turkey sausage skillet

Prep Time: 15 Minutes
Start to Finish: 25 Minutes
Servings: 4

EASY QUICK

1 tablespoon olive or vegetable oil

1 package (19.5 oz) lean Italian turkey sausages, casings removed, cut into 1/2-inch slices

1 large onion, coarsely chopped (1 cup)

1 cup Progresso® chicken broth (from 32-oz carton)

1 cup water

1 cup uncooked orzo or rosamarina pasta (6 oz)

1 lb fresh asparagus spears, trimmed, cut into 1-inch pieces

2 tablespoons sliced pimientos (from 4-oz jar)

1 In 12-inch nonstick skillet, heat the oil over medium-high heat. Add the sausage and onion; cook 2 minutes, stirring occasionally.

2 Stir in broth and water. Heat to boiling. Stir in orzo; boil 2 minutes. Add asparagus and pimientos. Reduce heat to medium. Cover; return to boiling. Cook 8 to 10 minutes or until pasta is tender.

High Altitude (3500-6500 ft): No change.

Nutritional Info: 1 Serving: Calories 470 (Calories from Fat 170); Total Fat 19g (Saturated Fat 4g, Trans Fat 0.5g); Cholesterol 125mg; Sodium 1140mg; Total Carbohydrate 34g (Dietary Fiber 3g, Sugars 4g); Protein 40g. % Daily Value: Vitamin A 15%; Vitamin C 10%; Calcium 6%; Iron 25%. Exchanges: 2 Starch, 1-1/2 Vegetable, 1-1/2 Very Lean Meat, 2 Lean Meat, 2-1/2 Fat. Carbohydrate Choices: 2.

Betty's Kitchen Tips

Success Hint: If not using a nonstick skillet, stir often to keep orzo from sticking to the bottom of the skillet.

Leftovers: Leftover chicken broth can be put into a Ziploc® Freezer bag and frozen for later use.

How-To: Coarsely chop onion in a food processor fitted with a chopping blade.

SANDWICHES & SIDES

p. 144

136

148

133

easy mashed potato casserole

Prep Time: 15 Minutes
Start to Finish: 45 Minutes
Servings: 8

EASY

2	teaspoons butter or margarine	1	cup half-and-half or whole milk
16	medium green onions, sliced (1 cup)	1/4	cup butter or margarine
1	medium yellow or orange bell pepper, chopped (1 cup)	1	box (7.2 oz) Betty Crocker® roasted garlic mashed potatoes (2 pouches)
3	cups hot water	1-1/2	cups shredded Cheddar cheese (6 oz)

1 Heat oven to 350°F. Spray 2-quart casserole with cooking spray. In 10-inch nonstick skillet, melt 2 teaspoons butter over medium-high heat. Cook onions and bell pepper in butter 1 minute, stirring occasionally. Remove from heat; set aside.

2 In 2-quart saucepan, heat water, half-and-half and 1/4 cup butter to boiling; remove from heat. Stir in both pouches of potatoes (and seasoning) just until moistened. Let stand about 1 minute or until liquid is absorbed. Beat with fork until smooth.

3 Spoon 1-1/3 cups of the potatoes into casserole; top with half of the onion mixture and 3/4 cup of the cheese. Spoon another 1-1/3 cups potatoes over cheese; carefully spread to cover. Sprinkle evenly with remaining onion mixture. Top with remaining potatoes; carefully spread to cover. Sprinkle with remaining 3/4 cup cheese.

4 Bake mashed potatoes about 30 minutes or until hot.

High Altitude: (3500-6500 ft): In step 3, do not sprinkle with remaining 3/4 cup cheese. In step 4, bake 35 minutes; sprinkle with remaining cheese. Bake about 5 minutes longer or until cheese is melted and casserole is hot.

Nutritional Info: 1 Serving: Calories 290 (Calories from Fat 160); Total Fat 18g (Saturated Fat 11g, Trans Fat 0.5g); Cholesterol 50mg; Sodium 470mg; Total Carbohydrate 23g (Dietary Fiber 2g, Sugars 4g); Protein 9g. % Daily Value: Vitamin A 15%; Vitamin C 30%; Calcium 15%; Iron 6%. Exchanges: 1-1/2 Starch, 1/2 High-Fat Meat, 2-1/2 Fat. Carbohydrate Choices: 1-1/2.

Betty's Kitchen Tips

Do-Ahead: Make this casserole up to 24 hours ahead of time; cover and refrigerate. You'll need to bake it about 45 minutes or until hot.

Substitution: Use Colby or Colby-Monterey Jack cheese blend for the Cheddar, if you like.

sage and garlic vegetable bake

Prep Time: 30 Minutes
Start to Finish: 1 Hour 45 Minutes
Servings: 4 (2 cups each)

LOW FAT

- 1 medium butternut squash, peeled, cut into 1-inch pieces (3 cups)
- 2 medium parsnips, peeled, cut into 1-inch pieces (2 cups)
- 2 cans (14 oz each) stewed tomatoes, undrained
- 2 cups Green Giant® frozen cut green beans (from 1-lb bag)
- 1/2 cup coarsely chopped onion
- 1/2 cup uncooked quick-cooking barley
- 1/2 cup water
- 1 teaspoon dried sage leaves
- 1/2 teaspoon seasoned salt
- 2 cloves garlic, finely chopped

1 Heat oven to 375°F. In ungreased 3-quart casserole, mix all ingredients, breaking up large pieces of tomatoes.

2 Cover casserole. Bake 1 hour to 1 hour 15 minutes or until vegetables and barley are tender.

High Altitude: (3500-6500 ft): Increase water to 3/4 cup.

Nutritional Info: 1 Serving: Calories 280 (Calories from Fat 10); Total Fat 1g (Saturated Fat 0g, Trans Fat 0g); Cholesterol 0mg; Sodium 750mg; Total Carbohydrate 61g (Dietary Fiber 12g, Sugars 20g); Protein 6g. % Daily Value: Vitamin A 210%; Vitamin C 40%; Calcium 15%; Iron 20%. Exchanges: 2 Starch, 2 Other Carbohydrate. Carbohydrate Choices: 4.

Betty's Kitchen Tips

Variation: Try carrots in this recipe instead of the parsnips.

Did You Know? Butternut squash is peanut shaped and has a peel that ranges from cream to yellow. Inside, the squash is bright orange and sweet.

roasted cauliflower with asiago and orange

Prep Time: 10 Minutes
Start to Finish: 40 Minutes
Servings: 10 (1/2 cup each)

EASY

3 tablespoons olive oil	1/4 teaspoon pepper
1/2 teaspoon salt	2 lb cauliflower florets
1/2 teaspoon grated orange peel	1 cup shredded Asiago cheese

1 Heat oven to 450°F. In large bowl, mix oil, salt, orange peel and pepper; toss in cauliflower until evenly coated. Place mixture in ungreased 15x10x1-inch pan.

2 Bake 20 to 25 minutes; stir. Sprinkle with cheese. Bake 1 to 2 minutes longer or until cheese is melted.

High Altitude: (3500-6500 ft): No change.

Nutritional Info: 1 Serving: Calories 120 (Calories from Fat 80); Total Fat 9g (Saturated Fat 3.5g, Trans Fat 0g); Cholesterol 10mg; Sodium 270mg; Total Carbohydrate 5g (Dietary Fiber 2g, Sugars 3g); Protein 4g. % Daily Value: Vitamin A 2%; Vitamin C 35%; Calcium 10%; Iron 2%. Exchanges: 1 Vegetable, 2 Fat. Carbohydrate Choices: 1/2.

Betty's Kitchen Tips

Substitution: Shredded Parmesan can be used instead of the shredded Asiago.

Serve-With: This vegetable dish would go great with seafood, including salmon, shrimp or halibut.

Success Hint: To add visual interest, garnish with additional orange peel.

root beer barbecue beef sandwiches

Prep Time: 30 Minutes
Start to Finish: 10 Hours 30 Minutes
Servings: 16 Sandwiches

- 1   boneless beef rump roast (4 lb)
- 2   cups barbecue sauce
- 1   cup root beer
- Dash salt and pepper, if desired
- 16   sandwich buns, split

1 In 3-1/2- to 4-quart slow cooker, place beef. In 4-cup measuring cup or bowl, mix 1-1/2 cups of the barbecue sauce and the root beer; pour over beef.

2 Cover; cook on Low heat setting 10 to 12 hours.

3 About 20 minutes before serving, remove beef from slow cooker; place on large plate. Pour juices from slow cooker into 12-inch skillet. Cook over medium-high heat about 15 minutes, stirring occasionally, until juices are thickened and reduced to about 3 cups. Meanwhile, shred beef with 2 forks; return to slow cooker.

4 Stir remaining 1/2 cup barbecue sauce into reduced juices in skillet; pour over shredded beef in slow cooker. Stir in salt and pepper to taste. Spoon about 1/2 cup beef mixture into each bun.

High Altitude: (3500-6500 ft): No change.

Nutritional Info: 1 Sandwich: Calories 310 (Calories from Fat 50); Total Fat 5g (Saturated Fat 1.5g, Trans Fat 0g); Cholesterol 60mg; Sodium 570mg; Total Carbohydrate 36g (Dietary Fiber 1g, Sugars 15g); Protein 29g. % Daily Value: Vitamin A 0%; Vitamin C 0%; Calcium 8%; Iron 25%. Exchanges: 1-1/2 Starch, 1 Other Carbohydrate, 3 Lean Meat. Carbohydrate Choices: 2-1/2.

LOW FAT

Betty's Kitchen Tip

• Serve these hearty sandwiches with coleslaw from the deli and baked beans.

green beans with leeks

Prep Time: 15 Minutes
Start to Finish: 40 Minutes
Servings: 12 (1/2 cup each)

EASY

1/4	cup butter or margarine
2	medium leeks (3/4 lb), rinsed, white part and some of the green thinly sliced (about 2 cups)
1/4	cup Gold Medal® all-purpose flour
1/4	teaspoon salt
1/4	teaspoon pepper

1	can (14 oz) chicken broth
1/3	cup Parmesan cheese
1/4	teaspoon ground nutmeg
1	bag (12 oz) Green Giant® frozen cut green beans, thawed
1/2	cup French-fried onions (from 2.8-oz can)

1 Heat oven to 350°F. In 12-inch skillet, heat butter over medium heat. Add leeks; cook 5 to 7 minutes, stirring occasionally, until leeks are tender and soft.

2 Stir in flour, salt and pepper, using wire whisk. Cook, stirring constantly, until mixture is smooth and bubbly. Gradually stir in broth. Heat to boiling, stirring constantly. Boil and stir 1 minute. Stir in cheese and nutmeg. Cook 1 to 2 minutes, stirring occasionally, until cheese is melted. Stir in green beans. Pour mixture into ungreased 1-1/2-quart casserole. Sprinkle with onions.

3 Bake green beans 20 to 25 minutes or until bubbly.

High Altitude: (3500-6500 ft): Bake green beans 25 to 30 minutes.

Nutritional Info: 1 Serving: Calories 100 (Calories from Fat 60); Total Fat 6g (Saturated Fat 3.5g, Trans Fat 0g); Cholesterol 10mg; Sodium 290mg; Total Carbohydrate 8g (Dietary Fiber 1g, Sugars 1g); Protein 3g. % Daily Value: Vitamin A 10%; Vitamin C 2%; Calcium 6%; Iron 4%. Exchanges: 1 Vegetable, 1-1/2 Fat. Carbohydrate Choices: 1/2.

Betty's Kitchen Tip

• Rinse the leeks well under cold running water to remove any soil or grit.

chicken caesar sandwiches

Prep Time: 20 Minutes
Start to Finish: 6 Hours 55 Minutes
Servings: 12 sandwiches

- 2 lb boneless skinless chicken thighs
- 1 package (1.2 oz) Caesar dressing mix
- 1 can (10-3/4 oz) condensed cream of chicken soup
- 1/3 cup shredded Parmesan cheese
- 1/4 cup chopped fresh parsley
- 1/2 teaspoon coarse ground black pepper
- 2 cups shredded romaine lettuce
- 12 mini burger buns (about 2-1/2 inches in diameter)

1 Spray 3- to 4-quart slow cooker with cooking spray. Place chicken in cooker.

2 Cover; cook on Low heat setting 6 to 7 hours.

3 Using slotted spoon, remove chicken from cooker; place on cutting board. Discard liquid in cooker. With 2 forks, pull chicken into shreds. In cooker, mix dressing mix (dry), soup, cheese, parsley and pepper; gently fold in chicken.

4 Increase heat setting to High. Cover and cook 30 to 35 minutes longer or until mixture is hot.

5 To serve, spoon 1/4 cup chicken mixture onto lettuce in each bun. Chicken mixture can be kept warm on Low heat setting up to 2 hours; stir occasionally.

High Altitude: (3500-6500 ft): No change.

Nutritional Info: 1 Sandwich: Calories 250 (Calories from Fat 70); Total Fat 7g (Saturated Fat 2g, Trans Fat 0g); Cholesterol 55mg; Sodium 670mg; Total Carbohydrate 23g (Dietary Fiber 1g, Sugars 3g); Protein 23g. % Daily Value: Vitamin A 15%; Vitamin C 4%; Calcium 10%; Iron 15%. Exchanges: 1-1/2 Starch, 2-1/2 Lean Meat. Carbohydrate Choices: 1-1/2.

LOW FAT

Betty's Kitchen Tip

- Boneless skinless turkey thighs work great in this recipe, too. Just use the same amount of turkey as chicken.

spicy chipotle grilled vegetables

Prep Time: 30 Minutes
Start to Finish: 30 Minutes
Servings: 6 (3/4 cup each)

QUICK LOW FAT

- 2 cloves garlic, finely chopped
- 1 tablespoon olive or vegetable oil
- 1 teaspoon kosher (coarse) salt
- 2 medium zucchini, halved lengthwise, cut into 1-inch slices (2 cups)
- 1 small red bell pepper, cut into 1-inch pieces (3/4 cup)

- 1 lb fresh asparagus spears, cut into 2-inch pieces (about 3-1/2 cups)
- 8 oz baby pattypan squash, cut in half
- 1 canned chipotle chile in adobo sauce, seeds removed, finely chopped
- 1 tablespoon grated orange peel
- 1/2 cup orange juice

1 Heat gas or charcoal grill. In large resealable food-storage plastic bag, place garlic, oil, salt, zucchini, bell pepper, asparagus and squash; seal bag and toss to coat. Place vegetables in grill basket (grill "wok").

2 Place grill basket on grill over medium heat. Cover grill; cook 15 to 20 minutes, stirring occasionally, until vegetables are crisp-tender.

3 Meanwhile, in small bowl, stir together chile, orange peel and orange juice; set aside.

4 In large bowl, toss cooked vegetables with orange juice mixture. Serve warm.

High Altitude: (3500-6500 ft): No change.

Nutritional Info: 1 Serving: Calories 70 (Calories from Fat 0); Total Fat 0.5g (Saturated Fat 0g, Trans Fat 0g); Cholesterol 0mg; Sodium 480mg; Total Carbohydrate 14g (Dietary Fiber 4g, Sugars 6g); Protein 3g. % Daily Value: Vitamin A 25%; Vitamin C 35%; Calcium 6%; Iron 15%. Exchanges: 1/2 Other Carbohydrate, 1-1/2 Vegetable. Carbohydrate Choices: 1.

Betty's Kitchen Tips

Did You Know? Kosher salt has larger grains than ordinary table salt and contains no additives.

Serve-With: The spicy, fresh flavors of these veggies work nicely with just about any grilled meat. Try them with grilled burgers or chicken drumsticks.

classic baked corn pudding

Prep Time: 20 Minutes
Start to Finish: 1 Hour 35 Minutes
Servings: 16 (1/2 cup each)

- 1/2 cup butter or margarine
- 1 small onion, chopped (1/4 cup)
- 1/2 cup Gold Medal® all-purpose flour
- 1/2 teaspoon salt
- 1/2 teaspoon pepper
- 4 cups milk (1 quart)
- 6 eggs, slightly beaten
- 2 cups shredded Cheddar cheese (8 oz)
- 3 bags (12 oz each) Green Giant® Niblets® frozen corn, thawed
- 1/2 cup chopped fresh parsley or 2 tablespoons parsley flakes
- 3/4 cup Progresso® plain dry bread crumbs
- 3 tablespoons butter or margarine, melted

1 Heat oven to 350°F. Spray 13x9-inch (3-quart) baking dish or casserole with cooking spray.

2 In 4-quart Dutch oven, melt 1/2 cup butter over medium heat. Cook onion in butter 3 to 4 minutes, stirring frequently, until tender. Stir in flour, salt and pepper until well blended. Stir in milk. Cook 4 to 5 minutes, stirring constantly, until thickened. Gradually stir in eggs and cheese. Stir in corn and parsley. Pour into baking dish. In small bowl, mix bread crumbs and 3 tablespoons melted butter; sprinkle over corn mixture.

3 Bake 55 to 65 minutes or until mixture is set and knife inserted in center comes out clean. Let stand 5 to 10 minutes before serving.

High Altitude: (3500-6500 ft): No change.

Nutritional Info: 1 Serving: Calories 280 (Calories from Fat 150); Total Fat 16g (Saturated Fat 10g, Trans Fat 0g); Cholesterol 120mg; Sodium 310mg; Total Carbohydrate 21g (Dietary Fiber 2g, Sugars 6g); Protein 10g. % Daily Value: Vitamin A 20%; Vitamin C 4%; Calcium 15%; Iron 6%. Exchanges: 1 Starch, 1/2 Other Carbohydrate, 1 Medium-Fat Meat, 2 Fat. Carbohydrate Choices: 1-1/2.

Betty's Kitchen Tips

Variation: For a change of flavor, add 1/2 teaspoon dried basil leaves with the parsley.

Substitution: You can use three 15.25-oz cans of Green Giant® whole kernel sweet corn, drained, instead of the frozen corn.

turkey, bacon and avocado wraps

Prep Time: 20 Minutes
Start to Finish: 5 Hours 20 Minutes
Servings: 8 wraps

LOW FAT

- 4 slices bacon, cut into 1/2-inch pieces
- 2 lb turkey breast tenderloins, cut crosswise into 1-inch slices
- 3/4 cup barbecue sauce
- 2 tablespoons Old El Paso® taco seasoning mix (from 1-oz package)

- 1 medium ripe avocado, pitted, peeled and mashed
- 2 cups shredded lettuce
- 1/2 cup drained roasted red or yellow bell peppers (from 7-oz jar), large pieces cut up
- 8 Old El Paso® flour tortillas (6 or 8 inch), heated

1 In 12-inch nonstick skillet, cook bacon over medium heat 4 to 6 minutes, stirring occasionally, until almost crisp. Add turkey slices to skillet; cook 4 to 6 minutes, stirring occasionally, until turkey is brown on all sides.

2 Spray 3- to 4-quart slow cooker with cooking spray. Place turkey mixture in cooker. Top with barbecue sauce and taco seasoning mix; stir to mix well.

3 Cover; cook on Low heat setting 5 to 6 hours.

4 Remove turkey from cooker; place on cutting board. With 2 forks, break up turkey; return to cooker. Layer avocado, lettuce, turkey mixture and bell peppers on tortillas; roll up.

High Altitude: (3500-6500 ft): No change.

Nutritional Info: 1 Wrap: Calories 300 (Calories from Fat 70); Total Fat 8g (Saturated Fat 1.5g, Trans Fat 1g); Cholesterol 80mg; Sodium 790mg; Total Carbohydrate 27g (Dietary Fiber 2g, Sugars 9g); Protein 30g. % Daily Value: Vitamin A 10%; Vitamin C 20%; Calcium 6%; Iron 15%. Exchanges: 2 Starch, 3 Lean Meat. Carbohydrate Choices: 2.

Betty's Kitchen Tips

Serve-With: Refried beans and a fruit salad with cantaloupe and pineapple chunks are perfect partners for these sandwiches.

How-To: To warm tortillas, place them on a microwavable plate and cover with microwavable waxed paper; microwave on High 45 to 60 seconds.

Success Hint: Tender, low-fat meats like the turkey tenderloins in this recipe will get dry and tough if overcooked, so follow the cooking times carefully.

hot roast beef sandwiches au jus

Prep Time: 20 Minutes
Start to Finish: 6 Hours 20 Minutes
Servings: 10 sandwiches

1	beef eye of round roast (2-1/2 lb), trimmed of fat
6	cloves garlic, peeled
2	teaspoons coarse ground black pepper
1	large onion, thinly sliced
1/2	cup condensed beef broth (from 10-1/2-oz can)
10	kaiser rolls, split, toasted
2	large tomatoes, each cut into 5 slices

1 Using sharp knife, make 6 evenly spaced deep slits in beef roast. Insert garlic clove into each slit. Sprinkle pepper evenly over entire roast; rub pepper into roast.

2 Spray 3- to 4-quart slow cooker with cooking spray. Place onion slices in cooker; pour broth over onion. Add beef.

3 Cover; cook on Low heat setting 6 to 8 hours.

4 Remove beef from cooker; place on cutting board. Cut beef across grain into thin slices. Return beef to cooker to moisten. Fill each toasted roll with beef, onion and 1 tomato slice. If desired, spoon small amount of broth from cooker over beef.

High Altitude: (3500-6500 ft): No change.

Nutritional Info: 1 Sandwich: Calories 350 (Calories from Fat 130); Total Fat 14g (Saturated Fat 5g, Trans Fat 1g); Cholesterol 60mg; Sodium 420mg; Total Carbohydrate 30g (Dietary Fiber 2g, Sugars 2g); Protein 25g. % Daily Value: Vitamin A 6%; Vitamin C 6%; Calcium 6%; Iron 25%. Exchanges: 2 Starch, 2-1/2 Medium-Fat Meat. Carbohydrate Choices: 2.

Betty's Kitchen Tip

• Keep cleanup to a minimum by lightly spraying the inside of the slow cooker with cooking spray before using.

do-ahead garlic mashed potatoes

Prep Time: 35 Minutes
Start to Finish: 1 Hour 45 Minutes
Servings: 8

- -

3 lb red or white potatoes (about 9 medium), peeled, cut into pieces
6 cloves garlic, peeled
3/4 cup milk

1/2 cup whipping cream
1/2 cup butter or margarine
1 teaspoon salt
Dash pepper

- -

1 In 3-quart saucepan, place potatoes and garlic; add enough water to cover. Heat to boiling; reduce heat. Cover and cook 20 to 25 minutes or until potatoes are tender. Drain and return to saucepan.

2 Heat potatoes over low heat about 1 minute, shaking pan often to keep potatoes from sticking and burning, to dry potatoes. Mash potatoes and garlic in pan with potato masher until no lumps remain.

3 In 1-quart saucepan, heat milk, whipping cream, butter, salt and pepper over medium-low heat, stirring occasionally, until butter is melted; reserve and refrigerate 1/4 cup mixture. Add remaining milk mixture in small amounts to potatoes, mashing after each addition, until potatoes are light and fluffy. Spray 2-quart casserole with cooking spray. Spoon potatoes into casserole; cover and refrigerate up to 24 hours.

4 Heat oven to 350°F. Uncover casserole; pour reserved milk mixture over potatoes. Bake 40 to 45 minutes or until hot. Stir potatoes before serving.

High Altitude: (3500-6500 ft): Heat oven to 375°F.

Nutritional Info: 1 Serving: Calories 300 (Calories from Fat 150); Total Fat 17g (Saturated Fat 11g, Trans Fat 0.5g); Cholesterol 50mg; Sodium 400mg; Total Carbohydrate 33g (Dietary Fiber 3g, Sugars 3g); Protein 4g. % Daily Value: Vitamin A 10%; Vitamin C 10%; Calcium 6%; Iron 2%. Exchanges: 2 Starch, 3 Fat. Carbohydrate Choices: 2.

Betty's Kitchen Tips

Special Touch: Garnish the finished baked casserole with chopped fresh chives.

Time-Saver: You can use garlic from a jar for this recipe. Follow the directions on the jar for the correct amount to use.

buffalo chicken sandwiches

Prep Time: 15 Minutes
Start to Finish: 7 Hours 20 Minutes
Servings: 12 sandwiches

EASY

1 package (3.35 lb) boneless skinless chicken thighs (about 14 thighs)	1 English (seedless) cucumber
1-3/4 cups Buffalo wing sauce	12 large sandwich buns, split
	3/4 cup crumbled blue cheese

1 Spray 3-1/2- to 4-quart slow cooker with cooking spray. Place chicken in cooker. Pour 1 cup of the Buffalo wing sauce over chicken. Cover; cook on Low heat setting 7 to 8 hours.

2 Remove chicken from cooker; place in medium bowl. Place strainer over another medium bowl. Strain juices from cooker; skim fat from juices. Reserve 1-1/2 cups juices. Stir chicken to separate into pieces. Return chicken to cooker; stir in reserved juices. Increase heat setting to High. Cover; cook about 15 minutes or until thoroughly heated.

3 Meanwhile, cut cucumber in half crosswise. With vegetable peeler, cut 1 strip of peel lengthwise from 1 cucumber half; discard strip that is mostly peel. Continue cutting thin strips lengthwise from cucumber, making about 18 strips. Repeat with other half of cucumber. Set strips aside.

4 Fill each bun with 1/2 cup chicken mixture, 1 tablespoon of the remaining wing sauce, about 3 strips of cucumber and 1 tablespoon blue cheese.

High Altitude: (3500-6500 ft): No change.

Nutritional Info: 1 Sandwich: Calories 400 (Calories from Fat 140); Total Fat 15g (Saturated Fat 5g, Trans Fat 0.5g); Cholesterol 85mg; Sodium 1390mg; Total Carbohydrate 31g (Dietary Fiber 1g, Sugars 6g); Protein 34g. % Daily Value: Vitamin A 4%; Vitamin C 20%; Calcium 15%; Iron 25%. Exchanges: 2 Starch, 4 Lean Meat, 1/2 Fat. Carbohydrate Choices: 2.

Betty's Kitchen Tips

Success Hint: For a quick appetizer, fill purchased mini phyllo (filo) shells with the chicken mixture, and top with finely diced celery and a dollop of creamy dressing.

Variation: Are you blue at the thought of using blue cheese? Substitute another cheese if desired.

dilled carrots and pea pods

Prep Time: 15 Minutes
Start to Finish: 15 Minutes
Servings: 4

EASY QUICK LOW FAT

1-1/2	cups ready-to-eat baby-cut carrots (about 8 oz)
1-1/2	cups fresh snow pea pods (about 5 oz), strings removed
1	tablespoon butter or margarine
2	teaspoons chopped fresh or 1/2 teaspoon dried dill weed
1/8	teaspoon salt

1 In 2-quart saucepan, heat 1 inch water to boiling. Add carrots; cover and heat to boiling. Reduce heat; cover and cook about 4 minutes or until carrots are crisp-tender. Do not drain water.

2 Add pea pods to carrots in saucepan. Heat uncovered to boiling. Boil uncovered 2 to 3 minutes, stirring occasionally, until pea pods are crisp-tender. Drain vegetables; return to saucepan.

3 Stir butter, dill weed and salt into vegetables until butter is melted.

High Altitude: (3500-6500 ft): No change.

Nutritional Info: 1 Serving: Calories 70 (Calories from Fat 30); Total Fat 3g (Saturated Fat 1-1/2g, Trans Fat 0g); Cholesterol 10mg; Sodium 135mg; Total Carbohydrate 8g (Dietary Fiber 2g, Sugars 4g); Protein 1g. % Daily Value: Vitamin A 170%; Vitamin C 15%; Calcium 2%; Iron 4%. Exchanges: 1-1/2 Vegetable, 1/2 Fat. Carbohydrate Choices: 1/2.

Betty's Kitchen Tips

How-To: To remove the strings from pea pods, snap off the stem end from each one, then pull the string across the pea pod.

Did You Know? Snow pea pods are very similar to snap pea pods, and they can be used interchangeably. Both are edible pea pods with tender, sweet peas inside.

Substitution: One package (6 oz) frozen snow pea pods can be substituted for the fresh pea pods. Thaw them before cooking in step 2.

two-cheese potato gratin

Prep Time: 30 Minutes
Start to Finish: 1 Hour 35 Minutes
Servings: 12 (1/2 cup each)

1/2 cup butter or margarine	10 cups thinly sliced (about 1/8 inch) Yukon gold potatoes (about 3 lb)
1/2 cup Gold Medal® all-purpose flour	1-1/2 cups shredded Gruyère cheese (6 oz)
3 cups milk	1-1/2 cups shredded Cheddar cheese (6 oz)
1 tablespoon Dijon mustard	
1/2 teaspoon salt	

1 Heat oven to 350°F. Grease 13x9-inch (3-quart) baking dish with shortening, or spray with cooking spray.

2 In 2-quart saucepan, melt butter over medium heat. Stir in flour with wire whisk until smooth. Gradually stir in milk. Heat to boiling. Reduce heat to low; cook about 5 minutes, stirring frequently, until sauce is slightly thickened. Stir in mustard and salt.

3 Place half of the potatoes in baking dish; top with half of the sauce and half of each of the cheeses. Repeat layers.

4 Bake 50 to 55 minutes or until potatoes are tender and top is golden brown. Let stand 5 to 10 minutes before serving.

High Altitude: (3500-6500 ft): Be sure to slice potatoes about 1/8 inch thick. In step 4, bake 1 hour to 1 hour 5 minutes.

Nutritional Info: 1 Serving: Calories 320 (Calories from Fat 160); Total Fat 18g (Saturated Fat 11g, Trans Fat 0.5g); Cholesterol 55mg; Sodium 350mg; Total Carbohydrate 27g (Dietary Fiber 3g, Sugars 4g); Protein 12g. % Daily Value: Vitamin A 15%; Vitamin C 10%; Calcium 30%; Iron 15%. Exchanges: 2 Starch, 1 High-Fat Meat, 1-1/2 Fat. Carbohydrate Choices: 2.

Betty's Kitchen Tips

Did You Know? Gruyère cheese has a rich, sweet, nutty flavor and melts easily.

Success Hint: Yukon gold potatoes, with a yellow-gold color and creamy texture, hold their shape without being waxy.

cheeseburger sandwiches

Prep Time: 20 Minutes
Start to Finish: 6 Hours 20 Minutes
Servings: 12 sandwiches

1-1/2 lb lean (at least 80%) ground beef
1/2 teaspoon garlic-pepper blend
1 package (8 oz) prepared cheese product loaf, diced (2 cups)
2 tablespoons milk
1 medium green bell pepper, chopped (1 cup)
1 small onion, chopped (1/4 cup)
2 cloves garlic, finely chopped
12 burger buns, split

1 In 12-inch skillet, place beef; sprinkle with garlic-pepper blend. Cook over medium heat 8 to 10 minutes, stirring occasionally, until beef is brown; drain.

2 Spray 3- to 4-quart slow cooker with cooking spray. Mix beef and remaining ingredients except buns in cooker.

3 Cover; cook on Low heat setting 6 to 7 hours. Serve beef mixture in buns.

High Altitude: (3500-6500 ft): No change.

Nutritional Info: 1 Sandwich: Calories 280 (Calories from Fat 120); Total Fat 13g (Saturated Fat 6g, Trans Fat 0.5g); Cholesterol 50mg; Sodium 520mg; Total Carbohydrate 21g (Dietary Fiber 1g, Sugars 4g); Protein 17g. % Daily Value: Vitamin A 4%; Vitamin C 8%; Calcium 20%; Iron 15%. Exchanges: 1-1/2 Starch, 2 Medium-Fat Meat. Carbohydrate Choices: 1-1/2.

Betty's Kitchen Tips

Purchasing: Garlic-pepper blend is a zesty blend of garlic powder and cracked pepper. Look for it with the other spices at your supermarket.

Substitution: Ground turkey or pork can be used instead of ground beef.

Serve-With: These sandwiches are great for casual get-togethers or tailgating. Serve them with chips and a tray of raw veggies and dip. Top off the meal with brownies.

teriyaki-sesame-chicken wraps

Prep Time: 30 Minutes
Start to Finish: 7 Hours 45 Minutes
Servings: 12 wraps

3	lb boneless skinless chicken thighs		1/2	cup hoisin sauce
1/2	cup teriyaki sauce		12	flour tortillas (10 inch)
1	tablespoon finely chopped gingerroot		3/4	cup shredded carrots
4	cloves garlic, finely chopped		1	medium bell pepper, cut into bite-size strips
1	tablespoon sesame seed		1/2	cup sliced green onions (8 medium)
1	teaspoon toasted sesame oil		3/4	cup chow mein noodles

1 Spray 4- to 5-quart slow cooker with cooking spray. Place chicken in cooker. In small bowl, mix teriyaki sauce, gingerroot and garlic; pour over chicken.

2 Cover; cook on Low heat setting 7 to 8 hours.

3 Stir chicken mixture to break apart large pieces of chicken. Stir in sesame seed and sesame oil. Increase heat setting to High. Cover; cook about 15 minutes or until thoroughly heated.

4 Spread 2 teaspoons hoisin sauce on each tortilla. Using slotted spoon, spread about 1/3 cup chicken mixture down center of each tortilla. Top chicken mixture with 1 tablespoon shredded carrot, a few bell pepper strips, 2 teaspoons green onions and 1 tablespoon noodles. Roll up tortilla; cut diagonally in half.

High Altitude: (3500-6500 ft): No change.

Nutritional Info: 1 Wrap: Calories 480 (Calories from Fat 160); Total Fat 18g (Saturated Fat 5g, Trans Fat 1g); Cholesterol 80mg; Sodium 1170mg; Total Carbohydrate 47g (Dietary Fiber 2g, Sugars 4g); Protein 34g. % Daily Value: Vitamin A 25%; Vitamin C 8%; Calcium 15%; Iron 30%. Exchanges: 3 Starch, 3-1/2 Lean Meat, 1 Fat. Carbohydrate Choices: 3.

Betty's Kitchen Tips

Variation: Instead of using tortillas, wrap the same ingredients in large lettuce leaves.

Success Hint: For an easy Asian salad, toss chicken with mixed greens, green onions, mandarin orange segments and Asian dressing. Top with chow mein noodles.

grilled summer squash medley

Prep Time: 30 Minutes
Start to Finish: 30 Minutes
Servings: 4

QUICK

- 2 small zucchini, cut into 1/4-inch slices
- 2 small yellow summer squash, cut into 1/4-inch slices
- 6 baby pattypan squash, cut in half
- 1/4 cup citrus vinaigrette dressing
- 2 medium plum (Roma) tomatoes, sliced
- 2 tablespoons chopped fresh cilantro

1 Heat gas or charcoal grill. In large bowl, toss zucchini, summer squash, pattypan squash and dressing. With slotted spoon, place squash in grill basket (grill "wok"). Reserve dressing in bowl.

2 Place grill basket on grill over medium heat. Cover grill; cook 10 to 13 minutes, shaking basket or stirring squash occasionally, until crisp-tender. Return squash to bowl with dressing. Add tomatoes and cilantro; toss to coat.

High Altitude: (3500-6500 ft): No change.

Nutritional Info: 1 Serving: Calories 100 (Calories from Fat 40); Total Fat 4.5g (Saturated Fat 0g, Trans Fat 0g); Cholesterol 0mg; Sodium 270mg; Total Carbohydrate 12g (Dietary Fiber 4g, Sugars 6g); Protein 3g. % Daily Value: Vitamin A 10%; Vitamin C 35%; Calcium 4%; Iron 6%. Exchanges: 2 Vegetable, 1 Fat. Carbohydrate Choices: 1.

Betty's Kitchen Tip

• Look for the citrus vinaigrette dressing with the salad dressings and sauces. If it's not available, balsamic and Asian vinaigrettes work well in this recipe.

mixed vegetable bake

Prep Time: 15 Minutes
Start to Finish: 50 Minutes
Servings: 6 (1 cup each)

EASY

- 1 lb medium red potatoes, (about 4), cut into 1/8-inch slices
- 1 large onion, cut in half and into 1/4-inch slices
- 2 medium carrots, peeled, cut into 1/4-inch slices
- 1/4 cup extra-virgin olive oil
- 2 teaspoons finely chopped garlic

- 1 teaspoon dried thyme leaves
- 1 teaspoon dried tarragon leaves
- 1/2 teaspoon salt
- 1/2 teaspoon pepper
- 1 medium red bell pepper, cut into 1/4-inch slices
- 1 medium zucchini, cut into 1/4-inch slices

1 Heat oven to 400°F. Spray bottom of 13x9-inch (3-quart) baking dish with cooking spray.

2 Place potatoes, onion and carrots in baking dish; toss with half each of the oil, garlic, thyme, tarragon, salt and pepper. Bake 10 minutes.

3 Meanwhile, in medium bowl, toss bell pepper and zucchini with remaining oil and seasonings. Stir into mixture in baking dish. Bake 30 to 35 minutes longer or until vegetables are tender; stirring halfway through bake time.

High Altitude: (3500-6500 ft): No change.

Nutritional Info: 1 Serving: Calories 180 (Calories from Fat 80); Total Fat 9g (Saturated Fat 1.5g, Trans Fat 0g); Cholesterol 0mg; Sodium 220mg; Total Carbohydrate 21g (Dietary Fiber 4g, Sugars 4g); Protein 2g. % Daily Value: Vitamin A 80%; Vitamin C 35%; Calcium 4%; Iron 10%. Exchanges: 1 Starch, 1 Vegetable, 1-1/2 Fat. Carbohydrate Choices: 1-1/2.

Betty's Kitchen Tip

• This recipe would go great with grilled steak or chicken.

MAIN&SIDE SALADS

p. 175

170

177

172

layered mexican party salad

Prep Time: 20 Minutes
Start to Finish: 30 Minutes
Servings: 12 (1 cup each)

QUICK

- 1 box Betty Crocker® Suddenly Salad® classic pasta salad mix
- 3 tablespoons cold water
- 2 tablespoons vegetable oil
- 1 teaspoon ground cumin
- 1 can (15 oz) Progresso® black beans, drained, rinsed
- 1 can (15.25 oz) Green Giant® whole kernel corn, drained

- 4 cups torn romaine lettuce
- 1 container (12 oz) refrigerated guacamole dip
- 1-1/2 cups finely shredded Mexican 4-cheese blend (6 oz)
- 3 plum (Roma) tomatoes, chopped
- 1 can (2-1/4 oz) sliced ripe olives, drained
- 3 cups nacho-flavored tortilla chips

1 Cook, drain and rinse pasta as directed on box. Meanwhile, in large bowl, stir together seasoning mix, cold water, oil and cumin.

2 Add drained pasta, beans and corn to seasoning mixture; toss gently to coat.

3 In 4-quart glass salad bowl or 13x9-inch glass baking dish, layer lettuce and pasta mixture. Spread guacamole dip evenly over top. Sprinkle with cheese and tomatoes; top with olives.

4 Just before serving, arrange chips around edge of bowl. Serve immediately, or cover and refrigerate until serving time.

High Altitude (3500-6500 ft): No change.

Nutritional Info: 1 Serving: Calories 300 (Calories from Fat 100); Total Fat 12g (Saturated Fat 3.5g, Trans Fat 0g); Cholesterol 15mg; Sodium 840mg; Total Carbohydrate 38g (Dietary Fiber 7g, Sugars 5g); Protein 10g. % Daily Value: Vitamin A 25%; Vitamin C 25%; Calcium 15%; Iron 15%. Exchanges: 1-1/2 Starch, 1 Other Carbohydrate, 1/2 High-Fat Meat, 1-1/2 Fat. Carbohydrate Choices: 2-1/2.

Betty's Kitchen Tips

Time-Saver: Purchase a bag of ready-to-eat torn romaine lettuce to save time.

Do-Ahead: Make this salad up to 24 hours before serving.

seven-layer slaw

Prep Time: 10 Minutes
Start to Finish: 2 Hours 10 Minutes
Servings: 6 (about 1 cup each)

EASY

- 2 cups coleslaw mix (from 16-oz bag)
- 2 cups shredded carrots
- 2 cups broccoli slaw (from 16-oz bag)
- 1 medium yellow or red bell pepper, chopped (1 cup)
- 1 cup coleslaw dressing

Additional broccoli slaw, if desired

1 In bottom of 2-1/2-quart clear glass bowl, evenly spread 1 cup of the coleslaw mix. Layer with 1 cup of the carrots, 1 cup of the broccoli slaw and the bell pepper. Layer with remaining coleslaw mix, carrots and broccoli slaw.

2 Pour dressing over layered slaw. Sprinkle with additional broccoli slaw. Cover; refrigerate at least 2 hours but no longer than 24 hours. Toss before serving.

High Altitude (3500-6500 ft): No change.

Nutritional Info: 1 Serving: Calories 215 (Calories from Fat 145); Total Fat 16g (Saturated Fat 2g, Trans Fat 0g); Cholesterol 30mg; Sodium 570mg; Total Carbohydrate 19g (Dietary Fiber 3g, Sugars 14g); Protein 2g. % Daily Value: Vitamin A 62%; Vitamin C 100%; Calcium 4%; Iron 4%. Exchanges: 1 Other Carbohydrate, 1 Vegetable, 2-1/2 Fat. Carbohydrate Choices: 1.

Betty's Kitchen Tips

Purchasing: Pick up coleslaw mix, broccoli slaw and shredded carrots in bags in the produce department.

Did You Know? The vegetables in this slaw are great sources of vitamins A and C.

layered cobb salad

Prep Time: 30 Minutes
Start to Finish: 30 Minutes
Servings: 6 (about 1-1/2 cups each)

QUICK

Dressing

2/3	cup olive or vegetable oil
1/3	cup red wine vinegar
1	teaspoon Dijon mustard
1/2	teaspoon salt
1/4	teaspoon pepper
1	clove garlic, finely chopped

Salad

8	cups chopped romaine lettuce (12 oz)
2	cups cut-up cooked chicken
6	slices precooked bacon, chopped
4	plum (Roma) tomatoes, chopped (about 2 cups)
1/2	cup crumbled blue cheese (2 oz)
4	hard-cooked eggs, chopped
2	medium avocados, pitted, peeled and cubed (about 2 cups)

1 In small bowl, beat dressing ingredients with wire whisk until well blended. Refrigerate until ready to serve.

2 In 6- to 8-quart glass bowl, place half of the chopped lettuce. Top with half each of the chicken, bacon, tomatoes, cheese and eggs. Repeat layers.

3 Just before serving, top salad with avocados. Pour dressing over salad; toss to coat.

High Altitude (3500-6500 ft): No change.

Nutritional Info: 1 Serving: Calories 550 (Calories from Fat 410); Total Fat 45g (Saturated Fat 10g, Trans Fat 0g); Cholesterol 200mg; Sodium 730mg; Total Carbohydrate 10g (Dietary Fiber 5g, Sugars 3g); Protein 25g. % Daily Value: Vitamin A 80%; Vitamin C 45%; Calcium 10%; Iron 15%. Exchanges: 1/2 Starch, 3-1/2 High-Fat Meat, 3-1/2 Fat. Carbohydrate Choices: 1/2.

Betty's Kitchen Tips

Purchasing: Romaine can come in several different packages to get to 8 cups.
• One head of romaine weighs about 18 oz = 12 to 13 cups
• One 18-oz bag of hearts of romaine = about 12 to 13 cups
• One 10-oz bag hearts of romaine = about 7-1/2 cups

Success Hint: The traditional way to serve a cobb salad is with the ingredients arranged in rows on lettuce. We've given it a new twist by serving it in layers.

easy club salad

Prep Time: 15 Minutes
Start to Finish: 15 Minutes
Servings: 4

EASY QUICK

• •

> 1 bag (16 ounces) lettuce or 1 small head lettuce, torn into bite-size pieces (6 cups)
> 1-1/2 cups cut-up cooked chicken (9 ounces)
> 1 medium tomato, cut into eighths
> 1/3 cup Thousand Island dressing
> 1/3 cup Betty Crocker® Bac~Os® bacon flavor bits or chips
>
> Hard-cooked egg slices, if desired

• •

1 In large bowl, toss lettuce, chicken, tomato, dressing and bacon bits.

2 Garnish salad with egg slices and serve.

High Altitude (3500-6500 ft): No change.

Nutritional Info: 1 Serving: Calories 210 (Calories from Fat 110); Total Fat 12g (Saturated Fat 2.5g, Trans Fat 0g); Cholesterol 50mg; Sodium 370mg; Total Carbohydrate 7g (Dietary Fiber 2g, Sugars 4g); Protein 19g. % Daily Value: Vitamin A 15%; Vitamin C 10%; Calcium 6%; Iron 8%. Exchanges: 1 Vegetable, 2-1/2 Lean Meat, 1 Fat. Carbohydrate Choices: 1/2.

Betty's Kitchen Tips

Time-Saver: In a hurry? Just use 2 cans (4.5 oz each) chunk chicken, drained, instead of the cooked chicken.

Did You Know? What makes a club a club? Club sandwiches are double-decker delights made of three slices of bread alternated with layers of chicken or turkey, bacon, lettuce and tomato.

Substitution: You can use the type of lettuce you have on hand. Mixed salad greens, romaine and baby spinach leaves are all good choices.

summer vinaigrette potato salad

Prep Time: 20 Minutes
Start to Finish: 3 Hours 20 Minutes
Servings: 16 (1/2 cup each)

Salad

5	cups water
2	teaspoons salt
2-1/2	lb unpeeled Yukon Gold potatoes, cut into 3/4-inch pieces (about 8 cups)
1-1/2	cups chopped cucumber (1 medium)
1	cup chopped yellow bell pepper (1 medium)
1/2	cup thinly sliced celery (1 medium stalk)
1/4	cup chopped green onions (4 medium)

Dressing

1/2	cup canola or vegetable oil
1/4	cup lemon juice
1/4	cup chopped fresh basil leaves
2	tablespoons chopped fresh parsley
2	teaspoons chopped fresh thyme leaves
1-1/2	teaspoons salt

1 In 4-quart saucepan, heat water and 2 teaspoons salt to boiling. Add potatoes; return to boiling. Cook uncovered 5 to 8 minutes or just until tender.

2 Meanwhile, in large bowl, mix dressing ingredients; set aside.

3 Drain potatoes. Add potatoes and remaining salad ingredients to dressing; toss to coat. Cover; refrigerate 3 hours to blend flavors.

High Altitude (3500-6500 ft): No change.

Nutritional Info: 1 Serving: Calories 140 (Calories from Fat 60); Total Fat 7g (Saturated Fat 0.5g, Trans Fat 0g); Cholesterol 0mg; Sodium 530mg; Total Carbohydrate 17g (Dietary Fiber 2g, Sugars 1g); Protein 1g. % Daily Value: Vitamin A 2%; Vitamin C 20%; Calcium 0%; Iron 2%. Exchanges: 1 Starch, 1 Fat. Carbohydrate Choices: 1.

Betty's Kitchen Tips

Variation: If you like tomatoes, add 2 medium tomatoes, chopped, to the mix.

Do-Ahead: You can make this salad up to 24 hours ahead, but the olive oil will solidify a bit so you'll have to let it stand and then stir it right before serving.

chipotle ranch chicken and pasta salad

Prep Time: 20 Minutes
Start to Finish: 1 Hour 20 Minutes
Servings: 4

1	box Betty Crocker® Suddenly Salad® chipotle ranch pasta salad mix
1/2	cup Green Giant® Valley Fresh Steamers™ Niblets® frozen corn
3	tablespoons milk
1/3	cup mayonnaise
2	cups cubed cooked chicken
1/2	cup coarsely chopped tomato
4	medium green onions, sliced (1/4 cup)

Lime wedges, if desired

1 Empty pasta mix into 3-quart saucepan 2/3 full of boiling water. Gently boil uncovered 15 minutes, stirring occasionally; add corn during last 3 minutes of cooking.

2 Drain pasta with corn; rinse with cold water. Shake to drain well.

3 Meanwhile, in large bowl, stir together seasoning mix (from salad mix) and milk until blended. Stir in mayonnaise. Stir in pasta with corn, chicken, tomato and green onions. Refrigerate at least 1 hour. Serve with lime wedges.

High Altitude (3500-6500 ft): No change.

Nutritional Info: 1 Serving: Calories 420 (Calories from Fat 170); Total Fat 19g (Saturated Fat 3g, Trans Fat 0g); Cholesterol 65mg; Sodium 560mg; Total Carbohydrate 36g (Dietary Fiber 2g, Sugars 4g); Protein 27g. % Daily Value: Vitamin A 15%; Vitamin C 10%; Calcium 6%; Iron 15%. Exchanges: 2 Starch, 1/2 Other Carbohydrate, 3 Lean Meat, 1-1/2 Fat. Carbohydrate Choices: 2-1/2.

Betty's Kitchen Tip

• For a lighter dressing, substitute reduced-fat mayonnaise.

poppy seed-fruit salad

Prep Time: 15 Minutes
Start to Finish: 15 Minutes
Servings: 8

EASY QUICK LOW FAT

1/4	cup honey		1	cup cubed pineapple
1/4	cup frozen (thawed) limeade concentrate		1	cup fresh blueberries
2	teaspoons poppy seed		1	cup cubed watermelon
1	cup fresh strawberries, cut in half		1/4	cup slivered almonds, toasted, if desired*

1 In medium bowl, mix honey, limeade concentrate and poppy seed.

2 Add fruit to honey mixture; carefully toss. Sprinkle with almonds.

*Note: To toast nuts, cook in an ungreased heavy skillet over medium-low heat 5 to 7 minutes, stirring frequently until browning begins, then stirring constantly until nuts are golden brown.

High Altitude (3500-6500 ft): No change.

Nutritional Info: 1 Serving: Calories 110 (Calories from Fat 0); Total Fat 0g (Saturated Fat 0g, Trans Fat 0g); Cholesterol 0mg; Sodium 0mg; Total Carbohydrate 25g (Dietary Fiber 1g, Sugars 21g); Protein 0g. % Daily Value: Vitamin A 2%; Vitamin C 30%; Calcium 2%; Iron 2%. Exchanges: 1/2 Fruit, 1 Other Carbohydrate. Carbohydrate Choices: 1-1/2.

Betty's Kitchen Tips

Variation: Try other combinations of fresh fruit with this zingy dressing. Pineapple, blackberries and cantaloupe make a nice combination, too.

Serve-With: Serve this salad alongside Ham Steak with Mustard Sauce on p. 73.

peppered shrimp and mango salad

Prep Time: 20 Minutes
Start to Finish: 20 Minutes
Servings: 4 (about 2 cups each)   **QUICK**

20	uncooked deveined large shrimp, thawed if frozen, tail shells removed (about 3/4 lb)
1/2	teaspoon salt
1/2	teaspoon pepper
1	tablespoon sesame or vegetable oil
1	bag (5 oz) ready-to-eat mixed salad greens
1-1/2	cups diced mangoes (about 1-1/2 medium)
1/2	cup sliced radishes (about 5 medium)
1/3	cup Asian sesame dressing

1 Toss the shrimp with the salt and pepper.

2 In 10-inch skillet, heat oil over high heat. Add shrimp; cook about 3 minutes, stirring frequently, until shrimp are pink. Remove from heat.

3 In large bowl, toss salad greens, mangoes, radishes and dressing. Top with shrimp.

High Altitude (3500-6500 ft): No change.

Nutritional Info: 1 Serving: Calories 200 (Calories from Fat 120); Total Fat 13g (Saturated Fat 2g, Trans Fat 0g); Cholesterol 60mg; Sodium 590mg; Total Carbohydrate 13g (Dietary Fiber 2g, Sugars 9g); Protein 7g. % Daily Value: Vitamin A 45%; Vitamin C 20%; Calcium 4%; Iron 8%. Exchanges: 1 Fruit, 2 Vegetable, 1 Very Lean Meat, 2 Fat. Carbohydrate Choices: 1.

Betty's Kitchen Tips

Time-Saver: Purchase quick-peel shrimp to speed up prep time. The shells are already split and the shrimp deveined, so the shells come off easily.

Substitution: Use jarred mangoes if ripe mangoes are not available.

lemon-chicken pasta salad

Prep Time: 15 Minutes
Start to Finish: 25 Minutes
Servings: 4 (1-1/2 cups each)

EASY QUICK

- 1 box Betty Crocker® Suddenly Salad® ranch & bacon pasta salad mix
- 1 cup reduced-fat mayonnaise
- 2 teaspoons grated lemon peel
- 2 tablespoons fresh lemon juice

- 2 cups cubed cooked chicken
- 1-1/2 cups fresh snow pea pods, strings removed, cut diagonally into 1/2-inch pieces
- 1/2 cup sliced almonds

Leaf lettuce, if desired

1 Empty pasta mix into 3-quart saucepan 2/3 full of boiling water. Gently boil uncovered 12 minutes, stirring occasionally.

2 Drain pasta; rinse with cold water. Shake to drain well.

3 In large bowl, stir together seasoning mix (from salad mix), mayonnaise, lemon peel and lemon juice. Stir in pasta, chicken, pea pods and almonds. Serve on lettuce leaves. Serve immediately, or refrigerate until serving.

High Altitude (3500-6500 ft): No change.

Nutritional Info: 1 Serving: Calories 600 (Calories from Fat 270); Total Fat 30g (Saturated Fat 5g, Trans Fat 0g); Cholesterol 80mg; Sodium 880mg; Total Carbohydrate 47g (Dietary Fiber 3g, Sugars 8g); Protein 33g. % Daily Value: Vitamin A 30%; Vitamin C 20%; Calcium 8%; Iron 20%. Exchanges: 2 Starch, 1 Other Carbohydrate, 1 Vegetable, 3-1/2 Lean Meat, 3-1/2 Fat. Carbohydrate Choices: 3.

Betty's Kitchen Tips

Do-Ahead: Make this salad up to 24 hours before serving. Just before serving, stir in a few drops of milk if needed to make it creamy again.

Substitution: No leftover cooked chicken on hand? You can buy frozen chopped cooked chicken, canned chunk chicken or deli rotisserie chicken.

lo mein noodle salad

Prep Time: 20 Minutes
Start to Finish: 20 Minutes
Servings: 12 (1/2 cup each)

QUICK

Salad

- 1 package (8 oz) lo mein noodles
- 1 bag (10 oz) frozen shelled edamame (green) soybeans
- 1 large red bell pepper, chopped (1-1/2 cups)
- 4 medium green onions, sliced (1/4 cup)

Dressing

- 1/3 cup rice vinegar
- 1/3 cup peanut butter
- 1/4 cup soy sauce
- 2 tablespoons packed brown sugar
- 2 tablespoons vegetable oil
- 1/4 teaspoon crushed red pepper flakes

1 Break lo mein noodles into thirds. Cook as directed on package. Rinse with cold water; drain.

2 Cook edamame as directed on bag; drain.

3 In medium bowl, place bell pepper, onions, noodles and edamame.

4 In small bowl, beat dressing ingredients with wire whisk until well blended. Spoon over noodle mixture; toss to coat. Serve immediately, or cover and refrigerate until serving time.

High Altitude (3500-6500 ft): No change.

Nutritional Info: 1 Serving: Calories 200 (Calories from Fat 70); Total Fat 8g (Saturated Fat 1.5g, Trans Fat 0g); Cholesterol 0mg; Sodium 340mg; Total Carbohydrate 24g (Dietary Fiber 3g, Sugars 5g); Protein 8g. % Daily Value: Vitamin A 10%; Vitamin C 15%; Calcium 2%; Iron 10%. Exchanges: 1-1/2 Starch, 1/2 Lean Meat, 1 Fat. Carbohydrate Choices: 1-1/2.

Betty's Kitchen Tips

Success Hint: Use 1 to 2 tablespoons chopped fresh cilantro as a garnish.

Purchasing: Shelled edamame are sometimes called "mukimame."

fresh fruit with orange sour cream

Prep Time: 15 Minutes
Start to Finish: 15 Minutes
Servings: 8 (1/2 cup each)

EASY QUICK LOW FAT

- 2 cups cubed cantaloupe
- 1 cup seedless green grapes, halved if large
- 1 cup fresh blueberries
- 1/2 cup sour cream
- 1 teaspoon grated orange peel
- 1 tablespoon sugar
- 1 tablespoon orange juice

1 In medium bowl, place cantaloupe, grapes and blueberries.

2 In small bowl, beat remaining ingredients with wire whisk until well blended. Stir sour cream mixture into fruit.

High Altitude (3500-6500 ft): No change.

Nutritional Info: 1 Serving: Calories 80 (Calories from Fat 25); Total Fat 3g (Saturated Fat 2g, Trans Fat 0g); Cholesterol 10mg; Sodium 15mg; Total Carbohydrate 12g (Dietary Fiber 1g, Sugars 10g); Protein 1g. % Daily Value: Vitamin A 30%; Vitamin C 35%; Calcium 2%; Iron 0%. Exchanges: 1 Fruit, 1/2 Fat. Carbohydrate Choices: 1.

Betty's Kitchen Tips

Health-Twist: Use reduced-fat sour cream to lower the fat content even more.

Variation: Try lemon or lime peel and juice in place of the orange.

steakhouse salad

Prep Time: 35 Minutes
Start to Finish: 35 Minutes
Servings: 4 (2 cups each)

12 small red potatoes, quartered	1 lb beef flank steak
2 tablespoons olive or vegetable oil	1 bag (6 oz) washed fresh baby spinach leaves
2 teaspoons kosher (coarse) salt	1 medium tomato, cut into bite-size pieces
1/2 teaspoon pepper	1/4 cup tangy tomato bacon dressing

1 Heat oven to 375°F. In large bowl, toss potatoes, 1 tablespoon of the oil, 1 teaspoon of the salt and 1/4 teaspoon of the pepper. Spread on cookie sheet with sides. Roast 20 to 25 minutes, stirring occasionally, until tender.

2 Meanwhile, sprinkle beef steak with remaining 1 teaspoon salt and 1/4 teaspoon pepper. In 12-inch nonstick skillet, heat remaining 1 tablespoon oil over medium heat. Add beef; cover and cook 8 to 10 minutes, turning once, until desired doneness.

3 Remove beef from skillet to cutting board; cover with foil and let rest 5 minutes.

4 Cut beef into thin bite-size pieces. In large bowl, toss beef, potatoes, spinach, tomato and dressing.

High Altitude (3500-6500 ft): No change.

Nutritional Info: 1 Serving: Calories 790 (Calories from Fat 360); Total Fat 40g (Saturated Fat 8g, Trans Fat 0g); Cholesterol 55mg; Sodium 1440mg; Total Carbohydrate 71g (Dietary Fiber 10g, Sugars 5g); Protein 36g. % Daily Value: Vitamin A 90%; Vitamin C 50%; Calcium 15%; Iron 60%. Exchanges: 3 Starch, 1/2 Other Carbohydrate, 3 Vegetable, 3 Medium-Fat Meat, 4-1/2 Fat. Carbohydrate Choices: 5.

 Kitchen Tips

Success Hint: Start the steak about 5 minutes after you start roasting the potatoes; they'll be done at about the same time.

Variation: For wilted spinach, toss all ingredients, cover bowl with plastic wrap and allow steam from the beef and potatoes to wilt the spinach.

roasted pepper and pepperoni tossed salad

Prep Time: 30 Minutes
Start to Finish: 30 Minutes
Servings: 6

QUICK

- 1 medium red bell pepper
- 1 package (5 oz) pepperoni links, diced
- 3 tablespoons olive or vegetable oil
- 2 tablespoons sherry vinegar
- 1/2 teaspoon garlic salt
- 1 bag (10 oz) ready-to-eat romaine lettuce
- 1/2 cup grape tomatoes
- 1 can (15 oz) Progresso® chick peas, drained, rinsed

1 Cut bell pepper in half; remove seeds. Place halves, skin sides up, on foil-lined broiler pan. Broil 3 to 4 inches from heat about 5 minutes or until skin blackens. Place in plastic bag; let stand 10 minutes to steam. Peel skin from pepper.

2 Meanwhile, line microwavable plate with microwavable paper towels. Spread diced pepperoni on plate; cover loosely with microwavable paper towel. Microwave on High 2 minutes to remove excess fat.

3 Cut the roasted pepper into thin bite-size pieces.

4 In small bowl, beat oil, vinegar and garlic salt with wire whisk until well blended. In large bowl, toss lettuce, roasted pepper, pepperoni, tomatoes and chick peas with oil-and-vinegar dressing.

High Altitude (3500-6500 ft): No change.

Nutritional Info: 1 Serving (1-1/2 cups): Calories 310 (Calories from Fat 170); Total Fat 19g (Saturated Fat 4.5g, Trans Fat 0g); Cholesterol 25mg; Sodium 580mg; Total Carbohydrate 22g (Dietary Fiber 6g, Sugars 2g); Protein 12g. % Daily Value: Vitamin A 70%; Vitamin C 30%; Calcium 6%; Iron 15%. Exchanges: 1/2 Starch, 3 Vegetable, 1 Very Lean Meat, 3 Fat. Carbohydrate Choices: 1-1/2.

Betty's Kitchen Tips

Time-Saver: Use jarred roasted red peppers instead of roasting your own.

Success Hint: If the outer casing on the pepperoni is tough, remove it from the pepperoni before dicing and microwaving.

mediterranean couscous salad

Prep Time: 20 Minutes
Start to Finish: 1 Hour 20 Minutes
Servings: 8 (1/2 cup each)

- -

1 cup Progresso® chicken broth (from 32-oz carton)	1/4 cup chopped fresh or 1 tablespoon dried dill weed
3/4 cup uncooked couscous	2 tablespoons lemon juice
1 cup cubed plum (Roma) tomatoes (3 medium)	2 tablespoons olive or vegetable oil
1 cup cubed unpeeled cucumber (1 small)	1/8 teaspoon salt
1/2 cup halved pitted kalamata olives	2 tablespoons crumbled feta cheese
1/4 cup chopped green onions (about 4 medium)	

- -

1 In 2-quart saucepan, heat broth to boiling. Stir in couscous; remove from heat. Cover; let stand 5 minutes.

2 In large bowl, place tomatoes, cucumber, olives, onions and dill weed. Stir in couscous.

3 In small bowl, beat lemon juice, oil and salt with wire whisk until well blended; pour over vegetable mixture and toss. Cover; refrigerate 1 hour to blend flavors.

4 Just before serving, sprinkle with the cheese.

High Altitude (3500-6500 ft): No change.

Nutritional Info: 1 Serving: Calories 120 (Calories from Fat 45); Total Fat 5g (Saturated Fat 1g, Trans Fat 0g); Cholesterol 0mg; Sodium 250mg; Total Carbohydrate 16g (Dietary Fiber 2g, Sugars 2g); Protein 3g. % Daily Value: Vitamin A 10%; Vitamin C 6%; Calcium 4%; Iron 4%. Exchanges: 1 Starch, 1 Fat. Carbohydrate Choices: 1.

Betty's Kitchen Tip

• Any variety of tomato will work in this recipe. We call for plum (Roma) tomatoes because they are firm in texture and don't contain a lot of seeds.

mixed fresh fruit with lime and ginger

Prep Time: 15 Minutes
Start to Finish: 1 Hour 20 Minutes
Servings: 11 (1/2 cup each)

- 1/4 cup sugar
- 2 tablespoons water
- 1/2 teaspoon grated lime peel
- 2 tablespoons lime juice
- 2 cups bite-size pieces honeydew melon
- 2 tablespoons finely chopped crystallized ginger
- 2 cups halved fresh strawberries

Additional grated lime peel, if desired

1 In 1-quart saucepan, heat sugar and water to boiling. Remove from heat; stir in 1/2 teaspoon lime peel and the lime juice. Cool 10 minutes.

2 In medium bowl, place melon and ginger. Pour sugar mixture over melon mixture. Cover; refrigerate about 1 hour to blend flavors.

3 Just before serving, stir strawberries into melon mixture. Serve garnished with additional lime peel.

High Altitude (3500-6500 ft): No change.

Nutritional Info: 1 Serving: Calories 45 (Calories from Fat 0); Total Fat 0g (Saturated Fat 0g, Trans Fat 0g); Cholesterol 0mg; Sodium 5mg; Total Carbohydrate 10g (Dietary Fiber 1g, Sugars 9g); Protein 0g. % Daily Value: Vitamin A 0%; Vitamin C 40%; Calcium 0%; Iron 0%. Exchanges: 1/2 Fruit. Carbohydrate Choices: 1/2.

EASY LOW FAT

Betty's Kitchen Tips

Success Hint: This versatile dish could be served for breakfast or as a side at a picnic.

Purchasing: You'll find crystallized ginger in plastic containers with the other baking ingredients at the grocery store.

gemelli with fresh green and yellow beans

Prep Time: 25 Minutes
Start to Finish: 1 Hour 25 Minutes
Servings: 18 servings (1/2 cup each)

2 cups uncooked gemelli pasta (8 oz)
4 oz fresh green beans, cut into 2-inch pieces (1 cup)
4 oz fresh yellow wax beans, cut into 2-inch pieces (1 cup)
1 pint (2 cups) grape or cherry tomatoes, halved

1/4 cup vegetable oil
1/4 cup tarragon vinegar
1/2 teaspoon salt
3/4 cup shaved Parmesan cheese (3 oz)
1/4 teaspoon freshly ground black pepper

1 Cook pasta as directed on package, adding green and yellow beans for last 5 minutes of cooking time; drain. Rinse with cold water to cool; drain well.

2 In large bowl, mix pasta, beans and tomatoes.

3 In small bowl, beat oil, vinegar and salt with wire whisk until well blended; stir into pasta mixture. Stir in 1/2 cup of the cheese. Cover; refrigerate at least 1 hour to blend flavors.

4 Just before serving, stir salad; top with remaining 1/4 cup cheese and sprinkle with pepper.

High Altitude (3500-6500 ft): No change.

Nutritional Info: 1 Serving: Calories 100 (Calories from Fat 40); Total Fat 4.5g (Saturated Fat 1.5g, Trans Fat 0g); Cholesterol 0mg; Sodium 180mg; Total Carbohydrate 12g (Dietary Fiber 1g, Sugars 0g); Protein 4g. % Daily Value: Vitamin A 2%; Vitamin C 2%; Calcium 6%; Iron 4%. Exchanges: 1 Starch, 1/2 Fat. Carbohydrate Choices: 1.

Betty's Kitchen Tips

Purchasing: You can buy shaved Parmesan cheese in the deli section of your grocery store.
Success Hint: Garnish the salad with parsley or tarragon.

barbecued chicken salad

Prep Time: 30 Minutes
Start to Finish: 30 Minutes
Servings: 4 (about 1 cup each)

QUICK

4	slices thick-sliced bacon (about 5 oz), diced
1/2	cup mayonnaise or salad dressing
1/3	cup barbecue sauce
1/2	teaspoon salt
4	cups bite-size pieces deli rotisserie chicken (from 2- to 2-1/2-lb chicken)
1/2	cup finely chopped red onion
1	jalapeño chile, seeded, finely chopped
4	large Bibb lettuce leaves
2	tablespoons chopped fresh parsley

1 In 10-inch skillet, cook bacon over medium heat 7 to 9 minutes, stirring occasionally, until crisp. Drain bacon on paper towels.

2 In small bowl, beat mayonnaise, barbecue sauce and salt with wire whisk until blended.

3 In large bowl, stir chicken, bacon, onion, jalapeño chile and mayonnaise mixture until well mixed. Serve on lettuce leaves. Sprinkle with parsley.

High Altitude (3500-6500 ft): No change.

Nutritional Info: 1 Serving: Calories 380 (Calories from Fat 260); Total Fat 29g (Saturated Fat 5g, Trans Fat 0g); Cholesterol 60mg; Sodium 1860mg; Total Carbohydrate 13g (Dietary Fiber 0g, Sugars 10g); Protein 18g. % Daily Value: Vitamin A 15%; Vitamin C 6%; Calcium 4%; Iron 8%. Exchanges: 1 Vegetable, 3 High-Fat Meat, 1 Fat. Carbohydrate Choices: 1.

Betty's Kitchen Tips

Variation: For a spicier or sweeter salad, use a spicier or sweeter barbecue sauce.

Success Hint: For a more developed flavor, refrigerate the chicken salad overnight or up to 24 hours before serving on the lettuce.

chicken pasta salad with grapes and poppy seed dressing

Prep Time: 15 Minutes
Start to Finish: 25 Minutes
Servings: 4 (1-1/2 cups each)

EASY   QUICK

1	box Betty Crocker® Suddenly Salad® classic pasta salad mix
1/2	cup refrigerated poppy seed dressing
1-1/2	cups cut-up cooked chicken

3/4	cup halved seedless red grapes
1/2	cup thinly sliced celery
1/4	cup slivered almonds, toasted*

1 Empty pasta mix into 3-quart saucepan 2/3 full of boiling water. Gently boil uncovered 12 minutes, stirring occasionally.

2 Drain pasta; rinse with cold water. Shake to drain well.

3 In large bowl, stir together seasoning mix (from salad mix) and dressing. Add pasta and remaining ingredients; toss to combine. Serve immediately, or refrigerate until serving.

***Note:** To toast almonds, cook in ungreased heavy skillet over medium heat 5 to 7 minutes, stirring frequently until almonds begin to brown, then stirring constantly until light brown.

High Altitude (3500-6500 ft): No change.

Nutritional Info: 1 Serving: Calories 520 (Calories from Fat 200); Total Fat 22g (Saturated Fat 3.5g, Trans Fat 0g); Cholesterol 45mg; Sodium 1280mg; Total Carbohydrate 57g (Dietary Fiber 3g, Sugars 20g); Protein 23g. % Daily Value: Vitamin A 4%; Vitamin C 6%; Calcium 6%; Iron 15%. Exchanges: 1-1/2 Starch, 2-1/2 Other Carbohydrate, 2-1/2 Lean Meat, 2-1/2 Fat. Carbohydrate Choices: 4.

Betty's Kitchen Tips

Variation: Dried cherries can be used instead of the red grapes.

Success Hint: You can use frozen diced cooked chicken, thawed, or cut-up deli rotisserie chicken.

black bean-chili salad

Prep Time: 10 Minutes
Start to Finish: 10 Minutes
Servings: 4

EASY QUICK

Dressing

- 1/4 cup red wine vinegar
- 2 tablespoons vegetable oil
- 1/2 teaspoon chili powder
- 1/4 teaspoon ground cumin
- 1 small clove garlic, finely chopped

Salad

- 1 cup Green Giant® Valley Fresh Steamers™ Niblets® frozen corn, thawed, drained
- 1 cup finely chopped peeled jicama
- 1 medium tomato, seeded, chopped (3/4 cup)
- 2 medium green onions, sliced (2 tablespoons)
- 2 cans (15 oz each) Progresso® black beans, drained, rinsed

1 In large glass or plastic bowl, mix dressing ingredients.

2 Stir salad ingredients into dressing until well mixed.

High Altitude (3500-6500 ft): No change.

Nutritional Info: 1 Serving: Calories 290 (Calories from Fat 70); Total Fat 8g (Saturated Fat 1g, Trans Fat 0g); Cholesterol 0mg; Sodium 710mg; Total Carbohydrate 42g (Dietary Fiber 12g, Sugars 2g); Protein 12g. % Daily Value: Vitamin A 10%; Vitamin C 10%; Calcium 8%; Iron 20%. Exchanges: 2-1/2 Starch, 1/2 Vegetable, 1/2 Lean Meat, 1 Fat. Carbohydrate Choices: 3.

Betty's Kitchen Tips

Did You Know? What's jicama? Sometimes referred to as the "Mexican potato," this sweet and nutty root vegetable can be enjoyed raw or cooked. Look for it in the produce section of the store.

Purchasing: Most large supermarkets carry jicama. If that's not an option in your area, check out Mexican and farmers' markets.

caprese salad with greens

Prep Time: 10 Minutes
Start to Finish: 10 Minutes
Servings: 4

EASY QUICK

4	cups torn mixed salad greens or arugula
1	cup halved grape tomatoes
1	cup bocconcini (small fresh mozzarella cheese balls), cut in half
1/4	cup julienne-cut fresh basil leaves
1/4	cup finely chopped red onion
1/4	cup red wine vinaigrette
2	tablespoons pine nuts, toasted, if desired*

1 In large bowl, toss all ingredients except nuts.

2 Divide salad among 4 salad plates. Sprinkle with nuts.

*Note: To toast nuts, cook in an ungreased heavy skillet over medium-low heat 5 to 7 minutes, stirring frequently until browning begins, then stirring constantly until golden brown.

High Altitude (3500-6500 ft): No change.

Nutritional Info: 1 Serving: Calories 150 (Calories from Fat 90); Total Fat 9g (Saturated Fat 4.5g, Trans Fat 0g); Cholesterol 20mg; Sodium 190mg; Total Carbohydrate 6g (Dietary Fiber 1g, Sugars 2g); Protein 10g. % Daily Value: Vitamin A 25%; Vitamin C 15%; Calcium 30%; Iron 4%. Exchanges: 1 Vegetable, 1-1/2 Medium-Fat Meat. Carbohydrate Choices: 1/2.

Betty's Kitchen Tips

Substitution: If bocconcini is not available, substitute 3/4 cup cubed fresh mozzarella cheese.

Success Hint: To re-create the special touch of a fine-dining restaurant, top each salad with freshly ground black pepper and a pinch of sea salt.

antipasto pasta salad

Prep Time: 15 Minutes
Start to Finish: 25 Minutes
Servings: 6 (1-1/2 cups each)

EASY QUICK

1   box Betty Crocker® Suddenly Salad® Caesar pasta salad mix
1/2   cup Italian dressing
4   cups torn romaine lettuce
1   cup cubed salami

1   cup cherry tomatoes, halved
4   oz mozzarella or provolone cheese, cut into 1/2-inch cubes (1 cup)
1   can (2-1/4 oz) sliced ripe olives, drained

1   Empty pasta mix into 3-quart saucepan 2/3 full of boiling water. Gently boil uncovered 12 minutes, stirring occasionally.

2   Drain pasta; rinse with cold water. Shake to drain well.

3   In large bowl, stir together seasoning mix (from salad mix) and dressing. Toss with pasta and remaining ingredients. Stir in croutons and Parmesan topping (from salad mix) just before serving. Serve immediately, or refrigerate until serving.

High Altitude (3500-6500 ft): No change.

Nutritional Info: 1 Serving: Calories 310 (Calories from Fat 140); Total Fat 16g (Saturated Fat 4.5g, Trans Fat 0g); Cholesterol 25mg; Sodium 1190mg; Total Carbohydrate 31g (Dietary Fiber 2g, Sugars 7g); Protein 12g. % Daily Value: Vitamin A 45%; Vitamin C 10%; Calcium 15%; Iron 10%. Exchanges: 1-1/2 Starch, 1/2 Other Carbohydrate, 1 High-Fat Meat, 1 Fat. Carbohydrate Choices: 2.

Betty's Kitchen Tips

Time-Saver: Purchase a bag of ready-to-eat torn romaine lettuce to save time.

Do-Ahead: Make this salad a day ahead, but wait to stir in the lettuce, croutons and Parmesan topping until just before serving.

Variation: Make it your way. Use a package (3.5 oz) of sliced pepperoni instead of the salami; cut the slices in half. Add canned (drained) artichoke hearts, or use other olives from the deli.

mediterranean tuna salad

Prep Time: 15 Minutes
Start to Finish: 15 Minutes
Servings: 5

- 5 large tomatoes
- 2 cans (4.5 oz each) light tuna in olive oil, undrained
- 1 can (15.5 oz) great northern beans, drained, rinsed
- 1/4 cup chopped fresh Italian (flat-leaf) parsley
- 2 tablespoons capers, drained
- 3 tablespoons fresh lemon juice
- 2 teaspoons finely chopped garlic
- 1 teaspoon salt
- 1/4 teaspoon pepper
- 5 sprigs fresh Italian (flat-leaf) parsley, if desired

1 Cut very thin slice from bottom of each tomato so it will stand upright. Cut thin slice from top of each tomato; scoop out tomato flesh, leaving tomato shell. Remove seeds from tomato flesh; chop enough tomato flesh to measure 1 cup.

2 In medium bowl, toss chopped tomato, tuna, beans, chopped parsley, capers, lemon juice, garlic, salt and pepper.

3 Spoon tuna mixture into hollowed-out tomatoes. Garnish with parsley sprigs.

High Altitude (3500-6500 ft): No change.

Nutritional Info: 1 Serving: Calories 310 (Calories from Fat 90); Total Fat 10g (Saturated Fat 1.5g, Trans Fat 0g); Cholesterol 10mg; Sodium 1020mg; Total Carbohydrate 30g (Dietary Fiber 8g, Sugars 5g); Protein 23g. % Daily Value: Vitamin A 35%; Vitamin C 25%; Calcium 10%; Iron 25%. Exchanges: 1/2 Starch, 1 Low-Fat Milk, 2 Vegetable, 2 Lean Meat. Carbohydrate Choices: 2.

EASY QUICK LOW FAT

Betty's Kitchen Tips

How-To: Use a grapefruit spoon to easily hollow out the tomatoes.

Variation: Try using seared fresh tuna steaks in place of the canned tuna.

grilled caesar vegetable salad

Prep Time: 35 Minutes
Start to Finish: 35 Minutes
Servings: 4

1/3	cup Caesar dressing
1/4	cup chopped fresh parsley
4	large fresh portabella mushrooms, cut into fourths
4	medium yellow summer squash, cut into 1/2-inch slices
2	medium bell peppers (any color), cut into 1/2-inch strips
3	tablespoons olive or vegetable oil
1	cup cherry tomatoes, cut into fourths
1/3	cup shredded Parmesan cheese

1 Heat gas or charcoal grill. In small bowl, mix dressing and parsley; set aside. Brush mushrooms, squash and bell peppers with oil. If desired, place mushrooms, squash and bell peppers in grill basket (grill "wok").

2 Place vegetables directly on grill rack (or place grill basket on grill rack) over medium heat. Cover grill; cook 5 to 7 minutes, turning vegetables or shaking basket occasionally, until vegetables are crisp-tender.

3 To serve, arrange mushrooms around edge of serving platter and place remaining grilled vegetables in center; sprinkle with tomatoes. Drizzle dressing over vegetables. Sprinkle with cheese. Serve at room temperature.

High Altitude (3500-6500 ft): No change.

Nutritional Info: 1 Serving: Calories 320 (Calories from Fat 220); Total Fat 25g (Saturated Fat 4.5g, Trans Fat 0g); Cholesterol 10mg; Sodium 350mg; Total Carbohydrate 16g (Dietary Fiber 5g, Sugars 8g); Protein 9g. % Daily Value: Vitamin A 25%; Vitamin C 80%; Calcium 15%; Iron 10%. Exchanges: 3 Vegetable, 5 Fat. Carbohydrate Choices: 1.

Betty's Kitchen Tip

• To reduce the fat in this recipe, use fat-free Caesar dressing and spray the vegetables with cooking spray instead of brushing with olive oil.

mango-pecan salad

Prep Time: 20 Minutes
Start to Finish: 20 Minutes
Servings: 4

QUICK

- 1/4 cup chopped pecans
- 5 cups torn mixed salad greens
- 1 medium mango, seed removed, peeled and cut up (3/4 to 1 cup)
- 1/4 cup sliced green onions (about 4 medium)
- 1/4 cup balsamic vinaigrette or other oil-and-vinegar dressing
- 2 slices bacon, cooked, crumbled

1 Heat oven to 350°F. In shallow pan, spread pecans. Toast in oven 5 to 8 minutes, stirring occasionally, until light brown; cool.

2 In large serving bowl, toss salad greens, mango, green onions and vinaigrette. Top with bacon and pecans. Serve immediately.

High Altitude (3500-6500 ft): No change.

Nutritional Info: 1 Serving: Calories 180 (Calories from Fat 120); Total Fat 14g (Saturated Fat 2g, Trans Fat 0g); Cholesterol 0mg; Sodium 220mg; Total Carbohydrate 11g (Dietary Fiber 3g, Sugars 7g); Protein 3g. % Daily Value: Vitamin A 80%; Vitamin C 20%; Calcium 4%; Iron 6%. Exchanges: 1/2 Other Carbohydrate, 1/2 Vegetable, 1/2 High-Fat Meat, 1 Fat. Carbohydrate Choices: 1.

Betty's Kitchen Tips

Variation: No mango? Other fruits, such as raspberries, grapes or nectarines, will work well, too.

Substitution: Instead of toasting pecans, substitute candied pecans found in the snack section of the grocery store.

ratatouille tabbouleh salad

Prep Time: 20 Minutes
Start to Finish: 1 Hour
Servings: 4 (1 cup each)

LOW FAT

1 cup uncooked quick-cooking bulgur	1 cup finely sliced yellow summer squash
1-1/2 teaspoons salt	1 cup finely chopped red onion
2 cups boiling water	1 cup halved grape tomatoes
1 tablespoon olive or vegetable oil	1/2 cup chopped fresh Italian (flat-leaf) parsley
1 cup finely sliced zucchini	3 tablespoons balsamic vinegar

1 In medium bowl, place bulgur and 1/2 teaspoon of the salt. Pour boiling water over bulgur; let stand 1 hour. Drain any remaining liquid from bulgur.

2 Meanwhile, in 10-inch nonstick skillet, heat oil over medium-high heat. Add zucchini, yellow squash, onion, tomatoes and 1/2 teaspoon salt; cook about 6 minutes, stirring frequently, until vegetables are tender.

3 In large bowl, toss vegetable mixture, bulgur, parsley, vinegar and remaining 1/2 teaspoon salt.

High Altitude (3500-6500 ft): No change.

Nutritional Info: 1 Serving: Calories 200 (Calories from Fat 35); Total Fat 4g (Saturated Fat 0.5g, Trans Fat 0g); Cholesterol 0mg; Sodium 910mg; Total Carbohydrate 34g (Dietary Fiber 8g, Sugars 5g); Protein 5g. % Daily Value: Vitamin A 20%; Vitamin C 20%; Calcium 4%; Iron 10%. Exchanges: 1 Starch, 3 Vegetable, 1 Fat. Carbohydrate Choices: 2.

Betty's Kitchen Tips

Variation: Try using chopped fresh mint leaves instead of the parsley.

Substitution: You can use 1 cup chopped regular tomatoes instead of grape tomatoes, if you have them on hand.

CAKES&CHEESECAKES

p. 204

200

190

187

caramel-bottom cake

Prep Time: 20 Minutes
Start to Finish: 2 Hours 5 Minutes
Servings: 15

- 1 box Betty Crocker® SuperMoist® yellow cake mix
- 1/4 cup Gold Medal® all-purpose flour
- 1 cup water
- 1/3 cup vegetable oil
- 3 eggs

- 1 bag (8 oz) milk chocolate-coated toffee bits
- 1 can (13.4 oz) dulce de leche (caramelized sweetened condensed milk)

Sweetened whipped cream, if desired
Caramel topping, if desired

1 Heat oven to 350°F (or 325°F for dark or nonstick pan). Spray bottom and sides of 13x9-inch pan with baking spray with flour.

2 In large bowl, beat cake mix, flour, water, oil and eggs with electric mixer on low speed 30 seconds. Beat on medium speed 2 minutes, scraping bowl occasionally. Stir in 1/2 cup of the toffee bits. Pour into pan.

3 Reserve 1/2 cup dulce de leche. Spoon remaining dulce de leche by teaspoonfuls onto batter.

4 Bake 30 to 40 minutes or until toothpick inserted in center comes out clean. Cool 5 minutes. Drop reserved dulce de leche by spoonfuls over top of cake and spread evenly. Sprinkle with remaining toffee bits. Cool about 1 hour before serving. Top each serving with whipped cream and caramel topping.

High Altitude (3500-6500 ft): Increase flour to 1/3 cup.

Nutritional Info: 1 Serving: Calories 370 (Calories from Fat 130); Total Fat 14g (Saturated Fat 6g, Trans Fat 1g); Cholesterol 55mg; Sodium 310mg; Total Carbohydrate 54g (Dietary Fiber 0g, Sugars 39g); Protein 5g. % Daily Value: Vitamin A 4%; Vitamin C 0%; Calcium 10%; Iron 6%. Exchanges: 1/2 Starch, 3 Other Carbohydrate, 1/2 Medium-Fat Meat, 2-1/2 Fat. Carbohydrate Choices: 3-1/2.

Betty's Kitchen Tips

Substitution: You can substitute crushed chocolate-covered English toffee candy bars for the toffee bits.

Purchasing: Dulce de leche, a caramelized condensed milk, can be found near the sweetened condensed milk in the grocery store.

chocolate chip snack cake

Prep Time: 20 Minutes
Start to Finish: 1 Hour 55 Minutes
Servings: 9

1-3/4	cups Betty Crocker® SuperMoist® yellow cake mix (from 18.25-oz box)
1/2	cup sour cream
1/4	cup water
3	tablespoons butter or margarine, melted
1	egg
1-1/4	cups miniature semisweet chocolate chips
1/2	teaspoon vegetable oil

1 Heat oven to 350°F (or 325°F for dark or nonstick pan). Spray bottom and sides of 9- or 8-inch square pan with baking spray with flour.

2 In large bowl, beat cake mix, sour cream, water, butter and egg with electric mixer on low speed 30 seconds. Beat on medium speed 2 minutes, scraping bowl occasionally. Stir in 1/2 cup of the chocolate chips. Spread in pan.

3 Bake 25 to 35 minutes or until toothpick inserted in center comes out clean. Cool completely, about 1 hour.

4 In small microwavable bowl, microwave 1/2 cup of the chocolate chips and the oil uncovered on High 45 seconds, stirring every 15 seconds, until melted. Place in small resealable food-storage plastic bag; cut off tiny corner of bag. Drizzle over top of cake. Sprinkle with remaining 1/4 cup chocolate chips.

High Altitude (3500-6500 ft): Decrease sour cream to 1/3 cup. Bake 30 to 40 minutes.

Nutritional Info: 1 Serving: Calories 290 (Calories from Fat 140); Total Fat 16g (Saturated Fat 9g, Trans Fat 1g); Cholesterol 40mg; Sodium 190mg; Total Carbohydrate 34g (Dietary Fiber 1g, Sugars 23g); Protein 3g. % Daily Value: Vitamin A 4%; Vitamin C 0%; Calcium 6%; Iron 6%. Exchanges: 1 Starch, 1 Other Carbohydrate, 3 Fat. Carbohydrate Choices: 2.

Betty's Kitchen Tips

Did You Know? A stiff batter prevents the chocolate chips from sinking to the bottom of the pan.

Success Hint: Use the other half of the cake mix to make Raspberry Crumb Cake on p. 204.

Special Touch: The sour cream in this cake lends both a nice sharp bite and a moist crumb.

fruit-topped almond cake

Prep Time: 15 Minutes
Start to Finish: 1 Hour 50 Minutes
Servings: 8

EASY

Cake

1-3/4	cups Betty Crocker® SuperMoist® yellow cake mix (from 18.25-oz box)
1/2	cup water
1/2	cup slivered almonds, finely ground
3	tablespoons vegetable oil
1/2	teaspoon almond extract
2	eggs

Topping

3	cups assorted fresh berries (such as raspberries, strawberries, blueberries and blackberries)
3/4	cup apricot preserves
3	tablespoons apple juice
3	tablespoons sliced almonds, toasted, if desired

1 Heat oven to 350°F (or 325°F for dark or nonstick pan). Generously spray bottom and side of 8- or 9-inch round cake pan with baking spray with flour.

2 In large bowl, beat cake mix, water, ground almonds, oil, almond extract and eggs with electric mixer on low speed until moistened. Beat on medium speed 2 minutes, scraping bowl occasionally. Pour into pan.

3 Bake as directed on box for 8- or 9-inch rounds. Cool in pan 10 minutes. Remove from pan to cooling rack. Cool completely, about 1 hour.

4 Place berries in medium bowl. In 1-quart saucepan, heat preserves and apple juice to boiling, stirring frequently. Pour over berries; toss berries until coated with preserves mixture. Let stand 5 minutes.

5 Gently cut off any dome from top of cake, using serrated knife, to make top level. On serving plate, place cake, sliced side down. Arrange berries on cake; drizzle with syrup remaining in bowl. Sprinkle with sliced almonds if desired. Store leftover cake covered in refrigerator.

High Altitude (3500-6500 ft): No change.

Nutritional Info: 1 Serving: Calories 320 (Calories from Fat 100); Total Fat 12g (Saturated Fat 2g, Trans Fat 0.5g); Cholesterol 55mg; Sodium 200mg; Total Carbohydrate 49g (Dietary Fiber 4g, Sugars 29g); Protein 4g. % Daily Value: Vitamin A 0%; Vitamin C 10%; Calcium 8%; Iron 8%. Exchanges: 1 Fruit, 2 Other Carbohydrate, 1/2 Medium-Fat Meat, 2 Fat. Carbohydrate Choices: 3.

fudge ice cream dessert

Prep Time: 15 Minutes
Start to Finish: 6 Hours 25 Minutes
Servings: 15

EASY

1	box Betty Crocker® SuperMoist® chocolate fudge cake mix
1/3	cup butter or margarine, melted
3	eggs
1	can or jar (16 oz) hot fudge topping, heated
2	cups chopped creme-filled chocolate sandwich cookies (20 cookies)
1/2	gallon vanilla ice cream, slightly softened

1 Heat oven to 350°F. Line bottom and sides of 13x9-inch pan with foil, leaving foil overhanging at 2 opposite sides of pan. Spray bottom only of foil-lined pan with baking spray with flour.

2 In large bowl, mix cake mix, butter and eggs with spoon until blended (batter will be very thick). Spread or pat in pan with greased fingers.

3 Bake 17 to 19 minutes or until surface appears dry and is no longer shiny. Cool completely in pan, about 1 hour.

4 Spread warm fudge topping over cake. Sprinkle with 1 cup of the chopped cookies. Freeze about 30 minutes or until firm.

5 Spread ice cream over cookies. Cover; freeze at least 4 hours or overnight until firm. Sprinkle with remaining 1 cup chopped cookies.

6 Before serving, let dessert stand 15 to 20 minutes. For easier cutting, remove from pan using foil to lift. Store dessert covered in freezer.

High Altitude (3500-6500 ft): Stir 1 tablespoon Gold Medal all-purpose flour into dry cake mix.

Nutritional Info: 1 Serving: Calories 460 (Calories from Fat 170); Total Fat 19g (Saturated Fat 10g, Trans Fat 1.5g); Cholesterol 85mg; Sodium 500mg; Total Carbohydrate 66g (Dietary Fiber 2g, Sugars 43g); Protein 7g. % Daily Value: Vitamin A 10%; Vitamin C 0%; Calcium 15%; Iron 10%. Exchanges: 2-1/2 Starch, 2 Other Carbohydrate, 3-1/2 Fat. Carbohydrate Choices: 4-1/2.

Betty's Kitchen Tips

Success Hint: If you let the ice cream stand at room temperature for 15 to 20 minutes, it will soften slightly so you can spread it easily. To make ice cream even smoother for spreading, place it in a large bowl and stir with a sturdy wooden spoon. Just make sure you don't let the ice cream get overly soft or melt.

Variation: Have a favorite flavor of ice cream? Go ahead and use it instead of the vanilla. Chocolate chip, cookies and cream or cherry are all scrumptious choices.

strawberry and white chocolate buttercream cake

Prep Time: 25 Minutes
Start to Finish: 2 Hours 5 Minutes
Servings: 8

Cake

1-3/4	cups Betty Crocker® SuperMoist® butter recipe yellow cake mix (from 18.25-oz box)
1/2	cup water
1/4	cup butter or margarine, softened
1/2	teaspoon almond extract
1	egg

Filling and Topping

4	oz white chocolate baking bars or squares, chopped
2	tablespoons butter or margarine, cut into pieces, softened
1	cup whipping cream
1	tablespoon berry-flavored liqueur, if desired
2	cups fresh whole strawberries, thinly sliced

1 Heat oven to 350°F (or 325°F for dark or nonstick pan). Generously spray bottom and side of 8- or 9-inch round cake pan with baking spray with flour.

2 In large bowl, beat cake mix, water, 1/4 cup butter, the almond extract and egg with electric mixer on low speed until moistened. Beat on medium speed 2 minutes, scraping bowl occasionally. Pour into pan.

3 Bake as directed on box for 8- or 9-inch rounds. Cool in pan 10 minutes. Remove from pan to cooling rack. Cool completely, about 1 hour.

4 Meanwhile, place white chocolate and 2 tablespoons butter in small metal bowl. In 2-quart saucepan, heat 1/2 cup of the whipping cream just to boiling. Pour hot cream over white chocolate and butter; let stand until mixture is melted and smooth when stirred. Refrigerate chocolate mixture 1 hour, stirring occasionally, until cold.

5 In large bowl, beat remaining 1/2 cup whipping cream, the cold chocolate mixture and liqueur on high speed until stiff peaks form. Refrigerate until ready to use.

6 Cut cake horizontally in half, using long, sharp knife. On serving plate, place 1 layer, cut side up. Spread with 1/2 of the filling; top with 1/2 of the strawberries. Add remaining cake layer, cut side down. Spread remaining filling over top of cake; top with remaining strawberries. Store covered in refrigerator.

High Altitude (3500-6500 ft): No change.

Nutritional Info: 1 Serving: Calories 430 (Calories from Fat 290); Total Fat 32g (Saturated Fat 19g, Trans Fat 1g); Cholesterol 100mg; Sodium 270mg; Total Carbohydrate 29g (Dietary Fiber 3g, Sugars 14g); Protein 4g. % Daily Value: Vitamin A 15%; Vitamin C 20%; Calcium 8%; Iron 15%. Exchanges: 1 Starch, 1/2 Fruit, 1/2 Other Carbohydrate, 6-1/2 Fat. Carbohydrate Choices: 2.

morning glory carrot cake

Prep Time: 30 Minutes
Start to Finish: 3 Hours 10 Minutes
Servings: 15

Cake

- 1 box Betty Crocker® SuperMoist® yellow cake mix
- 1/3 cup Gold Medal® whole wheat flour
- 1 cup water
- 1/3 cup canola oil
- 1 teaspoon ground cinnamon
- 1/4 teaspoon ground nutmeg
- 4 eggs
- 2-1/2 cups finely shredded carrots (about 5 medium)
- 1/3 cup raisins
- 1/3 cup chopped walnuts

Frosting

- 3 cups powdered sugar
- 1 package (8 oz) cream cheese, softened
- 2 tablespoons butter or margarine, softened
- 1 teaspoon vanilla
- 3/4 cup flaked coconut, toasted*

1 Heat oven to 350°F (or 325°F for dark or nonstick pan). Spray bottom and sides of 13x9-inch pan with baking spray with flour.

2 In large bowl, beat cake mix, flour, water, oil, cinnamon, nutmeg and eggs with electric mixer on low speed 30 seconds. Beat on medium speed 2 minutes, scraping bowl occasionally. Stir in carrots, raisins and walnuts. Pour into pan.

3 Bake 30 to 40 minutes or until toothpick inserted in center comes out clean. Cool completely, about 2 hours.

4 In large bowl, beat powdered sugar, cream cheese, butter and vanilla on low speed until blended. Beat on medium speed until smooth and creamy. Spread frosting over cake. Sprinkle with coconut.

*Note: To toast coconut, spread it in an ungreased shallow pan and bake at 350°F for 5 to 7 minutes, stirring occasionally, until golden brown.

High Altitude (3500-6500 ft): Increase whole wheat flour to 1/2 cup. Bake 35 to 45 minutes.

Nutritional Info: 1 Serving: Calories 430 (Calories from Fat 170); Total Fat 19g (Saturated Fat 7g, Trans Fat 1g); Cholesterol 75mg; Sodium 320mg; Total Carbohydrate 60g (Dietary Fiber 1g, Sugars 42g); Protein 5g. % Daily Value: Vitamin A 70%; Vitamin C 0%; Calcium 8%; Iron 8%. Exchanges: 1-1/2 Starch, 2-1/2 Other Carbohydrate, 3-1/2 Fat. Carbohydrate Choices: 4.

Betty's Kitchen Tips

Variation: Not a fan of raisins? Omit them and increase the chopped walnuts to 2/3 cup.

Time-Saver: Instead of making your own frosting, use 1 container of Betty Crocker® Rich & Creamy cream cheese frosting.

warm caramel apple cake

Prep Time: 30 Minutes
Start to Finish: 1 Hour 25 Minutes
Servings: 15

Cake
1/2	cup butter or margarine
1/4	cup whipping cream
1	cup packed brown sugar
1/2	cup chopped pecans
2	large cooking apples, peeled, cored and thinly sliced (2-1/3 cups)
1	box (1 lb 2.25 oz) Betty Crocker® SuperMoist® yellow cake mix
1-1/4	cups water
1/3	cup vegetable oil
3	eggs
1/4	teaspoon apple pie spice

Topping
2/3	cup Betty Crocker® Whipped fluffy white frosting (from 12-oz container)
1/2	cup frozen (thawed) whipped topping

Caramel topping, if desired

1 Heat oven to 350°F. In heavy 1-quart saucepan, cook butter, whipping cream and brown sugar over low heat, stirring occasionally, just until butter is melted. Pour into 13x9-inch pan. Sprinkle with pecans; top with apples.

2 In large bowl, beat cake mix, water, oil, eggs and apple pie spice with electric mixer on low speed until moistened. Beat on medium speed 2 minutes. Carefully spoon batter over apple mixture.

3 Bake 40 to 45 minutes or until toothpick inserted near center comes out clean. Cool in pan 10 minutes. Loosen sides of cake from pan. Place heatproof serving platter upside down on pan; carefully turn platter and pan over. Let pan remain over cake 1 minute so caramel can drizzle over cake. Remove pan.

4 In small bowl, mix frosting and whipped topping. Serve warm cake topped with frosting mixture and drizzled with caramel topping, if desired.

High Altitude (3500-6500 ft): No change.

Nutritional Info: 1 Serving: Calories 400 (Calories from Fat 180); Total Fat 21g (Saturated Fat 8g, Trans Fat 1.5g); Cholesterol 65mg; Sodium 290mg; Total Carbohydrate 50g (Dietary Fiber 0g, Sugars 36g); Protein 3g. % Daily Value: Vitamin A 6%; Vitamin C 0%; Calcium 8%; Iron 6%. Exchanges: 1 Starch, 2-1/2 Other Carbohydrate, 4 Fat. Carbohydrate Choices: 3.

Betty's Kitchen Tip

• You can use cinnamon for the apple pie spice for a slightly different flavor.

lemon cream rolled cake

Prep Time: 20 Minutes
Start to Finish: 2 Hours 30 Minutes
Servings: 12

Cake

3	eggs
1-3/4	cups Betty Crocker® SuperMoist® yellow cake mix (from 18.25-oz box)
1/4	cup water
2	tablespoons lemon juice
2	tablespoons vegetable oil

2	tablespoons powdered sugar

Filling

1	cup whipping cream
2	tablespoons powdered sugar
4	teaspoons grated lemon peel

Garnish

1	tablespoon powdered sugar

1 Heat oven to 375°F (or 350°F for dark or nonstick pan). Line bottom only of 15x10x1-inch pan with foil or waxed paper; spray foil and sides of pan with baking spray with flour.

2 In large bowl, beat eggs with electric mixer on high speed about 5 minutes or until thick and lemon colored. Add cake mix, water, lemon juice and oil. Beat on low speed 30 seconds, then on medium speed 1 minute, scraping bowl occasionally. Pour into pan; spread batter evenly.

3 Bake 11 to 14 minutes or until cake springs back when lightly touched in center. If necessary, run knife around edge of pan to loosen cake. Turn cake upside down onto clean kitchen towel sprinkled with 2 tablespoons powdered sugar; carefully remove foil. While hot, carefully roll up cake and towel from narrow end. Cool completely, seam side down, on cooling rack, about 1 hour.

4 In chilled large glass or metal bowl, beat 1 cup whipping cream and 2 tablespoons powdered sugar on medium speed until foamy, then on high speed until stiff peaks form. Fold in lemon peel.

5 Unroll cake carefully and remove towel. Spread filling evenly over cake; roll up cake. On serving platter, arrange cake, seam side down; cover loosely and refrigerate at least 1 hour. Before serving, sprinkle with 1 tablespoon powdered sugar. Store covered in refrigerator.

High Altitude (3500-6500 ft): No change.

Nutritional Info: 1 Serving: Calories 190 (Calories from Fat 110); Total Fat 12g (Saturated Fat 6g, Trans Fat 0.5g); Cholesterol 80mg; Sodium 135mg; Total Carbohydrate 18g (Dietary Fiber 0g, Sugars 11g); Protein 2g. % Daily Value: Vitamin A 8%; Vitamin C 0%; Calcium 4%; Iron 2%. Exchanges: 1/2 Starch, 1/2 Other Carbohydrate, 2-1/2 Fat. Carbohydrate Choices: 1.

Betty's Kitchen Tip

• Make sure you spread the cake batter evenly in the pan before baking. The cake sets quickly, and you want the resulting cake roll to be even.

country apple streusel cake

Prep Time: 35 Minutes
Start to Finish: 1 Hour 35 Minutes
Servings: 15

Streusel Topping

3/4	cup Gold Medal® whole wheat flour
1/2	cup packed brown sugar
1/2	teaspoon ground cinnamon
1/2	cup cold butter or margarine

Cake

1-1/2	cups Gold Medal® whole wheat flour
1-1/2	cups Gold Medal® all-purpose flour
1-1/2	cups granulated sugar
3	teaspoons baking powder
1	teaspoon salt
1-1/4	cups milk
3/4	cup butter or margarine, softened
1-1/2	teaspoons vanilla
3	eggs
4	cups very thinly sliced peeled apples

1 Heat oven to 350°F. Spray 13x9-inch pan with cooking spray. In small bowl, mix topping ingredients with pastry blender or fork until crumbly; set aside.

2 In large bowl, beat all cake ingredients except apples with electric mixer on medium speed 3 minutes, scraping bowl frequently. Spread batter in pan. Arrange apple slices evenly over batter. Sprinkle evenly with topping.

3 Bake 55 to 60 minutes or until toothpick inserted in center comes out clean. Serve warm with ice cream or whipped cream.

High Altitude (3500-6500 ft): No change.

Nutritional Info: 1 Serving: Calories 400 (Calories from Fat 160); Total Fat 17g (Saturated Fat 10g, Trans Fat 0.5g); Cholesterol 85mg; Sodium 390mg; Total Carbohydrate 55g (Dietary Fiber 3g, Sugars 31g); Protein 6g. % Daily Value: Vitamin A 10%; Vitamin C 0%; Calcium 10%; Iron 8%. Exchanges: 2 Starch, 1-1/2 Other Carbohydrate, 3 Fat. Carbohydrate Choices: 3-1/2.

Betty's Kitchen Tip

• Braeburn and Granny Smith apples are ideal apples for this recipe.

layered pumpkin cheesecake

Prep Time: 40 Minutes
Start to Finish: 10 Hours 35 Minutes
Servings: 16

Crust

 2   cups gingersnap cookie crumbs
1/4   cup butter or margarine, melted

Cheesecake

 4   packages (8 oz each) cream cheese, softened

1-1/2   cups sugar
 4   eggs
 1   cup canned pumpkin (not pumpkin pie mix)
1-1/2   teaspoons ground ginger
 1   teaspoon ground cinnamon
1/4   teaspoon ground nutmeg

1 Heat oven to 300°F. Grease or spray 9-inch springform pan. Wrap outside of pan in heavy-duty foil. In bowl, mix crust ingredients. Press in bottom and 1 inch up side of pan. Bake 8 to 10 minutes or until set. Cool 5 minutes.

2 In large bowl, beat cream cheese with electric mixer on medium speed just until smooth and creamy; do not overbeat. On low speed, gradually beat in sugar. Beat in eggs, one at a time, just until blended. Spoon 3 cups of the mixture into pan; spread evenly. Add pumpkin, ginger, cinnamon and nutmeg to remaining cream cheese mixture; mix with wire whisk until smooth. Spoon over mixture in pan.

3 Bake 1 hour 25 minutes to 1 hour 30 minutes or until edges are set but center

of cheesecake still jiggles slightly when moved. Turn oven off; open oven door at least 4 inches. Leave cheesecake in oven 30 minutes. Remove from oven to cooling rack. Without releasing side of pan, run knife around edge of pan to loosen cheesecake. Cool in pan on cooling rack 30 minutes. Cover loosely; refrigerate at least 6 hours but no longer than 24 hours.

4 Run knife around edge of pan to loosen cheesecake again; carefully remove side of pan. Place cheesecake on serving plate. Cover and refrigerate any remaining cheesecake.

High Altitude (3500-6500 ft): No change.

Nutritional Info: 1 Serving: Calories 400 (Calories from Fat 230); Total Fat 26g (Saturated Fat 15g, Trans Fat 1g); Cholesterol 125mg; Sodium 300mg; Total Carbohydrate 34g (Dietary Fiber 1g, Sugars 25g); Protein 7g. % Daily Value: Vitamin A 70%; Vitamin C 0%; Calcium 8%; Iron 8%. Exchanges: 1 Starch, 1-1/2 Other Carbohydrate, 1/2 High-Fat Meat, 4 Fat. Carbohydrate Choices: 2.

Betty's Kitchen Tips

Success Hint: The key to a smooth top on a cheesecake is using the correct oven temperature and bake time plus beating the cream cheese mixture just until smooth.

Special Touch: Garnish this luscious dessert with whipping cream.

ginger carrot cake

Prep Time: 25 Minutes
Start to Finish: 2 Hours
Servings: 9

Cake

1	tablespoon Gold Medal® all-purpose flour
1/4	cup finely chopped crystallized ginger
1-1/4	cups Gold Medal® all-purpose flour
3/4	cup granulated sugar
3/4	cup vegetable oil
2	teaspoons ground cinnamon
1	teaspoon baking soda
2	teaspoons vanilla
1/2	teaspoon salt
1/4	teaspoon ground nutmeg
2	eggs
1-1/2	cups finely shredded carrots

Cream Cheese Frosting

1	package (3 oz) cream cheese, softened
1/4	cup butter or margarine, softened
2	cups powdered sugar
1	teaspoon vanilla

1 Heat oven to 350°F. Grease 8- or 9-inch square pan. Mix 1 tablespoon flour and ginger; set aside. In large bowl, beat remaining cake ingredients except carrots with electric mixer on low speed 30 seconds. Beat on medium speed 3 minutes. Stir in carrots and ginger-flour mixture. Pour into pan.

2 Bake 30 to 35 minutes or until toothpick inserted in center comes out clean. Cool completely on cooling rack, about 1 hour.

3 Beat cream cheese and butter on medium speed until smooth. Gradually stir in powdered sugar and vanilla until spreadable. Spread on cake. Store covered in refrigerator.

High Altitude (3500-6500 ft): No change.

Nutritional Info: 1 Serving: Calories 530 (Calories from Fat 250); Total Fat 28g (Saturated Fat 9g, Trans Fat 0g); Cholesterol 70mg; Sodium 360mg; Total Carbohydrate 64g (Dietary Fiber 1g, Sugars 44g); Protein 4g. % Daily Value: Vitamin A 70%; Vitamin C 0%; Calcium 2%; Iron 6%. Exchanges: 1 Starch, 3-1/2 Other Carbohydrate, 5-1/2 Fat. Carbohydrate Choices: 4.

Betty's Kitchen Tip

• Crystallized ginger gives the unique flavor to this traditional carrot cake recipe. Try it sprinkled on top.

tropical cheesecake

Prep Time: 25 Minutes
Start to Finish: 8 Hours 10 Minutes
Servings: 16

Crust

1	box Betty Crocker® SuperMoist® yellow cake mix
1/2	cup butter or margarine, softened
2	teaspoons grated lime peel

Filling

1/4	cup reserved cake mix
3	packages (8 oz each) cream cheese, softened
3/4	cup sugar

1/2	cup canned cream of coconut (not coconut milk)
1/2	teaspoon rum extract, if desired
3	eggs

Topping

1	large mango, seed removed, peeled and chopped (about 1-1/2 cups)
3	kiwifruit, peeled, chopped (about 1-1/2 cups)
1/4	cup shredded coconut, toasted*

1 Heat oven to 325°F. Spray bottom and side of 9-inch springform pan with baking spray with flour. Wrap foil around outside of pan to catch drips. Reserve 1/4 cup of the cake mix. In large bowl, beat remaining cake mix, the butter and lime peel with electric mixer on low speed until crumbly. Press in bottom and 2 inches up side of pan.

2 In same large bowl, beat reserved 1/4 cup cake mix, cream cheese, sugar, cream of coconut and rum extract on medium speed until smooth and creamy. Beat in eggs, one at a time, until mixed. Pour into crust.

3 Bake 1 hour to 1 hour 15 minutes or until cheesecake is set at least 2 inches from edge of pan but center of cheesecake still jiggles slightly when moved. Turn oven off; remove cheesecake from oven and run metal spatula around edge to loosen. Return cheesecake to oven; open oven door at least 4 inches. Leave cheesecake in oven 30 minutes (top may crack as it cools).

4 Remove cheesecake from oven; place on cooling rack. Without releasing side of pan, run metal spatula around edge of pan again to loosen cheesecake. Cool in pan on cooling rack 2 hours. Refrigerate 4 hours or overnight.

5 To serve, run metal spatula around edge of pan again and remove side of pan. Arrange mango and kiwifruit on top of cheesecake. Sprinkle with coconut. Store covered in refrigerator.

*Note: To toast coconut, spread it in an ungreased shallow pan and bake at 350°F for 5 to 7 minutes, stirring occasionally, until golden brown.

High Altitude (3500-6500 ft): Before heating oven, place small baking pan filled with 1 to 2 cups of water on oven rack below center rack to help prevent cheesecake from cracking.

Nutritional Info: 1 Serving: Calories 440 (Calories from Fat 240); Total Fat 27g (Saturated Fat 17g, Trans Fat 1.5g); Cholesterol 100mg; Sodium 390mg; Total Carbohydrate 42g (Dietary Fiber 1g, Sugars 28g); Protein 6g. % Daily Value: Vitamin A 20%; Vitamin C 15%; Calcium 10%; Iron 8%. Exchanges: 3 Other Carbohydrate, 1 Medium-Fat Meat, 4 Fat. Carbohydrate Choices: 3.

Betty's Kitchen Tip

• Leaving the baked cheesecake in the turned-off oven for 30 minutes allows the center to continue cooking and finish setting while the cake gradually begins to cool down.

chunky apple cake

Prep Time: 25 Minutes
Start to Finish: 3 Hours
Servings: 16

Cake

1	cup butter, softened
2	cups granulated sugar
3	eggs
1/2	teaspoon vanilla
2-1/2	cups Gold Medal® all-purpose flour
2	teaspoons baking soda
1/2	teaspoon salt

2	teaspoons ground cinnamon
3	cups coarsely chopped peeled baking apples
1	cup chopped walnuts

Frosting

1/2	cup butter (do not use margarine)
3-1/4	cups powdered sugar
1	teaspoon vanilla
1	to 3 tablespoons milk

1. Heat oven to 350°F. Spray 12-cup fluted tube cake pan with baking spray with flour.

2. In large bowl, beat 1 cup butter and the granulated sugar with electric mixer on medium speed until light and fluffy. Beat in eggs, one at a time. Stir in 1/2 teaspoon vanilla, the flour, baking soda, salt and cinnamon. Stir in apples and walnuts. Spoon into pan.

3. Bake 50 to 65 minutes or until toothpick inserted in center of cake comes out clean. Cool 10 minutes. Remove from pan to cooling rack. Cool completely, about 1 hour 30 minutes.

4. In 2-quart saucepan, heat 1/2 cup butter over medium heat, stirring constantly, until golden brown. Gradually beat in powdered sugar with spoon. Stir in 1 teaspoon vanilla and milk until desired spreading consistency. Generously spread frosting over top and partially down side of cake. Cut cake with serrated knife.

High Altitude (3500-6500 ft): No change.

Nutritional Info: 1 Serving: Calories 500 (Calories from Fat 210); Total Fat 23g (Saturated Fat 12g, Trans Fat 0.5g); Cholesterol 85mg; Sodium 370mg; Total Carbohydrate 69g (Dietary Fiber 1g, Sugars 51g); Protein 4g. % Daily Value: Vitamin A 10%; Vitamin C 0%; Calcium 2%; Iron 8%. Exchanges: 1 Starch, 3-1/2 Other Carbohydrate, 4-1/2 Fat. Carbohydrate Choices: 4-1/2.

Betty's Kitchen Tip

• Browned butter frosting has a sweet, nutty flavor that pairs well with this cake.

texas sheet cake

Prep Time: 10 Minutes
Start to Finish: 1 Hour 15 Minutes
Servings: 24

EASY

- 1 box Betty Crocker® SuperMoist® devil's food cake mix
- 1/4 cup sour cream
- 1-1/4 cups water
- 2 tablespoons unsweetened baking cocoa
- 2 tablespoons vegetable oil
- 3 eggs
- 1 container (1 lb) Betty Crocker® Rich & Creamy chocolate frosting
- 3/4 cup chopped pecans

1 Heat oven to 350°F (or 325°F for dark or nonstick pan). Spray bottom and sides of 15x10x1-inch pan with baking spray with flour.

2 In large bowl, beat cake mix, sour cream, water, cocoa, oil and eggs with electric mixer on low speed 30 seconds. Beat on medium speed 2 minutes, scraping bowl occasionally. Pour into pan.

3 Bake 15 to 20 minutes or until toothpick inserted in center comes out clean. Cool about 45 minutes.

4 Remove lid and foil cover from frosting. Microwave frosting in container on High 20 to 30 seconds, stirring once, until pourable. Spread frosting over cake; sprinkle with pecans.

High Altitude (3500-6500 ft): No change.

Nutritional Info: 1 Serving: Calories 210 (Calories from Fat 80); Total Fat 9g (Saturated Fat 2.5g, Trans Fat 1.5g); Cholesterol 30mg; Sodium 250mg; Total Carbohydrate 29g (Dietary Fiber 1g, Sugars 19g); Protein 2g. % Daily Value: Vitamin A 0%; Vitamin C 0%; Calcium 2%; Iron 8%. Exchanges: 1/2 Starch, 1-1/2 Other Carbohydrate, 1-1/2 Fat. Carbohydrate Choices: 2.

Betty's Kitchen Tips

Success Hint: To get the most flavor from the pecans, toast them before sprinkling on top of the cake.

Did You Know? Adding cocoa is a great way to give extra chocolate punch to a devil's food cake mix.

Do-Ahead: This is a great recipe for serving a crowd. Keep the ingredients on hand for last-minute occasions.

caramel-apple butter cheesecake

Prep Time: 40 Minutes
Start to Finish: 8 Hours 25 Minutes
Servings: 16

1-1/2	cups gingersnap cookie crumbs	1/4	cup sugar
1/4	cup butter or margarine, melted	2	tablespoons Gold Medal® all-purpose flour
20	caramels, unwrapped	3	eggs
3/4	cup apple butter		**Caramel Sauce**
3	packages (8 oz each) cream cheese, softened	30	caramels, unwrapped
		1/2	cup half-and-half

1 Heat oven to 300°F. Wrap outside of 9- or 10-inch springform pan in heavy-duty foil. In small bowl, mix cookie crumbs and butter. Press in bottom and 1/2 inch up sides of ungreased pan.

2 In medium microwavable bowl, microwave 20 caramels and 1/2 cup of the apple butter uncovered on High 2-1/2 to 3 minutes, stirring every 30 seconds, until melted. Stir in remaining 1/4 cup apple butter; set aside to cool.

3 In large bowl, beat cream cheese, sugar and flour with electric mixer on medium speed about 1 minute or until smooth and creamy. On low speed, beat in eggs, 1 at a time. Reserve 1/2 cup batter. Fold caramel mixture into remaining batter without mixing it in completely, leaving a few streaks. Pour over crust. Drop spoonfuls of reserved batter over the top. Cut through batter several times with knife for marbled design.

4 Bake 1 hour 15 minutes to 1 hour 25 minutes or until center looks almost set when pan is jiggled. Without releasing side of pan, run metal spatula carefully around cheesecake to loosen. Turn oven off; open oven door at least 4 inches. Leave cheesecake in oven 30 minutes, then remove from oven; cool completely at room temperature, about 2 hours. Cover and refrigerate at least 4 hours or overnight. Run metal spatula around cheesecake to loosen again. Remove side of pan; leave cheesecake on bottom of pan to serve.

5 In 1-quart saucepan, heat 30 caramels and the half-and-half over low heat, stirring frequently, until caramels are completely melted. Serve warm or cool over slices of cheesecake.

High Altitude (3500-6500 ft): No change.

Nutritional Info: 1 Serving: Calories 430 (Calories from Fat 210); Total Fat 24g (Saturated Fat 13g, Trans Fat 0.5g); Cholesterol 100mg; Sodium 320mg; Total Carbohydrate 47g (Dietary Fiber 1g, Sugars 29g); Protein 7g. % Daily Value: Vitamin A 15%; Vitamin C 0%; Calcium 10%; Iron 6%. Exchanges: 1 Starch, 2 Other Carbohydrate, 1/2 High-Fat Meat, 4 Fat. Carbohydrate Choices: 3.

chocolate chai latte cake

Prep Time: 15 Minutes
Start to Finish: 1 Hour 55 Minutes
Servings: 15

EASY

Cake

1	box Betty Crocker® SuperMoist® devil's food cake mix
1/4	cup chai latte-flavored international instant coffee mix (from 9.7-oz container)
1-1/3	cups water
1/2	cup vegetable oil
3	eggs
1	cup miniature semisweet chocolate chips

Frosting

2-1/2	cups powdered sugar
2	tablespoons butter or margarine, softened
3	tablespoons milk
1	tablespoon chai latte-flavored international instant coffee mix (from 9.7-oz container)

Ground cinnamon, if desired

1 Heat oven to 350°F (or 325°F for dark or nonstick pan). Spray bottom and sides of 13x9-inch pan with baking spray with flour.

2 In large bowl, beat cake mix, 1/4 cup dry chai latte mix, the water, oil and eggs with electric mixer on low speed 30 seconds. Beat on medium speed 2 minutes, scraping bowl occasionally. Stir in chocolate chips. Pour into pan.

3 Bake 29 to 39 minutes or until center of cake springs back when lightly touched. Cool completely, about 1 hour. (A crack may appear in top of cake, but frosting will cover it.)

4 In medium bowl, mix powdered sugar and butter until smooth; set aside. In small microwavable bowl, microwave milk on High 10 to 15 seconds until very warm. Stir in 1 tablespoon dry chai latte mix until dissolved; stir into powdered sugar mixture until smooth and spreadable. Spread over cake. Just before serving, dust with cinnamon.

High Altitude (3500-6500 ft): No change.

Nutritional Info: 1 Serving: Calories 390 (Calories from Fat 150); Total Fat 16g (Saturated Fat 5g, Trans Fat 1g); Cholesterol 45mg; Sodium 340mg; Total Carbohydrate 56g (Dietary Fiber 1g, Sugars 42g); Protein 3g. % Daily Value: Vitamin A 2%; Vitamin C 0%; Calcium 6%; Iron 10%. Exchanges: 1 Starch, 2-1/2 Other Carbohydrate, 3-1/2 Fat. Carbohydrate Choices: 4.

Betty's Kitchen Tips

Substitution: Dry instant espresso coffee can be substituted for the chai latte mix.

Purchasing: You'll find the chai latte mix near the coffee in your supermarket.

butternut squash cake

Prep Time: 20 Minutes
Start to Finish: 2 Hours
Servings: 15

Cake
- 3/4 cup butter, softened
- 1-1/2 cups granulated sugar
- 3 eggs
- 1-1/2 teaspoons baking powder
- 1/2 teaspoon baking soda
- 1/2 teaspoon salt
- 1/2 teaspoon ground ginger
- 1/2 teaspoon ground cinnamon
- 1/4 teaspoon ground nutmeg
- 2-1/2 cups Gold Medal® all-purpose flour
- 3/4 cup buttermilk
- 2 cups shredded peeled butternut squash (1 small)
- 1/2 cup chopped walnuts

Frosting
- 1/2 cup butter, softened
- 1 package (3 oz) cream cheese, softened
- 4 cups powdered sugar
- 2 to 4 tablespoons milk
- 1-1/2 teaspoons maple flavor
- 1/2 cup chopped walnuts

1 Heat oven to 350°F. Spray bottom of 13x9-inch pan with cooking spray.

2 In large bowl, beat 3/4 cup butter and the granulated sugar with electric mixer on medium speed until light and fluffy. Beat in eggs until fluffy. Beat in baking powder, baking soda, salt, ginger, cinnamon and nutmeg. Add flour alternately with buttermilk, scraping side of bowl. Beat 1 minute. Stir in squash and 1/2 cup walnuts. Spread in pan.

3 Bake 30 to 40 minutes or until toothpick inserted in center comes out clean. Cool completely.

4 In medium bowl, beat 1/2 cup butter and the cream cheese with electric mixer on medium speed until light and fluffy. Add powdered sugar, 2 tablespoons milk and the maple flavor. Beat until smooth and creamy, adding additional milk if needed. Frost cake. Sprinkle with 1/2 cup walnuts. Cover and refrigerate.

High Altitude (3500-6500 ft): No change.

Nutritional Info: 1 Serving: Calories 530 (Calories from Fat 220); Total Fat 24g (Saturated Fat 12g, Trans Fat 0.5g); Cholesterol 90mg; Sodium 320mg; Total Carbohydrate 72g (Dietary Fiber 1g, Sugars 53g); Protein 6g. % Daily Value: Vitamin A 50%; Vitamin C 2%; Calcium 8%; Iron 8%. Exchanges: 1-1/2 Starch, 3-1/2 Other Carbohydrate, 4-1/2 Fat. Carbohydrate Choices: 5.

Betty's Kitchen Tip
- A box grater or the shredding blade of a food processor works well for shredding the squash.

strawberries 'n cream cake

Prep Time: 15 Minutes
Start to Finish: 1 Hour 35 Minutes
Servings: 15

EASY

1	box Betty Crocker® SuperMoist® white cake mix
1-1/4	cups half-and-half
1	tablespoon vegetable oil
4	eggs
1/2	cup strawberry syrup
1	container (8 oz) frozen whipped topping, thawed
3	cups fresh whole strawberries, sliced
1/4	cup strawberry jam
2	tablespoons sugar

Lime peel twists

1. Heat oven to 350°F (or 325°F for dark or nonstick pan). Spray bottom and sides of 13x9-inch pan with baking spray with flour.

2. In large bowl, beat cake mix, half-and-half, oil and eggs with electric mixer on low speed 30 seconds. Beat on medium speed 2 minutes, scraping bowl occasionally. Pour into pan.

3. Bake 25 to 30 minutes or until toothpick inserted in center comes out clean. Cool 20 minutes. Poke cake every inch with tines of meat fork or a table knife. Pour syrup slowly over cake, allowing syrup to fill holes in cake. Cool completely, about 35 minutes longer.

4. Spread whipped topping over cake. In medium bowl, gently mix strawberries, jam and sugar. Top each serving with strawberry mixture; garnish with lime peel twist. Store covered cake and strawberry mixture separately in refrigerator.

High Altitude (3500-6500 ft): Bake 32 to 37 minutes.

Nutritional Info: 1 Serving: Calories 270 (Calories from Fat 90); Total Fat 11g (Saturated Fat 6g, Trans Fat 1g); Cholesterol 65mg; Sodium 260mg; Total Carbohydrate 40g (Dietary Fiber 1g, Sugars 24g); Protein 4g. % Daily Value: Vitamin A 4%; Vitamin C 15%; Calcium 8%; Iron 6%. Exchanges: 1 Fruit, 1-1/2 Other Carbohydrate, 1/2 Medium-Fat Meat, 1-1/2 Fat. Carbohydrate Choices: 2-1/2.

Betty's Kitchen Tips

Success Hint: Take your time pouring or spooning the syrup over the cake, letting it seep down into the holes.

Special Touch: We poked the cake with a meat fork because the tines are longer and larger, ensuring better saturation of the syrup.

mango layer cake

Prep Time: 20 Minutes
Start to Finish: 2 Hours
Servings: 12

Cake

1	box Betty Crocker® SuperMoist® white cake mix
3/4	cup mango nectar
1/2	cup water
1/4	cup vegetable oil
2	tablespoons grated lime peel
3	egg whites

Filling

1	container (12 oz) Betty Crocker® Whipped fluffy white frosting
2	to 3 medium mangoes, seeds removed, peeled and finely chopped (about 2 cups)
1/2	cup shredded coconut

1 Heat oven to 350°F (or 325°F for dark or nonstick pans). Generously spray bottoms and sides of 2 (9-inch) round cake pans with baking spray with flour.

2 In large bowl, beat cake mix, nectar, water, oil, lime peel and egg whites with electric mixer on low speed until moistened. Beat on medium speed 2 minutes, scraping bowl occasionally. Pour into pans.

3 Bake as directed on box for 9-inch rounds. Cool in pans 10 minutes. Remove from pans to cooling racks. Cool completely, about 1 hour.

4 On serving plate, place 1 cake, rounded side down. Spread with 1/2 of the frosting; top with 1 cup of the mangoes and half of coconut. Top with second cake, rounded side up. Spread with remaining frosting; top with remaining mangoes and half of coconut. Store covered in refrigerator.

High Altitude (3500-6500 ft): No change.

Nutritional Info: 1 Serving: Calories 390 (Calories from Fat 130); Total Fat 15g (Saturated Fat 4.5g, Trans Fat 3g); Cholesterol 0mg; Sodium 340mg; Total Carbohydrate 60g (Dietary Fiber 0g, Sugars 39g); Protein 3g. % Daily Value: Vitamin A 6%; Vitamin C 10%; Calcium 4%; Iron 6%. Exchanges: 1 Fruit, 3 Other Carbohydrate, 1/2 Lean Meat, 2-1/2 Fat. Carbohydrate Choices: 4.

Betty's Kitchen Tips

Purchasing: Mango nectar is a noncarbonated beverage made from the pulp of mangoes. Shop for it in the fruit juice aisle.

Special Touch: For a colorful accent, top the cake with fresh lime wedges.

How-To: An easy way to grate citrus peel is to use a Microplane grater. It was originally a woodworking tool, but it's now sold for kitchen use. The delicate grated lime peel in this recipe adds a complementary flavor to the cake.

pumpkin angel food cake with ginger-cream filling

Prep Time: 10 Minutes
Start to Finish: 3 Hours
Servings: 12

EASY

Cake

1   box (1 lb) Betty Crocker® white angel food cake mix

1   tablespoon Gold Medal® all-purpose flour

1-1/2   teaspoons pumpkin pie spice

3/4   cup canned pumpkin (not pumpkin pie mix)

1   cup cold water

Ginger-Cream Filling

2   cups whipping cream

1/4   cup powdered sugar

2   tablespoons finely chopped crystallized ginger

1 Move oven rack to lowest position. Heat oven to 350°F. In extra-large glass or metal bowl, beat cake ingredients with electric mixer on low speed 30 seconds. Beat on medium speed 1 minute. Pour into ungreased 10-inch angel food (tube) cake pan.

2 Bake 37 to 47 minutes or until crust is dark golden brown and cracks are dry. Immediately turn pan upside down onto heatproof funnel or glass bottle. Let hang about 2 hours or until cake is completely cool. Loosen cake from side of pan with knife or long metal spatula. Turn cake upside down onto serving plate.

3 In chilled large bowl, beat whipping cream and powdered sugar with electric mixer on high speed until stiff. Fold in ginger. Cut cake horizontally in half to make 2 even layers. Spread half of the filling on bottom layer; replace top of cake. Spread remaining filling on top of cake. Sprinkle with additional pumpkin pie spice if desired.

High Altitude (3500-6500 ft): No change.

Nutritional Info: 1 Serving: Calories 280 (Calories from Fat 110); Total Fat 12g (Saturated Fat 8g, Trans Fat 0g); Cholesterol 45mg; Sodium 330mg; Total Carbohydrate 38g (Dietary Fiber 0g, Sugars 27g); Protein 4g. % Daily Value: Vitamin A 60%; Vitamin C 0%; Calcium 10%; Iron 0%. Exchanges: 1 Starch, 1-1/2 Other Carbohydrate, 2-1/2 Fat. Carbohydrate Choices: 2-1/2.

Betty's Kitchen Tips

Substitution: Don't have crystallized ginger? Mix 1 teaspoon ground ginger with the powdered sugar when making the filling.

How-To: A serrated or electric knife will help you cleanly cut the cake into 2 layers, as well as slice the cake for serving.

piña colada pound cakes

Prep Time: 20 Minutes
Start to Finish: 2 Hours 20 Minutes
Servings: 2 loaf cakes (8 slices each)

- 1 box Betty Crocker® SuperMoist® white cake mix
- 3 eggs
- 1 can (14 oz) coconut milk (not cream of coconut)
- 2 teaspoons rum extract
- 1/2 cup flaked coconut
- 1 can (8 oz) crushed pineapple, drained, 3 tablespoons juice reserved
- 3/4 cup powdered sugar

1 Heat oven to 325°F (for all pans). Spray bottoms only of 2 (8x4-inch) loaf pans with baking spray with flour.

2 In large bowl, beat cake mix, eggs, coconut milk and rum extract with electric mixer on low speed 30 seconds. Beat on medium speed 2 minutes, scraping bowl occasionally. Stir in coconut and pineapple. Pour into pans.

3 Bake 55 to 60 minutes or until toothpick inserted in center comes out clean. Cool 10 minutes. Run knife around sides of pans to loosen cakes; remove from pans to cooling racks. Cool 50 minutes.

4 In small bowl, mix powdered sugar and reserved 3 tablespoons pineapple juice. Poke tops of cakes every inch with toothpick. Pour sugar mixture over cakes. Cut each cake into 8 thick slices, using serrated knife.

High Altitude (3500-6500 ft): Heat oven to 350°F. Bake 60 to 65 minutes.

Nutritional Info: 1 Slice: Calories 240 (Calories from Fat 80); Total Fat 9g (Saturated Fat 6g, Trans Fat 1g); Cholesterol 40mg; Sodium 240mg; Total Carbohydrate 36g (Dietary Fiber 0g, Sugars 22g); Protein 3g. % Daily Value: Vitamin A 0%; Vitamin C 0%; Calcium 4%; Iron 6%. Exchanges: 1 Starch, 1-1/2 Other Carbohydrate, 1-1/2 Fat. Carbohydrate Choices: 2-1/2.

Betty's Kitchen Tips

Success Hint: The slices of this cake are quite thick. If you cut the slices in half, you still get a lot of taste—just in a smaller portion.

Variation: This batter also bakes up nicely in layers. Bake 2 (9-inch) layers 26 to 30 minutes, then frost as desired.

Special Touch: For a different look, we cut the loaves into wedge shapes.

raspberry crumb cake

Prep Time: 20 Minutes
Start to Finish: 1 Hour 30 Minutes
Servings: 9

Cake

1-3/4	cups Betty Crocker® SuperMoist® yellow cake mix (from 18.25-oz box)
1/3	cup sour cream
2	tablespoons Gold Medal® all-purpose flour
2	tablespoons vegetable oil
2	tablespoons water
1	egg
3/4	cup fresh raspberries

Topping

1/2	cup sugar
1/3	cup sliced almonds
3	tablespoons Gold Medal® all-purpose flour
3	tablespoons butter or margarine, softened

Garnish

Fresh raspberries, if desired
Fresh mint leaves, if desired

1 Heat oven to 350°F (or 325°F for dark or nonstick pan). Spray bottom and sides of 9- or 8-inch square pan with baking spray with flour.

2 In large bowl, beat cake mix, sour cream, 2 tablespoons flour, the oil, water and egg with electric mixer on low speed 30 seconds. Beat on medium speed 2 minutes, scraping bowl occasionally. Spread in pan. Place raspberries on top of batter.

3 In small bowl, stir topping ingredients until well mixed. Sprinkle evenly over batter and raspberries.

4 Bake 28 to 38 minutes or until toothpick inserted in center comes out clean. Cool at least 30 minutes before serving. Garnish with fresh raspberries and mint leaves.

High Altitude (3500-6500 ft): No change.

Nutritional Info: 1 Serving: Calories 400 (Calories from Fat 130); Total Fat 15g (Saturated Fat 6g, Trans Fat 1.5g); Cholesterol 40mg; Sodium 410mg; Total Carbohydrate 62g (Dietary Fiber 1g, Sugars 36g); Protein 5g. % Daily Value: Vitamin A 4%; Vitamin C 2%; Calcium 6%; Iron 4%. Exchanges: 2 Starch, 2 Other Carbohydrate, 2-1/2 Fat. Carbohydrate Choices: 4.

Betty's Kitchen Tips

Substitution: Frozen berries (not packed in any syrup), thawed and drained, can be used in place of the fresh raspberries.

Success Hint: Use the other half of the cake mix to make Chocolate Chip Snack Cake on p. 181.

Special Touch: This is a great cake to bring to a friend's home, along with coffee or latte, in the morning or afternoon.

lemon buttermilk cake

Prep Time: 15 Minutes
Start to Finish: 1 Hour 30 Minutes
Servings: 24

EASY

Cake

1	box Betty Crocker® SuperMoist® lemon cake mix
1-1/4	cups buttermilk
1/3	cup vegetable oil
3	eggs

Frosting and Garnish

1/3	cup shortening
1/3	cup butter or margarine, softened
1	teaspoon grated lemon peel
2	tablespoons lemon juice
3	cups powdered sugar

1 Heat oven to 350°F (or 325°F for dark or nonstick pan). Spray bottom and sides of 15x10x1-inch pan with baking spray with flour.

2 In large bowl, beat cake mix, buttermilk, oil and eggs with electric mixer on low speed 30 seconds. Beat on medium speed 2 minutes, scraping bowl occasionally. Pour into pan.

3 Bake 15 to 20 minutes or until toothpick inserted in center comes out clean. Cool completely, about 1 hour.

4 In medium bowl, beat shortening, butter, grated lemon peel, lemon juice and powdered sugar on high speed until smooth and creamy; add more lemon juice if needed. Spread over cake.

High Altitude (3500-6500 ft): Bake 18 to 23 minutes.

Nutritional Info: 1 Serving: Calories 240 (Calories from Fat 100); Total Fat 11g (Saturated Fat 3.5g, Trans Fat 1g); Cholesterol 35mg; Sodium 180mg; Total Carbohydrate 33g (Dietary Fiber 0g, Sugars 24g); Protein 2g. % Daily Value: Vitamin A 2%; Vitamin C 0%; Calcium 4%; Iron 2%. Exchanges: 1/2 Starch, 1-1/2 Other Carbohydrate, 2-1/2 Fat. Carbohydrate Choices: 2.

Betty's Kitchen Tips

Special Touch: Take this great cake to a potluck, graduation party or picnic. For a large event, cut the cake into 48 small squares and serve in little paper baking cups.

Success Hint: Buttermilk is the not-so-secret ingredient in this moist, tasty cake.

orange cream angel food cake

Prep Time: 35 Minutes
Start to Finish: 5 Hours 25 Minutes
Servings: 12

Cake

1	box Betty Crocker® white angel food cake mix
1-1/4	cups cold water

Orange Cream

6	egg yolks
1	cup sugar

2	teaspoons cornstarch
2/3	cup orange juice

Pinch salt

3/4	cup butter or margarine, cut into pieces
1	cup whipping cream
1	tablespoon grated orange peel

Orange peel twists, if desired

1 Move oven rack to lowest position (remove other racks). Heat oven to 350°F. In extra-large glass or metal bowl, beat cake mix and cold water with electric mixer on low speed 30 seconds. Beat on medium speed 1 minute. Pour into ungreased 10-inch angel food (tube) cake pan. (Do not use fluted tube cake pan or 9-inch angel food pan or batter will overflow.)

2 Bake 37 to 47 minutes or until top is dark golden brown and cracks feel very dry and are not sticky. Do not underbake. Immediately turn pan upside down onto glass bottle until cake is completely cool, about 2 hours.

3 Meanwhile, in 2-quart saucepan, beat egg yolks, sugar, cornstarch, orange juice and salt with wire whisk until blended. Add butter; cook 2 to 3 minutes over medium heat, stirring frequently, until boiling. Boil 3 to 5 minutes, stirring constantly, until thickened and mixture coats the back of a spoon. Immediately pour orange mixture (orange curd) through fine-mesh strainer into medium bowl. Cover with plastic wrap, pressing wrap directly onto surface of orange curd. Refrigerate about 1 hour or until completely chilled.

4 In medium bowl, beat whipping cream on high speed until stiff peaks form. Fold whipped cream and grated orange peel into orange curd.

5 On serving plate, place cake with browned side down. Cut off top 1/3 of cake, using long, sharp knife; set aside. Scoop out 1-inch-wide and 1-inch-deep tunnel around cake. Set aside scooped-out cake for another use. Spoon 1-1/3 cups orange cream into tunnel. Replace top of cake to seal filling. Frost top and side of cake with remaining orange cream. Refrigerate at least 2 hours before serving. Garnish with orange twists. Store covered in refrigerator.

High Altitude (3500-6500 ft): Follow High Altitude directions for 10-inch angel food (tube) cake pan on cake mix box.

Nutritional Info: 1 Serving: Calories 420 (Calories from Fat 190); Total Fat 21g (Saturated Fat 13g, Trans Fat 0.5g); Cholesterol 160mg; Sodium 410mg; Total Carbohydrate 51g (Dietary Fiber 0g, Sugars 41g); Protein 5g. % Daily Value: Vitamin A 15%; Vitamin C 4%; Calcium 8%; Iron 0%. Exchanges: 3-1/2 Other Carbohydrate, 1/2 High-Fat Meat, 3-1/2 Fat. Carbohydrate Choices: 3-1/2.

Betty's Kitchen Tip

• When making fresh orange curd, it's important to stir constantly to help prevent any of the egg from cooking too quickly. If this does happen, strain the mixture through a fine-mesh strainer to easily remove any cooked bits.

chocolate lover's dream cake

Prep Time: 30 Minutes
Start to Finish: 3 Hours 45 Minutes
Servings: 16

Cake

- 1 box Betty Crocker® SuperMoist® chocolate fudge cake mix
- 1/2 cup chocolate milk
- 1/3 cup butter or margarine, melted
- 3 eggs
- 1 box (4-serving size) chocolate fudge instant pudding and pie filling mix
- 1 container (16 oz) sour cream
- 1 bag (12 oz) semisweet chocolate chips (2 cups)

Glaze

- 3/4 cup semisweet chocolate chips
- 3 tablespoons butter or margarine
- 3 tablespoons light corn syrup
- 1-1/2 teaspoons water

1 Heat oven to 350°F. Generously spray 12-cup fluted tube cake pan with baking spray with flour. In large bowl, mix cake mix, chocolate milk, butter, eggs, dry pudding mix and sour cream with spoon until well blended (batter will be very thick). Stir in 1 bag (12 oz) chocolate chips. Spoon into pan.

2 Bake 55 to 65 minutes or until top springs back when touched lightly in center. Cool in pan 10 minutes. Place cooling rack or heatproof serving plate upside down over pan; turn rack and pan over. Remove pan. Cool completely, about 2 hours.

3 In 1-quart saucepan, heat glaze ingredients over low heat, stirring frequently, until chocolate chips are melted and mixture is smooth. Drizzle glaze over cake. Store loosely covered at room temperature.

High Altitude (3500-6500 ft): Heat oven to 375°F. Stir 2 tablespoons Gold Medal all-purpose flour into dry cake mix. In cake, increase chocolate milk to 3/4 cup, decrease butter to 2 tablespoons.

Nutritional Info: 1 Serving: Calories 450 (Calories from Fat 210); Total Fat 24g (Saturated Fat 14g, Trans Fat 1g); Cholesterol 75mg; Sodium 430mg; Total Carbohydrate 54g (Dietary Fiber 3g, Sugars 36g); Protein 5g. % Daily Value: Vitamin A 8%; Vitamin C 0%; Calcium 8%; Iron 10%. Exchanges: 2 Starch, 1-1/2 Other Carbohydrate, 4-1/2 Fat. Carbohydrate Choices: 3-1/2.

Betty's Kitchen Tips

Variation: For a mild chocolate flavor, use milk chocolate chips instead of semisweet chocolate chips.

Success Hint: You don't want to lose even a drop of this batter, so measure the volume of your tube cake pan using water to make sure it holds 12 cups. If the pan is smaller than 12 cups, the batter will overflow during baking.

chocolate-cherry ice cream cake

Prep Time: 25 Minutes
Start to Finish: 9 Hours 20 Minutes
Servings: 12

- 16 creme-filled chocolate sandwich cookies
- 1/4 cup butter or margarine
- 1 quart (4 cups) cherry or cherry-vanilla ice cream, softened
- 8 creme-filled chocolate sandwich cookies, coarsely chopped
- 1 cup miniature semisweet chocolate chips
- 1 quart (4 cups) vanilla ice cream, softened
- 1/2 cup fudge topping

Sweetened whipped cream, if desired

12 fresh cherries with stems

1 Heat oven to 350°F. Place 16 cookies in food processor; cover and process until finely ground. Add butter; cover and process until mixed. Press in bottom of ungreased 9-inch springform pan. Bake 8 to 10 minutes or until firm. Cool completely, about 30 minutes.

2 Wrap outside of springform pan with foil. Spread cherry ice cream over cooled crust. Freeze 30 minutes.

3 Sprinkle chopped cookies and 1/2 cup of the chocolate chips over cherry ice cream; press slightly. Spread vanilla ice cream over top. Drop fudge topping in small spoonfuls over ice cream; swirl slightly into ice cream. Sprinkle with remaining 1/2 cup chocolate chips; press slightly. Freeze about 8 hours until firm.

4 To serve, let stand at room temperature 5 to 10 minutes. Carefully remove side of pan. Garnish individual servings with whipped cream and a cherry.

High Altitude (3500-6500 ft): No change.

Nutritional Info: 1 Serving: Calories 460 (Calories from Fat 210); Total Fat 24g (Saturated Fat 12g, Trans Fat 0.5g); Cholesterol 50mg; Sodium 270mg; Total Carbohydrate 55g (Dietary Fiber 3g, Sugars 39g); Protein 5g. % Daily Value: Vitamin A 10%; Vitamin C 0%; Calcium 15%; Iron 8%. Exchanges: 2 Starch, 1-1/2 Other Carbohydrate, 4-1/2 Fat. Carbohydrate Choices: 3-1/2.

Betty's Kitchen Tips

How-To: It's a snap to spread the fudge topping over the ice cream. Just spoon the topping into a resealable food-storage plastic bag, cut off a small tip from a corner and squeeze.

Success Hint: This special dessert keeps well in the freezer for up to two weeks. Make the dessert, freeze until firm, then cover with foil to store.

rhubarb coffee cake

Prep Time: 20 Minutes
Start to Finish: 2 Hours 40 Minutes
Servings: 15

1 box Betty Crocker® SuperMoist® yellow cake mix	1 package (3 oz) cream cheese, softened
1 cup milk	2 cups chopped fresh rhubarb
1 teaspoon vanilla	1/2 cup Gold Medal® all-purpose flour
3 eggs	3/4 cup sugar
	1/4 cup butter or margarine, softened

1 Heat oven to 325°F (for all pans). Spray bottom and sides of 13x9-inch pan with baking spray with flour.

2 In large bowl, beat cake mix, milk, vanilla, eggs and cream cheese with electric mixer on low speed 1 minute. Beat on medium speed 2 minutes, scraping bowl frequently; set aside.

3 In medium bowl, toss rhubarb and 1/4 cup of the flour. Fold rhubarb into batter; spread in pan.

4 In small bowl, mix sugar, remaining 1/4 cup flour and the butter until coarse crumbs form. Sprinkle over top of batter.

5 Bake 40 to 46 minutes or until lightly browned and toothpick inserted in center comes out clean. Cool about 1 hour 30 minutes before serving.

High Altitude (3500-6500 ft): Heat oven to 350°F. Add 1/4 cup Gold Medal all-purpose flour to dry cake mix. Cut rhubarb into small pieces.

Nutritional Info: 1 Serving: Calories 180 (Calories from Fat 70); Total Fat 7g (Saturated Fat 4g, Trans Fat 0.5g); Cholesterol 60mg; Sodium 150mg; Total Carbohydrate 26g (Dietary Fiber 0g, Sugars 17g); Protein 3g. % Daily Value: Vitamin A 6%; Vitamin C 0%; Calcium 8%; Iron 6%. Exchanges: 1 Starch, 1 Other Carbohydrate, 1 Fat. Carbohydrate Choices: 2.

Betty's Kitchen Tips

How-To: If using frozen rhubarb, measure the rhubarb while it's still frozen, then thaw it completely. Drain in a colander, but do not press out the liquid.

Success Hint: Use a serrated knife to easily cut the cake, and dip it in hot water before cutting each piece.

peaches 'n cream cake

Prep Time: 10 Minutes
Start to Finish: 1 Hour 45 Minutes
Servings: 12

EASY

Cake

1	box Betty Crocker® SuperMoist® yellow cake mix
1/4	cup Gold Medal® all-purpose flour
1	cup Yoplait® 99% Fat Free creamy harvest peach yogurt (from 32-oz container)
1/2	cup water
1/4	cup vegetable oil
1/2	teaspoon ground ginger
1/2	teaspoon ground nutmeg
3	eggs

Topping

1-1/2	cups frozen (thawed) reduced-fat whipped topping
1	cup Yoplait® 99% Fat Free creamy harvest peach yogurt (from 32-oz container)
2	cups frozen sliced peaches (from 16-oz bag), thawed, drained

1 Heat oven to 350°F (or 325°F for dark or nonstick pan). Spray bottom and sides of 13x9-inch pan with baking spray with flour.

2 In large bowl, beat cake mix, flour, 1 cup yogurt, the water, oil, ginger, nutmeg and eggs with electric mixer on low speed 30 seconds. Beat on medium speed 2 minutes, scraping bowl occasionally. Pour into pan.

3 Bake 30 to 35 minutes or until toothpick inserted in center comes out clean. Cool completely, about 1 hour.

4 In small bowl, mix whipped topping and 1 cup yogurt until blended. Serve cake with peaches and topping mixture.

High Altitude (3500-6500 ft): Bake 35 to 40 minutes.

Nutritional Info: 1 Serving: Calories 310 (Calories from Fat 90); Total Fat 10g (Saturated Fat 3.5g, Trans Fat 1g); Cholesterol 55mg; Sodium 320mg; Total Carbohydrate 48g (Dietary Fiber 0g, Sugars 28g); Protein 5g. % Daily Value: Vitamin A 10%; Vitamin C 35%; Calcium 10%; Iron 6%. Exchanges: 1/2 Fruit, 2-1/2 Other Carbohydrate, 1/2 Medium-Fat Meat, 2 Fat. Carbohydrate Choices: 3.

Betty's Kitchen Tips

Success Hint: Shiny aluminum pans are best for baking cakes because they reflect heat away from the cake and produce a tender, light brown crust.

Serve-With: Serve this cake with fresh instead of frozen sliced peaches, if they are available.

brown sugar bundt cake with rum-caramel sauce

Prep Time: 25 Minutes
Start to Finish: 4 Hours
Servings: 16

1-1/2	cups packed brown sugar
1	cup granulated sugar
1-1/2	cups butter or margarine, softened
1/2	cup milk
1	teaspoon vanilla
5	eggs

3	cups Gold Medal® all-purpose flour
1	teaspoon baking powder
1/4	teaspoon salt
1	cup caramel topping
2	tablespoons light rum or 1 teaspoon rum extract

1 Heat oven to 325°F. Grease 12-cup fluted tube cake pan with shortening (do not use cooking spray); coat with flour. In large bowl, beat sugars and butter with electric mixer on low speed until well blended. Add milk, vanilla and eggs. Beat on medium speed 2 minutes.

2 Beat in flour, baking powder and salt until mixture is smooth and well blended. Spread in pan.

3 Bake 1 hour 5 minutes to 1 hour 15 minutes or until toothpick inserted in center comes out clean. Cool 10 minutes. Remove from pan. Cool completely, about 2 hours.

4 In 1-quart saucepan, heat caramel topping and rum over low heat, stirring occasionally, until well blended and warm. Serve warm topping over slices of cake.

High Altitude (3500-6500 ft): No change.

Nutritional Info: 1 Serving: Calories 460 (Calories from Fat 170); Total Fat 19g (Saturated Fat 12g, Trans Fat 0.5g); Cholesterol 115mg; Sodium 290mg; Total Carbohydrate 65g (Dietary Fiber 1g, Sugars 43g); Protein 5g. % Daily Value: Vitamin A 15%; Vitamin C 0%; Calcium 8%; Iron 8%. Exchanges: 1-1/2 Starch, 3 Other Carbohydrate, 3-1/2 Fat. Carbohydrate Choices: 4.

FUN CAKES & CUPCAKES

p. 218

228

223

214

chocolate ganache mini-cakes

Prep Time: 45 Minutes
Start to Finish: 1 Hour 55 Minutes
Servings: 60 mini-cakes

Mini-Cakes
    1 box Betty Crocker® SuperMoist®
       devil's food cake mix
Water, vegetable oil and eggs called for on
cake mix box

Filling
    2/3 cup raspberry jam

Glaze and Garnish
    6 oz dark baking chocolate, chopped
    2/3 cup whipping cream
    1 tablespoon raspberry-flavored liqueur,
       if desired
Fresh raspberries, if desired

1 Heat oven to 350°F (or 325°F for dark or nonstick pans). Place miniature paper baking cup in each of 60 mini muffin cups. Make cake mix as directed on box, using water, oil and eggs. Fill muffin cups 3/4 full (about 1 heaping tablespoon each).

2 Bake 10 to 15 minutes or until toothpick inserted in center comes out clean. Cool in pans 5 minutes. Remove from pans to cooling racks. Cool completely, about 30 minutes.

3 By slowly spinning end of round handle of wooden spoon back and forth, make deep, 1/2-inch-wide indentation in center of top of each cupcake, not quite to bottom (wiggle end of spoon in cupcake to make opening large enough).

4 Spoon jam into small resealable food-storage plastic bag; seal bag. Cut 3/8-inch tip off 1 bottom corner of bag. Insert tip of bag into opening in each cupcake; squeeze bag to fill opening.

5 Place chocolate in medium bowl. In 1-quart saucepan, heat whipping cream just to boiling; pour over chocolate. Let stand 3 to 5 minutes until chocolate is melted and smooth when stirred. Stir in liqueur. Let stand 15 minutes, stirring occasionally, until mixture coats a spoon.

6 Spoon about 1 teaspoon chocolate glaze onto each mini-cake. Garnish each with a raspberry.

High Altitude (3500-6500 ft): Bake 12 to 17 minutes.

Nutritional Info: 1 Mini-Cake: Calories 70 (Calories from Fat 25); Total Fat 3g (Saturated Fat 1.5g, Trans Fat 0g); Cholesterol 0mg; Sodium 75mg; Total Carbohydrate 10g (Dietary Fiber 0g, Sugars 5g); Protein 0g. % Daily Value: Vitamin A 0%; Vitamin C 0%; Calcium 0%; Iron 4%. Exchanges: 1/2 Other Carbohydrate, 1/2 Fat. Carbohydrate Choices: 1/2.

Betty's Kitchen Tip

• If you refrigerate these mini-cakes, let them stand at room temperature at least 20 minutes before serving.

mr. sun cupcakes

Prep Time: 1 Hour 15 Minutes
Start to Finish: 2 Hours 20 Minutes
Servings: 24 cupcakes

- -

Cupcakes
   1   box Betty Crocker® SuperMoist®
       yellow cake mix
Water, vegetable oil and eggs called for on
cake mix box

Frosting and Decorations
Yellow food color
   1   container (1 lb) Betty Crocker® Rich &
       Creamy vanilla frosting
Powdered sugar
  48 large yellow, orange and/or red gumdrops
Betty Crocker® black decorating icing
(from 4.25-oz tube)

Betty Crocker® red decorating gel (from 0.68-oz tube)

- -

1 Heat oven to 350°F (or 325°F for dark or nonstick pans). Place paper baking cup in each of 24 regular-size muffin cups. Make and bake cake mix as directed on box for 24 cupcakes, using water, oil and eggs. Cool in pans 10 minutes. Remove from pans to cooling racks. Cool completely, about 30 minutes.

2 Stir 15 drops food color into frosting until bright yellow. Frost cupcakes.

3 Lightly sprinkle powdered sugar on work surface and rolling pin. Roll 4 gumdrops at a time into flat ovals about 1/8 inch thick. Cut thin sliver off top and bottom of each oval to make rectangles. Cut each rectangle in half crosswise to make 2 squares; cut each square diagonally in half to make 2 triangles.

4 Arrange 8 gumdrop triangles around edge of each cupcake for sun rays. Using small writing tip on black icing tube, pipe sunglasses on each cupcake. Using red gel, pipe smiling mouth on each cupcake. Refrigerate until ready to serve. Store covered in refrigerator.

High Altitude (3500-6500 ft): Follow High Altitude directions for cupcakes on cake mix box.

Nutritional Info: 1 Frosted Cupcake (Undecorated): Calories 200 (Calories from Fat 70); Total Fat 8g (Saturated Fat 2g, Trans Fat 1.5g); Cholesterol 25mg; Sodium 190mg; Total Carbohydrate 30g (Dietary Fiber 0g, Sugars 21g); Protein 1g. % Daily Value: Vitamin A 0%; Vitamin C 0%; Calcium 4%; Iron 2%. Exchanges: 2 Other Carbohydrate, 1-1/2 Fat. Carbohydrate Choices: 2.

Betty's Kitchen Tips

Do-Ahead: Roll and cut sun rays ahead of time so kids can easily assemble the cupcakes.

How-To: For brighter yellow frosting, use gel food color instead of liquid.

cookies 'n cream cupcakes

Prep Time: 35 Minutes
Prep Time: 1 Hour 40 Minutes
Servings: 24 cupcakes

Cupcakes

1 box Betty Crocker® SuperMoist® devil's food cake mix

Water, vegetable oil and eggs called for on cake mix box

Filling

3/4 cup Betty Crocker® Whipped fluffy white frosting

1/2 cup marshmallow creme

Frosting and Garnish

1 container (12 oz) Betty Crocker® Whipped fluffy white frosting

10 creme-filled chocolate sandwich cookies, coarsely broken (about 1 cup)

1 Heat oven to 350°F (or 325°F for dark or nonstick pans). Place paper baking cup in each of 24 regular-size muffin cups. Make and bake cake mix as directed on box for 24 cupcakes, using water, oil and eggs. Cool in pans 10 minutes. Remove from pans to cooling racks. Cool completely, about 30 minutes.

2 By slowly spinning end of round handle of wooden spoon back and forth, make deep, 3/4-inch-wide indentation in center of top of each cupcake, not quite to bottom (wiggle end of spoon in cupcake to make opening large enough).

3 In medium bowl, stir together filling ingredients. Spoon into small resealable food-storage plastic bag; seal bag. Cut 3/8-inch tip off 1 bottom corner of bag. Insert tip of bag into opening in each cupcake; squeeze bag to fill opening.

4 Frost cupcakes with 1 container frosting. Garnish each with about 2 teaspoons broken cookies.

High Altitude (3500-6500 ft): Follow High Altitude directions for cupcakes on cake mix box.

Nutritional Info: 1 Cupcake: Calories 240 (Calories from Fat 100); Total Fat 11g (Saturated Fat 2.5g, Trans Fat 2g); Cholesterol 25mg; Sodium 220mg; Total Carbohydrate 32g (Dietary Fiber 0g, Sugars 22g); Protein 2g. % Daily Value: Vitamin A 0%; Vitamin C 0%; Calcium 2%; Iron 6%. Exchanges: 2 Other Carbohydrate, 1/2 Medium-Fat Meat, 1-1/2 Fat. Carbohydrate Choices: 2.

Betty's Kitchen Tips

How-To: You can easily crush the cookies by placing them in a resealable food-storage plastic bag and pressing with a rolling pin a few times.

Success Hint: To easily scoop the marshmallow creme out of the jar, lightly spray a rubber spatula with cooking spray. The sticky marshmallow won't stick quite as much.

friendly ghost cupcakes

Prep Time: 35 Minutes
Start to Finish: 1 Hour 25 Minutes
Servings: 24 cupcakes

3	cups Original Bisquick® mix
1	cup granulated sugar
1	cup packed brown sugar
1/4	cup butter or margarine, softened
2	teaspoons pumpkin pie spice
1/4	cup milk
4	eggs
1	can (15 oz) pumpkin (not pumpkin pie mix)
1	package (3 oz) cream cheese, softened
1/2	cup butter or margarine, softened
2	teaspoons vanilla
4-1/2	cups powdered sugar
2	teaspoons miniature chocolate chips

1 Heat oven to 350°F. Place paper baking cup in each of 24 regular-size muffin cups.

2 In large bowl, beat Bisquick® mix, granulated sugar, brown sugar, 1/4 cup butter, the pumpkin pie spice, milk, eggs and pumpkin with electric mixer on low speed 30 seconds. Beat on medium speed 3 minutes. Divide batter evenly among muffin cups.

3 Bake 25 to 30 minutes or until toothpick inserted in center of cupcake comes out clean. Cool 5 minutes; remove from pan to cooling rack. Cool completely, about 30 minutes.

4 In large bowl, beat cream cheese and 1/2 cup butter on low speed about 30 seconds or until well blended. Beat in vanilla and 2 cups of the powdered sugar on low speed about 30 seconds or just until mixed, then on high speed about 1 minute or until fluffy. On medium speed, gradually beat in remaining 2-1/2 cups powdered sugar. If too soft to mound, add additional powdered sugar, one tablespoon at a time.

5 Spoon frosting into large resealable food-storage plastic bag; press out air and seal bag. Cut 1/2-inch tip from lower corner of bag. Squeeze bag to pipe about 2 tablespoons frosting into ghost-shaped mound on each cupcake. Press 2 chocolate chips, flat sides out, into frosting for eyes.

High Altitude (3500-6500 ft): No change.

Nutritional Info: 1 Cupcake: Calories 310 (Calories from Fat 90); Total Fat 10g (Saturated Fat 5g, Trans Fat 1g); Cholesterol 55mg; Sodium 250mg; Total Carbohydrate 52g (Dietary Fiber 1g, Sugars 40g); Protein 2g. % Daily Value: Vitamin A 60%; Vitamin C 0%; Calcium 4%; Iron 4%. Exchanges: 1/2 Starch, 3 Other Carbohydrate, 2 Fat. Carbohydrate Choices: 3-1/2.

lemon cupcakes with strawberry frosting

Prep Time: 40 Minutes
Start to Finish: 1 Hour 45 Minutes
Servings: 24 cupcakes

- -

Cupcakes

1   box Betty Crocker® SuperMoist® white cake mix

Water, vegetable oil and egg whites called for on cake mix box

3   tablespoons grated lemon peel

Frosting

4   to 6 medium strawberries (about 4 oz), hulled

1   container (12 oz) Betty Crocker® Whipped fluffy white frosting

Garnish, if desired

12   strawberries, sliced

Lemon peel curls

- -

1 Heat oven to 350°F (or 325°F for dark or nonstick pans). Place paper baking cup in each of 24 regular-size muffin cups. Make and bake cake mix as directed on box for 24 cupcakes, using water, oil and egg whites and adding grated lemon peel. Cool in pans 10 minutes. Remove from pans to cooling racks. Cool completely, about 30 minutes.

2 Place 4 oz strawberries in blender. Cover; pulse 20 seconds to puree strawberries. Pour 1/4 cup of the strawberry puree into medium bowl. Stir in fluffy white frosting until well mixed.

3 Generously frost cupcakes. Garnish tops with quartered strawberries and lemon peel curls.

High Altitude (3500-6500 ft): Follow High Altitude directions for cupcakes on the cake mix box.

Nutritional Info: 1 Cupcake: Calories 180 (Calories from Fat 70); Total Fat 7g (Saturated Fat 2g, Trans Fat 1.5g); Cholesterol 0mg; Sodium 160mg; Total Carbohydrate 26g (Dietary Fiber 0g, Sugars 16g); Protein 1g. % Daily Value: Vitamin A 0%; Vitamin C 4%; Calcium 2%; Iron 2%. Exchanges: 1-1/2 Other Carbohydrate, 1-1/2 Fat. Carbohydrate Choices: 2.

Betty's Kitchen Tips

How-To: An easy way to hull strawberries is to push one end of a plastic drinking straw into the point of the berry and push it through to pop off the green cap.

Purchasing: To buy the filigree shown on the cupcakes, go to www.fancyflours.com and search **cupcake wrappers**.

rex the dinosaur cake

Prep Time: 30 Minutes
Start to Finish: 3 Hours
Servings: 15

1 box Betty Crocker® SuperMoist® devil's food cake mix

Water, vegetable oil and eggs called for on cake mix box

Tray or cardboard (18x14 inch), covered with paper or foil

2 containers (1 lb each) Betty Crocker® Rich & Creamy vanilla frosting

Green food color gel

19 Hershey®'s Kisses® milk chocolates, unwrapped

Assorted round chocolate candies (candy-coated chocolate candies, miniature candy-coated chocolate baking bits, coating wafers, chocolate chips)

Betty Crocker® white decorating icing (from 4.25-oz tube)

1 Heat oven to 350°F (325°F for dark or nonstick pans). Spray bottoms and sides of 2 (8- or 9-inch) round cake pans with baking spray with flour. Make and bake cake mix as directed on box, using water, oil and eggs. Cool 10 minutes. Remove from pans to cooking racks. Cool completely, about 1 hour.

2 For body, cut 1-inch slice from edge of one cake. From cut edge, cut out small inverted U-shape piece. Place body on tray. From remaining cake, cut head and tail (see diagram). Arrange head and tail pieces next to body.

3 Spoon frosting into large bowl. Stir in enough food color until desired green color. To "crumb-coat" cake, spread thin layer of frosting over cake pieces to seal in crumbs. Freeze cake 30 to 60 minutes.

4 Frost cake pieces with remaining frosting. Use milk chocolate candies for spikes along back of dinosaur. Decorate body with assorted candies. Use 2 candy-coated chocolate candies for eyes and white decorator icing for center of eyes and teeth.

High Altitude (3500-6500 ft): Follow High Altitude directions for 2 (8- or 9-inch) round cake pans on cake mix box.

Nutritional Info: 1 Serving Frosted Cake (Undecorated): Calories 470 (Calories from Fat 180); Total Fat 20g (Saturated Fat 4g, Trans Fat 4.5g); Cholesterol 40mg; Sodium 440mg; Total Carbohydrate 69g (Dietary Fiber 0g, Sugars 51g); Protein 3g. % Daily Value: Vitamin A 0%; Vitamin C 0%; Calcium 4%; Iron 8%. Exchanges: 1 Starch, 3-1/2 Other Carbohydrate, 4 Fat. Carbohydrate Choices: 4-1/2.

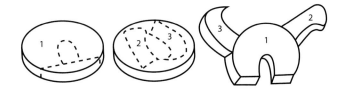

Cut one cake for the body.   Cut one cake for the head and tail.   Arrange pieces on tray to form dinosaur.

trick-or-treat brownie cupcakes

Prep Time: 30 Minutes
Start to Finish: 1 Hour 15 Minutes
Servings: 24 cupcakes

- 1 box (1 lb 2.3 oz) Betty Crocker® fudge brownie mix
- 1/2 cup vegetable oil
- 2 tablespoons water
- 2 eggs
- 1 cup white vanilla baking chips (6 oz)
- 1-3/4 cups powdered sugar
- 6 tablespoons butter or margarine, softened
- 3 tablespoons milk
- 6 to 8 drops red food color
- 6 to 8 drops yellow food color
- 24 miniature candy bars

1 Heat oven to 350°F. Spray 24 regular-size muffin cups with cooking spray. In medium bowl, mix brownie mix, oil, water and eggs. Divide batter among muffin cups. Bake 13 to 18 minutes or until centers are set and toothpick inserted near edge of cupcake comes out clean. Cool 30 minutes. Run metal spatula around edge of each brownie; lift out to remove from muffin cup.

2 In microwavable bowl, microwave vanilla chips uncovered on Medium (50%) 30 to 45 seconds, stirring every 15 seconds, until melted. Cool slightly.

3 In medium bowl, beat powdered sugar, butter, milk and food colors on medium speed until fluffy. Stir in melted vanilla chips. Spoon frosting over cooled cupcakes; top each with candy bar.

High Altitude (3500-6500 ft): No change.

Nutritional Info: 1 Cupcake: Calories 270 (Calories from Fat 110); Total Fat 12g (Saturated Fat 5g, Trans Fat 0g); Cholesterol 25mg; Sodium 130mg; Total Carbohydrate 38g (Dietary Fiber 1g, Sugars 30g); Protein 2g. % Daily Value: Vitamin A 2%; Vitamin C 0%; Calcium 2%; Iron 4%. Exchanges: 1/2 Starch, 2 Other Carbohydrate, 2-1/2 Fat. Carbohydrate Choices: 2-1/2.

Betty's Kitchen Tips

Special Touch: Sprinkle these treats with edible Halloween confetti or orange and red colored sugar.

Substitution: Substitute semisweet or milk chocolate chips for the white vanilla baking chips, if desired.

How-To: For extra-vibrant frosting, use paste food colors.

sunflower cupcakes

Prep Time: 1 Hour 15 Minutes
Start to Finish: 2 Hours 20 Minutes
Servings: 24 cupcakes

Cupcakes

1 box Betty Crocker® SuperMoist®
    yellow cake mix

Water, vegetable oil and eggs called for on
cake mix box

Filling

1/3 cup lemon curd (from 11-1/4-oz jar)

1 package (3 oz) cream cheese, softened

Frosting and Decorations

Yellow food color

1 container (12 oz) Betty Crocker® Whipped
    fluffy white frosting

4 to 5 tubes (4.25 oz each) Betty Crocker®
    yellow decorating icing

1/2 cup miniature semisweet chocolate chips

Sour candy straws, if desired

1 Heat oven to 350°F (or 325°F for dark or nonstick pans). Place paper baking cup in each of 24 regular-size muffin cups. Make and bake cake mix as directed on box for 24 cupcakes, using water, oil and eggs. Cool in pans 10 minutes. Remove from pans to cooling racks. Cool completely, about 30 minutes.

2 By slowly moving end of round handle of wooden spoon back and forth, make deep, 3/4-inch-wide indentation in center of top of each cupcake, not quite to bottom (wiggle end of spoon in cupcake to make opening large enough).

3 In medium bowl, beat lemon curd and cream cheese with electric mixer on medium speed until blended. Spoon into small resealable food-storage plastic bag; seal bag. Cut 3/8-inch tip off 1 bottom corner of bag. Insert tip of bag into top of each cupcake; squeeze bag to fill cupcake.

4 Stir 4 drops food color into frosting until pale yellow. Frost cupcakes.

5 Place unopened icing tube in tall drinking glass filled with hot tap water for 15 minutes. Remove from water; wipe dry. Knead tube gently with hands to soften. Using leaf tip on icing tube, pipe 2 concentric circles of leaves, starting with outside edge of cupcake and working toward center; leave quarter-size area in center with just frosting. Carefully spoon 1 teaspoon chocolate chips onto center of each cupcake; press into frosting. Arrange on tray using sour candy straws for stems and leaves. Refrigerate until ready to serve. Store in refrigerator.

High Altitude (3500-6500 ft): Follow High Altitude directions for cupcakes on box.

Nutritional Info: 1 Cupcake: Calories 290 (Calories from Fat 100); Total Fat 11g (Saturated Fat 3.5g, Trans Fat 1.5g); Cholesterol 35mg; Sodium 180mg; Total Carbohydrate 46g (Dietary Fiber 0g, Sugars 35g); Protein 2g. % Daily Value: Vitamin A 0%; Vitamin C 0%; Calcium 4%; Iron 4%. Exchanges: 1/2 Starch, 2-1/2 Other Carbohydrate, 2 Fat. Carbohydrate Choices: 3.

pull-apart butterfly cupcakes

Prep Time: 35 Minutes
Start to Finish: 1 Hour 40 Minutes
Servings: 24 cupcakes

Cupcakes
    1   box Betty Crocker® SuperMoist®
        yellow cake mix
Water, vegetable oil and eggs called for on
cake mix box

Frosting and Decorations
    1   container (1 lb) Betty Crocker® Rich &
        Creamy vanilla frosting
Red food color
Yellow food color
    2/3   cup Betty Crocker® Rich & Creamy
          chocolate frosting (from 1-lb container)
Assorted spring-colored candies and sugar

1   Heat oven to 350°F (or 325°F for dark or
    nonstick pans). Place paper baking cup in
    each of 24 regular-size muffin cups. Make
    and bake cake mix as directed on box for
    24 cupcakes, using water, oil and eggs.
    Cool in pans 10 minutes. Remove from
    pans to cooling racks. Cool completely,
    about 30 minutes.

2   Place vanilla frosting in small bowl. Stir
    in 5 drops red food color and 5 drops
    yellow food color to make orange frosting;
    set aside.

3   On large serving tray or cookie sheet
    covered with foil, arrange 24 cupcakes
    as shown in diagram. Frost center body
    of butterfly and antennae with chocolate
    frosting. (Push cupcakes together slightly
    to frost entire body and antennae, not just
    individual cupcakes.) Frost remaining
    cupcakes with orange frosting for wings.
    (Push cupcakes together slightly to frost
    entire wings, not just individual cupcakes.)
    Pipe chocolate frosting outline on wings,
    if desired. Decorate butterfly with candies
    and sugar.

High Altitude (3500-6500 ft): Follow High
Altitude directions for cupcakes on box.

Nutritional Info: 1 Frosted Cupcake (Undecorated): Calories 230
(Calories from Fat 80); Total Fat 9g (Saturated Fat 2g, Trans Fat
2g); Cholesterol 25mg; Sodium 210mg; Total Carbohydrate 35g
(Dietary Fiber 0g, Sugars 24g); Protein 1g. % Daily Value: Vitamin
A 0%; Vitamin C 0%; Calcium 4%; Iron 39%. Exchanges:
2-1/2 Other Carbohydrate, 1-1/2 Fat. Carbohydrate Choices: 2.

Arrange cupcakes in
this shape.

Betty's Kitchen Tip

• To order the decorations shown, go to
www.fancyflours.com and search for **royal icing
sugar decorations**.

fairy tale princess cake

Prep Time: 40 Minutes
Start to Finish: 3 Hours 40 Minutes
Servings: 30

- -

2   boxes Betty Crocker® SuperMoist®
    yellow cake mix
Water, vegetable oil and eggs called for on
cake mix boxes
2   containers (1 lb each) Betty Crocker®
    Rich & Creamy vanilla frosting

Red food color
1   fashion doll (11-1/2 inches tall)
1/4 cup Betty Crocker® star-shaped candy decors

- -

1 Heat oven to 325°F. Grease 1 (1-1/2-quart) ovenproof bowl (8 inches across top) and 2 (8-inch) round cake pans with shortening; coat with flour (do not use cooking spray).*

2 In large bowl, make both cake mixes as directed on box, using water, oil and eggs. (Two boxes of cake mix can be made at one time. Do not make more than 2 boxes; do not increase beating time.) Pour 3-1/2 cups batter into 1-1/2-quart bowl and 2-1/2 cups batter into each cake pan.

3 Bake cake pans 35 to 40 minutes and bowl 45 to 50 minutes or until toothpick inserted in center comes out clean. Cool 10 minutes. Remove cakes from pans and bowl; place rounded sides up on cooling racks. Cool completely, about 1 hour.

4 Spoon frosting into large bowl. Stir in enough food color until desired pink color. If necessary, cut off rounded tops of cakes baked in 8-inch pans. Cut 2-inch-diameter hole in center of all 3 cakes. Place one 8-inch cake on serving plate; spread 1/3 cup frosting over top. Top with second 8-inch cake; spread with 1/3 cup frosting. Top with bowl cake.

5 Wrap hair and lower half of doll with plastic wrap. Insert doll into center of cake. Trim side of cake if necessary to make a tapered "skirt."

6 To "crumb-coat" cake, spread thin layer of frosting over side and top of layered cake to seal in crumbs. Freeze 30 to 60 minutes.

7 Fit #24 star tip into decorating bag. Spoon 1/4 cup pink frosting into decorating bag; set aside. Starting at waist of doll, frost cake with downward strokes to make ruffled skirt. Use star tip to cover bodice of doll and add decoration to skirt if desired. Gently press star decors into frosting to decorate neckline and skirt. Unwrap hair.

*Note: Cake can be baked in 3 (8-inch) round cake pans and 1 (1-1/2-quart) ovenproof bowl. Use 3-1/2 cups batter in bowl and 1-2/3 cups batter in each cake pan. Bake cake pans 30 to 35 minutes and bowl 45 to 50 minutes.

High Altitude (3500-6500 ft): Bake cake in bowl 50 to 55 minutes.

Nutritional Info: 1 Serving: Calories 320 (Calories from Fat 120); Total Fat 13g (Saturated Fat 3g, Trans Fat 2.5g); Cholesterol 40mg; Sodium 300mg; Total Carbohydrate 48g (Dietary Fiber 0g, Sugars 33g); Protein 3g. % Daily Value: Vitamin A 0%; Vitamin C 0%; Calcium 6%; Iron 4%. Exchanges: 1 Starch, 2 Other Carbohydrate, 2-1/2 Fat. Carbohydrate Choices: 3.

Betty's Kitchen Tip

• To make fairy princess hat, cut a 3-1/2-inch circle out of pink construction paper. Roll the paper in a cone shape so that the top comes to a point; secure it with tape, and trim the bottom so it is flat. Embellish hat with ribbon and a yellow star candy. For magic wand, attach a yellow candy star and ribbons to a toothpick. Attach wand to hand with tape, if needed.

purse cake

Prep Time: 35 Minutes
Start to Finish: 3 Hours 15 Minutes
Servings: 12

---

1 box Betty Crocker® SuperMoist® cake mix (any flavor)

Water, vegetable oil and eggs called for on cake mix box

1 container (1 lb) Betty Crocker® Rich & Creamy vanilla frosting

Desired food color
1 piece green peelable string licorice
1 jellied ring candy

Assorted small multicolored hard candies

---

1 Heat oven to 350°F (or 325°F for dark or nonstick pans). Spray bottoms and sides of 2 (9-inch) round cake pans with baking spray with flour. Make and bake cake mix as directed on box, using water, oil and eggs. Cool 10 minutes; remove from pans to cooling racks. Cool completely, about 1 hour.

2 Use serrated knife to cut 1/4 off each cake to form a straight edge about 7 inches long, as shown in diagram (discard small pieces of cake or save for another use).

3 Spread about 2 tablespoons frosting on bottom of 1 cake. Place bottom of other cake on frosting, matching cut edges. On serving plate or tray, stand cake with cut side down. Cover; freeze cake for 1 hour or until firm.

4 Tint remaining frosting with food color. Frost cake. Use peelable string licorice for handle and jellied ring candy for clasp. Decorate purse as desired with assorted candies. Store cake loosely covered at room temperature.

High Altitude (3500-6500 ft): Follow High Altitude directions for 2 (9-inch) round cake pans on cake mix box.

Nutritional Info: 1 Serving Frosted Cake (Undecorated): Calories 410 (Calories from Fat 150); Total Fat 16g (Saturated Fat 3.5g, Trans Fat 3.5g); Cholesterol 55mg; Sodium 380mg; Total Carbohydrate 61g (Dietary Fiber 0g, Sugars 42g); Protein 3g. % Daily Value: Vitamin A 0%; Vitamin C 0%; Calcium 6%; Iron 4%. Exchanges: 1 Starch, 3 Other Carbohydrate, 3 Fat. Carbohydrate Choices: 4.

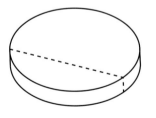

Cut one-fourth off each cake

Stand cake, cut sides down, on tray.

wedding cupcakes

Prep Time: 1 Hour
Start to Finish: 1 Hour 25 Minutes
Servings: 24 cupcakes

- -

Cupcakes
White paper baking cups
- 1 box Betty Crocker® SuperMoist® white cake mix

Water, vegetable oil and egg whites called for on cake mix box
- 2 containers (1 lb each) Betty Crocker® Rich & Creamy creamy white frosting

Decorating Options (all shown at right)
White Chocolate Curls

Pink rose petals

Handmade paper, cut into 8x1-1/4-inch strips

- -

1 Heat oven to 350°F (or 325°F for dark or nonstick pans). Place white paper baking cup in each of 24 regular-size muffin cups. Make and bake cake mix as directed on box for 24 cupcakes, using water, oil and egg whites. Cool in pans 10 minutes. Remove from pans to cooling racks. Cool completely, about 30 minutes.

2 Frost cupcakes with frosting. Choose from these decorating options: Top cupcakes with White Chocolate Curls (see below) or rose petals. Wrap handmade paper around each cupcake; attach with permanent double-stick tape.

3 For optional White Chocolate Curls, place a bar of room-temperature white chocolate on waxed paper. Make curls by pulling a vegetable peeler toward you in long, thin strokes while pressing firmly against the chocolate. (If curls crumble or stay too straight, chocolate may be too cold; placing the heel of your hand on the chocolate will warm it enough to get good curls.) Transfer each curl with a toothpick onto a frosted cupcake or to a waxed paper-lined cookie sheet.

High Altitude (3500-6500 ft): Follow High Altitude directions for cupcakes on box.

Nutritional Info: 1 Frosted Cupcake (Undecorated): Calories 270 (Calories from Fat 100); Total Fat 11g (Saturated Fat 2.5g, Trans Fat 2.5g); Cholesterol 25mg; Sodium 230mg; Total Carbohydrate 42g (Dietary Fiber 0g, Sugars 30g); Protein 1g. % Daily Value: Vitamin A 0%; Vitamin C 0%; Calcium 2%; Iron 2%. Exchanges: 3 Other Carbohydrate, 2 Fat. Carbohydrate Choices: 3.

Betty's Kitchen Tip

• Look for edible flowers and/or rose petals in the produce department of the grocery store. Edible flowers have not been treated with chemicals so they are safe to eat.

key lime cupcakes

Prep Time: 30 Minutes
Start to Finish: 1 Hour 35 Minutes
Servings: 24 cupcakes

Cupcakes

1	box Betty Crocker® SuperMoist® lemon cake mix
1	box (4-serving size) lime-flavored gelatin
3/4	cup water
1/3	cup Key lime juice
1/3	cup vegetable oil
3	eggs
2	or 3 drops green food color, if desired

Glaze

1	cup powdered sugar
2	to 2-1/2 tablespoons Key lime juice

Frosting

1	package (8 oz) cream cheese, softened
1/4	cup butter or margarine, softened
1	teaspoon vanilla
3-1/2	cups powdered sugar

Grated lime peel, if desired

1 Heat oven to 350°F. Place paper baking cup in each of 24 regular-size muffin cups. In large bowl, beat cake mix and gelatin with electric mixer on low speed 30 seconds. Add remaining cupcake ingredients. Beat with electric mixer on low speed 30 seconds; beat on medium speed 2 minutes, scraping bowl as necessary. Divide batter evenly among muffin cups, filling each about 2/3 full.

2 Bake 17 to 22 minutes or until toothpick inserted in center comes out clean. Cool in pan 10 minutes. Remove from pan to cooling rack. With toothpick or wooden skewer, pierce tops of cupcakes in several places.

3 In small bowl, mix 1 cup powdered sugar and enough of the 2 to 2-1/2 tablespoons lime juice until glaze is smooth and thin enough to drizzle. Drizzle and spread glaze over cupcakes. Cool completely, about 30 minutes.

4 In large bowl, beat cream cheese and butter on medium speed until light and fluffy. On low speed, beat in vanilla and 3-1/2 cups powdered sugar until mixed; beat on medium speed until fluffy. Frost cupcakes, mounding and swirling frosting in center. Garnish with lime peel. Store covered in refrigerator.

High Altitude (3500-6500 ft): Bake 19 to 24 minutes.

Nutritional Info: 1 Cupcake: Calories 280 (Calories from Fat 90); Total Fat 10g (Saturated Fat 4.5g, Trans Fat 0.5g); Cholesterol 40mg; Sodium 210mg; Total Carbohydrate 43g (Dietary Fiber 0g, Sugars 34g); Protein 2g. % Daily Value: Vitamin A 4%; Vitamin C 0%; Calcium 4%; Iron 4%. Exchanges: 1/2 Starch, 2-1/2 Other Carbohydrate, 2 Fat. Carbohydrate Choices: 3.

Betty's Kitchen Tip

• You can use fresh or bottled Key lime juice. If that is not available, use regular lime juice.

football cupcake pull-aparts

Prep Time: 40 Minutes
Start to Finish: 1 Hour 45 Minutes
Servings: 24 cupcakes

- 1 box Betty Crocker® SuperMoist® yellow cake mix

Water, vegetable oil and eggs called for on cake mix box

- 2 containers Betty Crocker® Rich & Creamy chocolate frosting
- 1/2 cup candy-coated chocolate candies
- 1 tube (4.25 oz) Betty Crocker® white decorating icing

1 Heat oven to 375°F (350°F for dark or nonstick pans). Place paper baking cup in each of 24 regular-size muffin cups. Make cake batter as directed on cake mix box. Divide batter evenly among muffin cups (about 2/3 full).

2 Bake 20 to 25 minutes or until toothpick inserted in center comes out clean. Cool in pans 10 minutes; remove from pans to cooling racks. Cool completely, about 30 minutes.

3 Spoon frosting into decorating bag with large star tip (size #5). Arrange cupcakes in football shape using 15 of the 24 cupcakes. Pipe thick lines of frosting over football-cupcake shape. Using spatula, spread frosting over cupcakes. Pipe decorative border of chocolate frosting around edge of football. Sprinkle decorative border with candy-coated chocolate candies. Pipe laces with white icing. Frost and decorate remaining cupcakes as desired, and serve alongside football.

High Altitude (3500-6500 ft): No change.

Nutritional Info: 1 Cupcake with Frosting: Calories 300 (Calories from Fat 100); Total Fat 11g (Saturated Fat 3g, Trans Fat 3g); Cholesterol 25mg; Sodium 260mg; Total Carbohydrate 48g (Dietary Fiber 0g, Sugars 35g); Protein 1g. % Daily Value: Vitamin A 0%; Vitamin C 0%; Calcium 4%; Iron 4%. Exchanges: 3 Other Carbohydrate, 2-1/2 Fat. Carbohydrate Choices: 3.

Betty's Kitchen Tips

How-To: Once cake is frosted, gently press together to give cake more of a football shape.

Special Touch: Get in the team spirit! Use candy-coated chocolate candies that represent your team colors.

mini pumpkin cakes

Prep Time: 45 Minutes
Start to Finish: 1 Hour
Servings: 48 mini cupcakes

- -

1 box (18.25 oz) Betty Crocker® SuperMoist® white cake mix

Water, vegetable oil and egg whites called for on cake mix box

2 teaspoons grated orange peel

6 to 8 drops red food color

6 to 8 drops yellow food color

1 container (1 lb) Betty Crocker® Rich & Creamy vanilla frosting

6 drops red food color

8 drops yellow food color

3 tubes (0.68 oz each) Betty Crocker® black decorating gel

3 rolls Betty Crocker® Fruit by the Foot® chewy fruit snack, any green variety (from 4.5-oz box), or small green candies

- -

1 Heat oven to 350°F. Place mini paper baking cup in each of 48 mini muffin cups. In large bowl, beat cake mix, water, oil and egg whites on low speed 30 seconds, then on medium speed 2 minutes, scraping bowl occasionally. Stir in orange peel and 6 to 8 drops each red and yellow food colors. Divide batter evenly among baking cups, about 1 heaping tablespoon each. Bake 10 to 12 minutes or until toothpick inserted in center comes out clean. Cool in pan 5 minutes; remove from pan and cool completely, about 10 minutes.

2 In medium bowl, stir together frosting, 6 drops red food color and 8 drops yellow food color. Frost top of each cupcake. Using black gel, draw two triangles on each cupcake to look like pumpkin eyes and draw a circle to look like a mouth.

3 Cut fruit snack into 48 (1-inch) pieces; tightly roll each piece to make a stem for each pumpkin. Place the stem at top of each pumpkin.

High Altitude (3500-6500 ft): No change.

Nutritional Info: 1 Mini Cupcake: Calories 100 (Calories from Fat 35); Total Fat 3.5g (Saturated Fat 1g, Trans Fat 1g); Cholesterol 0mg; Sodium 100mg; Total Carbohydrate 17g (Dietary Fiber 0g, Sugars 11g); Protein 0g. % Daily Value: Vitamin A 0%; Vitamin C 0%; Calcium 0%; Iron 0%. Exchanges: 1 Other Carbohydrate, 1 Fat. Carbohydrate Choices: 1.

Betty's Kitchen Tip

- If you don't have enough pans to bake all 48 mini cupcakes at once, bake 1 batch. Refrigerate remaining batter until you are ready to bake it.

cookies
GALORE

p. 270

255

232

271

black-and-white coconut macaroons

Prep Time: 1 Hour
Start to Finish: 2 Hours 25 Minutes
Servings: 40 macaroons

Cookies

3 cups lightly packed shredded coconut
1 pouch (1 lb 1.5 oz) Betty Crocker® sugar cookie mix
1/2 cup sweetened condensed milk (not evaporated)
1/2 to 1 teaspoon almond extract

1 teaspoon cream of tartar
2 egg whites

Glaze

2 cups semisweet chocolate chips (12 oz)
1 tablespoon shortening
1/3 cup macadamia nuts, finely chopped

1 Heat oven to 350°F. Line cookie sheets with cooking parchment paper. Using food processor, process coconut until finely ground.

2 In large bowl, stir together coconut and cookie mix. Add sweetened condensed milk and almond extract; mix well. Mixture will be crumbly. Stir in cream of tartar.

3 In small bowl, beat egg whites with electric mixer on medium speed until soft peaks form. Fold egg whites into cookie mixture. Using 1-1/2 tablespoon-size cookie scoop, firmly pack with coconut mixture and place mound on cookie sheet. Repeat with remaining mixture, placing mounds 2 inches apart. Press each mound to flatten slightly.

4 Bake 8 to 10 minutes or until edges just begin to lightly brown (do not overbake). Cool 2 minutes; remove from cookie sheets to cooling racks. Cool completely, about 15 minutes.

5 In 1-quart nonstick saucepan, melt chocolate chips and shortening over medium heat, stirring until chocolate is melted. Dip each cooled cookie halfway into melted chocolate, letting excess drip off. Place on sheet of parchment paper; sprinkle chocolate portion with nuts. Let stand until chocolate sets, about 1 hour. Store between sheets of parchment paper in tightly covered container.

High Altitude (3500-6500 ft): No change.

Nutritional Info: 1 Macaroon: Calories 160 (Calories from Fat 70); Total Fat 7g (Saturated Fat 4.5g, Trans Fat 0.5g); Cholesterol 0mg; Sodium 65mg; Total Carbohydrate 20g (Dietary Fiber 1g, Sugars 14g); Protein 1g. % Daily Value: Vitamin A 0%; Vitamin C 0%; Calcium 0%; Iron 4%. Exchanges: 1-1/2 Other Carbohydrate, 1-1/2 Fat. Carbohydrate Choices: 1.

triple chippers

Prep Time: 15 Minutes
Start to Finish: 45 Minutes
Servings: About 26 cookies

EASY

1-1/2	cups packed brown sugar
1	cup granulated sugar
1	cup butter or margarine, softened
1	cup shortening
2	teaspoons vanilla
2	eggs
3-3/4	cups Gold Medal® all-purpose flour
2	teaspoons baking soda
1	teaspoon salt
1-1/2	cups white vanilla baking chips
1/2	cup butterscotch chips
1	cup semisweet chocolate chips (6 oz)

1 Heat oven to 350°F. In large bowl, mix sugars, butter, shortening, vanilla and eggs with electric mixer on medium speed until creamy, or mix with spoon. Stir in flour, baking soda and salt. Stir in white, butterscotch and chocolate chips.

2 Onto ungreased large cookie sheet, drop dough by 1/4 cupfuls about 3 inches apart.

3 Bake 12 to 15 minutes or until light golden brown. Cool 4 minutes; remove from cookie sheet to cooling rack.

High Altitude (3500-6500 ft): No change.

Nutritional Info: 1 Cookie: Calories 410 (Calories from Fat 200); Total Fat 22g (Saturated Fat 11g, Trans Fat 1.5g); Cholesterol 35mg; Sodium 280mg; Total Carbohydrate 49g (Dietary Fiber 1g, Sugars 34g); Protein 3g. % Daily Value: Vitamin A 4%; Vitamin C 0%; Calcium 4%; Iron 6%. Exchanges: 1 Starch, 2 Other Carbohydrate, 4-1/2 Fat. Carbohydrate Choices: 3.

Betty's Kitchen Tips

How-To: To make drop cookies the same size and shape, use a spring-handled cookie or ice cream scoop. A #16 scoop holds 1/4 cup of dough.

Substitution: If you don't have butterscotch chips on hand, peanut butter chips make a tasty treat, too.

white chocolate-dipped cherry thins

Prep Time: 1 Hour 15 Minutes
Start to Finish: 4 Hours 30 Minutes
Servings: About 6 dozen cookies

1 cup sugar
1 cup butter or margarine, softened
1 teaspoon vanilla
1 teaspoon almond extract
1 egg
3 cups Gold Medal® all-purpose flour
1/2 teaspoon baking soda

1/2 teaspoon salt
1 container (8 oz) red candied cherries, finely chopped (about 1 cup)
1/4 cup chopped walnuts
1 package (20 oz) vanilla-flavored candy coating (almond bark)
Edible glitter, if desired

1 In large bowl, beat sugar, butter, vanilla, almond extract and egg with electric mixer on medium speed until well blended. On low speed, beat in flour, baking soda and salt. Stir in cherries and walnuts.

2 Divide dough in half. Shape each half into a roll, about 8 inches long and 2 inches in diameter. Wrap each roll in plastic wrap; refrigerate about 2 hours or until firm.

3 Heat oven to 375°F. Cut rolls into 1/8-inch slices. On ungreased cookie sheets, place slices 2 inches apart. Bake 6 to 8 minutes or until light brown. Cool slightly; remove from cookie sheets to cooling racks. Cool completely, about 15 minutes.

4 Meanwhile, in medium microwavable bowl, microwave candy coating as directed on package until melted and smooth. Dip about 1/3 of each cookie at an angle into coating, allowing excess coating to drip back into bowl. Place on waxed paper; sprinkle with glitter. Let stand about 1 hour or until coating is set.

High Altitude (3500-6500 ft): No change.

Nutritional Info: 1 Cookie: Calories 100 (Calories from Fat 50); Total Fat 5g (Saturated Fat 3g, Trans Fat 0g); Cholesterol 10mg; Sodium 50mg; Total Carbohydrate 12g (Dietary Fiber 0g, Sugars 8g); Protein 1g. % Daily Value: Vitamin A 0%; Vitamin C 0%; Calcium 0%; Iron 0%. Exchanges: 1 Other Carbohydrate, 1 Fat. Carbohydrate Choices: 1

Betty's Kitchen Tips

Time-Saver: Keep a roll or two of this cookie dough on hand ready to bake. Cookie dough can be covered and refrigerated up to 24 hours before baking. Dough can also be frozen in an airtight container up to 9 months. Thaw just until soft enough to slice.

Success Hint: Candy coating may set up while you are dipping the cookies. Just heat again in the microwave on High in 10-second intervals.

cinnamon-chocolate chip butterballs

Prep Time: 35 Minutes
Start to Finish: 1 Hour 25 Minutes
Servings: 3 dozen cookies

- 1-3/4 cups Gold Medal® all-purpose flour
- 1/2 cup powdered sugar
- 1-1/2 teaspoons ground cinnamon
- 1/2 teaspoon salt
- 1 cup cold butter
- 1 cup miniature semisweet chocolate chips
- 1 teaspoon vanilla
- 1/2 cup powdered sugar
- 1 teaspoon ground cinnamon

1 Heat oven to 400°F. In large bowl, mix flour, 1/2 cup powdered sugar, 1-1/2 teaspoons cinnamon and the salt. Cut in butter, using pastry blender or fork, until mixture looks like coarse crumbs. Stir in chocolate chips and vanilla (mixture will be crumbly).

2 Using hands, shape dough into 1-inch balls. On ungreased cookie sheets, place balls 1 inch apart.

3 Bake 6 to 8 minutes or until set but not brown. Immediately remove from cookie sheets to cooling racks. Cool slightly, about 20 minutes.

4 In small bowl, stir together 1/2 cup powdered sugar and 1 teaspoon cinnamon. Roll cookies in sugar mixture, shaking off excess back into bowl. Cool completely, about 30 minutes.

High Altitude (3500-6500 ft): No change.

Nutritional Info: 1 Cookie: Calories 110 (Calories from Fat 60); Total Fat 7g (Saturated Fat 4g, Trans Fat 0g); Cholesterol 15mg; Sodium 70mg; Total Carbohydrate 11g (Dietary Fiber 0g, Sugars 6g); Protein 1g. % Daily Value: Vitamin A 4%; Vitamin C 0%; Calcium 0%; Iron 2%. Exchanges: 1/2 Other Carbohydrate, 1-1/2 Fat. Carbohydrate Choices: 1.

Betty's Kitchen Tip

- If cookie dough sticks to your palms, occasionally wet your hands with cold water while shaping the dough into balls.

chocolate-peanut butter cookie treats

Prep Time: 1 Hour
Start to Finish: 1 Hour 15 Minutes
Servings: About 3 dozen cookies

Cookies

1	pouch (1 lb 1.5 oz) Betty Crocker® peanut butter cookie mix
3	tablespoons vegetable oil
1	tablespoon water
1	egg

Coating

1	cup semisweet chocolate chips (6 oz)
1/4	cup butter or margarine
1/4	cup peanut butter
1	teaspoon vanilla
1-1/2	to 2 cups powdered sugar

1 Heat oven to 375°F. In large bowl, stir cookie mix, oil, water and egg until soft dough forms.

2 Shape dough into 1-inch balls. On ungreased cookie sheets, place balls 2 inches apart.

3 Bake 8 to 9 minutes or until edges are light golden brown. Cool 2 minutes; remove from cookie sheets to cooling racks. Cool completely, about 15 minutes.

4 In small microwaveable bowl, microwave chocolate chips, butter and peanut butter uncovered on High 1 minute to 1 minute 30 seconds; stir until smooth. Stir in vanilla.

5 Place 1-1/2 cups powdered sugar in 1-gallon resealable food-storage plastic bag; set aside. Place 12 cooled cookies in large bowl. Pour 1/3 of chocolate mixture over cookies in bowl. Using rubber spatula, toss cookies gently to coat. Place cookies in bag with powdered sugar; seal bag. Gently turn bag to coat cookies. Remove cookies from bag to cooling rack to set. Repeat with 12 more cookies and 1/2 of remaining chocolate mixture; repeat again until all cookies are coated, adding additional powdered sugar to bag as needed.

High Altitude (3500-6500 ft): No change.

Nutritional Info: 1 Cookie: Calories 140 (Calories from Fat 60); Total Fat 7g (Saturated Fat 2.5g, Trans Fat 0g); Cholesterol 10mg; Sodium 90mg; Total Carbohydrate 18g (Dietary Fiber 0g, Sugars 13g); Protein 2g. % Daily Value: Vitamin A 0%; Vitamin C 0%; Calcium 0%; Iron 2%. Exchanges: 1/2 Starch, 1/2 Other Carbohydrate, 1-1/2 Fat. Carbohydrate Choices: 1.

the ultimate spritz

Prep Time: 1 Hour 5 Minutes
Start to Finish: 1 Hour 5 Minutes
Servings: About 5 dozen cookies

- -

    1   cup butter or margarine, softened
  1/2 cup sugar
    1   egg
2-1/2 cups Gold Medal® all-purpose flour
  1/4 teaspoon salt
  1/4 teaspoon almond extract or vanilla
Few drops food color, if desired
Colored sugars, red cinnamon candies, candy sprinkles, candy-coated miniature chocolate baking bits, if desired

- -

1 Heat oven to 400°F. In large bowl, beat butter and sugar with electric mixer on medium speed, or mix with spoon. Stir in flour, salt, egg, almond extract and food color.

2 Fit desired disk in cookie press, following manufacturer's directions. Place dough in cookie press. On ungreased cookie sheets, form desired shapes. Decorate as desired.

3 Bake 5 to 8 minutes or until set but not brown. Immediately remove from cookie sheets to cooling racks. To decorate cookies after baking, use a drop of corn syrup to attach decorations to cookies.

High Altitude (3500-6500 ft): No change.

Nutritional Info: 1 Cookie: Calories 50 (Calories from Fat 30); Total Fat 3g (Saturated Fat 2g, Trans Fat 0g); Cholesterol 10mg; Sodium 35mg; Total Carbohydrate 6g (Dietary Fiber 0g, Sugars 2g); Protein 0g. % Daily Value: Vitamin A 0%; Vitamin C 0%; Calcium 0%; Iron 0%. Exchanges: 1/2 Other Carbohydrate, 1/2 Fat. Carbohydrate Choices: 1/2.

LOW FAT

Betty's Kitchen Tips

Variation: Make It Your Way Chocolate Spritz are easily made by stirring 2 ounces unsweetened chocolate, melted and cooled, into the butter-sugar mixture.

Did you know? The name for these cookies comes from the German word spritzen, meaning "to squirt" because the soft dough is squirted or pushed through a cookie press to make fancy designs.

Variation: To make Spice Spritz, stir in 1 teaspoon ground cinnamon, 1/2 teaspoon ground nutmeg and 1/4 teaspoon ground allspice with the flour.

espresso thumbprint cookies

Prep Time: 1 Hour
Start to Finish: 1 Hour 15 Minutes
Servings: About 3-1/2 dozen cookies

Cookies

3/4	cup sugar
3/4	cup butter or margarine, softened
1/2	teaspoon vanilla
1	egg
1-3/4	cups Gold Medal® all-purpose flour
3	tablespoons unsweetened baking cocoa

1/4	teaspoon salt

Crushed hard peppermint candies, if desired

Espresso Filling

1/4	cup whipping cream
2	teaspoons instant espresso coffee granules
1	cup milk chocolate chips
1	tablespoon coffee-flavored liqueur, if desired

1 Heat oven to 350°F. In large bowl, beat sugar, butter, vanilla and egg with electric mixer on medium speed, or mix with spoon, until well blended. Stir in flour, cocoa and salt until dough forms.

2 Shape dough by rounded teaspoonfuls into 1-inch balls. On ungreased cookie sheets, place balls about 2 inches apart. Press thumb or end of wooden spoon into center of each cookie, but do not press all the way to cookie sheet.

3 Bake 7 to 11 minutes or until edges are firm. If necessary, quickly remake indentations with end of wooden spoon. Immediately remove from cookie sheets to cooling racks. Cool completely, about 30 minutes.

4 Meanwhile, in 1-quart saucepan, mix whipping cream and instant coffee. Heat over medium heat, stirring occasionally, until steaming and coffee is dissolved. Remove from heat; stir in chocolate chips until melted. Stir in liqueur. Cool about 10 minutes or until thickened.

5 Spoon rounded 1/2 teaspoon espresso filling into indentation in each cookie. Top with crushed candies.

High Altitude (3500-6500 ft): No change.

Nutritional Info: 1 Cookie: Calories 90 (Calories from Fat 45); Total Fat 5g (Saturated Fat 3.5g, Trans Fat 0g); Cholesterol 15mg; Sodium 45mg; Total Carbohydrate 10g (Dietary Fiber 0g, Sugars 6g); Protein 1g. % Daily Value: Vitamin A 2%; Vitamin C 0%; Calcium 0%; Iron 2%. Exchanges: 1/2 Starch, 1 Fat. Carbohydrate Choices: 1/2.

chocolate chip and peanut butter cookies

Prep Time: 55 Minutes
Start to Finish: 1 Hour 10 Minutes
Servings: About 4 dozen cookies

1	box Betty Crocker® SuperMoist® yellow cake mix
1-1/4	cups crunchy peanut butter
1/4	cup packed brown sugar
1/4	cup butter or margarine, softened
2	eggs
1	bag (11.5 oz) milk chocolate chips (2 cups)

1 Heat oven to 350°F (or 325°F for dark or nonstick cookie sheets). In large bowl, beat cake mix, peanut butter, brown sugar, butter and eggs with electric mixer on medium speed until well blended. Stir in chocolate chips.

2 On ungreased cookie sheets, drop dough by rounded tablespoonfuls 2 inches apart.

3 Bake 9 to 11 minutes or until edges are set (centers will be soft). Cool 1 minute; remove from cookie sheets to cooling racks.

High Altitude (3500-6500 ft): After dropping dough on cookie sheets, flatten dough slightly with palm of hand.

Nutritional Info: 1 Cookie: Calories 140 (Calories from Fat 70); Total Fat 7g (Saturated Fat 3g, Trans Fat 0g); Cholesterol 15mg; Sodium 115mg; Total Carbohydrate 15g (Dietary Fiber 0g, Sugars 10g); Protein 3g. % Daily Value: Vitamin A 0%; Vitamin C 0%; Calcium 4%; Iron 2%. Exchanges: 1 Starch, 1-1/2 Fat. Carbohydrate Choices: 1.

Betty's Kitchen Tip

• To soften butter, let it stand at room temperature for 30 to 45 minutes.

spiced chocolate chip cookies

Prep Time: 20 Minutes
Start to Finish: 1 Hour 15 Minutes
Servings: 5 dozen cookies

1	cup butter or margarine, softened
1-1/2	cups packed brown sugar
1	teaspoon vanilla
1	egg
2	cups Gold Medal® all-purpose flour
1	teaspoon baking soda

1-1/2	teaspoons ground cinnamon
1	teaspoon ground ginger
1/2	teaspoon salt
1	package (12 oz) semisweet chocolate chips (2 cups)
1	cup chopped walnuts

1 Heat oven to 375°F. In large bowl, beat butter, brown sugar, vanilla and egg with electric mixer on medium speed, or mix with spoon. On low speed, beat in remaining ingredients except chocolate chips and walnuts. Stir in chocolate chips and walnuts.

2 On ungreased cookie sheet, drop dough by rounded teaspoonfuls about 1 inch apart.

3 Bake 7 to 9 minutes or until light brown (centers will be soft). Cool 1 to 2 minutes; remove from cookie sheet to cooling rack.

High Altitude (3500-6500 ft): No change.

Nutritional Info: 1 Cookie: Calories 110 (Calories from Fat 60); Total Fat 6g (Saturated Fat 3g, Trans Fat 0g); Cholesterol 10mg; Sodium 65mg; Total Carbohydrate 13g (Dietary Fiber 0g, Sugars 8g); Protein 1g. % Daily Value: Vitamin A 2%; Vitamin C 0%; Calcium 0%; Iron 2%. Exchanges: 1 Other Carbohydrate, 1 Fat. Carbohydrate Choices: 1.

Betty's Kitchen Tip

• Other nuts, such as pecans, can be used instead of walnuts.

chocolate peanut butter cloud cookies

Prep Time: 40 Minutes
Start to Finish: 1 Hour 20 Minutes
Servings: 5 dozen cookies

· ·

Cookies

1	box (18.25 oz) Betty Crocker® SuperMoist® chocolate fudge cake mix
3/4	cup creamy peanut butter
1/3	cup water
1	teaspoon vanilla
4	eggs
1-1/2	cups semisweet chocolate chips

Frosting

1-1/2	containers (12 oz each) Betty Crocker® Whipped fluffy white frosting
3/4	cup creamy peanut butter
2	teaspoons milk

· ·

1 Heat oven to 375°F. Spray cookie sheet with cooking spray.

2 In large bowl, beat cake mix, 3/4 cup peanut butter, the water, vanilla and eggs on medium speed about 2 minutes or until blended. Gently stir in chocolate chips. Onto cookie sheet, drop dough by rounded teaspoonfuls about 2 inches apart.

3 Bake 7 to 9 minutes or until set. Cool 1 minute; remove from cookie sheet to cooling rack. Cool completely, about 10 minutes.

4 In medium bowl, stir together frosting ingredients. Frost cookies with frosting.

High Altitude (3500-6500 ft): No change.

Nutritional Info: 1 Cookie: Calories 140 (Calories from Fat 60); Total Fat 7g (Saturated Fat 2.5g, Trans Fat 0.5g); Cholesterol 15mg; Sodium 115mg; Total Carbohydrate 16g (Dietary Fiber 0g, Sugars 11g); Protein 2g. % Daily Value: Vitamin A 0%; Vitamin C 0%; Calcium 0%; Iron 4%. Exchanges: 1/2 Starch, 1/2 Other Carbohydrate, 1-1/2 Fat. Carbohydrate Choices: 1.

Betty's Kitchen Tips

How-To: For a decorative touch, spoon frosting into pastry bag fitted with star tip, then squirt on each cookie. You can also use a star tip inside a food-storage plastic bag!

Success Hint: The secret ingredient in this recipe, cake mix, makes these cookies very light and the perfect chocolate base for the creamy frosting.

glazed toffee bonbons

Prep Time: 1 Hour 10 Minutes
Start to Finish: 1 Hour 30 Minutes
Servings: About 4 dozen cookies

Cookies

1/2	cup butter or margarine, softened
1/2	cup packed brown sugar
1/2	teaspoon vanilla
1	egg
1-3/4	cups Gold Medal® all-purpose flour
1/4	teaspoon baking soda
1/4	teaspoon salt

3	bars (1.4 oz each) chocolate-covered English toffee candy, finely chopped

Glaze

1/4	cup butter or margarine
1/2	cup packed brown sugar
3	tablespoons milk
1-1/3	cups powdered sugar
1/3	cup semisweet chocolate chips
1/3	cup white vanilla baking chips

1 Heat oven to 325°F. In large bowl, beat 1/2 cup butter, 1/2 cup brown sugar, the vanilla and egg with electric mixer on medium speed until light and fluffy. On low speed, beat in flour, baking soda and salt. Reserve 1/3 of the chopped candy for garnish. Stir remaining chopped candy into dough. Shape dough into 1-inch balls. On ungreased cookie sheets, place balls 1 inch apart.

2 Bake 11 to 14 minutes or until edges start to brown and tops of cookies feel set when tapped. Place cooling racks on waxed paper. Immediately remove cookies from cookie sheets to cooling racks.

3 Meanwhile, in 1-quart saucepan, heat 1/4 cup butter, 1/2 cup brown sugar and 2 tablespoons of the milk over medium-low heat, stirring frequently, until mixture just comes to a boil and sugar is dissolved. Stir in powdered sugar; beat with wire whisk if necessary to remove lumps. Immediately dip tops of cookies into glaze, or spread glaze on tops of cookies. (Cookies don't need to be completely cooled, just firm and set.) Place on rack; let stand about 10 minutes until glaze is set. If glaze starts to set in saucepan, reheat over medium-low heat and beat with whisk until softened.

4 Place chocolate chips and vanilla chips in separate small microwavable bowls. Microwave each on High 1-1/2 to 2 minutes, stirring every 30 seconds, until melted and smooth. Using tip of spoon, drizzle each flavor generously over cookies. Sprinkle with remaining candy. Refrigerate 20 minutes to set quickly.

High Altitude (3500-6500 ft): No change.

Nutritional Info: 1 Cookie: Calories 100 (Calories from Fat 40); Total Fat 4.5g (Saturated Fat 3g, Trans Fat 0g); Cholesterol 15mg; Sodium 55mg; Total Carbohydrate 15g (Dietary Fiber 0g, Sugars 11g); Protein 1g. % Daily Value: Vitamin A 2%; Vitamin C 0%; Calcium 0%; Iron 0%. Exchanges: 1 Other Carbohydrate, 1 Fat. Carbohydrate Choices: 1.

Betty's Kitchen Tip

• You don't need to wait to drizzle the second melted chip mixture over the first melted chip mixture—just be sure to not touch the soft melted chocolate.

candy corn cookies

Prep Time: 1 Hour
Start to Finish: 2 Hours 30 Minutes
Servings: About 9-1/2 dozen cookies

- 1 pouch (1 lb 1.5 oz) Betty Crocker® sugar cookie mix
- 1/3 cup butter or margarine, melted
- 1 egg

Orange paste food color
- 2 oz semisweet chocolate, melted, cooled

1 Line 8x4-inch loaf pan with waxed paper, extending paper up over sides of pan. In medium bowl, stir cookie mix, melted butter and egg until soft dough forms.

2 On work surface, place 3/4 cup dough. Knead desired amount of orange food color into dough until color is uniform. Press dough evenly in bottom of pan.

3 Divide remaining dough in half. Gently press one half of remaining dough into pan on top of orange dough. On work surface, knead chocolate into remaining dough until color is uniform. Press over plain dough in pan, pressing gently to edge of pan. Refrigerate 1 1/2 to 2 hours or until firm.

4 Heat oven to 375°F. Remove dough from pan. Cut crosswise into 1/4-inch slices. Cut each slice into 5 wedges. On ungreased cookie sheet, place 1 inch apart.

5 Bake 7 to 9 minutes or until cookies are set and edges are very light golden brown. Cool 1 minute; remove from cookie sheet. Cool completely. Store in tightly covered container.

High Altitude (3500-6500 ft): No change.

Nutritional Info: 1 Cookie: Calories 25 (Calories from Fat 10); Total Fat 1g (Saturated Fat 0.5g, Trans Fat 0g); Cholesterol 0mg; Sodium 15mg; Total Carbohydrate 4g (Dietary Fiber 0g, Sugars 2g); Protein 0g. % Daily Value: Vitamin A 0%; Vitamin C 0%; Calcium 0%; Iron 0%. Exchanges: 1/2 Other Carbohydrate. Carbohydrate Choices: 0.

scary cat cookies

Prep Time: 30 Minutes
Start to Finish: 1 Hour 15 Minutes
Servings: About 15 cookies

3	oz semisweet baking chocolate
1	cup butter, softened
1/2	cup sugar
2-1/4	cups Gold Medal® all-purpose flour
1	teaspoon vanilla
1	egg
1	tube (4.25 oz) Betty Crocker® white decorating icing

Yellow candy sprinkles

15	miniature candy-coated chocolate baking bits
1	package pull-apart yellow licorice twists, cut into 1-inch pieces
1	package pull-apart pink licorice twists, cut into tiny pieces

1 Heat oven to 350°F. Grease cookie sheets.

2 In 1-quart saucepan, melt chocolate over low heat, stirring constantly. In large bowl, beat butter and sugar with electric mixer on medium speed, or mix with spoon. Stir in melted chocolate, flour, vanilla and egg.

3 Shape dough into 30 (1-inch) balls. Pull a little bit of dough from each of 15 balls to make tails; set aside. Cut about 1/4-inch slit in same balls, using scissors. Separate dough at slit for cat's ears. On cookie sheets, place balls about 2 inches apart. Place remaining balls below each cat head on cookie sheets for body of each. Shape small pieces of dough into 15 (2-1/2-inch) ropes. Place end of rope under each body.

4 Bake 12 to 14 minutes or until set. Remove from cookie sheets to cooling racks. Cool 30 minutes. Use icing to attach sprinkles for eyes and baking bits for noses. Add yellow licorice pieces for whiskers and pink licorice pieces for tongues.

High Altitude (3500-6500 ft): No change.

Nutritional Info: 1 Cookie: Calories 240 (Calories from Fat 130); Total Fat 15g (Saturated Fat 9g, Trans Fat 0g); Cholesterol 45mg; Sodium 90mg; Total Carbohydrate 25g (Dietary Fiber 1g, Sugars 10g); Protein 2g. % Daily Value: Vitamin A 8%; Vitamin C 0%; Calcium 0%; Iron 6%. Exchanges: 1/2 Starch, 1 Other Carbohydrate, 3 Fat. Carbohydrate Choices: 1-1/2.

Betty's Kitchen Tips

Substitution: Instead of greasing the cookie sheets, line them with parchment paper.

How-To: You can melt the chocolate in the microwave instead of a saucepan, if you like. Follow directions on the box.

Success Hint: Use a small dab of chocolate frosting, peanut butter or melted chocolate to adhere the candy to the cats' faces.

chocolate-peppermint shortbread

Prep Time: 15 Minutes
Start to Finish: 1 Hour 10 Minutes
Servings: 32 cookies

EASY

Shortbread

1	cup butter or margarine, softened
1/2	cup granulated sugar
4	oz bittersweet baking chocolate, melted, cooled
1/2	teaspoon peppermint extract
2-1/4	cups Gold Medal® all-purpose flour
1/3	cup unsweetened baking cocoa

Glaze and Topping

1/2	cup powdered sugar
2	tablespoons unsweetened baking cocoa
1 to 2	tablespoons milk
2	tablespoons chopped miniature peppermint candy canes

1 Heat oven to 325°F. Spray 2 (9-inch) glass pie plates with cooking spray.

2 In large bowl, beat butter, granulated sugar, chocolate and peppermint extract with electric mixer on medium speed until light and fluffy. On low speed, beat in flour and 1/3 cup cocoa. Divide dough in half. With lightly floured hands, press dough evenly in pie plates.

3 Bake 22 to 24 minutes or until edges just begin to pull away from sides of pie plates. Cool in pie plates 5 minutes. Carefully cut each round into 16 wedges. Cool completely in pie plates on cooling rack, about 30 minutes.

4 In small bowl, mix powdered sugar, 2 tablespoons cocoa and enough of the milk until glaze is smooth and thin enough to drizzle. Drizzle glaze over wedges; sprinkle with candies.

High Altitude (3500-6500 ft): No change.

Nutritional Info: 1 Cookie: Calories 140 (Calories from Fat 70); Total Fat 8g (Saturated Fat 5g, Trans Fat 0g); Cholesterol 15mg; Sodium 45mg; Total Carbohydrate 15g (Dietary Fiber 1g, Sugars 7g); Protein 1g. % Daily Value: Vitamin A 4%; Vitamin C 0%; Calcium 0%; Iron 6%. Exchanges: 1 Other Carbohydrate, 1-1/2 Fat. Carbohydrate Choices: 1.

Betty's Kitchen Tips

Success Hint: Cut the rounds into wedges while they are warm, but do not remove them from the pie plates until they are completely cool so they won't break.

Special Touch: For the best red color, look for candy canes that have bright red striping. The round peppermint candies have a larger proportion of white candy to the red color.

cherry tea cakes

Prep Time: 1 Hour 10 Minutes
Start to Finish: 1 Hour 40 Minutes
Servings: About 5 dozen cookies

1	cup powdered sugar
1	cup butter or margarine, softened
2	teaspoons maraschino cherry liquid
1/2	teaspoon almond extract
3 or 4	drops red food color
2-1/4	cups Gold Medal® all-purpose flour
1/2	teaspoon salt
1/2	cup drained maraschino cherries, chopped
1/2	cup white vanilla baking chips

1. Heat oven to 350°F. In large bowl, beat powdered sugar, butter, cherry liquid, almond extract and food color with electric mixer on medium speed until blended. On low speed, beat in flour and salt. Stir in cherries.

2. Shape dough into 1-inch balls. On ungreased cookie sheets, place balls 2 inches apart.

3. Bake 8 to 10 minutes or until edges are light golden brown. Remove from cookie sheets to cooling racks. Cool 20 to 30 minutes.

4. In 1-quart resealable freezer plastic bag, place baking chips; seal bag. Microwave on High 35 to 50 seconds, squeezing chips in bag every 15 seconds, until chips are melted and smooth. Cut small tip from bottom corner of bag; drizzle melted chips over cookies.

High Altitude (3500-6500 ft): No change.

Nutritional Info: 1 Cookie: Calories 60 (Calories from Fat 35); Total Fat 3.5g (Saturated Fat 2.5g, Trans Fat 0g); Cholesterol 10mg; Sodium 45mg; Total Carbohydrate 7g (Dietary Fiber 0g, Sugars 4g); Protein 0g.% Daily Value: Vitamin A 0%; Vitamin C 0%; Calcium 0%; Iron 0%. Exchanges: 1/2 Other Carbohydrate, 1/2 Fat. Carbohydrate Choices: 1/2.

cherry-chocolate cookie cups

Prep Time: 45 Minutes
Start to Finish: 1 Hour 30 Minutes
Servings: 48 cookies

1	pouch (1 lb 1.5 oz) Betty Crocker® sugar cookie mix
1/3	cup unsweetened baking cocoa
1/2	cup butter or margarine, softened
2	tablespoons water
1	egg

1	bag (12 oz) white vanilla baking chips
1/4	cup whipping cream
1/4	cup amaretto
1/2	cup finely chopped candied cherries

Red decorator sugar crystals or 8 candied cherries, each cut into 6 pieces

1 Heat oven to 350°F. Lightly spray 48 mini muffin cups with cooking spray. In medium bowl, stir cookie mix and cocoa until well mixed. Stir in butter, water and egg until soft dough forms.

2 Shape dough into 48 (1-inch) balls. (If dough is sticky, use moistened fingers.) Press 1 ball into bottom and up side of each muffin cup.

3 Bake 8 to 9 minutes or until edges are set. Gently press end of handle of wooden spoon into bottom and against side of each cookie cup to flatten, being careful not to

make holes in dough. Bake 2 to 3 minutes longer or until bottom is set. Cool in pan on cooling rack 20 to 30 minutes.

4 Meanwhile, in medium microwavable bowl, mix baking chips and cream. Microwave on High 30 seconds; stir. Microwave 20 to 30 seconds longer or until mixture is smooth and chips are melted. Stir in amaretto and chopped cherries. Let stand 10 to 15 minutes until slightly thickened; stir.

5 Using tip of knife or metal spatula, lift cookie cups out of pan, gently twisting and lifting up; place on cooling racks. Repress centers with spoon if necessary. Spoon about 1-1/2 teaspoons cherry mixture into each cup. Sprinkle with red sugar or top with cherry piece.

High Altitude (3500-6500 ft): No change.

Nutritional Info: 1 Cookie: Calories 110 (Calories from Fat 50); Total Fat 5g (Saturated Fat 3g, Trans Fat 0g); Cholesterol 10mg; Sodium 60mg; Total Carbohydrate 14g (Dietary Fiber 0g, Sugars 10g); Protein 1g. % Daily Value: Vitamin A 0%; Vitamin C 0%; Calcium 0%; Iron 0%. Exchanges: 1 Other Carbohydrate, 1 Fat. Carbohydrate Choices: 1.

Betty's Kitchen Tip

• Don't like amaretto? Orange-flavored liqueur also tastes great. Try your favorite flavor of liqueur, or omit it.

orange cream cookies

Prep Time: 45 Minutes
Start to Finish: 45 Minutes
Servings: 3 dozen cookies

- 1 pouch (1 lb 1.5 oz) Betty Crocker® sugar cookie mix
- 3 tablespoons butter or margarine, melted
- 1 teaspoon orange extract
- 1 teaspoon vanilla
- 1 egg
- 5 drops yellow food color
- 2 drops red food color
- 1 bag (12 oz) white vanilla baking chips (2 cups)

1. Heat oven to 350°F. In large bowl, stir all ingredients except baking chips until soft dough forms. Stir in baking chips.

2. On ungreased cookie sheets, drop dough with 1-1/2 tablespoon-size cookie scoop or by rounded tablespoonfuls about 2 inches apart.

3. Bake 9 to 10 minutes or just until dough is set (do not overbake). Cool 1 minute; remove from cookie sheets to cooling racks.

High Altitude (3500-6500 ft): No change.

Nutritional Info: 1 Cookie: Calories 120 (Calories from Fat 45); Total Fat 5g (Saturated Fat 3g, Trans Fat 0.5g); Cholesterol 10mg; Sodium 70mg; Total Carbohydrate 16g (Dietary Fiber 0g, Sugars 12g); Protein 1g. % Daily Value: Vitamin A 0%; Vitamin C 0%; Calcium 0%; Iron 0%. Exchanges: 1/2 Starch, 1/2 Other Carbohydrate, 1 Fat. Carbohydrate Choices: 1.

Betty's Kitchen Tip

• To make lemon cookies, substitute lemon extract for the orange extract and eliminate the 2 drops of red food color.

caramel macchiato thumbprints

Prep Time: 55 Minutes
Start to Finish: 1 Hour 25 Minutes
Servings: 3 dozen cookies

---

2   teaspoons instant espresso coffee powder or granules
1   tablespoon hot water
1   pouch (1 lb 1.5 oz) Betty Crocker® sugar cookie mix
1/4   cup Gold Medal® all-purpose flour
1/2   cup butter or margarine, melted

2   teaspoons vanilla
1   egg
18   caramels (from 14-oz bag), unwrapped
2   tablespoons milk
1/2   cup semisweet chocolate chips
1   teaspoon shortening

---

1 Heat oven to 375°F. In large bowl, dissolve coffee powder in hot water. Stir in cookie mix, flour, butter, vanilla and egg until very soft dough forms.

2 Shape dough into 1-1/2-inch balls. On ungreased cookie sheets, place balls 2 inches apart. Using thumb or handle of wooden spoon, make indentation in center of each cookie.

3 Bake 8 to 10 minutes or until edges are light golden brown. Cool 2 minutes; remove from cookie sheets to cooling racks.

4 In small microwavable bowl, microwave caramels and milk uncovered on High 1 minute to 1 minute 30 seconds, stirring

once, until caramels are melted. Spoon 1/2 teaspoon caramel into indentation in each cookie. Cool 15 minutes.

5 In another small microwavable bowl, microwave chocolate chips and shortening uncovered on High 1 minute to 1 minute 30 seconds or until chips can be stirred smooth. Drizzle chocolate over cookies. Let stand about 30 minutes or until chocolate is set.

High Altitude (3500-6500 ft): No change.

Nutritional Info: 1 Cookie: Calories 120 (Calories from Fat 45); Total Fat 5g (Saturated Fat 2.5g, Trans Fat 0.5g); Cholesterol 15mg; Sodium 75mg; Total Carbohydrate 17g (Dietary Fiber 0g, Sugars 10g); Protein 1g. % Daily Value: Vitamin A 0%; Vitamin C 0%; Calcium 0%; Iron 0%. Exchanges: 1/2 Starch, 1/2 Other Carbohydrate, 1 Fat. Carbohydrate Choices: 1.

Betty's Kitchen Tips

Did You Know? Dough can be covered and refrigerated 20 minutes to make it easier to shape.

Success Hint: To drizzle chocolate easily, put melted chocolate in small resealable food-storage plastic bag; cut small tip from 1 corner of bag. Squeeze bag gently to drizzle chocolate over cookies.

lemonade biscotti

Prep Time: 1 Hour 10 Minutes
Start to Finish: 1 Hour 55 Minutes
Servings: 32 biscotti

- 1/2 cup butter or margarine, melted
- 1/4 cup frozen (thawed) lemonade concentrate
- 2 teaspoons grated lemon peel
- 1 teaspoon lemon extract
- 2 eggs
- 1 pouch (1 lb 1.5 oz) Betty Crocker® sugar cookie mix
- 1-1/2 cups Gold Medal® all-purpose flour
- 1/2 cup chopped dried cherries

1 Heat oven to 350°F. Line large cookie sheet with foil. In large bowl, stir butter, lemonade concentrate, lemon peel, lemon extract and eggs until well mixed. Add remaining ingredients; stir until soft dough forms.

2 Divide dough in half. On cookie sheet, shape each half of dough into a 12x2-inch log.

3 Bake 25 to 30 minutes or until edges are golden brown. Cool 15 minutes.

4 Carefully lift foil to move cookie logs to cutting board. With serrated knife, carefully cut each log crosswise on a slight diagonal into 3/4-inch slices. Place slices cut side down on cookie sheet.

5 Bake 15 to 20 minutes, gently turning cookies over once during baking. Cool 2 minutes; remove from cookie sheet to cooling rack.

High Altitude (3500-6500 ft): No change.

Nutritional Info: 1 Biscotti: Calories 130 (Calories from Fat 40); Total Fat 4.5g (Saturated Fat 2g, Trans Fat 0.5g); Cholesterol 20mg; Sodium 70mg; Total Carbohydrate 19g (Dietary Fiber 0g, Sugars 10g); Protein 1g. % Daily Value: Vitamin A 2%; Vitamin C 0%; Calcium 0%; Iron 4%. Exchanges: 1-1/2 Other Carbohydrate, 1 Fat. Carbohydrate Choices: 1.

Betty's Kitchen Tip

- Biscotti are good keepers, so it's easy to keep some on hand for unexpected visitors.

chocolate-mallow cookie pies

Prep Time: 50 Minutes
Start to Finish: 1 Hour 10 Minutes
Servings: 18 sandwich cookies

Cookies

1	pouch (1 lb 1.5 oz) Betty Crocker® sugar cookie mix
1/3	cup unsweetened baking cocoa
2	tablespoons Gold Medal® all-purpose flour
1/3	cup sour cream
1/4	cup butter, softened
1	teaspoon vanilla
1	egg

Filling

2/3	cup marshmallow creme
1/3	cup butter, softened
1/2	teaspoon vanilla
2/3	cup powdered sugar

Topping

1	tablespoon powdered sugar
1/8	teaspoon unsweetened baking cocoa

1 Heat oven to 350°F. In large bowl, stir together cookie mix, cocoa and flour. Add sour cream, 1/4 cup butter, 1 teaspoon vanilla and the egg; stir until stiff dough forms.

2 Shape dough into 36 (1-inch) balls. On ungreased cookie sheets, place balls 2 inches apart. Press each ball to flatten slightly.

3 Bake 8 to 9 minutes or until set (do not overbake). Cool 2 minutes; remove from cookie sheets to cooling racks. Cool completely, about 15 minutes.

4 In small bowl, beat filling ingredients with electric mixer until light and fluffy. For each sandwich cookie, spread about 2 teaspoons filling on bottom of 1 cooled cookie. Top with second cookie, bottom side down; gently press cookies together.

5 In small bowl, stir together topping ingredients; sprinkle over tops of cookie pies. Store between sheets of waxed paper in tightly covered container.

High Altitude (3500-6500 ft): No change.

Nutritional Info: 1 Sandwich Cookie: Calories 220 (Calories from Fat 90); Total Fat 10g (Saturated Fat 5g, Trans Fat 1.5g); Cholesterol 30mg; Sodium 130mg; Total Carbohydrate 31g (Dietary Fiber 0g, Sugars 19g); Protein 2g. % Daily Value: Vitamin A 4%; Vitamin C 0%; Calcium 0%; Iron 4%. Exchanges: 1/2 Starch, 1-1/2 Other Carbohydrate, 2 Fat. Carbohydrate Choices: 2.

spiced hazelnut thumbprints

Prep Time: 1 Hour
Start to Finish: 1 Hour
Servings: About 2-1/2 dozen cookies

- 1/2 cup butter or margarine, softened
- 6 tablespoons sugar
- 1 teaspoon vanilla
- 1 egg yolk
- 1 cup Gold Medal® all-purpose flour
- 1/2 cup hazelnuts (filberts), toasted, skins removed and nuts ground (6 tablespoons)
- 1/2 teaspoon ground cinnamon
- 1/4 teaspoon ground cloves
- 1/4 teaspoon salt
- 1/3 cup strawberry or raspberry preserves

1 Heat oven to 350°F. In large bowl, beat butter and sugar with electric mixer on medium speed until light and fluffy. Beat in vanilla and egg yolk until blended. On low speed, beat in flour, hazelnuts, cinnamon, cloves and salt.

2 Shape dough into 1-inch balls. On ungreased cookie sheets, place balls 2 inches apart.

3 Bake 10 minutes. Using end of handle of wooden spoon, press a well into center of each cookie. Fill each well with 1/2 teaspoon preserves. Bake about 10 minutes longer or until edges are light golden. Cool 2 minutes; remove from cookie sheets to cooling racks.

High Altitude (3500-6500 ft): No change.

Nutritional Info: 1 Cookie: Calories 70 (Calories from Fat 35); Total Fat 4g (Saturated Fat 2g, Trans Fat 0g); Cholesterol 15mg; Sodium 45mg; Total Carbohydrate 8g (Dietary Fiber 0g, Sugars 4g); Protein 0g. % Daily Value: Vitamin A 2%; Vitamin C 0%; Calcium 0%; Iron 0%. Exchanges: 1/2 Other Carbohydrate, 1 Fat. Carbohydrate Choices: 1/2.

Betty's Kitchen Tip

- Any other nut may be used in place of the hazelnuts. Use what you have on hand.

brown sugar snowflakes

Prep Time: 1 Hour 30 Minutes
Start to Finish: 3 Hours 30 Minutes
Servings: About 2-1/2 dozen cookies

Cookies
3/4	cup butter, softened
3/4	cup packed brown sugar
1	egg
2-1/4	cups Gold Medal® all-purpose flour
1/2	teaspoon baking soda

1/4	teaspoon salt

Frosting
1-1/2	teaspoons meringue powder
1	tablespoon cold water
1/2	cup powdered sugar

Granulated sugar, if desired

1. In large bowl, beat butter and brown sugar with electric mixer on medium-high speed until light and fluffy. Beat in egg until blended. On low speed, beat in flour, baking soda and salt.

2. Divide dough into 4 parts; shape each part into a flat disk. Wrap each disk separately in plastic wrap. Refrigerate at least 2 hours until completely chilled.

3. Heat oven to 350°F. Line cookie sheets with cooking parchment paper. On floured surface, roll 1 disk at a time to 1/4-inch thickness (keep remaining dough refrigerated). Cut with snowflake cutters; place on cookie sheets. Reroll scraps once, chilling dough again before cutting.

4. Bake 8 to 11 minutes or until light golden. Cool 2 minutes; remove from cookie sheets to cooling racks. Cool completely, about 30 minutes.

5. In medium bowl, beat meringue powder and cold water with electric mixer on medium speed until peaks form. Gradually beat in powdered sugar until soft peaks form, about 1 minute. Spoon frosting into decorating bag fitted with medium round tip; pipe frosting on cookies. Sprinkle with granulated sugar. Let stand about 5 minutes or until frosting is set.

High Altitude (3500-6500 ft): No change.

Nutritional Info: 1 Cookie: Calories 110 (Calories from Fat 45); Total Fat 5g (Saturated Fat 3g, Trans Fat 0g); Cholesterol 20mg; Sodium 80mg; Total Carbohydrate 15g (Dietary Fiber 0g, Sugars 7g); Protein 1g. % Daily Value: Vitamin A 4%; Vitamin C 0%; Calcium 0%; Iron 2%. Exchanges: 1 Other Carbohydrate, 1 Fat. Carbohydrate Choices: 1.

Betty's Kitchen Tips

Success Hint: Roll dough between sheets of parchment paper to keep it from sticking to the counter.

Variation: Use dark brown sugar for a little more molasses flavor.

german chocolate chiparoos

Prep Time: 30 Minutes
Start to Finish: 1 Hour
Servings: 2 dozen cookies

- 1/2 cup butter or margarine, softened
- 1 egg
- 1 pouch (1 lb 1.5 oz) Betty Crocker® chocolate chip cookie mix
- 1/3 cup unsweetened baking cocoa
- 1/4 cup water
- 1 container (1 lb) Betty Crocker® Rich & Creamy coconut pecan frosting

1 Heat oven to 375°F. In medium bowl, stir together butter and egg. Stir in cookie mix, cocoa and water until soft dough forms.

2 Onto ungreased cookie sheet, drop dough by rounded tablespoonfuls about 2 inches apart.

3 Bake 7 to 9 minutes or until cookies are set. Cool 1 minute; remove from cookie sheet to cooling rack. Cool completely, about 15 minutes.

4 Generously frost cookies with coconut pecan frosting.

High Altitude (3500-6500 ft): No change.

Nutritional Info: 1 Cookie: Calories 200 (Calories from Fat 90); Total Fat 10g (Saturated Fat 5g, Trans Fat 1g); Cholesterol 25mg; Sodium 140mg; Total Carbohydrate 26g (Dietary Fiber 1g, Sugars 18g); Protein 1g. % Daily Value: Vitamin A 2%; Vitamin C 0%; Calcium 0%; Iron 2%. Exchanges: 1/2 Starch, 1 Other Carbohydrate, 2 Fat. Carbohydrate Choices: 2.

Betty's Kitchen Tip

• To help with mixing the softened butter and egg, try cutting the butter into small pieces.

apple-oat cookies

Prep Time: 40 Minutes
Start to Finish: 1 Hour 40 Minutes
Servings: About 3 dozen cookies

- -

3/4	cup butter or margarine, softened
1	cup granulated sugar
1/2	cup packed brown sugar
1	teaspoon vanilla
2	eggs
1-3/4	cups Gold Medal® all-purpose flour
1	teaspoon baking soda

1-1/2	teaspoons ground cinnamon
1/2	teaspoon salt
2	cups old-fashioned or quick-cooking oats
1	medium apple, peeled and shredded (about 1 cup shredded)
1	cup powdered sugar
2	to 3 tablespoons apple juice or milk

- -

1 Heat oven to 375°F. Spray cookie sheet with cooking spray. In large bowl, beat butter, granulated sugar and brown sugar with electric mixer on medium speed until creamy. Beat in vanilla and eggs, scraping sides occasionally, until blended.

2 In medium bowl, mix flour, baking soda, cinnamon and salt. Gradually beat flour mixture into sugar mixture. Stir in oats and apple. Onto cookie sheet, drop dough by rounded tablespoonfuls 2 inches apart.

3 Bake about 10 minutes or until edges are light golden brown. Cool 1 minute; remove from cookie sheet to cooling rack. Cool completely, about 15 minutes.

4 In medium bowl, beat powdered sugar and apple juice until smooth, using wire whisk or fork. Drizzle over cooled cookies on cooling rack. Let stand about 1 hour or until glaze is set.

High Altitude (3500-6500 ft): No change.

Nutritional Info: 1 Cookie: Calories 130 (Calories from Fat 40); Total Fat 4.5g (Saturated Fat 2.5g, Trans Fat 0g); Cholesterol 20mg; Sodium 100mg; Total Carbohydrate 20g (Dietary Fiber 0g, Sugars 12g); Protein 1g. % Daily Value: Vitamin A 2%; Vitamin C 0%; Calcium 0%; Iron 4%. Exchanges: 1-1/2 Other Carbohydrate, 1 Fat. Carbohydrate Choices: 1.

 **Kitchen Tips**

Time-Saver: For easy cleanup when glazing cookies, place waxed paper or paper towels under the cooling rack.

Success Hint: For fuller cookies and less spread while baking, refrigerate dough between baking batches.

frosted tropical coconut bursts

Prep Time: 1 Hour 10 Minutes
Start to Finish: 1 Hour 10 Minutes
Servings: 3 dozen cookies

• •

Cookies

1	pouch (1 lb 1.5 oz) Betty Crocker® sugar cookie mix
1/2	cup butter or margarine, softened
1	egg
1	cup dried tropical three-fruit mix
1/2	cup coconut

Glaze

1	cup powdered sugar
1/2	teaspoon coconut extract
1	to 2 tablespoons milk

• •

1 Heat oven to 375°F. In large bowl, stir cookie mix, butter and egg until soft dough forms. Stir in fruit mix and coconut until well mixed.

2 On ungreased cookie sheets, drop dough by rounded tablespoonfuls 2 inches apart.

3 Bake 8 to 9 minutes or until golden brown around edges. Cool 2 minutes; remove from cookie sheets to cooling racks. Cool completely, about 15 minutes.

4 In small bowl, stir powdered sugar, extract and enough milk until glaze is spreadable. Spread glaze over tops of cooled cookies.

High Altitude (3500-6500 ft): No change.

Nutritional Info: 1 Cookie: Calories 120 (Calories from Fat 40); Total Fat 4.5g (Saturated Fat 2.5g, Trans Fat 0.5g); Cholesterol 15mg; Sodium 65mg; Total Carbohydrate 17g (Dietary Fiber 0g, Sugars 12g); Protein 0g. % Daily Value: Vitamin A 2%; Vitamin C 0%; Calcium 0%; Iron 0%. Exchanges: 1 Other Carbohydrate, 1 Fat. Carbohydrate Choices: 1

Betty's Kitchen Tip

• With their tropical taste, these cookies make great gifts for friends or neighbors during a cold weather spell.

chocolate-mint thumbprints

Prep Time: 1 Hour
Start to Finish: 2 Hours 15 Minutes
Servings: About 3 dozen cookies

- -

1 cup butter, softened	1/2 teaspoon baking powder
1 cup powdered sugar	1/4 teaspoon salt
1-1/2 teaspoons peppermint extract	3/4 cup dark chocolate chips
2 egg yolks	3 tablespoons whipping cream
16 drops green food color	3 tablespoons butter
2-1/4 cups Gold Medal® all-purpose flour	18 thin rectangular crème de menthe chocolate candies, unwrapped, cut in half diagonally

- -

1 Heat oven to 350°F. Line cookie sheets with cooking parchment paper.

2 In large bowl, beat 1 cup butter and the powdered sugar with electric mixer on medium speed until light and fluffy. Beat in peppermint extract, egg yolks and food color until blended. On low speed, beat in flour, baking powder and salt.

3 Shape dough into 1-inch balls; place 2 inches apart on cookie sheets. Using end of handle of wooden spoon, press a deep well into center of each cookie.

4 Bake 10 to 12 minutes or until set. Reshape wells with end of handle of wooden spoon. Cool 2 minutes; remove from cookie sheets to cooling racks. Cool completely, about 15 minutes.

5 In medium microwavable bowl, microwave chocolate chips, cream and 3 tablespoons butter on High 1 minute, stirring frequently, until chocolate is melted and mixture is smooth. Fill each well with about 1 teaspoon chocolate mixture; garnish with candy piece. Let stand about 1 hour until chocolate is set.

High Altitude (3500-6500 ft): No change.

Nutritional Info: 1 Cookie: Calories 130 (Calories from Fat 70); Total Fat 8g (Saturated Fat 5g, Trans Fat 0g); Cholesterol 30mg; Sodium 70mg; Total Carbohydrate 12g (Dietary Fiber 0g, Sugars 6g); Protein 1g. % Daily Value: Vitamin A 4%; Vitamin C 0%; Calcium 0%; Iron 2%. Exchanges: 1 Other Carbohydrate, 1-1/2 Fat. Carbohydrate Choices: 1.

Betty's Kitchen Tip

• The color of these delicious cookies makes them perfect for holidays such as Christmas and St. Patrick's Day.

orange-pecan-ginger cookies

Prep Time: 1 Hour 15 Minutes
Start to Finish: 4 Hours 30 Minutes
Servings: About 6 dozen cookies

LOW FAT

3/4	cup butter or margarine, softened
1/2	cup granulated sugar
1/2	cup packed brown sugar
1	tablespoon grated orange peel
1	tablespoon orange juice
1	egg

2-1/2	cups Gold Medal® all-purpose flour
1	teaspoon baking powder
1/2	teaspoon salt
1/2	cup chopped pecans
1/4	cup chopped crystallized ginger
1/4	cup decorator sugar crystals

1 In large bowl, beat butter, granulated sugar and brown sugar with electric mixer on medium speed until light and fluffy. Beat in orange peel, orange juice and egg until blended. On low speed, beat in flour, baking powder and salt. Stir in pecans and ginger.

2 Divide dough in half. Shape each half into 10-inch log. Sprinkle 2 tablespoons of the sugar crystals on sheet of plastic wrap; roll 1 log in sugar to coat. Wrap log in plastic wrap. Repeat with remaining log and sugar crystals. Refrigerate 3 hours or until very firm.

3 Heat oven to 375°F. Cut logs into 1/4-inch slices. On ungreased cookie sheets, place slices 2 inches apart.

4 Bake 8 to 10 minutes or until edges start to brown and tops are light golden brown. Immediately remove from cookie sheets to cooling racks. Cool completely, about 15 minutes.

High Altitude (3500-6500 ft): No change.

Nutritional Info: 1 Cookie: Calories 60 (Calories from Fat 25); Total Fat 2.5g (Saturated Fat 1.5g, Trans Fat 0g); Cholesterol 10mg; Sodium 40mg; Total Carbohydrate 8g (Dietary Fiber 0g, Sugars 4g); Protein 0g. % Daily Value: Vitamin A 0%; Vitamin C 0%; Calcium 0%; Iron 0%. Exchanges: 1/2 Other Carbohydrate, 1/2 Fat. Carbohydrate Choices: 1/2.

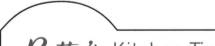

Betty's Kitchen Tips

How-To: These crisp, delicious cookies would be a welcome holiday treat. Stack 6 or 8 cookies, and tie with a pretty ribbon to present as a small gift.

Special Touch: For a pretty presentation, melt about 2/3 cup semisweet or milk chocolate chips in a long, narrow microwavable dish, such as a butter dish. Dip about 1/4 inch of one edge of each cookie into chocolate; place on waxed paper about 40 minutes until set.

chocolate-marshmallow pillows

Prep Time: 45 Minutes
Start to Finish: 1 Hour 5 Minutes
Servings: 2 dozen cookies

Cookies

1	pouch (1 lb 1.5 oz) Betty Crocker® double chocolate chunk cookie mix
1/4	cup vegetable oil
2	tablespoons water
1	egg
2/3	cup chopped pecans
12	large marshmallows, cut in half

Frosting

1	cup semisweet chocolate chips (6 oz)
1/3	cup whipping cream
1	teaspoon butter or margarine
1	teaspoon vanilla
1/2	cup powdered sugar

1 Heat oven to 350°F. In large bowl, stir cookie mix, oil, water, egg and pecans until soft dough forms.

2 On ungreased cookie sheets, drop dough by rounded tablespoonfuls 2 inches apart.

3 Bake 7 minutes. Remove from oven; immediately press marshmallow half lightly, cut side down, on top of cookie. Bake 1 to 2 minutes longer or just until marshmallows begin to soften. Cool 2 minutes; remove from cookie sheets to cooling racks. Cool completely, about 15 minutes.

4 Meanwhile, in 1-quart nonstick saucepan, melt chocolate chips over low heat, stirring until smooth. Remove from heat. Add whipping cream, butter and vanilla; blend well. Stir in powdered sugar until smooth.

5 Spread frosting over each cooled cookie, covering marshmallow. Let stand until frosting is set.

High Altitude (3500-6500 ft): No change.

Nutritional Info: 1 Cookie: Calories 200 (Calories from Fat 90); Total Fat 10g (Saturated Fat 3g, Trans Fat 1g); Cholesterol 15mg; Sodium 70mg; Total Carbohydrate 26g (Dietary Fiber 0g, Sugars 17g); Protein 1g. % Daily Value: Vitamin A 0%; Vitamin C 0%; Calcium 0%; Iron 4%. Exchanges: 1/2 Starch, 1 Other Carbohydrate, 2 Fat. Carbohydrate Choices: 2.

Betty's Kitchen Tips

How-To: Lightly spray kitchen scissors with cooking spray to make cutting marshmallows easy.

Substitution: A pouch of Betty Crocker® chocolate chip cookie mix can be used for the double chocolate chunk mix.

snowman sugar cookies

Prep Time: 1 Hour 20 Minutes
Start to Finish: 3 Hours 20 Minutes
Servings: 3 dozen cookies

LOW FAT

1	cup butter or margarine, softened
1	package (3 oz) cream cheese, softened
3/4	cup sugar
1	teaspoon vanilla
1	egg
3	cups Gold Medal® all-purpose flour
1/8	teaspoon salt

1	pouch (7 oz) Betty Crocker® Cookie Icing white icing
1	pouch (7 oz) Betty Crocker® Cookie Icing blue icing

Decorator sugar crystals
Orange string licorice
Miniature semisweet chocolate chips

1 In large bowl, beat butter, cream cheese, sugar, vanilla and egg with electric mixer on medium speed until light and fluffy. Stir in flour and salt until blended. Cover and refrigerate dough at least 2 hours but no longer than 24 hours.

2 Heat oven to 375°F. On lightly floured cloth-covered surface, roll 1/4 of dough at a time to 1/8-inch thickness. (Keep remaining dough refrigerated until ready to roll.) Cut dough with snowman cookie cutters; place about 1 inch apart on ungreased cookie sheets.

3 Bake 7 to 10 minutes or until light brown. Immediately remove from cookie sheets to cooling racks. Cool completely. Frost cookies with white icing. Decorate snowmen using blue icing for hat and scarf; sprinkle with sugar crystals. Add orange licorice for nose and chocolate chips for eyes.

High Altitude (3500-6500 ft): No change.

Nutritional Info: 1 Cookie: Calories 60 (Calories from Fat 30); Total Fat 3g (Saturated Fat 2g, Trans Fat 0g); Cholesterol 10mg; Sodium 25mg; Total Carbohydrate 6g (Dietary Fiber 0g, Sugars 2g); Protein 0g. % Daily Value: Vitamin A 0%; Vitamin C 0%; Calcium 0%; Iron 0%. Exchanges: 1/2 Other Carbohydrate, 1/2 Fat. Carbohydrate Choices: 1/2.

Betty's Kitchen Tips

Variation: To make Santa Sugar Cookies, use Santa cookie cutter. Frost cookies with red icing; sprinkle with red sugar crystals. Decorate as desired using icing, red gumdrop and cinnamon candy. Go to bettycrocker.com for decorating tips.

Do-Ahead: To freeze cookies, place unfrosted cookies in airtight freezer container and label. Freeze for up to 3 months. Cookies will thaw while you decorate them.

holiday house cookies

Prep Time: 1 Hour 20 Minutes
Start to Finish: 1 Hour 20 Minutes
Servings: 8 large cookies

- -

   1   pouch (1 lb 1.5 oz) Betty Crocker®
       gingerbread cookie mix
1/2   cup butter or margarine, softened
   1   tablespoon water
   1   egg
   1   container (1 lb) Betty Crocker® Rich &
       Creamy vanilla or creamy white frosting

Assorted small candies

- -

1 Heat oven to 375°F. In medium bowl, stir cookie mix, butter, water and egg until soft dough forms. Divide dough in half.

2 Working with half of dough at a time, roll on floured surface into 9x6-inch rectangle. Cut rectangle into 6 (3-inch) squares. Place 4 squares on ungreased cookie sheet. Cut remaining 2 squares diagonally in half to form 4 triangles. Place 1 triangle on one side of each square for roof; press dough to seal.

3 Bake 8 to 11 minutes or until set. Cool 5 minutes. Remove from cookie sheet to cooling rack. Cool completely, about 15 minutes. Repeat with remaining dough.

4 Decorate with frosting and candies as desired.

High Altitude (3500-6500 ft): No change.

Nutritional Info: 1 Large Cookie: Calories 360 (Calories from Fat 150); Total Fat 17g (Saturated Fat 9g, Trans Fat 1.5g); Cholesterol 55mg; Sodium 390mg; Total Carbohydrate 48g (Dietary Fiber 0g, Sugars 24g); Protein 3g. % Daily Value: Vitamin A 8%; Vitamin C 0%; Calcium 0%; Iron 6%. Exchanges: 1 Starch, 2 Other Carbohydrate, 3-1/2 Fat. Carbohydrate Choices: 3.

Betty's Kitchen Tip

• Roll dough to an even thickness by rolling over 2 wooden dowels or rulers. Use dowels or rulers of the desired thickness, and place them on opposite sides of the dough.

choco-damia banana cookies

Prep Time: 50 Minutes
Start to Finish: 1 Hour 10 Minutes
Servings: 3 dozen cookies

7	tablespoons butter or margarine
1	cup semisweet chocolate chips (6 oz)
1	pouch (1 lb 1.5 oz) Betty Crocker® chocolate chip cookie mix
2/3	cup mashed ripe bananas (about 2 small)
1	teaspoon instant coffee granules or crystals

1	egg
1	cup chopped macadamia nuts
2 or 3	drops orange or yellow food color, if desired
2/3	cup Betty Crocker® Rich & Creamy cream cheese frosting (from 1-lb container)

1 Heat oven to 375°F. In large microwavable bowl, microwave butter and chocolate chips uncovered on High 1 minute to 1 minute 30 seconds, stirring every 30 seconds, until melted and smooth. Stir in cookie mix, bananas, coffee granules, egg and nuts until well blended.

2 On ungreased cookie sheets, drop dough by rounded tablespoonfuls 2 inches apart.

3 Bake 9 to 11 minutes or until set. Cool 2 minutes; remove from cookie sheets to cooling racks. Cool completely, about 30 minutes.

4 Stir food color into frosting. Place frosting in 1-quart food-storage plastic bag; partially seal bag. Cut small tip from corner of bag. Squeeze bag to drizzle frosting over cookies.

High Altitude (3500-6500 ft): No change.

Nutritional Info: 1 Cookie: Calories 170 (Calories from Fat 80); Total Fat 9g (Saturated Fat 3.5g, Trans Fat 0.5g); Cholesterol 10mg; Sodium 90mg; Total Carbohydrate 22g (Dietary Fiber 0g, Sugars 16g); Protein 1g. % Daily Value: Vitamin A 0%; Vitamin C 0%; Calcium 0%; Iron 2%. Exchanges: 1-1/2 Other Carbohydrate, 2 Fat. Carbohydrate Choices: 1-1/2.

tasty trail-mix treats

Prep Time: 40 Minutes
Start to Finish: 40 Minutes
Servings: 3 dozen cookies

- 1 pouch (1 lb 1.5 oz) Betty Crocker® oatmeal cookie mix
- 2 tablespoons wheat germ
- 2 tablespoons ground flaxseed
- 3/4 teaspoon ground cinnamon
- 1/3 cup canola or vegetable oil
- 4 tablespoons water
- 2 egg whites
- 1/2 cup sweetened dried cranberries
- 1/2 cup coarsely chopped walnuts
- 1/3 cup dark chocolate chips

1. Heat oven to 375°F. In large bowl, stir cookie mix, wheat germ, flaxseed, cinnamon, oil, water and egg whites until well blended. Stir in remaining ingredients.

2. On ungreased cookie sheets, drop dough by teaspoonfuls 2 inches apart.

3. Bake 8 to 10 minutes until edges are light golden brown. Cool 2 minutes; remove from cookie sheets to cooling racks.

High Altitude (3500-6500 ft): No change.

Nutritional Info: 1 Cookie: Calories 100 (Calories from Fat 40); Total Fat 4.5g (Saturated Fat 0.5g, Trans Fat 0g); Cholesterol 0mg; Sodium 55mg; Total Carbohydrate 14g (Dietary Fiber 0g, Sugars 8g); Protein 1g. % Daily Value: Vitamin A 0%; Vitamin C 0%; Calcium 0%; Iron 0%. Exchanges: 1 Other Carbohydrate, 1 Fat. Carbohydrate Choices: 1.

Betty's Kitchen Tips

Special Touch: These cookies are a welcome treat after outdoor activities.

Success Hint: You can freeze these cookies for up to 2 months.

cardamom sugar crisps

Prep Time: 50 Minutes
Start to Finish: 2 Hours
Servings: 4 to 5 dozen cookies

LOW FAT

3/4	cup butter or margarine, softened
3/4	cup packed brown sugar
1/2	teaspoon vanilla
1	egg
1-1/2	cups Gold Medal® all-purpose flour
1/4	teaspoon salt
1	teaspoon ground cardamom

1/4	teaspoon ground cinnamon
3	tablespoons granulated sugar
1-1/2	cups powdered sugar
1	teaspoon vanilla
2 to 3	tablespoons milk
3	tablespoons decorator sugar crystals

1 Heat oven to 350°F. In medium bowl, beat butter, brown sugar, 1/2 teaspoon vanilla and egg with electric mixer on medium speed until smooth. On low speed, beat in flour, salt, cardamom and cinnamon. Refrigerate dough about 1 hour or until firm.

2 Shape dough into 1-inch balls. On ungreased cookie sheets, place balls 2 inches apart. Gently press bottom of drinking glass onto dough to grease, then press into granulated sugar and onto dough balls to flatten to about 1-1/2 inches in diameter.

3 Bake 7 to 9 minutes or until edges are just beginning to brown and centers of cookies are set. Immediately remove from cookie sheets to cooling racks. Cool 10 minutes.

4 In small bowl, mix powdered sugar, 1 teaspoon vanilla and enough of the milk until glaze is smooth and thin enough to drizzle. Drizzle glaze over cookies; sprinkle with sugar crystals.

High Altitude (3500-6500 ft): No change.

Nutritional Info: 1 Cookie: Calories 80 (Calories from Fat 25); Total Fat 3g (Saturated Fat 2g, Trans Fat 0g); Cholesterol 10mg; Sodium 35mg; Total Carbohydrate 12g (Dietary Fiber 0g, Sugars 9g); Protein 0g. % Daily Value: Vitamin A 0%; Vitamin C 0%; Calcium 0%; Iron 0%. Exchanges: 1 Other Carbohydrate, 1/2 Fat. Carbohydrate Choices: 1.

Betty's Kitchen Tip

• Cardamom, one of the oldest spices in the world, comes from the seeds of a gingerlike plant.

ginger crinkles

Prep Time: 40 Minutes
Start to Finish: 40 Minutes
Servings: About 3 dozen cookies

- 1 cup sugar
- 3/4 cup butter or margarine, softened
- 1/4 cup molasses
- 1 egg
- 2 cups Gold Medal® all-purpose flour
- 1 tablespoon ground ginger
- 2 teaspoons baking soda
- 1 teaspoon ground cinnamon
- 1/4 teaspoon ground cloves
- 1/4 teaspoon salt
- 3 tablespoons sugar

1 Heat oven to 375°F. In large bowl, beat 1 cup sugar and the butter with electric mixer on medium speed until soft and fluffy, or mix with spoon. Beat in molasses and egg. Stir in remaining ingredients except 3 tablespoons sugar until well blended.

2 In small bowl, place 3 tablespoons sugar. Shape dough by tablespoonfuls into balls; roll in sugar. On ungreased cookie sheet, place 2 inches apart.

3 Bake 6 to 8 minutes or until golden brown. Remove from cookie sheet to cooling rack.

High Altitude (3500-6500 ft): No change.

Nutritional Info: 1 Cookie: Calories 100 (Calories from Fat 35); Total Fat 4g (Saturated Fat 2.5g, Trans Fat 0g); Cholesterol 15mg; Sodium 115mg; Total Carbohydrate 14g (Dietary Fiber 0g, Sugars 8g); Protein 1g. % Daily Value: Vitamin A 2%; Vitamin C 0%; Calcium 0%; Iron 2%. Exchanges: 1 Starch, 1/2 Fat. Carbohydrate Choices: 1.

Betty's Kitchen Tips

Success Hint: For even baking, make sure balls of dough are the same shape and size.

Special Touch: These old-fashioned, chewy cookies are an easy homemade cookie-jar favorite your family is sure to enjoy.

choco-hazelnut latte cookies

Prep Time: 50 Minutes
Start to Finish: 1 Hour 10 Minutes
Servings: 32 cookies

1 pouch (1 lb 1.5 oz) Betty Crocker® sugar cookie mix	1 egg
1/3 cup unsweetened baking cocoa	1-1/2 cups toasted hazelnuts, chopped
3 tablespoons instant coffee granules or crystals	1 cup miniature semisweet chocolate chips
1/2 cup butter or margarine, softened	2/3 cup Betty Crocker® Rich & Creamy chocolate frosting (from 1-lb container)
3 tablespoons hazelnut-flavored syrup for beverages (from 12.7-oz bottle)	4 1/2 teaspoons hazelnut-flavored syrup for beverages (from 12.7-oz bottle)

1 Heat oven to 350°F. In large bowl, stir together cookie mix, cocoa and instant coffee. Add butter, 3 tablespoons syrup and the egg; stir until soft dough forms. Stir in 1 cup of the nuts and the chocolate chips.

2 On ungreased cookie sheets, drop dough with rounded 1-1/2 tablespoon-size cookie scoop or by rounded tablespoonfuls 2 inches apart. Press each mound to flatten slightly.

3 Bake 8 to 10 minutes or until set. Cool 3 minutes; remove from cookie sheets to cooling racks. Cool completely, about 15 minutes.

4 In small bowl, stir frosting and 4-1/2 teaspoons syrup. Spread about 1 teaspoon frosting on each cookie. Sprinkle with remaining 1/2 cup nuts.

High Altitude (3500-6500 ft): No change.

Nutritional Info: 1 Cookie: Calories 190 (Calories from Fat 90); Total Fat 10g (Saturated Fat 3.5g, Trans Fat 1g); Cholesterol 15mg; Sodium 85mg; Total Carbohydrate 22g (Dietary Fiber 1g, Sugars 14g); Protein 2g. % Daily Value: Vitamin A 2%; Vitamin C 0%; Calcium 0%; Iron 4%. Exchanges: 1/2 Starch, 1 Other Carbohydrate, 2 Fat.

Betty's Kitchen Tip

• To toast hazelnuts, heat oven to 350°F. Spread nuts in ungreased shallow pan. Bake uncovered 6 to 10 minutes, stirring occasionally, until light brown.

on-the-trail monster cookies

Prep Time: 1 Hour
Start to Finish: 1 Hour
Servings: About 3 dozen cookies

1	cup granulated sugar
1	cup packed brown sugar
1	cup peanut butter
1/2	cup butter or margarine, softened
1/2	cup butter-flavor or regular shortening
2	teaspoons vanilla
2	eggs
1-1/2	cups quick-cooking or old-fashioned oats
2	cups Gold Medal® all-purpose flour
1	teaspoon baking powder
1	teaspoon baking soda
2	cups candy-coated chocolate candies
1	cup peanuts
3/4	cup raisins

1 Heat oven to 375°F. In large bowl, beat sugars, peanut butter, butter, shortening, vanilla and eggs with electric mixer on medium speed until smooth, or mix with spoon. Stir in oats. Stir in flour, baking powder and baking soda thoroughly. Stir in candies, peanuts and raisins.

2 Onto ungreased cookie sheets, drop dough by slightly less than 1/4 cupfuls about 2 inches apart. Flatten to 3/4-inch thickness with bottom of glass.

3 Bake 12 to 14 minutes or just until cookies are set and begin to brown. Cool 2 minutes; remove from cookie sheets to cooling racks.

High Altitude (3500-6500 ft): No change.

Nutritional Info: 1 Cookie: Calories 270 (Calories from Fat 130); Total Fat 14g (Saturated Fat 5g, Trans Fat 0.5g); Cholesterol 20mg; Sodium 115mg; Total Carbohydrate 32g (Dietary Fiber 2g, Sugars 21g); Protein 5g. % Daily Value: Vitamin A 4%; Vitamin C 0%; Calcium 4%; Iron 6%. Exchanges: 1/2 Starch, 1-1/2 Other Carbohydrate, 1/2 High-Fat Meat, 2 Fat. Carbohydrate Choices: 2.

Betty's Kitchen Tip

• For cookies with a less-monstrous size but the same big taste, drop dough by rounded tablespoonfuls, and flatten slightly. Bake 8 to 10 minutes.

buckeye delights

Prep Time: 1 Hour 5 Minutes
Start to Finish: 2 Hours 5 Minutes
Servings: 36 cookie cups

Cookie Base

1	pouch (1 lb 1.5 oz) Betty Crocker® sugar cookie mix
1/3	cup unsweetened baking cocoa
1/2	cup butter or margarine, softened
1	egg

Filling

1/2	cup powdered sugar
1/2	cup peanut butter

2	tablespoons butter or margarine, softened
1	teaspoon vanilla
1/4	teaspoon salt

Topping

1/2	cup whipping cream
1	cup plus 2 tablespoons semisweet chocolate chips
1	tablespoon peanut butter

1 Heat oven to 350°F. Place mini foil candy cups (about 1-1/4 inch) in each of 36 mini muffin cups. In large bowl, stir cookie base ingredients until soft dough forms. Press about 1 tablespoon dough into each foil cup. Bake 8 to 10 minutes or until puffy and set. Cool completely, about 30 minutes. Remove from pan.

2 In small bowl, mix filling ingredients until well blended. Press about 1 teaspoon mixture on top of each cooled cookie.

3 In 1-quart saucepan, heat whipping cream just to boiling over low heat, stirring occasionally; remove from heat. Stir in 1 cup of the chocolate chips. Refrigerate about 30 minutes or until cooled. Spread about 2 teaspoons chocolate mixture over each cookie cup.

4 Place remaining 2 tablespoons chocolate chips and 1 tablespoon peanut butter in resealable food-storage plastic bag; partially seal bag. Microwave uncovered on High 30 to 60 seconds or until softened; knead to mix. Cut off small tip from one corner of bag. Squeeze bag to drizzle chocolate mixture over each cookie cup. Refrigerate about 30 minutes or until set. Store covered in refrigerator.

High Altitude (3500-6500 ft): No change.

Nutritional Info: 1 Cookie Cup: Calories 160 (Calories from Fat 80); Total Fat 9g (Saturated Fat 4.5g, Trans Fat 0.5g); Cholesterol 20mg; Sodium 100mg; Total Carbohydrate 17g (Dietary Fiber 0g, Sugars 11g); Protein 2g. % Daily Value: Vitamin A 2%; Vitamin C 0%; Calcium 0%; Iron 4%. Exchanges: 1 Starch, 1-1/2 Fat. Carbohydrate Choices: 1.

Betty's Kitchen Tip

• Buckeye candies are peanut butter balls dipped in chocolate. The name comes from their resemblance to the nut of the buckeye tree.

ginger-lemon delights

Prep Time: 50 Minutes
Start to Finish: 1 Hour 10 Minutes
Servings: 3 dozen cookies

Cookies

1	pouch (1 lb 1.5 oz) Betty Crocker® sugar cookie mix
1/2	cup shortening
1/4	cup mild-flavor (light) molasses
1	tablespoon ground ginger
1-1/4	teaspoons ground cinnamon
1	teaspoon ground cloves
1	egg

Glaze and Topping

1	cup powdered sugar
1	teaspoon grated lemon peel
4	teaspoons lemon juice
1/4	cup finely chopped crystallized ginger

1 Heat oven to 375°F. In large bowl, stir cookie ingredients until very soft dough forms (dough will be sticky).

2 On ungreased cookie sheets, drop dough with 1 tablespoon-size cookie scoop or by tablespoonfuls about 2 inches apart.

3 Bake 8 to 10 minutes or until edges are light golden brown. Cool 2 minutes; remove from cookie sheets to cooling racks. Cool completely, about 30 minutes.

4 In small bowl, stir powdered sugar, lemon peel and lemon juice until smooth. Spread glaze on cookies. Sprinkle with crystallized ginger.

High Altitude (3500-6500 ft): No change.

Nutritional Info: 1 Cookie: Calories 110 (Calories from Fat 40); Total Fat 4.5g (Saturated Fat 1g, Trans Fat 1g); Cholesterol 5mg; Sodium 45mg; Total Carbohydrate 16g (Dietary Fiber 0g, Sugars 11g); Protein 0g. % Daily Value: Vitamin A 0%; Vitamin C 0%; Calcium 0%; Iron 0%. Exchanges: 1 Other Carbohydrate, 1 Fat. Carbohydrate Choices: 1.

carrot-spice cookies

Prep Time: 1 Hour
Start to Finish: 1 Hour 25 Minutes
Servings: About 4 dozen cookies

LOW FAT

Cookies
- 1   box Betty Crocker® SuperMoist® carrot cake mix
- 1/4   cup Gold Medal® all-purpose flour
- 1/2   cup butter or margarine, melted
- 2   eggs
- 1   cup sweetened dried cranberries

Glaze
- 1/2   cup Betty Crocker® Rich & Creamy cream cheese frosting (from 1-lb container)

1 Heat oven to 350°F. In large bowl, beat cake mix, flour, butter and eggs with electric mixer on low speed 1 minute. Stir in cranberries.

2 On ungreased cookie sheets, drop dough by teaspoonfuls about 2 inches apart.

3 Bake 10 to 12 minutes or until edges are set. Immediately remove from cookie sheets to cooling racks. Cool completely, about 10 minutes.

4 In small microwavable bowl, microwave frosting on High 10 to 15 seconds or until frosting is thin enough to drizzle. Drizzle frosting over cookies.

High Altitude (3500-6500 ft): Bake 11 to 13 minutes.

Nutritional Info: 1 Cookie: Calories 80 (Calories from Fat 30); Total Fat 3g (Saturated Fat 1.5g, Trans Fat 0g); Cholesterol 15mg; Sodium 85mg; Total Carbohydrate 12g (Dietary Fiber 0g, Sugars 7g); Protein 0g. % Daily Value: Vitamin A 4%; Vitamin C 0%; Calcium 2%; Iron 0%. Exchanges: 1 Other Carbohydrate, 1/2 Fat. Carbohydrate Choices: 1.

Betty's Kitchen Tips

Variation: Try using raisins instead of the dried cranberries.

Success Hint: Measure flour by spooning it lightly into a dry-ingredient measuring cup, then leveling it off with the straight edge of a spatula or knife.

butterscotch-oatmeal cookies

Prep Time: 1 Hour 5 Minutes
Start to Finish: 1 Hour 20 Minutes
Servings: About 4 dozen cookies

- 1 cup butter or margarine, softened
- 1/4 cup sugar
- 1 teaspoon ground cinnamon
- 1 egg
- 1 box Betty Crocker® SuperMoist® yellow cake mix
- 2 cups quick-cooking oats
- 1 cup butterscotch chips
- 1 cup chopped walnuts

1 Heat oven to 350°F. In large bowl, beat butter, sugar, cinnamon and egg with electric mixer on medium speed until creamy. Stir in cake mix and oats until blended. Stir in butterscotch chips and walnuts.

2 On ungreased cookie sheets, drop dough by teaspoonfuls about 2 inches apart.

3 Bake 10 to 12 minutes or until light brown. Immediately remove from cookie sheets to cooling racks.

High Altitude (3500-6500 ft): No change.

Nutritional Info: 1 Cookie: Calories 130 (Calories from Fat 70); Total Fat 8g (Saturated Fat 4g, Trans Fat 0g); Cholesterol 15mg; Sodium 115mg; Total Carbohydrate 15g (Dietary Fiber 0g, Sugars 8g); Protein 1g. % Daily Value: Vitamin A 2%; Vitamin C 0%; Calcium 2%; Iron 2%. Exchanges: 1/2 Starch, 1/2 Other Carbohydrate, 1 Fat. Carbohydrate Choices: 1.

Betty's Kitchen Tips

Did You Know? Both old-fashioned and quick-cooking oats are whole oats that have been steamed and rolled. Because the quick-cooking variety is cut into small pieces before steaming, it gives baked goods a softer texture.

Variation: We like using butterscotch chips in these yummy cookies, but you can try making them with chocolate chips instead.

pistachio-cranberry biscotti

Prep Time: 25 Minutes
Start to Finish: 2 Hours 10 Minutes
Servings: 4 dozen cookies

1/2 cup butter or margarine, softened	3 teaspoons baking powder
1 cup sugar	1/4 teaspoon salt
1 teaspoon grated orange peel	3/4 cup sweetened dried cranberries
3 eggs	1/2 cup pistachio nuts
2-1/2 cups Gold Medal® all-purpose flour	2/3 cup white vanilla baking chips, melted
1 cup pistachio nuts, finely ground (1 cup)	

---

1 Heat oven to 325°F. Line cookie sheet with cooking parchment paper.

2 In large bowl, beat butter and sugar with electric mixer on medium-high speed until light and fluffy. Add orange peel and eggs, one at a time, beating thoroughly after each addition. On low speed, beat in flour, ground nuts, baking powder and salt. Stir in cranberries and 1/2 cup nuts.

3 Divide dough in half. On 1 side of cookie sheet, shape half of dough into 10-inch log. Repeat with remaining dough on same cookie sheet.

4 Bake 30 to 35 minutes or until toothpick inserted in center comes out clean. Cool 25 minutes; remove from cookie sheet to cutting board. Cut logs crosswise into 1/2-inch slices; discard ends. Place slices, cut sides down, on cookie sheet.

5 Bake about 18 minutes longer, turning once, until biscotti are crisp and light brown. Immediately remove from cookie sheet to cooling rack. Cool completely, about 30 minutes. Drizzle one side with melted baking chips; let stand until set before storing.

High Altitude (3500-6500 ft): No change.

Nutritional Info: 1 Cookie: Calories 110 (Calories from Fat 45); Total Fat 5g (Saturated Fat 2.5g, Trans Fat 0g); Cholesterol 20mg; Sodium 70mg; Total Carbohydrate 14g (Dietary Fiber 0g, Sugars 8g); Protein 2g. % Daily Value: Vitamin A 0%; Vitamin C 0%; Calcium 2%; Iron 4%. Exchanges: 1/2 Starch, 1/2 Other Carbohydrate, 1 Fat. Carbohydrate Choices: 1.

Betty's Kitchen Tip

• This recipe also tastes great with dried cherries instead of cranberries.

BARS & CANDIES

p. 299

286

296

303

cranberry-cherry pound cake bars

Prep Time: 35 Minutes
Start to Finish: 3 Hours 35 Minutes
Servings: 24 bars

Crust

3/4	cup butter or margarine, softened
1/2	cup granulated sugar
1/2	teaspoon vanilla
1-1/2	cups Gold Medal® all-purpose flour

Cake

1/2	cup butter or margarine, softened
1	cup granulated sugar
1/4	teaspoon almond extract
2	eggs
1-2/3	cups Gold Medal® all-purpose flour

1/4	teaspoon baking powder
1/4	teaspoon baking soda
1/4	cup cranberry juice
1/4	cup whipping cream
1	bag (5 oz) whole dried cherries (about 1 cup)
1	cup sweetened dried cranberries

Glaze

1	cup powdered sugar
2	tablespoons cranberry juice

1 Heat oven to 350°F. Lightly spray 13x9-inch pan with cooking spray. In medium bowl, beat 3/4 cup butter, 1/2 cup granulated sugar and the vanilla with electric mixer on medium speed until well blended. On low speed, beat in 1-1/2 cups flour until soft dough forms. Press dough in bottom of pan.

2 In large bowl, beat 1/2 cup butter, 1 cup granulated sugar and the almond extract on medium speed until well blended. Beat in eggs, one at a time, until creamy. On low speed, beat in 1-2/3 cups flour, the baking powder and baking soda. Beat in 1/4 cup juice and the cream.

Fold in cherries and cranberries. Spread over crust.

3 Bake 45 to 50 minutes or until toothpick inserted in center comes out clean and top is golden brown. Cool completely, about 2 hours.

4 In small bowl, beat glaze ingredients with wire whisk until smooth; drizzle over bars. Let stand about 10 minutes or until glaze is set. Run table knife around edges of bars to loosen. For bars, cut into 6 rows by 4 rows, using serrated knife.

High Altitude: (3500-6500 ft): No change.

Nutritional Info: 1 Bar: Calories 270 (Calories from Fat 100); Total Fat 11g (Saturated Fat 7g, Trans Fat 0g); Cholesterol 45mg; Sodium 95mg; Total Carbohydrate 40g (Dietary Fiber 1g, Sugars 26g); Protein 2g. % Daily Value: Vitamin A 8%; Vitamin C 0%; Calcium 0%; Iron 6%. Exchanges: 1 Starch, 1-1/2 Other Carbohydrate, 2 Fat. Carbohydrate Choices: 2-1/2.

Betty's Kitchen Tip

• Here's a wonderful bar to serve midmorning or for brunch with coffee or milk for the holidays!

chewy orange-date bars

Prep Time: 15 Minutes
Start to Finish: 2 Hours 20 Minutes
Servings: 48 bars

EASY

- 1 box Betty Crocker® SuperMoist® yellow cake mix
- 3/4 cup quick-cooking oats
- 3/4 cup butter or margarine, melted
- 1 tablespoon grated orange peel
- 3 eggs
- 2 cups chopped dates (from two 8-oz packages)
- 2 cups chopped walnuts

1 Heat oven to 350°F (or 325°F for dark or nonstick pan). Spray bottom and sides of 15x10x1-inch pan with baking spray with flour.

2 In large bowl, beat cake mix, oats, butter, orange peel and eggs with electric mixer on medium speed about 2 minutes or until batter is thick. Stir in dates and walnuts. Spread in pan.

3 Bake 20 to 25 minutes or until top is golden brown and toothpick inserted in center comes out clean. Cool on cooling rack 10 minutes. Run knife around sides of pan to loosen bars. Cool completely, about 1 hour 30 minutes. For bars, cut into 8 rows by 6 rows.

High Altitude: (3500-6500 ft): Bake 22 to 27 minutes.

Nutritional Info: 1 Bar: Calories 130 (Calories from Fat 70); Total Fat 7g (Saturated Fat 2.5g, Trans Fat 0g); Cholesterol 20mg; Sodium 100mg; Total Carbohydrate 15g (Dietary Fiber 1g, Sugars 9g); Protein 2g. % Daily Value: Vitamin A 4%; Vitamin C 0%; Calcium 2%; Iron 4%. Exchanges: 1 Starch, 1 Fat. Carbohydrate Choices: 1.

Betty's Kitchen Tips

Special Touch: Sprinkle the top of these bars with powdered sugar for an extra-special look.

Time-Saver: You can chop whole pitted dates or buy chopped dates.

nanaimo cookie bars

Prep Time: 25 Minutes
Start to Finish: 1 Hour 45 Minutes
Servings: 36 bars

Cookie Base

- 1 pouch (1 lb 1.5 oz) Betty Crocker® double chocolate chunk cookie mix
- 1 cup graham cracker crumbs
- 1/2 cup chopped nut topping or chopped walnuts
- 1/2 cup coconut
- 1 cup butter or margarine, melted
- 1 egg

Filling

- 4 cups powdered sugar
- 4 tablespoons vanilla instant pudding and pie filling mix
- 1/3 cup butter or margarine, softened
- 1/4 cup milk

Topping

- 1 bag (12 oz) semisweet chocolate chips (2 cups)
- 1/4 cup butter or margarine

1 Heat oven to 350°F. Line bottom and sides of 13x9-inch pan with foil, leaving foil hanging over 2 opposite sides of pan. In large bowl, stir cookie base ingredients until well mixed. Spread into pan; press lightly. Bake 16 to 18 minutes or until set. Cool completely, about 30 minutes.

2 In another large bowl, stir together powdered sugar and pudding mix. Add

1/3 cup butter and the milk; beat with electric mixer on medium speed until smooth (filling will be very thick). Spoon over cookie base; press evenly to cover. Refrigerate while making topping.

3 In small microwaveable bowl, microwave topping ingredients uncovered on High 1 minute to 1 minute 30 seconds, stirring every 30 seconds until melted and smooth. Spread over filling. Refrigerate uncovered until set, about 30 minutes.

4 Use foil to lift bars from pan; pull foil from sides of bars. Cut into 9 rows by 4 rows. Store covered in refrigerator.

High Altitude: (3500-6500 ft): No change.

Nutritional Info: 1 Bar: Calories 270 (Calories from Fat 130); Total Fat 14g (Saturated Fat 8g, Trans Fat 0g); Cholesterol 25mg; Sodium 150mg; Total Carbohydrate 34g (Dietary Fiber 0g, Sugars 26g); Protein 1g. % Daily Value: Vitamin A 6%; Vitamin C 0%; Calcium 0%; Iron 4%. Exchanges: 2-1/2 Other Carbohydrate, 2-1/2 Fat. Carbohydrate Choices: 2.

peanut butter-fudge bars

Prep Time: 20 Minutes
Start to Finish: 2 Hours 45 Minutes
Servings: 24 bars

Brownie Layer
- 1 pouch (10.25 oz) Betty Crocker® fudge brownie mix
- 3 tablespoons vegetable oil
- 2 tablespoons water
- 1 egg

Cookie Layer
- 1 pouch (1 lb 1.5 oz) Betty Crocker® peanut butter cookie mix
- 1/2 cup butter or margarine, softened
- 1/3 cup creamy peanut butter
- 2 eggs

Topping
- 1-1/2 cups milk chocolate chips (9 oz)
- 1/3 cup butterscotch chips
- 1/3 cup creamy peanut butter

1 Heat oven to 350°F. Grease bottom only of 13x9-inch pan with cooking spray or shortening. In medium bowl, stir brownie layer ingredients 50 strokes with spoon until blended. Spread evenly in pan.

2 In large bowl, beat cookie layer ingredients with electric mixer on medium speed until soft dough forms. Drop by spoonfuls over brownie layer; gently spread to pan edges.

3 Bake 32 to 35 minutes or until edges are golden brown and center looks slightly underdone. Cool in pan on cooling rack 5 minutes.

4 Meanwhile, in medium microwavable bowl, microwave both chips uncovered on High 2 to 3 minutes, stirring every minute, until mixture can be stirred smooth. Stir in 1/3 cup peanut butter until smooth.

5 Pour over warm bars; spread evenly. If desired, sprinkle with chopped peanuts. Cool completely, about 1 hour. Refrigerate about 45 minutes or until topping is set. Store covered at room temperature.

High Altitude: (3500-6500 ft): No change.

Nutritional Info: 1 Bar: Calories 310 (Calories from Fat 150); Total Fat 17g (Saturated Fat 7g, Trans Fat 0g); Cholesterol 40mg; Sodium 220mg; Total Carbohydrate 34g (Dietary Fiber 1g, Sugars 23g); Protein 5g. % Daily Value: Vitamin A 4%; Vitamin C 0%; Calcium 2%; Iron 6%. Exchanges: 2-1/2 Other Carbohydrate, 1/2 High-Fat Meat, 2-1/2 Fat. Carbohydrate Choices: 2.

chocolate-frosted mint bars

Prep Time: 25 Minutes
Start to Finish: 2 Hours 45 Minutes
Servings: 36 bars

Cream Cheese Mixture

- 1 package (8 oz) cream cheese, softened
- 1/4 cup granulated sugar
- 1 egg
- 1 teaspoon mint extract
- 4 drops green food color

Chocolate Mixture

- 1 cup butter or margarine
- 4 oz unsweetened baking chocolate, cut into pieces
- 2 cups granulated sugar
- 2 teaspoons vanilla
- 4 eggs
- 1 cup Gold Medal® all-purpose flour

Frosting

- 2 tablespoons butter or margarine
- 2 tablespoons corn syrup
- 2 tablespoons water
- 2 oz unsweetened baking chocolate, cut into pieces
- 1 teaspoon vanilla
- 1 cup powdered sugar

1 Heat oven to 350°F. Grease bottom and sides of 13x9-inch pan with shortening or cooking spray; lightly flour. In small bowl, beat cream cheese and 1/4 cup granulated sugar with spoon until smooth. Stir in 1 egg, mint extract and food color until well mixed; set aside.

2 In 3-quart saucepan, melt 1 cup butter and 4 oz chocolate over very low heat, stirring constantly; remove from heat. Cool 15 minutes or until slightly cooled.

3 Stir 2 cups sugar and 2 teaspoons vanilla into chocolate mixture. Add 4 eggs, one at a time, beating well with spoon after each addition. Stir in flour. Spread in pan. Carefully spoon cream cheese mixture over brownie mixture. Lightly swirl cream cheese mixture into brownie mixture with knife for marbled design.

4 Bake 45 to 50 minutes or until set. Cool in pan on cooling rack 30 minutes. Refrigerate 1 hour.

5 In 2-quart saucepan, heat 2 tablespoons butter, the corn syrup and water to rolling boil, stirring frequently; remove from heat. Stir in 2 oz chocolate until melted. Stir in 1 teaspoon vanilla and the powdered sugar; beat with spoon until smooth. Spread frosting over cooled brownies. For bars, cut into 6 rows by 6 rows. Store covered in refrigerator.

High Altitude: (3500-6500 ft): No change.

Nutritional Info: 1 Bar: Calories 200 (Calories from Fat 100); Total Fat 11g (Saturated Fat 7g, Trans Fat 0g); Cholesterol 50mg; Sodium 70mg; Total Carbohydrate 21g (Dietary Fiber 1g, Sugars 16g); Protein 2g. % Daily Value: Vitamin A 6%; Vitamin C 0%; Calcium 0%; Iron 6%. Exchanges: 1/2 Starch, 1 Other Carbohydrate, 2 Fat. Carbohydrate Choices: 1-1/2.

chunky chocolate and almond bars

Prep Time: 20 Minutes
Start to Finish: 2 Hours 35 Minutes
Servings: 48 bars

Crust
1	box Betty Crocker® SuperMoist® chocolate fudge cake mix
1/2	cup butter or margarine, softened

Topping
4	eggs
1	cup dark corn syrup
1/4	cup butter or margarine, melted
2	cups salted roasted whole almonds, coarsely chopped
6	oz dark or bittersweet baking chocolate, chopped

1 Heat oven to 350°F (or 325°F for dark or nonstick pan). Place cake mix in medium bowl. Using pastry blender or fork, cut in 1/2 cup butter until crumbly. Press firmly in ungreased 13x9-inch pan. Bake 12 to 14 minutes or until set.

2 In large bowl, beat eggs, corn syrup and 1/4 cup melted butter with wire whisk until smooth. Stir in almonds and chocolate. Pour over crust.

3 Bake 25 to 30 minutes longer or until golden brown and set. Cool 30 minutes. Refrigerate about 1 hour or until chocolate is firm. For bars, cut into 8 rows by 6 rows. Store covered in refrigerator.

High Altitude: (3500-6500 ft): No change.

Nutritional Info: 1 Bar: Calories 150 (Calories from Fat 80); Total Fat 9g (Saturated Fat 3.5g, Trans Fat 0g); Cholesterol 25mg; Sodium 135mg; Total Carbohydrate 15g (Dietary Fiber 1g, Sugars 9g); Protein 2g. % Daily Value: Vitamin A 2%; Vitamin C 0%; Calcium 4%; Iron 8%. Exchanges: 1 Starch, 1-1/2 Fat. Carbohydrate Choices: 1.

Betty's Kitchen Tips

Success Hint: Much like the center of a pecan pie, the center of these bars is very moist and may even look raw. Not to worry—that's how they should look.

Did You Know? Dark corn syrup has color added and a caramel flavor, which gives it a darker color and a stronger flavor than light corn syrup.

irish cream-coffee bars

Prep Time: 25 Minutes
Start to Finish: 1 Hour 55 Minutes
Servings: 25 bars

Bars

1	pouch (1 lb 1.5 oz) Betty Crocker® sugar cookie mix
1/2	cup chopped pecans
1/2	cup cold butter or margarine
1	egg
1	can (14 oz) sweetened condensed milk (not evaporated)
2	tablespoons Irish cream liqueur
1	teaspoon instant coffee granules or crystals

Topping

1	cup whipping cream
3	tablespoons packed brown sugar
1	tablespoon Irish cream liqueur
1	teaspoon vanilla
1/8	teaspoon ground cinnamon
25	cinnamon sticks (2 inch)

1 Heat oven to 350°F. Spray bottom and sides of 8-inch square pan with cooking spray. In large bowl, place cookie mix and pecans. Cut in butter, using pastry blender or fork, until mixture looks like coarse crumbs. With fork, stir in egg. Press 1/2 of cookie mixture in bottom of pan.

2 Bake 15 to 18 minutes or until golden brown. Reserve remaining cookie mixture. Meanwhile, in small bowl, stir milk, 2 tablespoons liqueur and the coffee granules until well blended.

3 Pour coffee mixture evenly over warm crust. Sprinkle reserved cookie mixture over top. Bake 25 to 30 minutes longer or until golden brown. Cool 30 minutes at room temperature. Refrigerate 1 hour to cool completely. Let stand 10 minutes before cutting into bars (5 rows by 5 rows). Store bars covered at room temperature.

4 Just before serving, in small bowl, beat whipping cream, brown sugar, 1 tablespoon liqueur and the vanilla with electric mixer on high speed until soft peaks form. Top each bar with dollop of whipped cream; sprinkle with ground cinnamon. Insert cinnamon stick into each dollop of whipped cream.

High Altitude: (3500-6500 ft): No change.

Nutritional Info: 1 Bar: Calories 230 (Calories from Fat 110); Total Fat 12g (Saturated Fat 6g, Trans Fat 1g); Cholesterol 35mg; Sodium 110mg; Total Carbohydrate 26g (Dietary Fiber 0g, Sugars 19g); Protein 2g . % Daily Value: Vitamin A 6%; Vitamin C 0%; Calcium 6%; Iron 2%. Exchanges: 1 Starch, 1/2 Other Carbohydrate, 2-1/2 Fat. Carbohydrate Choices: 2.

festive vanilla fudge

Prep Time: 10 Minutes
Start to Finish: 1 Hour 10 Minutes
Servings: 32 candies

EASY

1	bag (12 oz) white vanilla baking chips (2 cups)
1/4	cup whipping cream
1	tablespoon honey
3/4	cup chopped salted mixed nuts
3/4	cup red and green candy-coated chocolate candies

1 Line bottom and sides of 8-inch square pan with foil, leaving foil overhanging 2 opposite sides of pan; spray foil with cooking spray.

2 In large microwavable bowl, mix baking chips, cream and honey. Microwave on High about 1 minute 30 seconds, stirring every 30 seconds, until chips are melted and mixture is smooth. Stir in nuts. Cool about 30 minutes or until just slightly warm. Quickly stir in 1/2 cup of the candies. Spread evenly in pan. Sprinkle remaining 1/4 cup candies over top; press lightly into top. Refrigerate about 30 minutes or until completely set.

3 Remove fudge from pan onto cutting board by lifting with foil; peel back foil. With large sharp knife, cut into 4 rectangles. Cut each rectangle crosswise into 8 pieces.

High Altitude: (3500-6500 ft): No change.

Nutritional Info: 1 Candy: Calories 110 (Calories from Fat 60); Total Fat 6g (Saturated Fat 3.5g, Trans Fat 0g); Cholesterol 0mg; Sodium 40mg; Total Carbohydrate 11g (Dietary Fiber 0g, Sugars 10g); Protein 1g. % Daily Value: Vitamin A 0%; Vitamin C 0%; Calcium 2%; Iron 0%. Exchanges: 1/2 Starch, 1/2 Other Carbohydrate, 1 Fat. Carbohydrate Choices: 1.

Betty's Kitchen Tips

Purchasing: During the holidays, candy-coated chocolate candies are usually available in a red and green combination. If you can't find just the red and green mixture, sort a multicolored bag to get enough of the red and green for this recipe. Use the remaining candies to stir into drop cookies or just for snacking.

Substitution: White baking bars or white chocolate candy bars (12 oz total) can be substituted for the vanilla chips, but they are a bit more expensive.

coconut bonbon bars

Prep Time: 35 Minutes
Start to Finish: 4 Hours 10 Minutes
Servings: 36 bars

Cookie Base
- 1 pouch (1 lb 1.5 oz) Betty Crocker® double chocolate chunk cookie mix
- 1/4 cup vegetable oil
- 2 tablespoons water
- 1 egg

Filling
- 1/2 cup butter, softened
- 1 can (14 oz) sweetened condensed milk (not evaporated)
- 1 teaspoon vanilla
- 6 cups powdered sugar
- 1-1/2 cups coconut
- 1/2 cup finely chopped blanched almonds

Topping
- 1/2 cup whipping cream
- 1 bag (12 oz) semisweet chocolate chips (2 cups)
- 1/2 cup butter (do not use margarine)

1 Heat oven to 350°F. In large bowl, stir cookie base ingredients until soft dough forms. Press in bottom of ungreased 13x9-inch pan. Bake 12 minutes. Cool completely, about 30 minutes.

2 Meanwhile, in large bowl, beat softened butter, milk and vanilla with electric mixer on medium speed until smooth. Gradually beat in powdered sugar. Stir in coconut and almonds until well blended. Spread filling evenly over cooled cookie base. Cover; refrigerate about 1 hour or until filling is set.

3 Meanwhile, in 2-quart nonstick saucepan, heat topping ingredients over medium-low heat, stirring constantly, until melted and smooth. Cool about 10 minutes or until lukewarm.

4 Pour topping over filling; spread to cover filling. Refrigerate uncovered about 2 hours or until set. Before cutting into bars, let stand 10 minutes at room temperature. For bars, cut into 9 rows by 4 rows. Store covered in refrigerator.

High Altitude: (3500-6500 ft): No change.

Nutritional Info: 1 Bar: Calories 330 (Calories from Fat 140); Total Fat 15g (Saturated Fat 8g, Trans Fat 0g); Cholesterol 25mg; Sodium 125mg; Total Carbohydrate 45g (Dietary Fiber 1g, Sugars 38g); Protein 2g. % Daily Value: Vitamin A 4%; Vitamin C 0%; Calcium 4%; Iron 4%. Exchanges: 1/2 Starch, 2-1/2 Other Carbohydrate, 3 Fat. Carbohydrate Choices: 3.

Betty's Kitchen Tip

• To cut bars easily, line bottom and sides of 13x9-inch pan with foil, leaving foil overhanging at 2 opposite sides of pan. Use foil to lift bars from pan, and pull foil from sides of bars before cutting.

orange-toffee-almond truffles

Prep Time: 10 Minutes
Start to Finish: 3 Hours
Servings: About 30 truffles

EASY

- 1-1/3 cups semisweet chocolate chips (8 oz)
- 1/2 cup whipping cream
- 1/2 teaspoon grated orange peel
- 1/2 cup toffee bits
- 1 cup sliced almonds, chopped, toasted

1 In large microwavable bowl, microwave chocolate chips uncovered on High about 1 minute or until softened; stir until smooth. (If not completely softened, continue microwaving in 15-second increments, stirring after each, until smooth.)

2 Stir whipping cream into chocolate until very smooth and glossy. Stir in orange peel and toffee bits. Cover and refrigerate about 2 hours or until firm.

3 Place almonds in small bowl. Shape chocolate mixture into 1-inch balls. Immediately roll balls in almonds, pressing to coat. Place on ungreased cookie sheet or in paper candy cups. Refrigerate about 30 minutes or until firm. Remove from refrigerator 20 minutes before serving.

High Altitude: (3500-6500 ft): No change.

Nutritional Info: 1 Truffle: Calories 90 (Calories from Fat 60); Total Fat 6g (Saturated Fat 3g, Trans Fat 0g); Cholesterol 10mg; Sodium 20mg; Total Carbohydrate 8g (Dietary Fiber 0g, Sugars 6g); Protein 1g. % Daily Value: Vitamin A 0%; Vitamin C 0%; Calcium 0%; Iron 0%. Exchanges: 1/2 Starch, 1 Fat. Carbohydrate Choices: 1/2.

Betty's Kitchen Tip

• At each place at the table, place a truffle wrapped in tulle and tied with a ribbon. Add a gift tag for a pretty and delicious place card.

mocha marble fudge

Prep Time: 10 Minutes
Start to Finish: 2 Hours 10 Minutes
Servings: 64 candies

EASY LOW FAT

Butter for greasing
1   can (14 oz) sweetened condensed milk (not evaporated)
1   tablespoon instant espresso coffee powder or coffee granules

1   bag (12 oz) white vanilla baking chips (2 cups)
1   cup semisweet chocolate chips (6 oz)
1/2   teaspoon vanilla

1 Line bottom and sides of 8- or 9-inch square pan with foil, leaving foil overhanging 2 opposite sides of pan; grease foil with butter.

2 In 2-quart nonstick saucepan, mix 3/4 cup of the milk and the espresso powder. Stir in white baking chips. Heat over medium-low heat 5 to 7 minutes, stirring occasionally, until chips are melted and mixture is smooth. Spread in pan.

3 In same saucepan, mix remaining milk, the chocolate chips and vanilla. Heat over medium-low heat 5 to 7 minutes, stirring occasionally, until chips are melted and mixture is smooth. Drop by spoonfuls over espresso layer. Swirl mixtures with table knife. Gently press with hand to smooth top.

4 Refrigerate about 2 hours or until cooled and firm. Remove from pan, using foil to lift. Cut into 1-inch pieces.

High Altitude: (3500-6500 ft): No change.

Nutritional Info: 1 Candy: Calories 60 (Calories from Fat 25); Total Fat 3g (Saturated Fat 2g, Trans Fat 0g); Cholesterol 0mg; Sodium 20mg; Total Carbohydrate 8g (Dietary Fiber 0g, Sugars 8g); Protein 1g. % Daily Value: Vitamin A 0%; Vitamin C 0%; Calcium 2%; Iron 0%. Exchanges: 1/2 Other Carbohydrate, 1/2 Fat. Carbohydrate Choices: 1/2.

Betty's Kitchen Tips

Success Hint: For an extra coffee "hit," top each square of fudge with a chocolate-covered coffee bean.

Special Touch: To serve or to present as a gift, place each candy in a small holiday paper candy cup.

coffee-chocolate chip bars

Prep Time: 20 Minutes
Start to Finish: 2 Hours 50 Minutes
Servings: 48 bars

Crust
1   box Betty Crocker® SuperMoist®
     white cake mix
1/3 cup butter or margarine, softened
2   egg whites

Filling and Topping
1   package (8 oz) cream cheese, softened
2   whole eggs
1   cup powdered sugar
1-1/2 teaspoons instant espresso coffee powder
2   cups miniature semisweet chocolate chips

1 Heat oven to 350°F (or 325°F for dark or nonstick pan). In large bowl, beat cake mix, butter and egg whites with electric mixer on low speed until crumbly. Press in ungreased 13x9-inch pan.

2 In medium bowl, beat cream cheese and 2 whole eggs on medium speed until smooth. On low speed, gradually beat in powdered sugar and espresso coffee powder. Stir in 1 cup of the chocolate chips. Spread over crust.

3 Bake 22 to 26 minutes or until set. Cool completely, about 1 hour.

4 In medium microwavable bowl, microwave remaining 1 cup chocolate chips uncovered on High 30 to 45 seconds, stirring once, until softened and chips can be stirred smooth. Spoon into resealable food-storage plastic bag; seal bag. Cut small tip from 1 bottom corner of bag; drizzle chocolate over bars. Refrigerate about 1 hour or until chocolate is firm. For bars, cut into 8 rows by 6 rows. Store covered in refrigerator.

High Altitude: (3500-6500 ft): Bake 26 to 30 minutes.

Nutritional Info: 1 Bar: Calories 120 (Calories from Fat 50); Total Fat 6g (Saturated Fat 3.5g, Trans Fat 0g); Cholesterol 15mg; Sodium 100mg; Total Carbohydrate 16g (Dietary Fiber 0g, Sugars 10g); Protein 1g. % Daily Value: Vitamin A 2%; Vitamin C 0%; Calcium 0%; Iron 2%. Exchanges: 1/2 Starch, 1/2 Other Carbohydrate, 1 Fat. Carbohydrate Choices: 1.

Betty's Kitchen Tips

How-To: Use an egg separator to safely separate the egg white from the yolk. A separator consists of a small bowl-shaped center that holds the yolk with a surrounding space that allows the white to slip through into a bowl.

Purchasing: In most grocery stores, you'll find instant espresso coffee powder in the same aisle as the instant coffee.

spooky monster brownie pops

Prep Time: 30 Minutes
Start to Finish: 2 Hours
Servings: 24 pops

- 1 box (1 lb 2.3 oz) Betty Crocker® fudge brownie mix
- Water, vegetable oil and eggs called for on brownie mix box
- 24 craft sticks (flat wooden sticks with round ends)
- 1 package (16 oz) vanilla-flavored candy coating (almond bark)
- 8 to 10 drops green food color
- 48 small green candies
- 1/2 cup Betty Crocker® Rich & Creamy chocolate frosting (from 1-lb container)

1 Heat oven to 350°F. Line bottom and sides of 13x9-inch pan with foil, leaving foil overhanging on 2 opposite sides of pan. Spray foil with cooking spray. Bake and cool brownie mix as directed on box for 13x9-inch pan.

2 Place brownies in freezer 30 minutes. Remove brownies from pan, using foil to lift; peel foil from sides of brownies. Cut into 24 rectangular bars, 6 rows lengthwise by 4 rows across, each about 1-1/2 by 3 1/4 inches. Gently insert stick into end of each bar, peeling foil from bars. Place on cookie sheet; freeze 30 minutes.

3 In microwavable bowl, microwave candy coating uncovered on High about 1 minute or until smooth when stirred. Stir in food color. Spread on brownies. Insert 2 candies into sides of each brownie to look like ears. Place on waxed paper or foil to dry.

4 To decorate, spoon frosting into small resealable food-storage plastic bag; seal bag. Cut small hole in bottom corner of bag. Squeeze bag to pipe frosting on top of each brownie to look like hair. Draw eyebrows, eyes and zigzag mouth to look like Frankenstein face.

High Altitude: (3500-6500 ft): No change.

Nutritional Info: 1 Pop: Calories 300 (Calories from Fat 130); Total Fat 14g (Saturated Fat 5g, Trans Fat 0g); Cholesterol 20mg; Sodium 115mg; Total Carbohydrate 39g (Dietary Fiber 1g, Sugars 31g); Protein 2g. % Daily Value: Vitamin A 0%; Vitamin C 0%; Calcium 4%; Iron 4%. Exchanges: 1 Starch, 1-1/2 Other Carbohydrate, 2-1/2 Fat. Carbohydrate Choices: 2-1/2.

Betty's Kitchen Tips

Substitution: Substitute white vanilla baking chips for the almond bark if desired.

Purchasing: Hair tips can be purchased at a cake decorating store or online.

gooey caramel-chocolate bars

Prep Time: 25 Minutes
Start to Finish: 3 Hours
Servings: 48 bars

Crust

1   box Betty Crocker® SuperMoist® chocolate fudge cake mix
1/2   cup butter or margarine, softened
3   eggs
1   cup semisweet chocolate chips

Filling

1   bag (14 oz) caramels, unwrapped

1/4   cup butter or margarine
1   can (14 oz) sweetened condensed milk (not evaporated)

Topping

1/2   cup reserved cake mix
1/2   cup quick-cooking oats
3   tablespoons butter or margarine, softened

1 Heat oven to 350°F (or 325°F for dark or nonstick pan). Reserve 1/2 cup cake mix for topping. In large bowl, beat remaining cake mix, 1/2 cup butter and the eggs with electric mixer on medium speed until dough forms. Stir in chocolate chips. Spread in ungreased 13x9-inch pan. Bake 14 to 18 minutes or until set.

2 Meanwhile, in 2-quart saucepan, heat caramels, 1/4 cup butter and the milk over medium heat about 8 minutes, stirring frequently, until caramels are melted and mixture is smooth.

3 Spread caramel filling evenly over partially baked crust. In small bowl, mix reserved 1/2 cup cake mix, the oats and 3 tablespoons butter with fork until crumbly. Sprinkle over caramel filling.

4 Bake 18 to 22 minutes longer or until top is set. Cool completely, about 2 hours. Run knife around sides of pan to loosen bars. For bars, cut into 8 rows by 6 rows.

High Altitude: (3500-6500 ft): In step 1, bake 16 to 20 minutes.

Nutritional Info: 1 Bar: Calories 160 (Calories from Fat 60); Total Fat 7g (Saturated Fat 4g, Trans Fat 0g); Cholesterol 25mg; Sodium 150mg; Total Carbohydrate 22g (Dietary Fiber 0g, Sugars 15g); Protein 2g. % Daily Value: Vitamin A 4%; Vitamin C 0%; Calcium 4%; Iron 4%. Exchanges: 1/2 Starch, 1 Other Carbohydrate, 1-1/2 Fat. Carbohydrate Choices: 1-1/2.

Betty's Kitchen Tip

• Get your kids involved in making these bars by letting them unwrap the caramels. Just make sure the caramels don't disappear!

fully loaded bars

Prep Time: 20 Minutes
Start to Finish: 1 Hour 50 Minutes
Servings: 36 bars

3/4	cup packed brown sugar
3/4	cup butter or margarine, softened
1	egg
1-1/2	cups Gold Medal® all-purpose flour
1	cup old-fashioned or quick-cooking oats
1	bag (14 oz) caramels, unwrapped
1/3	cup half-and-half
1	cup semisweet chocolate chunks
1	cup coarsely chopped mixed nuts
1/4	cup broken pretzel twists

1 Heat oven to 350°F (325°F for dark or nonstick pan). Grease 13x9-inch pan with shortening or cooking spray. In large bowl, beat brown sugar, butter and egg with electric mixer on medium speed, or mix with spoon. Stir in flour and oats. Spread in pan.

2 Bake 15 to 20 minutes or until light golden brown. Meanwhile, in 1-quart saucepan, heat caramels and half-and-half over low heat, stirring occasionally, until caramels are melted.

3 Pour caramel mixture over crust. Sprinkle with chocolate chunks, nuts and pretzels.

4 Bake 5 to 8 minutes or until chocolate is softened. Cool about 1 hour or until chocolate is set. For bars, cut into 6 rows by 6 rows.

High Altitude: (3500-6500 ft): No change.

Nutritional Info: 1 Bar: Calories 180 (Calories from Fat 80); Total Fat 9g (Saturated Fat 4g, Trans Fat 0g); Cholesterol 20mg; Sodium 80mg; Total Carbohydrate 23g (Dietary Fiber 1g, Sugars 12g); Protein 2g. % Daily Value: Vitamin A 2%; Vitamin C 0%; Calcium 4%; Iron 4%. Exchanges: 1-1/2 Other Carbohydrate, 2 Fat. Carbohydrate Choices: 1-1/2.

Betty's Kitchen Tip

• Pop these crunchy-chewy bars into the refrigerator to quickly cool them.

toffee-pecan bars

Prep Time: 30 Minutes
Start to Finish: 2 Hours
Servings: 48 bars

Crust

3/4	cup butter or margarine, softened
1/3	cup packed brown sugar
1	egg
2	cups Gold Medal® all-purpose flour

Filling

1	cup butter or margarine
3/4	cup packed brown sugar
1/4	cup light corn syrup
2	cups coarsely chopped pecans
1	cup swirled milk chocolate and caramel chips (from 10-oz bag)

1 Heat oven to 375°F. Grease bottom and sides of 15x10x1-inch pan with shortening or cooking spray (do not use dark pan).

2 In large bowl, beat 3/4 cup butter and 1/3 cup brown sugar with electric mixer on medium speed until light and fluffy. Add egg; beat until well blended. On low speed, beat in flour until dough begins to form. Press dough in pan.

3 Bake 12 to 17 minutes or until edges are light golden brown. Meanwhile, in 2-quart saucepan, heat 1 cup butter, 3/4 cup brown sugar and the corn syrup to boiling over medium heat, stirring frequently. Boil 2 minutes without stirring.

4 Quickly stir pecans into corn syrup mixture; spread over partially baked crust. Bake 20 to 23 minutes or until filling is golden brown and bubbly.

5 Immediately sprinkle chocolate chips evenly over hot bars. Let stand 5 minutes to soften. With rubber spatula, gently swirl melted chips over bars. Cool completely, about 1 hour. For bars, cut into 6 rows by 4 rows to make 24 squares, then cut each square in half to make triangles. Store in refrigerator.

High Altitude: (3500-6500 ft): No change.

Nutritional Info: 1 Bar: Calories 160 (Calories from Fat 100); Total Fat 11g (Saturated Fat 5g, Trans Fat 0g); Cholesterol 20mg; Sodium 50mg; Total Carbohydrate 14g (Dietary Fiber 0g, Sugars 9g); Protein 1g. % Daily Value: Vitamin A 4%; Vitamin C 0%; Calcium 0%; Iron 2%. Exchanges: 1/2 Starch, 1/2 Other Carbohydrate, 2 Fat. Carbohydrate Choices: 1.

Betty's Kitchen Tips

Variation: Try using raspberry-flavored chocolate chips instead of the swirled chips.

Substitution: Coarsely chopped walnuts can be used instead of the pecans.

pistachio-cranberry fudge

Prep Time: 20 Minutes
Start to Finish: 2 Hours 20 Minutes
Servings: 72 candies

- 1-1/2 bags (12-oz size) semisweet chocolate chips (3 cups)
- 2 cups miniature marshmallows or 16 large marshmallows, cut in half
- 1 can (14 oz) sweetened condensed milk (not evaporated)
- 1 teaspoon vanilla
- 1 cup pistachio nuts
- 1/2 cup sweetened dried cranberries or chopped candied cherries
- 1/4 cup white vanilla baking chips, melted, if desired

1 Line 9-inch square pan with foil, leaving 1 inch of foil hanging over 2 opposite sides of pan. Grease foil with butter.

2 In 8-cup microwavable measuring cup or bowl, microwave chocolate chips, marshmallows and milk uncovered on High 3 to 5 minutes, stirring every minute, until marshmallows and chips are melted and can be stirred smooth.

3 Stir in vanilla, nuts and cranberries. Immediately pour into pan. Drizzle with melted vanilla baking chips. Refrigerate about 2 hours or until firm.

4 Using foil edges to lift, remove fudge from pan. Cut into 9 rows by 8 rows, or cut into diamond shapes.

High Altitude: (3500-6500 ft): No change.

Nutritional Info: 1 Candy: Calories 70 (Calories from Fat 30); Total Fat 3g (Saturated Fat 2g, Trans Fat 0g); Cholesterol 0mg; Sodium 10mg; Total Carbohydrate 10g (Dietary Fiber 0g, Sugars 9g); Protein 1g. % Daily Value: Vitamin A 0%; Vitamin C 0%; Calcium 0%; Iron 0%. Exchanges: 1/2 Starch, 1/2 Fat. Carbohydrate Choices: 1/2.

LOW FAT

Betty's Kitchen Tips

Substitution: For a scrumptious new flavor twist, omit the cranberries, substitute hazelnuts for the pistachios and add 2 tablespoons hazelnut liqueur with the nuts.

Variation: If you like luscious, creamy chocolate fudge, just leave out the nuts and cranberries for a smooth, rich chocolate treat.

easy peppermint marshmallows

Prep Time: 20 Minutes
Start to Finish: 8 Hours 20 Minutes
Servings: 77 marshmallows

LOW FAT

Butter for greasing
1/3 cup powdered sugar
2-1/2 tablespoons unflavored gelatin
1/2 cup cold water
1-1/2 cups granulated sugar

1 cup corn syrup
1/4 teaspoon salt
1/2 cup water
1 teaspoon pure peppermint extract
8 to 10 drops red food color

1 Generously grease bottom and sides of 11x7-inch (2-quart) glass baking dish with butter; dust with 1 tablespoon of the powdered sugar. In bowl of stand mixer, sprinkle gelatin over 1/2 cup cold water to soften; set aside.

2 In 2-quart saucepan, heat granulated sugar, corn syrup, salt and 1/2 cup water over low heat, stirring constantly, until sugar is dissolved. Heat to boiling; cook without stirring about 30 minutes to 240°F on candy thermometer or until small amount of mixture dropped into cup of very cold water forms a ball that holds its shape but is pliable; remove from heat.

3 Slowly pour syrup into softened gelatin while beating on low speed. Increase speed to high; beat 8 to 10 minutes or until mixture is white and has almost tripled in volume. Add peppermint extract; beat on high speed 1 minute. Pour into baking dish, patting lightly with wet hands. Drop food color randomly onto top of marshmallow mixture. Pull table knife through food color to create swirl pattern over top. Let stand uncovered at least 8 hours or overnight.

4 Dust cutting board with about 1 tablespoon powdered sugar. Place remaining powdered sugar in small bowl. To remove marshmallow mixture, loosen sides from dish and gently lift in one piece onto cutting board. Using sharp knife greased with butter, cut into 1-inch squares (11 rows by 7 rows). Dust bottom and sides of each marshmallow square by dipping into bowl of powdered sugar. Store in airtight container at room temperature up to 3 weeks.

High Altitude: (3500-6500 ft): No change.

Nutritional Info: 1 Marshmallow: Calories 35 (Calories from Fat 0); Total Fat 0g (Saturated Fat 0g, Trans Fat 0g); Cholesterol 0mg; Sodium 10mg; Total Carbohydrate 8g (Dietary Fiber 0g, Sugars 6g); Protein 0g. % Daily Value: Vitamin A 0%; Vitamin C 0%; Calcium 0%; Iron 0%. Exchanges: 1/2 Other Carbohydrate. Carbohydrate Choices: 1/2.

Betty's Kitchen Tip

• Package marshmallows in a plastic bag, and tie with curly ribbon. Place bags of marshmallows in oversized mugs along with packages of gourmet cocoa.

mexican brownies

Prep Time: 30 Minutes
Start to Finish: 3 Hours 30 Minutes
Servings: 20 brownies

- 1 box (1 lb 6.5 oz) Betty Crocker® Original Supreme Premium brownie mix (with chocolate syrup pouch)
- 1 tablespoon ground cinnamon

Water, vegetable oil and eggs called for on brownie mix box

- 1 cup semisweet chocolate chips (6 oz)
- 1/2 cup butter or margarine
- 1 cup packed brown sugar
- 1/4 cup milk
- 2 cups powdered sugar
- 1 cup chopped pecans, toasted

1 Heat oven to 350°F (325°F for dark or nonstick pan). Spray bottom only of 13x9-inch square pan with cooking spray.

2 In medium bowl, stir together dry brownie mix and cinnamon. Add the pouch of chocolate syrup, water, oil and eggs; stir until well blended. Stir in chocolate chips. Spread in pan.

3 Bake 28 to 30 minutes or until toothpick inserted 2 inches from side of pan comes out almost clean. Cool completely, about 2 hours.

4 In 2-quart saucepan, melt butter over medium heat. Stir in brown sugar. Heat to boiling, stirring constantly. Reduce heat to low; boil and stir 2 minutes. Stir in milk. Heat to boiling. Remove from heat; cool to lukewarm, about 30 minutes.

5 Gradually beat powdered sugar into brown sugar mixture with wire whisk until blended, then beat until smooth. If frosting becomes too stiff, stir in additional milk, 1 teaspoon at a time. Spread frosting over brownies; sprinkle with pecans. For brownies, cut into 5 rows by 4 rows. Store tightly covered.

High Altitude: (3500-6500 ft): Follow High Altitude directions for 13x9-inch pan on brownie mix box, adding cinnamon and chocolate chips as directed in recipe.

Nutritional Info: 1 Brownie: Calories 380 (Calories from Fat 150); Total Fat 17g (Saturated Fat 6g, Trans Fat 0g); Cholesterol 35mg; Sodium 170mg; Total Carbohydrate 55g (Dietary Fiber 1g, Sugars 45g); Protein 2g. % Daily Value: Vitamin A 4%; Vitamin C 0%; Calcium 2%; Iron 10%. Exchanges: 1 Starch, 2-1/2 Other Carbohydrate, 3-1/2 Fat. Carbohydrate Choices: 3-1/2.

Betty's Kitchen Tips

How-To: To toast pecans in the microwave, place 1 teaspoon vegetable oil and 1 cup nuts in 2-cup glass measuring cup. Microwave uncovered on High 2 minutes 30 seconds to 3 minutes 30 seconds, stirring every 30 seconds, until light brown.

Did You Know? Cinnamon, caramel and pecans are typical ingredients in Mexican desserts.

tropical layered bark

Prep Time: 15 Minutes
Start to Finish: 1 Hour
Servings: About 9 dozen candies

EASY LOW FAT

12　oz chocolate-flavored candy coating, cut up

3/4　cup coarsely chopped cashews

12　oz vanilla-flavored candy coating (almond bark), cut up

3/4　cup dried tropical three-fruit mix (from 7-oz bag)

1 Line cookie sheet with waxed paper. In 1-quart microwavable bowl, microwave chocolate coating on High 1 minute; stir. Microwave in 15-second increments, stirring after each, until melted. Stir in cashews. Spread in thin 12x9-inch rectangle on cookie sheet. Refrigerate 15 minutes.

2 In another 1-quart microwavable bowl, microwave vanilla coating on High 1 minute; stir. Microwave in 15-second increments, stirring after each, until melted. Stir in 1/2 cup of the dried fruit. Quickly and carefully spoon and quickly spread half of the vanilla mixture over

half of the chocolate layer (edges may not be completely covered). Repeat spreading remaining vanilla mixture over remaining chocolate layer. Sprinkle remaining 1/4 cup dried fruit evenly over top; press in lightly.

3 Let stand about 30 minutes or until completely cooled and set. Cut into 1-inch pieces. Store covered at room temperature.

High Altitude: (3500-6500 ft): No change.

Nutritional Info: 1 Candy: Calories 45 (Calories from Fat 20); Total Fat 2.5g (Saturated Fat 1.5g, Trans Fat 0g); Cholesterol 0mg; Sodium 5mg; Total Carbohydrate 5g (Dietary Fiber 0g, Sugars 4g); Protein 0g. % Daily Value: Vitamin A 0%; Vitamin C 0%; Calcium 0%; Iron 0%. Exchanges: 1/2 Other Carbohydrate, 1/2 Fat. Carbohydrate Choices: 1/2.

Betty's Kitchen Tips

Substitution: The tropical fruit mix contains dried mango, papaya and pineapple. If this mix isn't available, you can often find individual packages of each fruit, or you could use another mixture of dried fruit.

Success Hint: Be sure the chocolate layer is very cold when you add the vanilla layer so the chocolate doesn't melt and mix with the vanilla layer.

pumpkin cheesecake squares

Prep Time: 20 Minutes
Start to Finish: 3 Hours 5 Minutes
Servings: 16 bars

Base
1	cup Gold Medal® all-purpose flour
3/4	cup packed brown sugar
1/2	cup butter or margarine
1	cup quick-cooking oats
1/2	cup finely chopped walnuts

Filling
1	package (8 oz) cream cheese, softened
3/4	cup sugar
1	can (15 oz) pumpkin (not pumpkin pie mix)
1-1/2	teaspoons ground cinnamon
1	teaspoon ground ginger
3	eggs

Topping
2	cups sour cream
1/3	cup sugar
1/2	teaspoon vanilla

High Altitude: (3500-6500 ft): No change.

Nutritional Info: 1 Bar: Calories 340 (Calories from Fat 170); Total Fat 19g (Saturated Fat 11g, Trans Fat 0.5g); Cholesterol 50mg; Sodium 110mg; Total Carbohydrate 37g (Dietary Fiber 2g, Sugars 26g); Protein 4g. % Daily Value: Vitamin A 100%; Vitamin C 0%; Calcium 8%; Iron 15%. Exchanges: 1 Starch, 1-1/2 Other Carbohydrate, 3-1/2 Fat. Carbohydrate Choices: 2-1/2.

1 Heat oven to 350°F. Spray 13x9-inch pan with cooking spray. In medium bowl, mix flour and brown sugar. Using pastry blender, cut in butter until mixture looks like coarse crumbs. Stir in oats and walnuts. Press in bottom of pan; bake 15 minutes.

2 In large bowl, beat filling ingredients with electric mixer on medium speed until well blended. Pour over hot base. Bake 20 to 25 minutes or until set and dry in center.

3 Meanwhile, in small bowl, mix topping ingredients. Drop mixture by spoonfuls over pumpkin layer; spread evenly over hot filling. Bake about 5 minutes or until topping is set. Cool completely, about 2 hours. Cut into 4 rows by 4 rows. If desired, sprinkle with additional chopped walnuts. Store covered in refrigerator.

Betty's Kitchen Tip

• Don't want to make a pie? Try these bars instead. They can be made up to a day ahead of time.

apple streusel cheesecake bars

Prep Time: 20 Minutes
Start to Finish: 3 Hours 40 Minutes
Servings: 24 bars

---

1 pouch (1 lb 1.5 oz) Betty Crocker® oatmeal cookie mix

1/2 cup cold butter or margarine

2 packages (8 oz each) cream cheese, softened

1/2 cup sugar

2 tablespoons Gold Medal® all-purpose flour

1 teaspoon vanilla

1 egg

1 can (21 oz) apple pie filling

1/2 teaspoon ground cinnamon

1/4 cup chopped walnuts

---

1 Heat oven to 350°F. Spray 13x9-inch pan with cooking spray. In large bowl, place cookie mix. Using pastry blender (or pulling 2 table knives through mixture in opposite directions), cut in butter until mixture looks like coarse crumbs. Reserve 1-1/2 cups crumb mixture; press remaining crumbs in bottom of pan. Bake 10 minutes.

2 Meanwhile, in large bowl, beat cream cheese, sugar, flour, vanilla and egg with electric mixer on medium speed until smooth.

3 Spread cream cheese mixture evenly over partially baked crust. In medium bowl, mix pie filling and cinnamon. Spoon evenly over cream cheese mixture. Sprinkle reserved crumbs over top. Sprinkle with walnuts.

4 Bake 35 to 40 minutes or until light golden brown. Cool about 30 minutes. Refrigerate to chill, about 2 hours. Cut into 6 rows by 4 rows. Cover and refrigerate any remaining bars.

High Altitude: (3500-6500 ft): No change.

Nutritional Info: 1 Bar: Calories 240 (Calories from Fat 110); Total Fat 12g (Saturated Fat 7g, Trans Fat 0g); Cholesterol 40mg; Sodium 160mg; Total Carbohydrate 29g (Dietary Fiber 0g, Sugars 19g); Protein 3g. % Daily Value: Vitamin A 8%; Vitamin C 0%; Calcium 2%; Iron 4%. Exchanges: 1 Starch, 1 Other Carbohydrate, 2 Fat. Carbohydrate Choices: 2.

lemon cheesecake bars

Prep Time: 20 Minutes
Start to Finish: 4 Hours 50 Minutes
Servings: 48 bars

- 1 box Betty Crocker® SuperMoist® lemon cake mix
- 1/3 cup butter or margarine, softened
- 3 eggs
- 1 package (8 oz) cream cheese, softened
- 1 cup powdered sugar
- 2 teaspoons grated lemon peel
- 2 tablespoons lemon juice

1 Heat oven to 350°F (or 325°F for dark or nonstick pan). In large bowl, beat cake mix, butter and 1 of the eggs with electric mixer on low speed until crumbly. Press in bottom of ungreased 13x9-inch pan.

2 In medium bowl, beat cream cheese on medium speed until smooth. On low speed, gradually beat in powdered sugar. Stir in lemon peel and lemon juice until smooth. Reserve 1/2 cup for topping; refrigerate. Into remaining cream cheese mixture, beat remaining 2 eggs on medium speed until blended. Spread over cake mixture.

3 Bake 25 to 28 minutes or until set. Cool completely, about 1 hour. Spread with reserved cream cheese mixture. Refrigerate about 3 hours or until firm. For bars, cut into 8 rows by 6 rows. Store covered in refrigerator.

High Altitude: (3500-6500 ft): No change.

Nutritional Info: 1 Bar: Calories 90 (Calories from Fat 35); Total Fat 4g (Saturated Fat 2g, Trans Fat 0g); Cholesterol 20mg; Sodium 95mg; Total Carbohydrate 11g (Dietary Fiber 0g, Sugars 8g); Protein 1g. % Daily Value: Vitamin A 2%; Vitamin C 0%; Calcium 2%; Iron 0%. Exchanges: 1/2 Other Carbohydrate, 1 Fat. Carbohydrate Choices: 1.

Betty's Kitchen Tips

Variation: To make Lemon-Blueberry Cheesecake Bars, stir in 1 cup dried blueberries after beating the remaining 2 eggs into the cream cheese mixture. Continue as directed.

Special Touch: Save a little grated lemon peel to sprinkle over the tops of the bars for a garnish.

chocolate-topped sea salt caramels

Prep Time: 1 Hour 10 Minutes
Start to Finish: 2 Hours 40 Minutes
Servings: 48 caramels

Butter for greasing
1   cup butter (do not use margarine)
2-1/2   cups packed brown sugar (1 lb)
1/2   teaspoon coarse sea salt
1   cup light corn syrup
1   can (14 oz) sweetened condensed milk (not evaporated)

1   teaspoon vanilla
1/2   cup semisweet chocolate chips
1/2   teaspoon vegetable oil
1   teaspoon coarse sea salt

1 Line bottom and sides of 11x7-inch glass baking dish or pan with foil, leaving 1 inch foil overhanging on 2 opposite sides of pan; grease foil with butter.

2 In 3-quart heavy saucepan, melt butter over medium heat. Stir in brown sugar, 1/2 teaspoon salt, the corn syrup and milk. Cook over medium heat, stirring constantly, until mixture begins to boil.

3 Reduce heat to medium-low. Cook 40 to 50 minutes or until 248°F on candy thermometer (firm ball stage). Remove from heat; stir in vanilla. Pour into pan. Refrigerate about 1 hour or until completely cooled.

4 In small microwavable bowl, microwave chocolate chips and oil on High 30 to 40 seconds, stirring every 10 seconds, until chocolate is melted. Using spatula, spread chocolate evenly over caramel layer. Sprinkle with 1 teaspoon salt. Refrigerate about 30 minutes or until chocolate is set.

5 Remove caramels from baking dish to cutting surface, using foil to lift; peel back foil. Cut into 8 rows by 6 rows. Store at room temperature.

High Altitude: (3500-6500 ft): No change.

Nutritional Info: 1 Caramel: Calories 140 (Calories from Fat 45); Total Fat 5g (Saturated Fat 3.5g, Trans Fat 0g); Cholesterol 15mg; Sodium 120mg; Total Carbohydrate 22g (Dietary Fiber 0g, Sugars 19g); Protein 0g. % Daily Value: Vitamin A 2%; Vitamin C 0%; Calcium 4%; Iron 0%. Exchanges: 1-1/2 Other Carbohydrate, 1 Fat. Carbohydrate Choices: 1-1/2.

Betty's Kitchen Tips

Substitution: If you don't have coarse sea salt, any coarse salt will do.

Special Touch: To serve, place caramels in mini decorative paper baking cups if desired.

fig bars

Prep Time: 30 Minutes
Start to Finish: 1 Hour 50 Minutes
Servings: 16 bars

Crust

1/2	cup butter or margarine, softened
1/4	cup granulated sugar
1/4	teaspoon vanilla
1	cup Gold Medal® all-purpose flour

Filling

1/4	cup granulated sugar
1	cup boiling water
1	bag (9 oz) dried Mission figs, chopped (1 cup)

Topping

1/4	cup Gold Medal® all-purpose flour
1/4	cup packed brown sugar
3	tablespoons cold butter (do not use margarine)
1/4	cup quick-cooking oats
1/4	cup chopped walnuts

1 Heat oven to 350°F. Spray 9-inch square pan with cooking spray. In small bowl, beat 1/2 cup butter, 1/4 cup granulated sugar and the vanilla with electric mixer on medium speed until well blended. On low speed, beat in 1 cup flour until soft dough forms. Press dough in bottom of pan. Bake 10 to 15 minutes or until the center is set.

2 Meanwhile, in 2-quart saucepan, cook filling ingredients over medium-high heat 5 to 10 minutes, stirring frequently, until figs are tender and most of liquid is absorbed. Spread over crust.

3 In small bowl, mix 1/4 cup flour, the brown sugar and 3 tablespoons butter, using pastry blender or fork, until crumbly. Stir in oats and walnuts. Sprinkle over filling.

4 Bake 15 to 20 minutes longer or until edges are bubbly and topping is light golden brown. Cool completely, about 1 hour. For bars, cut into 4 rows by 4 rows.

High Altitude: (3500-6500 ft): No change.

Nutritional Info: 1 Bar: Calories 210 (Calories from Fat 90); Total Fat 9g (Saturated Fat 5g, Trans Fat 0g); Cholesterol 20mg; Sodium 60mg; Total Carbohydrate 28g (Dietary Fiber 2g, Sugars 17g); Protein 2g. % Daily Value: Vitamin A 4%; Vitamin C 0%; Calcium 4%; Iron 6%. Exchanges: 1 Starch, 1 Other Carbohydrate, 1-1/2 Fat. Carbohydrate Choices: 2.

Betty's Kitchen Tip

• Instead of walnuts, try roasted pecans. Serve with cinnamon ice cream.

chocolate-drizzled cherry bars

Prep Time: 20 Minutes
Start to Finish: 1 Hour 55 Minutes
Servings: 64 bars

- 3/4 cup butter or margarine, softened
- 3/4 cup sugar
- 1 egg
- 2-1/4 cups Gold Medal® all-purpose flour
- 1/4 teaspoon salt
- 1/4 cup cherry-flavored gelatin (from 4-serving-size box)
- 3/4 cup semisweet chocolate chips
- 3/4 teaspoon vegetable oil

1 Heat oven to 350°F. In large bowl, beat butter and sugar with electric mixer on medium speed until creamy. Beat in egg until well blended. On low speed, beat in flour, salt and dry gelatin until soft dough forms. Press dough in bottom of ungreased 13x9-inch pan.

2 Bake 11 to 14 minutes or until center is set. Cool completely, about 30 minutes.

3 In resealable freezer plastic bag, mix chocolate chips and oil; seal bag. Microwave on High 30 to 45 seconds, squeezing chocolate in bag every 15 seconds, until smooth. Cut 1/4-inch tip from corner of bag; drizzle chocolate over bars. Let stand about 1 hour or until chocolate is set. For bars, cut into 8 by 4 rows; cut each bar in half diagonally to make triangles.

High Altitude: (3500-6500 ft): No change.

Nutritional Info: 1 Bar: Calories 50 (Calories from Fat 25); Total Fat 3g (Saturated Fat 2g, Trans Fat 0g); Cholesterol 10mg; Sodium 30mg; Total Carbohydrate 5g (Dietary Fiber 0g, Sugars 2g); Protein 0g. % Daily Value: Vitamin A 0%; Vitamin C 0%; Calcium 0%; Iron 0%. Exchanges: 1/2 Other Carbohydrate, 1/2 Fat. Carbohydrate Choices: 1/2.

LOW FAT

Betty's Kitchen Tip

• Try with strawberry gelatin—except use the entire 4-serving-size box.

toasted almond-cappuccino-oatmeal bars

Prep Time: 30 Minutes
Start to Finish: 2 Hours 30 Minutes
Servings: 24 bars

Bars

2   pouches (1 lb 1.5 oz each) Betty Crocker® oatmeal chocolate chip cookie mix

Butter and eggs called for on cookie mix pouches

1/2   cup cappuccino international instant coffee mix (dry)

1   tablespoon water

Glaze and Topping

2   to 3 tablespoons water

1/4   cup cappuccino international instant coffee mix (dry)

3/4   cup powdered sugar

1/2   cup sliced almonds, toasted

1 Heat oven to 350°F. Spray 13x9-inch pan with cooking spray.

2 In large bowl, stir together filling ingredients until dough forms. Gently press dough in bottom of pan, using floured fingers. Bake 27 to 30 minutes or until deep golden brown. Cool completely, about 1 hour.

3 In small microwavable bowl, mix 2 tablespoons water and 2 tablespoons of the cappuccino mix. Microwave on High 15 to 20 seconds or until cappuccino mix is dissolved. Stir in powdered sugar

until well blended; if necessary, stir in remaining 1 tablespoon water.

4 In another small bowl, mix almonds and remaining 2 tablespoons cappuccino mix. Drizzle glaze over bars; sprinkle with almond mixture. Let stand 30 minutes until glaze is set. For bars, cut into 6 rows by 4 rows.

High Altitude: (3500-6500 ft): No change.

Nutritional Info: 1 Bar: Calories 250 (Calories from Fat 70); Total Fat 8g (Saturated Fat 3.5g, Trans Fat 0g); Cholesterol 20mg; Sodium 240mg; Total Carbohydrate 42g (Dietary Fiber 0g, Sugars 24g); Protein 4g. % Daily Value: Vitamin A 2%; Vitamin C 0%; Calcium 0%; Iron 4%. Exchanges: 1 Starch, 2 Other Carbohydrate, 1-1/2 Fat. Carbohydrate Choices: 3.

Betty's Kitchen Tips

Variation: Instead of cappuccino flavor, try using French vanilla, hazelnut or mocha instant coffee mix.

Substitution: Instead of almonds, you can use chopped hazelnuts.

caramel-pecan pretzels

Prep Time: 35 Minutes
Start to Finish: 55 Minutes
Servings: 40 candies

LOW FAT

- 40 tree- and star-shaped pretzel twists
- 20 caramels, unwrapped, each cut in half horizontally into 2 thin squares
- 40 pecan halves
- 1/2 cup dark chocolate chips
- 1/2 cup white vanilla baking chips

1 Heat oven to 250°F. On large cookie sheet, place pretzels in single layer. Place caramel piece on center of each pretzel. Bake 6 to 8 minutes or until caramels have softened. Remove from oven. Press pecan half into each caramel piece. Place close together on sheet of waxed paper.

2 In separate 1-quart resealable freezer plastic bags, place chocolate chips and vanilla chips; seal bags. Microwave each on High 35 to 50 seconds, squeezing chips in bag every 15 seconds, until chips are melted and smooth.

3 Cut small tip from bottom corner of each bag. Drizzle melted chocolate over pretzels. Carefully drizzle melted vanilla chips over chocolate. (If careful when drizzling, there is no need to let the chocolate set before drizzling the vanilla chips.) Refrigerate about 20 minutes or until chocolate is set.

High Altitude: (3500-6500 ft): No change.

Nutritional Info: 1 Candy: Calories 60 (Calories from Fat 25); Total Fat 3g (Saturated Fat 1g, Trans Fat 0g); Cholesterol 0mg; Sodium 35mg; Total Carbohydrate 8g (Dietary Fiber 0g, Sugars 5g); Protein 0g. % Daily Value: Vitamin A 0%; Vitamin C 0%; Calcium 0%; Iron 0%. Exchanges: 1/2 Other Carbohydrate, 1/2 Fat. Carbohydrate Choices: 1/2.

Betty's Kitchen Tips

Success Hint: There are several brands of small pretzel twists. For the best success, choose the twists that are the most compact with the smallest openings.

Purchasing: When buying caramels, choose ones that give a little when they are pressed; they're the freshest.

black-and-white truffles

Prep Time: 30 Minutes
Start to Finish: 1 Hour 45 Minutes
Servings: About 72 truffles

- 1 package (1 lb 2 oz) creme-filled chocolate sandwich cookies
- 1 package (8 oz) cream cheese, softened
- 36 oz (from two 24-oz packages) vanilla-flavored candy coating (almond bark)
- 1/2 cup semisweet chocolate chips
- 1/2 teaspoon vegetable oil

1 Line 2 cookie sheets with waxed paper. Place cookies in large food processor. Cover; process with on-and-off pulses until consistency of fine crumbs. In large bowl, stir cookie crumbs and cream cheese until well blended and mixture forms a doughlike consistency.

2 Chop 8 oz of the candy coating; stir into dough mixture. Roll dough into 1-inch balls; place half on each cookie sheet. Freeze about 30 minutes or until very firm.

3 In small microwavable bowl, microwave half of remaining 28 oz candy coating on High 1 minute 30 seconds; stir. Continue microwaving and stirring in 15-second intervals until melted and smooth.

4 Remove half of the balls from freezer. Using 2 forks, dip and roll each ball in coating; return to cookie sheet. Melt remaining candy coating; dip the remaining balls.

5 In 1-quart resealable freezer plastic bag, place chocolate chips and oil; seal bag. Microwave on High 35 to 50 seconds, squeezing chips in bag every 15 seconds, until chips are melted and mixture is smooth. Cut small tip from bottom corner of each bag. Drizzle chocolate over truffles. Refrigerate 30 to 45 minutes or until chocolate is set. Store covered in the refrigerator.

High Altitude: (3500-6500 ft): No change.

Nutritional Info: 1 Truffle: Calories 130 (Calories from Fat 70); Total Fat 7g (Saturated Fat 4g, Trans Fat 0g); Cholesterol 5mg; Sodium 60mg; Total Carbohydrate 14g (Dietary Fiber 0g, Sugars 12g); Protein 1g. % Daily Value: Vitamin A 0%; Vitamin C 0%; Calcium 4%; Iron 0%. Exchanges: 1/2 Starch, 1/2 Other Carbohydrate, 1-1/2 Fat. Carbohydrate Choices: 1.

Betty's Kitchen Tip

- The chilled dough will help the melted coating set somewhat quickly.

scream! cheese swirl brownies

Prep Time: 15 Minutes
Start to Finish: 2 Hours 45 Minutes
Servings: 24 brownies

••••••••••••••••••••••••••••••••••

Filling

2	packages (3 oz each) cream cheese, softened
1	egg
1/4	cup sugar
4	drops red food color
4	drops yellow food color
1/2	teaspoon vanilla

Brownies

1	box (1 lb 6.5 oz) Betty Crocker® Original Supreme brownie mix (with chocolate syrup pouch)
1/3	cup vegetable oil
1/4	cup water
2	eggs

••••••••••••••••••••••••••••••••••

1 Heat oven to 350°F (325°F for dark or nonstick pan). Grease bottom only of 13x9-inch pan with shortening or cooking spray. In small bowl, beat filling ingredients with electric mixer on low speed until smooth. Set aside.

2 In large bowl, stir brownie ingredients until well blended. Make brownie batter as directed on box. Spread 3/4 of brownie batter in pan. Spoon filling by tablespoonfuls evenly onto brownie batter. Spoon remaining brownie batter over filling. For marbled design, pull knife through batter and filling in wide curves; turn pan and repeat.

3 Bake 26 to 30 minutes or until set. Cool completely at room temperature, about 1 hour. Refrigerate at least 1 hour until chilled. For brownies, cut with plastic knife into 6 rows by 4 rows. Cover and refrigerate any remaining brownies.

EASY

High Altitude: Follow High Altitude directions on brownie mix box—except add 1/4 cup flour to dry mix. Bake 32 to 36 minutes.

Nutritional Info: 1 Brownie: Calories 170 (Calories from Fat 70); Total Fat 7g (Saturated Fat 2.5g, Trans Fat 0g); Cholesterol 35mg; Sodium 115mg; Total Carbohydrate 24g (Dietary Fiber 0g, Sugars 17g); Protein 2g. % Daily Value: Vitamin A 2%; Vitamin C 0%; Calcium 0%; Iron 6%. Exchanges: 1/2 Starch, 1 Other Carbohydrate, 1-1/2 Fat. Carbohydrate Choices: 1-1/2.

Betty's Kitchen Tip

• Softening cream cheese is easy. Just microwave unwrapped cream cheese in a microwavable bowl on High for 15 to 20 seconds.

chocolate-cashew brownies

Prep Time: 45 Minutes
Start to Finish: 2 Hours 5 Minutes
Servings: 24 brownies

Brownies

1	cup butter or margarine, softened
3/4	cup granulated sugar
1/2	cup packed brown sugar
1	teaspoon vanilla
2	eggs
1-3/4	cups Gold Medal® all-purpose flour
3/4	cup unsweetened baking cocoa
1	teaspoon salt
1/2	teaspoon baking soda

1	cup semisweet chocolate chips (6 oz)
3/4	cup miniature marshmallows
1/2	cup chopped cashews

Frosting

3	cups powdered sugar
1/4	cup butter or margarine, softened
1/2	teaspoon vanilla
3	to 4 tablespoons half-and-half or milk
1/4	teaspoon unsweetened baking cocoa

1 Heat oven to 350°F. Spray 13x9-inch pan with cooking spray.

2 In large bowl, beat 1 cup butter with electric mixer on medium speed until smooth and creamy. Beat in granulated and brown sugars, 1 teaspoon vanilla and eggs until smooth. On low speed, beat in flour, 3/4 cup cocoa, the salt and baking soda until soft dough forms. Stir in chocolate chips, marshmallows and cashews. Spread mixture in pan.

3 Bake 15 to 20 minutes or until set. Cool completely, about 1 hour.

4 In small bowl, mix all frosting ingredients except cocoa, adding enough of the half-and-half until frosting is smooth and spreadable. Frost brownies. Sprinkle with 1/4 teaspoon cocoa and additional cashews if desired. Let stand 30 minutes or until frosting is set. Cut into 6 rows by 4 rows.

High Altitude: (3500-6500 ft): No change.

Nutritional Info: 1 Brownie: Calories 300 (Calories from Fat 130); Total Fat 14g (Saturated Fat 8g, Trans Fat 0g); Cholesterol 40mg; Sodium 150mg; Total Carbohydrate 41g (Dietary Fiber 1g, Sugars 30g); Protein 3g. % Daily Value: Vitamin A 6%; Vitamin C 0%; Calcium 0%; Iron 8%. Exchanges: 1 Starch, 1-1/2 Other Carbohydrate, 2-1/2 Fat. Carbohydrate Choices: 3.

glazed lemon wedges

Prep Time: 15 Minutes
Start to Finish: 1 Hour 40 Minutes
Servings: 24 cookie wedges

EASY

• •

Cookies

1	box Betty Crocker® SuperMoist® butter recipe yellow cake mix
1/2	cup butter or margarine, softened
2	tablespoons grated lemon peel
1	egg

Glaze

1	cup powdered sugar
1	teaspoon grated lemon peel
3	tablespoons lemon juice

Garnish

Grated lemon peel, if desired

• •

1 Heat oven to 350°F (or 325°F for dark or nonstick pans). Spray bottoms and sides of 2 (8-inch) round cake pans with baking spray with flour or line with foil.

2 In large bowl, beat cake mix, butter, 2 tablespoons lemon peel and the egg with electric mixer on low speed until crumbly. Beat on medium speed until dough forms. Press half of dough in each pan.

3 Bake 18 to 22 minutes or until edges are light golden brown. Cool 10 minutes.

4 In small bowl, mix glaze ingredients until smooth. Spoon glaze over warm shortbread; spread to edges of pans. Cool completely, about 50 minutes. Garnish with lemon peel. Cut each shortbread into 12 wedges.

High Altitude: (3500-6500 ft): No change.

Nutritional Info: 1 Cookie Wedge: Calories 140 (Calories from Fat 50); Total Fat 6g (Saturated Fat 3g, Trans Fat 0.5g); Cholesterol 20mg; Sodium 170mg; Total Carbohydrate 22g (Dietary Fiber 0g, Sugars 14g); Protein 1g. % Daily Value: Vitamin A 2%; Vitamin C 0%; Calcium 4%; Iron 2%. Exchanges: 1-1/2 Other Carbohydrate, 1 Fat. Carbohydrate Choices: 1-1/2.

Betty's Kitchen Tips

Special Touch: Garnish with grated lemon peel or lemon peel strips.

Success Hint: When grating lemon peel, be sure to grate only the yellow part of the skin. The white part, or pith, is very bitter.

carrot cake bars with cinnamon-cream cheese frosting

Prep Time: 20 Minutes
Start to Finish: 2 Hours 30 Minutes
Servings: 46 bars

Bars

1	box (1 lb 2 oz) Betty Crocker® SuperMoist® carrot cake mix
1	cup butter or margarine, softened
2	eggs
3	tablespoons milk
1	teaspoon ground cinnamon
1/2	teaspoon maple flavor

Frosting

1	package (8 oz) cream cheese, softened
1/4	cup butter or margarine, softened
2	to 3 teaspoons milk
1	teaspoon vanilla
1/2	teaspoon ground cinnamon
4	cups powdered sugar

1 Heat oven to 350°F. Spray 15x10x1-inch pan with baking spray with flour.

2 In large bowl, beat bar ingredients with electric mixer on medium speed until well blended. Spread evenly in pan.

3 Bake 15 to 18 minutes or until top is evenly golden brown and bars spring back when touched lightly in center. Cool completely, about 2 hours.

4 In medium bowl, beat cream cheese, butter, milk, vanilla and cinnamon with electric mixer on low speed until smooth. Gradually beat in powdered sugar, 1 cup at a time, until smooth and spreadable. Spread frosting evenly over cooled bars. Store covered in refrigerator.

High Altitude: (3500-6500 ft): No change.

Nutritional Info: 1 Bar: Calories 150 (Calories from Fat 70); Total Fat 7g (Saturated Fat 4.5g, Trans Fat 0g); Cholesterol 25mg; Sodium 120mg; Total Carbohydrate 19g (Dietary Fiber 0g, Sugars 14g); Protein 1g. % Daily Value: Vitamin A 6%; Vitamin C 0%; Calcium 2%; Iron 0%. Exchanges: 1-1/2 Other Carbohydrate, 1-1/2 Fat. Carbohydrate Choices: 1.

peanut butter crunch bars

Prep Time: 15 Minutes
Start to Finish: 2 Hours 45 Minutes
Servings: 36 bars

EASY

1	cup sugar
1/2	cup butter or margarine, softened
1/2	cup peanut butter
2	tablespoons milk
1	teaspoon vanilla
1	egg
1-1/2	cups Gold Medal® whole wheat flour
1/2	teaspoon baking soda
1/2	teaspoon salt
1	cup semisweet chocolate chips (6 oz)
1/2	cup chopped honey-roasted peanuts

1 Heat oven to 350°F. Spray 13x9-inch pan with cooking spray. In large bowl, beat sugar, butter and peanut butter until light and fluffy. Add milk, vanilla and egg; beat until well blended. Add flour, baking soda and salt; mix well. Spread in pan.

2 Bake 19 to 24 minutes or until edges are golden brown. Immediately sprinkle with chocolate chips; let stand 5 minutes.

3 Using metal spatula, spread softened chips to frost bars. Sprinkle with peanuts. Cool completely in pan on cooling rack, about 2 hours. For bars, cut into 6 rows by 6 rows.

High Altitude: (3500-6500 ft): No change.

Nutritional Info: 1 Bar: Calories 130 (Calories from Fat 60); Total Fat 7g (Saturated Fat 3g, Trans Fat 0g); Cholesterol 15mg; Sodium 95mg; Total Carbohydrate 13g (Dietary Fiber 1g, Sugars 9g); Protein 2g. % Daily Value: Vitamin A 0%; Vitamin C 0%; Calcium 0%; Iron 2%. Exchanges: 1/2 Starch, 1/2 Other Carbohydrate, 1-1/2 Fat. Carbohydrate Choices: 1.

Betty's Kitchen Tip
• Try using your other favorite chips, such as dark or milk chocolate.

cinnamon bun bars

Prep Time: 15 Minutes
Start to Finish: 1 Hour 40 Minutes
Servings: 24 bars

EASY

1 box (1 lb 2.25 oz) Betty Crocker® SuperMoist® butter recipe yellow cake mix
1/2 cup butter, softened
2 tablespoons milk
2 eggs

3/4 cup packed brown sugar
1/3 cup caramel topping
1/3 cup butter, melted
3/4 cup chopped pecans
1 teaspoon ground cinnamon

1 Heat oven to 350°F. Spray 13x9-inch pan with cooking spray.

2 In large bowl, beat cake mix, softened butter, milk and eggs with electric mixer on medium speed about 1 minute or until blended. Spread evenly in pan.

3 In medium bowl, mix brown sugar, caramel topping, melted butter, pecans and cinnamon. Drop by spoonfuls on top of batter and spread evenly.

4 Bake 25 to 28 minutes or until topping is deep golden brown and slightly puffed throughout. Cool completely, about 1 hour. For bars, cut into 6 rows by 4 rows. Store covered.

High Altitude: (3500-6500 ft): No change.

Nutritional Info: 1 Bar: Calories 210 (Calories from Fat 100); Total Fat 11g (Saturated Fat 5g, Trans Fat 1g); Cholesterol 35mg; Sodium 210mg; Total Carbohydrate 27g (Dietary Fiber 0g, Sugars 18g); Protein 2g. % Daily Value: Vitamin A 4%; Vitamin C 0%; Calcium 4%; Iron 4%. Exchanges: 1/2 Starch, 1-1/2 Other Carbohydrate, 2 Fat. Carbohydrate Choices: 2.

Betty's Kitchen Tips

Success Hint: To easily cut these bars, spray the knife with cooking spray so it doesn't stick!

Variation: Try using your own favorite nut, such as walnuts, hazelnuts or almonds, in place of the pecans.

caramels

Prep Time: 45 Minutes
Start to Finish: 2 Hours 45 Minutes
Servings: 64 candies

- -

  2 cups sugar
1/2 cup butter or margarine
  2 cups whipping cream
3/4 cup light corn syrup

- -

1 Grease bottom and sides of 8-inch square (2-quart) glass baking dish with butter.

2 In 3-quart heavy saucepan, heat all ingredients to boiling over medium heat, stirring constantly. Boil uncovered about 35 minutes, stirring frequently, until candy thermometer reads 245°F or until small amount of mixture dropped into cup of very cold water forms a firm ball that holds its shape until pressed.

3 Immediately spread caramel mixture in baking dish. Cool completely, about 2 hours.

4 Cut into 8 rows by 8 rows to make 1-inch squares. Wrap candies individually in waxed paper or plastic wrap. Store in tightly covered container.

High Altitude: (3500-6500 ft): Use 5-quart saucepan. Boil over medium heat about 15 minutes, stirring frequently, until the candy thermometer reads 240°F.

Nutritional Info: 1 Candy: Calories 70 (Calories from Fat 35); Total Fat 4g (Saturated Fat 2.5g, Trans Fat 0g); Cholesterol 10mg; Sodium 15mg; Total Carbohydrate 10g (Dietary Fiber 0g, Sugars 8g); Protein 0g. % Daily Value: Vitamin A 2%; Vitamin C 0%; Calcium 0%; Iron 0%. Exchanges: 1/2 Other Carbohydrate, 1 Fat. Carbohydrate Choices: 1/2.

Betty's Kitchen Tip

• To make Chocolate Caramels, heat 2 oz unsweetened baking chocolate with the sugar mixture.

"lime in the coconut" frosted cheesecake bars

Prep Time: 15 Minutes
Start to Finish: 3 Hours 25 Minutes
Servings: 24 bars

EASY

Cookie Base
- 1 pouch (1 lb 1.5 oz) Betty Crocker® sugar cookie mix
- 2 tablespoons Gold Medal® all-purpose flour
- 1/3 cup butter or margarine, softened
- 1 egg, slightly beaten

Filling
- 2 packages (8 oz each) cream cheese, softened
- 1 can (16 oz) cream of coconut (not coconut milk)
- 3 tablespoons lime juice
- 1 teaspoon vanilla
- 2 eggs

Topping
- 1 container (12 oz) Betty Crocker® Whipped cream cheese frosting
- 1-1/4 cups coconut, toasted
- 2 teaspoons grated lime peel

1 Heat oven to 350°F. Spray bottom and sides of 13x9-inch pan with cooking spray. In large bowl, stir cookie base ingredients until soft dough forms. Press evenly in bottom of pan. Bake 15 to 18 minutes or until golden brown. Cool 15 minutes.

2 Meanwhile, in large bowl, beat cream cheese with electric mixer on medium speed until light and fluffy. Beat in cream of coconut until well blended. Beat in lime juice, vanilla and 2 eggs until smooth. Spread over cookie base.

3 Bake 40 to 45 minutes or until set and light golden brown on edges. Cool in pan on cooling rack 30 minutes. Refrigerate for 1 hour to cool completely.

4 Carefully spread frosting over filling. Sprinkle with coconut and lime peel. Cover; refrigerate 30 minutes. For bars, cut into 6 rows by 4 rows. Store covered in refrigerator.

High Altitude: (3500-6500 ft): No change.

Nutritional Info: 1 Bar: Calories 340 (Calories from Fat 200); Total Fat 23g (Saturated Fat 14g, Trans Fat 2g); Cholesterol 55mg; Sodium 180mg; Total Carbohydrate 29g (Dietary Fiber 0g, Sugars 20g); Protein 4g. % Daily Value: Vitamin A 8%; Vitamin C 0%; Calcium 2%; Iron 6%. Exchanges: 1 Starch, 1 Other Carbohydrate, 4-1/2 Fat. Carbohydrate Choices: 2.

Betty's Kitchen Tip

• To toast coconut, spread on ungreased cookie sheet and bake at 350°F for 10 to 15 minutes, stirring occasionally, until coconut is light golden brown.

raspberry truffle cups

Prep Time: 30 Minutes
Start to Finish: 1 Hour 35 Minutes
Servings: 24 truffle cups

---

6 oz vanilla-flavored candy coating (almond bark), cut into pieces

6 oz semisweet baking chocolate, cut into pieces

2 tablespoons butter or margarine, cut into pieces

1/3 cup whipping cream

2 tablespoons raspberry-flavored liqueur or raspberry pancake syrup

24 fresh raspberries

---

1 Melt candy coating as directed on package. Spread 1 teaspoon coating evenly in bottom and up side of each of 24 miniature paper candy cups. Let stand until hardened.

2 In 2-quart saucepan, melt chocolate over low heat, stirring constantly. Remove from heat. Stir in remaining ingredients except raspberries. Refrigerate about 35 minutes, stirring frequently, until mixture is thickened and mounds when dropped from a spoon.

3 Place raspberry in each candy-coated cup. Spoon chocolate mixture into decorating bag with star tip. Pipe mixture into candy-coated cups over raspberry. Place cups on cookie sheet. Refrigerate until chocolate mixture is firm, about 30 minutes. If desired, peel paper from truffle cups before serving. Store tightly covered in refrigerator.

High Altitude: (3500-6500 ft): No change.

Nutritional Info: 1 Truffle Cup: Calories 100 (Calories from Fat 60); Total Fat 6g (Saturated Fat 4g, Trans Fat 0g); Cholesterol 10mg; Sodium 15mg; Total Carbohydrate 9g (Dietary Fiber 0g, Sugars 9g); Protein 0g. % Daily Value: Vitamin A 0%; Vitamin C 0%; Calcium 0%; Iron 0%. Exchanges: 1/2 Starch, 1 Fat. Carbohydrate Choices: 1/2.

Betty's Kitchen Tips

Variation: For Crème de Menthe Truffle Cups, add 1/4 cup finely ground almonds to the chocolate mixture and substitute crème de menthe for the raspberry liqueur.

Variation: For Cherry Truffle Cups, substitute cherry-flavored liqueur for the raspberry liqueur and 24 candied cherry halves for the raspberries.

glazed dried fruit and nut bars

Prep Time: 25 Minutes
Start to Finish: 1 Hour 10 Minutes
Servings: 32 bars

• •

Cookie Crust

1	pouch (1 lb 1.5 oz) Betty Crocker® sugar cookie mix
1/2	cup butter or margarine, softened
2	to 3 teaspoons grated orange peel
1/2	teaspoon vanilla
1	egg, slightly beaten

Filling

1	jar (12 oz) orange marmalade
1	bag (5 oz) dried cherries (about 1 cup)
1	cup sweetened dried cranberries
3/4	cup cashew halves and pieces
1/2	cup unblanched whole almonds
1/2	cup chopped pitted dates

• •

1 Heat oven to 350°F. In large bowl, stir cookie crust ingredients until well blended. Press dough in bottom of ungreased 13x9-inch pan. Bake 14 to 16 minutes or until golden brown. Cool 10 minutes.

2 Meanwhile, in 2-quart saucepan, heat orange marmalade to boiling over medium-high heat, stirring constantly. Boil 3 to 4 minutes, stirring frequently, until slightly thickened. Stir in remaining filling ingredients until well mixed. Spread evenly over cookie crust.

3 Bake about 15 minutes longer or until edges are golden brown and filling is set. Cool completely, about 30 minutes. For bars, cut into 8 rows by 4 rows.

High Altitude: (3500-6500 ft): No change.

Nutritional Info: 1 Bar: Calories 190 (Calories from Fat 60); Total Fat 7g (Saturated Fat 2.5g, Trans Fat 0.5g); Cholesterol 15mg; Sodium 70mg; Total Carbohydrate 29g (Dietary Fiber 1g, Sugars 20g); Protein 2g. % Daily Value: Vitamin A 2%; Vitamin C 0%; Calcium 0%; Iron 4%. Exchanges: 2 Other Carbohydrate, 1-1/2 Fat Carbohydrate Choices: 2.

Betty's Kitchen Tips

Variation: Mix up these bars with other dried fruits and nuts, like golden raisins, dried apricots, hazelnuts or walnuts.

Special Touch: Try with salted roasted nuts for that great salty-sweet flavor combination!

eggnog cheesecake bars

Prep Time: 20 Minutes
Start to Finish: 2 Hours 25 Minutes
Servings: 24 bars

Crust

2	cups graham cracker crumbs (32 squares)
3/4	cup butter or margarine, melted
1/2	cup blanched whole almonds, finely chopped
1/4	cup packed brown sugar
1	tablespoon ground cinnamon

Filling

2	packages (8 oz each) cream cheese, softened

1/4	cup granulated sugar
1/4	cup packed brown sugar
2	teaspoons ground nutmeg
1/2	cup whipping cream
1	teaspoon vanilla
2	eggs

Topping

1/2	cup blanched whole almonds, finely chopped, toasted

1 Heat oven to 350°F. In large bowl, stir crust ingredients until well blended. Press mixture in bottom of ungreased 13x9-inch pan. Bake 8 minutes.

2 In clean large bowl, beat cream cheese with electric mixer on medium speed until softened. Gradually beat in granulated sugar, 1/4 cup brown sugar, the nutmeg, cream and vanilla. Beat in eggs, one at a time, until creamy. Pour mixture over the crust.

3 Bake 30 to 35 minutes longer or until center is set. Sprinkle with 1/2 cup toasted almonds; press in slightly. Cool 1-1/2 hours. For bars, cut into 6 rows by 4 rows, using thin knife and wiping blade occasionally. Store covered in refrigerator.

High Altitude: (3500-6500 ft): No change.

Nutritional Info: 1 Bar: Calories 460 (Calories from Fat 320); Total Fat 36g (Saturated Fat 19g, Trans Fat 1g); Cholesterol 110mg; Sodium 300mg; Total Carbohydrate 28g (Dietary Fiber 2g, Sugars 18g); Protein 7g. % Daily Value: Vitamin A 20%; Vitamin C 0%; Calcium 10%; Iron 8%. Exchanges: 2 Other Carbohydrate, 1 High-Fat Meat, 5-1/2 Fat. Carbohydrate Choices: 2.

Betty's Kitchen Tips

Substitution: Try crushed vanilla wafer cookies instead of the graham cracker crumbs.

How-To: To toast almonds, bake in shallow pan at 350°F for 3 to 5 minutes, stirring occasionally, until golden brown.

chocolate-raspberry triangles

Prep Time: 30 Minutes
Start to Finish: 1 Hour 50 Minutes
Servings: 48 bars

1-1/2	cups Gold Medal® all-purpose flour
3/4	cup sugar
3/4	cup butter or margarine, softened
1	package (10 oz) frozen raspberries in syrup, thawed and drained
1/4	cup orange juice
1	tablespoon cornstarch
3/4	cup miniature semisweet chocolate chips

1 Heat oven to 350°F. In small bowl, mix flour, sugar and butter until crumbly. Press in ungreased 13x9-inch pan. Bake 15 minutes.

2 Meanwhile, in 1-quart saucepan, mix raspberries, orange juice and cornstarch. Heat to boiling, stirring constantly. Boil and stir 1 minute. Cool 10 minutes.

3 Sprinkle chocolate chips over crust. Carefully spread raspberry mixture over chocolate chips.

4 Bake about 20 minutes or until raspberry mixture is set. Refrigerate about 1 hour or until chocolate is firm. For triangles, cut into 4 rows by 3 rows, then cut each square into 4 triangles.

High Altitude: (3500-6500 ft): No change.

Nutritional Info: 1 Bar: Calories 70 (Calories from Fat 35); Total Fat 3.5g (Saturated Fat 2.5g, Trans Fat 0g); Cholesterol 10mg; Sodium 20mg; Total Carbohydrate 10g (Dietary Fiber 0g, Sugars 6g); Protein 0g. % Daily Value: Vitamin A 0%; Vitamin C 0%; Calcium 0%; Iron 0%. Exchanges: 1/2 Other Carbohydrate, 1 Fat. Carbohydrate Choices: 1/2.

ultimate turtle brownies

Prep Time: 30 Minutes
Start to Finish: 3 Hours 5 Minutes
Servings: 36 brownies

1 box (1 lb 6.5 oz) Betty Crocker® Original Supreme brownie mix (with chocolate syrup pouch)

Water, vegetable oil and eggs called for on brownie mix box

1 bag (14 oz) caramels, unwrapped
1/4 cup whipping cream
1 bag (11.5 oz) semisweet chocolate chunks (2 cups)
1 cup coarsely chopped pecans

1 Heat oven to 350°F. Spray bottom and sides of 13x9-inch pan with baking spray with flour. In medium bowl, stir brownie mix, pouch of chocolate syrup, water, oil and eggs until well blended. Spread 1/2 of batter (about 1-1/2 cups) in the pan. Bake 15 minutes.

2 Meanwhile, in large microwavable bowl, microwave caramels and whipping cream uncovered on High 2 to 3 minutes, stirring occasionally, until smooth.

3 Pour caramel over partially baked brownie; spread to edges. Sprinkle with 1 cup of the chocolate chunks and 1/2 cup of the pecans. Drop remaining brownie batter by spoonfuls onto caramel layer. Sprinkle with remaining 1 cup chocolate chunks and 1/2 cup pecans.

4 Bake 33 to 36 minutes or until center is almost set. Cool 1 hour at room temperature. Cover; refrigerate 1 hour before serving. For brownies, cut into 6 rows by 6 rows. Store brownies covered at room temperature.

High Altitude: (3500-6500 ft): Follow High Altitude directions for 13x9-inch pan on brownie mix box.

Nutritional Info: 1 Brownie: Calories 210 (Calories from Fat 80); Total Fat 9g (Saturated Fat 3g, Trans Fat 0g); Cholesterol 15mg; Sodium 90mg; Total Carbohydrate 29g (Dietary Fiber 1g, Sugars 20g); Protein 2g. % Daily Value: Vitamin A 0%; Vitamin C 0%; Calcium 2%; Iron 6%. Exchanges: 1/2 Starch, 1-1/2 Other Carbohydrate, 2 Fat. Carbohydrate Choices: 2.

Betty's Kitchen Tips

Success Hint: Need to bake for a potluck or picnic? You can make these bars the day ahead and store at room temperature.

Time-Saver: Buy a bag of already-chopped pecans to save on prep time.

teddy bear fudge

Prep Time: 20 Minutes
Start to Finish: 2 Hours 20 Minutes
Servings: 6 candies

- 6 (3x1/2-inch) teddy bear-shaped cookie cutters
- 1-1/2 cups semisweet chocolate chips (9 oz)
- 1 cup peanut butter chips (6 oz)
- 1 can (14 oz) sweetened condensed milk (not evaporated)
- 2 tablespoons butter or margarine, softened
- 1 teaspoon vanilla
- 6 cellophane gift bags

1 Place each cookie cutter on 5-inch square of foil. Seal foil tightly around outside of cookie cutters. Place on cookie sheet. Lightly spray cookie cutters with cooking spray.

2 In 4-cup microwavable measuring cup or bowl, microwave chocolate chips, peanut butter chips, sweetened condensed milk and butter uncovered on High 1 to 2 minutes, stirring every 30 seconds, until chips are almost melted. Stir in vanilla.

3 Pour mixture into teddy bear molds, filling to tops of molds. Refrigerate uncovered about 2 hours or until firm.

4 Carefully remove foil. Place cookie cutter with fudge into cellophane bags. Or gently press fudge out of molds to serve. Store covered in refrigerator.

High Altitude: (3500-6500 ft): No change.

Nutritional Info: 1 Candy: Calories 630 (Calories from Fat 280); Total Fat 31g (Saturated Fat 15g, Trans Fat 0g); Cholesterol 35mg; Sodium 190mg; Total Carbohydrate 77g (Dietary Fiber 3g, Sugars 70g); Protein 11g. % Daily Value: Vitamin A 6%; Vitamin C 0%; Calcium 20%; Iron 10%. Exchanges: 5 Other Carbohydrate, 1-1/2 High-Fat Meat, 4 Fat. Carbohydrate Choices: 5.

Betty's Kitchen Tips

Variation: You can use an 8-inch square pan instead of the cookie cutters. Line the pan with aluminum foil, and pour the fudge into the pan. Cover and refrigerate 2 hours. Cut into 1-1/2-inch squares.

Special Touch: Use white or red decorating icing, purchased in tubes, to decorate the teddy bears.

frosted cinnamon-ginger bars

Prep Time: 15 Minutes
Start to Finish: 1 Hour 35 Minutes
Servings: 24 bars

EASY

Bars
3/4	cup butter or margarine, softened
1/2	cup packed brown sugar
1	egg
1/3	cup molasses
2-1/2	cups Gold Medal® all-purpose flour
2	teaspoons baking soda
1/2	teaspoon ground cinnamon

1/2	teaspoon ground ginger
1/2	teaspoon ground cloves
1/4	teaspoon salt

Topping
1/2	teaspoon granulated sugar
1/4	teaspoon ground cinnamon
1	cup Betty Crocker® Whipped vanilla frosting (from 12-oz container)

1 Heat oven to 350°F. In large bowl, beat butter and brown sugar with electric mixer on medium speed until well blended. Beat in egg until well blended. Beat in molasses until creamy. On low speed, beat in remaining bar ingredients until soft dough forms. Press dough in bottom of ungreased 13x9-inch pan.

2 Bake 15 to 18 minutes or until edges look dry and center springs back when touched gently with finger. Cool bars completely, about 1 hour.

3 In small bowl, mix granulated sugar and 1/4 teaspoon cinnamon. Spread frosting over bars; sprinkle with cinnamon-sugar mixture. For bars, cut into 6 rows by 4 rows.

High Altitude: (3500-6500 ft): No change.

Nutritional Info: 1 Bar: Calories 170 (Calories from Fat 70); Total Fat 8g (Saturated Fat 4g, Trans Fat 0.5g); Cholesterol 25mg; Sodium 180mg; Total Carbohydrate 23g (Dietary Fiber 0g, Sugars 12g); Protein 1g. % Daily Value: Vitamin A 4%; Vitamin C 0%; Calcium 0%; Iron 4%. Exchanges: 1/2 Starch, 1 Other Carbohydrate, 1-1/2 Fat. Carbohydrate Choices: 1-1/2.

Betty's Kitchen Tips

Variation: Add 1-1/2 cups chopped walnuts to the batter.
Substitution: Use Betty Crocker® Whipped cream cheese frosting instead.

rich chocolate fudge

Prep Time: 15 Minutes
Start to Finish: 1 Hour 45 Minutes
Servings: 64 candies

- 1 can (14 oz) sweetened condensed milk (not evaporated)
- 1 bag (12 oz) semisweet chocolate chips (2 cups)
- 1 oz unsweetened baking chocolate, chopped, if desired
- 1-1/2 cups chopped nuts, if desired
- 1 teaspoon vanilla

1 Grease bottom and sides of 8-inch square pan with butter.

2 In 2-quart saucepan, heat milk, chocolate chips and unsweetened chocolate over low heat, stirring constantly, until chocolate is melted and mixture is smooth. Remove from heat.

3 Quickly stir in nuts and vanilla. Spread in pan. Refrigerate about 1 hour 30 minutes or until firm. Cut into 8 rows by 8 rows to make 1-inch squares.

High Altitude: (3500-6500 ft): No change.

Nutritional Info: 1 Candy: Calories 60 (Calories from Fat 25); Total Fat 2.5g (Saturated Fat 1.5g, Trans Fat 0g); Cholesterol 0mg; Sodium 10mg; Total Carbohydrate 8g (Dietary Fiber 0g, Sugars 7g); Protein 0g. % Daily Value: Vitamin A 0%; Vitamin C 0%; Calcium 2%; Iron 0%. Exchanges: 1/2 Other Carbohydrate, 1/2 Fat. Carbohydrate Choices: 1/2.

EASY LOW FAT

Betty's Kitchen Tip

- Line the pan with foil for super-quick cleanup and to easily lift the fudge out of the pan so you can cut it evenly.

triple-nut bars

Prep Time: 35 Minutes
Start to Finish: 1 Hour 50 Minutes
Servings: 36 bars

Crust

3/4	cup butter or margarine, softened
1/2	cup packed brown sugar
1/2	teaspoon almond extract
1-1/2	cups Gold Medal® all-purpose flour

Topping

1	cup butter or margarine
1-1/2	cups packed brown sugar
1/4	cup honey
1/4	cup light corn syrup
1/2	teaspoon vanilla
1	cup walnut pieces
1	cup unblanched or blanched whole almonds
1	cup pecan halves

1 Heat oven to 350°F. In medium bowl, beat 3/4 cup butter, 1/2 cup brown sugar and the almond extract with electric mixer on medium-low speed until blended. On low speed, beat in flour until soft dough forms. Press dough in bottom of ungreased 13x9-inch pan. Bake 17 to 20 minutes or until golden brown.

2 Meanwhile, in 2-quart saucepan, cook 1 cup butter, 1-1/2 cups brown sugar, the honey, corn syrup and vanilla over medium-high heat 12 to 15 minutes, stirring frequently, until mixture comes to a full rolling boil. Boil 1 to 2 minutes, stirring frequently. Remove from heat.

3 Sprinkle walnuts, almonds and pecans over crust. Pour brown sugar mixture over nuts. Bake 13 to 15 minutes longer or until top of mixture is bubbly. Cool completely, about 1 hour. For bars, cut into 6 rows by 6 rows.

High Altitude: (3500-6500 ft): No change.

Nutritional Info: 1 Bar: Calories 230 (Calories from Fat 140); Total Fat 15g (Saturated Fat 6g, Trans Fat 0g); Cholesterol 25mg; Sodium 70mg; Total Carbohydrate 21g (Dietary Fiber 1g, Sugars 15g); Protein 2g. % Daily Value: Vitamin A 6%; Vitamin C 0%; Calcium 2%; Iron 4%. Exchanges: 1-1/2 Other Carbohydrate, 3 Fat. Carbohydrate Choices: 1-1/2.

pistachio-cranberry divinity

Prep Time: 30 Minutes
Start to Finish: 1 Hour
Servings: 20 candies

LOW FAT

1	egg white
1/4	cup water
1/4	cup light corn syrup
1-1/2	cups sugar
1/2	teaspoon vanilla
1/2	cup chopped pistachio nuts
1/4	cup sweetened dried cranberries, coarsely chopped

1 Line large cookie sheet with waxed paper. In medium bowl, beat egg white with electric mixer on high speed until soft peaks form; set aside.

2 In 2-quart heavy saucepan, mix water, corn syrup and sugar. Cook over medium heat, stirring constantly, until sugar is dissolved. Without stirring, cook mixture over medium heat 8 to 10 minutes or until syrup reaches 250°F on the candy thermometer.

3 When syrup is 250°F, continue beating egg white on high speed while slowly pouring syrup into egg white. Beat 2 to 3 minutes or until mixture holds a soft peak and does not flatten when dropped from a spoon.

4 Fold in vanilla, nuts and cranberries. Quickly spoon mixture by rounded teaspoonfuls onto cookie sheet. Let stand about 30 minutes or until completely set.

High Altitude: (3500-6500 ft): No change.

Nutritional Info: 1 Candy: Calories 100 (Calories from Fat 15); Total Fat 1.5g (Saturated Fat 0g, Trans Fat 0g); Cholesterol 0mg; Sodium 5mg; Total Carbohydrate 20g (Dietary Fiber 0g, Sugars 18g); Protein 0g. % Daily Value: Vitamin A 0%; Vitamin C 0%; Calcium 0%; Iron 0%. Exchanges: 1-1/2 Other Carbohydrate. Carbohydrate Choices: 1.

Betty's Kitchen Tip

• The candy can also be spooned into a foil-lined and buttered 8-inch square pan. Let stand until set, then cut into squares.

almond macaroon brownie bars

Prep Time: 20 Minutes
Start to Finish: 1 Hour 20 Minutes
Servings: 48 brownies

Brownies

- 1 box (1 lb 6.5 oz) Betty Crocker® Original Supreme brownie mix (with chocolate syrup pouch)
- 1/4 cup water
- 1/3 cup vegetable oil
- 3 eggs

Filling

- 3 cups flaked coconut
- 1 cup slivered almonds, toasted

- 1/4 teaspoon almond extract
- 1 can (14 oz) sweetened condensed milk (not evaporated)

Drizzle

- 1/2 cup semisweet chocolate chips
- 1/2 teaspoon vegetable oil

1 Heat oven to 350°F (325°F for dark or nonstick pan). Spray bottom of 13x9-inch pan with cooking spray. Make brownie mix as directed on box using 1/4 cup water, 1/3 cup vegetable oil, 3 eggs and chocolate syrup pouch. Spread batter in pan. Bake 28 to 30 minutes or until a toothpick inserted 2 inches from edge of pan comes out almost clean.

2 Meanwhile, in large bowl, mix filling ingredients. Remove brownies from oven. Carefully spoon and spread filling evenly over brownies. Bake 10 to 15 minutes longer (filling will not brown). Cool completely, about 1 hour.

3 In small microwavable bowl, microwave chocolate chips and 1/2 teaspoon oil on High 30 to 40 seconds, stirring every 10 seconds, until chips are melted. Spoon into resealable food-storage plastic bag; seal bag. Cut small tip from corner of bag; drizzle chocolate over filling. For bars, cut 8 rows by 6 rows.

High Altitude: (3500-6500 ft): No change.

Nutritional Info: 1 Brownie: Calories 300 (Calories from Fat 130); Total Fat 14g (Saturated Fat 8g, Trans Fat 0g); Cholesterol 15mg; Sodium 140mg; Total Carbohydrate 40g (Dietary Fiber 1g, Sugars 31g); Protein 4g. % Daily Value: Vitamin A 0%; Vitamin C 0%; Calcium 6%; Iron 8%. Exchanges: 1-1/2 Starch, 1 Other Carbohydrate, 2-1/2 Fat. Carbohydrate Choices: 2-1/2.

just
DESSERTS

p. 334

328

339

333

chocolate-cashew-cranberry tart

Prep Time: 40 Minutes
Start to Finish: 4 Hours
Servings: 16

1	Pillsbury® refrigerated pie crust (from 15-oz box), softened as directed on box
1-1/4	cups dark chocolate chips (from 12-oz bag)
1/2	cup granulated sugar
1/2	cup packed light brown sugar
1/4	cup light corn syrup
1	cup whipping cream

1	teaspoon vanilla
1	bag (6 oz) sweetened dried cranberries (1-1/3 cups)
1	container (9.25 oz) roasted cashew halves and pieces
1	teaspoon vegetable oil

1 Heat oven to 425°F. Make 1 pie crust as directed on box for One-Crust Filled Pie, using 10-inch tart pan with removable bottom. Trim edges. Bake 9 to 11 minutes or until lightly browned and dry in appearance. If crust puffs in center, flatten gently with back of wooden spoon. Sprinkle 1 cup of the chocolate chips over hot crust. Let stand 5 minutes to soften. Gently spread evenly over crust. Refrigerate to set chocolate. Reduce oven temperature to 375°F.

2 In 2-quart saucepan, heat granulated sugar, brown sugar, corn syrup and cream to full rolling boil over medium-high heat, stirring constantly with wire whisk, until sugar is dissolved. Reduce heat to medium-low to just maintain a full boil. Cook 8 to 10 minutes, stirring frequently, until mixture thickens and starts to turn a slightly darker caramel color. Remove from heat; stir in vanilla and dried cranberries. Let stand 15 minutes. Stir in cashews. Spoon mixture evenly over chocolate in pie crust. Bake at 375°F for 20 to 25 minutes or until filling is bubbly and cashews are golden brown.

3 In microwavable bowl, microwave remaining 1/4 cup chocolate chips and the oil uncovered on High 1 to 1-1/2 minutes or until melted, stirring twice. Drizzle over tart. Cool completely, about 2 hours. Refrigerate 1 hour or until chocolate is set. Cover and refrigerate any remaining tart.

High Altitude (3500-6500 ft): No change.

Nutritional Info: 1 Serving: Calories 380 (Calories from Fat 180); Total Fat 20g (Saturated Fat 8g, Trans Fat 0g); Cholesterol 20mg; Sodium 170mg; Total Carbohydrate 46g (Dietary Fiber 2g, Sugars 31g); Protein 3g. % Daily Value: Vitamin A 4%; Vitamin C 0%; Calcium 2%; Iron 8%. Exchanges: 1 Starch, 2 Other Carbohydrate, 4 Fat. Carbohydrate Choices: 3

Betty's Kitchen Tip

• When placing the crust into the tart pan, ease it in rather than stretching it to fit. If the crust is stretched, it will spring back into shape or "slump" during the initial bake.

almond-pear pie

Prep Time: 20 Minutes
Start to Finish: 2 Hours 25 Minutes
Servings: 8

1	box Pillsbury® refrigerated pie crusts, softened as directed on box
1	can (8 oz) or tube (7 oz) almond paste
5	cups 1/2-inch slices peeled, ripe (but firm) pears (about 4 pears)
2	tablespoons sugar
2	tablespoons Gold Medal® all-purpose flour
1-1/4	teaspoons apple pie spice
1	tablespoon lemon juice
1	egg, beaten
1/4	cup sliced almonds
1	teaspoon sugar

1 Heat oven to 375°F. Make pie crusts as directed on box for Two-Crust Pie, using 9-inch glass pie plate. Shape almond paste into a disk. On lightly floured surface, roll or pat into 8-inch circle. Place in bottom of pie crust.

2 In large bowl, mix pears, 2 tablespoons sugar, the flour, apple pie spice and lemon juice; mix well. Spoon over almond paste in crust. Place top crust over pears. Seal edges and flute. Cut slits in crust to vent steam. Brush top crust with egg. Sprinkle with almonds and 1 teaspoon sugar.

3 Bake 55 to 65 minutes or until pears are tender and crust is deep golden brown. Cool at least 1 hour before serving.

High Altitude (3500-6500 ft): No change.

Nutritional Info: 1 Serving: Calories 360 (Calories from Fat 150); Total Fat 16g (Saturated Fat 3.5g, Trans Fat 0g); Cholesterol 30mg; Sodium 120mg; Total Carbohydrate 49g (Dietary Fiber 5g, Sugars 26g); Protein 5g. % Daily Value: Vitamin A 0%; Vitamin C 4%; Calcium 6%; Iron 6%. Exchanges: 1/2 Starch, 1/2 Fruit, 2 Other Carbohydrate, 1/2 High-Fat Meat, 2-1/2 Fat. Carbohydrate Choices: 3

Betty's Kitchen Tips

Success Hint: Pears are best picked when hard and green (underripe). They finish ripening after picking. Plan on ripening pears at home for a few days before you use them.

Purchasing: Anjou pears are a great fall and winter pear. They are juicy when ripe but hold their shape well.

dutch pear pie

Prep Time: 20 Minutes
Start to Finish: 1 Hour 40 Minutes
Servings: 8

Crust

1	Pillsbury® refrigerated pie crust (from 15-oz box), softened as directed on box

Filling

1	cup sour cream
1/2	cup granulated sugar
1	tablespoon Gold Medal® all-purpose flour
1	teaspoon vanilla

1	egg, beaten
3	cups coarsely chopped fresh pears (2 to 3 medium pears)

Crumb Topping

1	cup Gold Medal® all-purpose flour
1/2	cup packed brown sugar
1/2	cup butter or margarine

1 Heat oven to 425°F. Place pie crust in 9-inch glass pie plate; do not prick crust. Carefully line pastry with double thickness of foil, gently pressing foil to bottom and side of crust. Let foil extend over edge to prevent excessive browning. Bake 10 minutes. Carefully remove foil; bake 2 to 4 minutes longer or until crust just begins to brown and has become set. If crust bubbles, gently push bubbles down with back of spoon.

2 Meanwhile, in medium bowl, mix filling ingredients. Pour into warm baked pie shell. Mix crumb topping ingredients with pastry blender or fork until mixture looks like fine crumbs; sprinkle over filling.

3 Reduce oven temperature to 350°F. Bake 40 to 50 minutes or until top is light golden brown. After 30 minutes of baking, cover top of pie with foil to prevent excessive browning. Cool at least 30 minutes before serving. Cover and refrigerate any remaining pie.

High Altitude (3500-6500 ft): No change.

Nutritional Info: 1 Serving: Calories 490 (Calories from Fat 220); Total Fat 25g (Saturated Fat 13g, Trans Fat 0.5g); Cholesterol 80mg; Sodium 220mg; Total Carbohydrate 62g (Dietary Fiber 2g, Sugars 33g); Protein 3g. % Daily Value: Vitamin A 10%; Vitamin C 2%; Calcium 6%; Iron 6%. Exchanges: 1 Starch, 3 Other Carbohydrate, 5 Fat. Carbohydrate Choices: 4

Betty's Kitchen Tips

Success Hint: Purchase pears ahead of time to ensure ripeness. To speed ripening, place pears in a paper or plastic bag at room temperature for several days. Pears are ready when they yield slightly when pressed.

Special Touch: Serve each slice with a dollop of whipped cream or a scoop of vanilla ice cream.

fresh berry crisp

Prep Time: 10 Minutes
Start to Finish: 40 Minutes
Servings: 6

EASY

- 3 cups fresh strawberries, sliced
- 3 tablespoons cornstarch
- 2 tablespoons granulated sugar
- 1 pint (2 cups) fresh blueberries
- 1 pint (2 cups) fresh raspberries
- 2/3 cup packed brown sugar
- 1/2 cup Gold Medal® whole wheat flour
- 1/2 cup old-fashioned or quick-cooking oats
- 1/2 teaspoon ground cinnamon
- 1/4 teaspoon salt
- 1/3 cup butter or margarine, softened

Ice cream or whipped cream, if desired

1. Heat oven to 350°F. In 2-quart saucepan, mash 2 cups of the strawberries; stir in cornstarch and granulated sugar. Cook over medium heat, stirring constantly, until mixture boils. Boil and stir 1 minute. Carefully stir in blueberries, raspberries and remaining strawberries. Pour berry mixture into ungreased 8-inch square (2-quart) glass baking dish or 9-inch pie plate.

2. In small bowl, mix remaining ingredients except ice cream with pastry blender or fork until crumbly; sprinkle over berry mixture.

3. Bake about 30 minutes or until topping is golden brown. Serve warm with ice cream.

High Altitude (3500-6500 ft): No change.

Nutritional Info: 1 Serving: Calories 370 (Calories from Fat 100); Total Fat 12g (Saturated Fat 7g, Trans Fat 0g); Cholesterol 25mg; Sodium 180mg; Total Carbohydrate 62g (Dietary Fiber 7g, Sugars 39g); Protein 3g. % Daily Value: Vitamin A 8%; Vitamin C 50%; Calcium 6%; Iron 10%. Exchanges: 1 Starch, 1 Fruit, 2 Other Carbohydrate, 2-1/2 Fat. Carbohydrate Choices: 4

Betty's Kitchen Tips

Success Hint: Use slightly tart apples with a crisp texture, such as Haralson apples. For a sweeter apple, choose Fuji, Prairie Spy or Gala.

Special Touch: Sprinkle with powdered sugar, and serve with warm maple syrup.

caramelized banana shortcakes

Prep Time: 10 Minutes
Start to Finish: 30 Minutes
Servings: 6

EASY QUICK

Shortcakes

2-1/3	cups Original Bisquick® mix
3	tablespoons packed brown sugar
1	teaspoon ground cinnamon
1/2	cup milk
3	tablespoons butter or margarine, melted

Filling

6	tablespoons butter or margarine
1/2	cup packed brown sugar
6	medium bananas (2-3/4 lb), peeled, diagonally cut into 1/2-inch slices (4-1/2 cups)
1/2	teaspoon ground cinnamon

Topping

3/4	cup hot fudge topping, warmed

1 Heat oven to 400°F.

2 In medium bowl, stir Bisquick mix, 3 tablespoons brown sugar and the cinnamon until well blended. Stir in milk and 3 tablespoons melted butter until soft dough forms. Drop by 6 heaping spoonfuls onto ungreased cookie sheet.

3 Bake 10 to 12 minutes or until golden brown.

4 Meanwhile, in 10-inch skillet, melt 6 tablespoons butter over medium heat. Stir in 1/2 cup brown sugar. Cook, stirring constantly, about 2 minutes or until dissolved. Add bananas to pan; coat with caramel mixture. Stir in ground cinnamon; remove from heat.

5 To serve, split warm shortcakes; fill with warm banana filling. Drizzle each with 2 tablespoons hot fudge topping.

High Altitude (3500-6500 ft): No change.

Nutritional Info: 1 Serving: Calories 630 (Calories from Fat 250); Total Fat 27g (Saturated Fat 15g, Trans Fat 2.5g); Cholesterol 50mg; Sodium 840mg; Total Carbohydrate 88g (Dietary Fiber 5g, Sugars 41g); Protein 7g. % Daily Value: Vitamin A 15%; Vitamin C 8%; Calcium 10%; Iron 10%. Exchanges: 2 Starch, 1 Fruit, 3 Other Carbohydrate, 5 Fat. Carbohydrate Choices: 6

Betty's Kitchen Tips

Success Hint: Make sure the bananas in this recipe aren't too ripe, so they don't get too soft after cooking.

Variation: Try substituting another spice, such as nutmeg or allspice, for the cinnamon in the shortcakes.

mixed-berry granola crunch

Prep Time: 10 Minutes
Start to Finish: 30 Minutes
Servings: 9

EASY QUICK

- 1 bag (12 oz) frozen unsweetened blueberries (about 2-1/2 cups)
- 1 bag (12 oz) frozen unsweetened red raspberries (about 2-1/2 cups)
- 1 tablespoon lemon juice
- 1/2 cup sugar
- 2 tablespoons cornstarch
- 2 cups organic oats & honey granola cereal
- 1/2 teaspoon ground cinnamon
- 2 tablespoons butter or margarine, melted, cooled

Vanilla ice cream, if desired

1 In ungreased 8-inch square (2-quart) glass baking dish, place blueberries, raspberries and lemon juice. Microwave uncovered on High 4 to 6 minutes, stirring once, until thawed.

2 In small bowl, mix sugar and cornstarch. Pour sugar mixture over berries; stir to coat berries. Microwave berries uncovered on High 10 to 12 minutes or until fruit is bubbling all over and mixture is thickened.

3 In medium bowl, mix cereal and cinnamon. Stir in butter until well mixed. Sprinkle over berries. Serve warm or at room temperature with ice cream.

High Altitude (3500-6500 ft): No change.

Nutritional Info: 1 Serving: Calories 150 (Calories from Fat 35); Total Fat 4g (Saturated Fat 1.5g, Trans Fat 0g); Cholesterol 5mg; Sodium 40mg; Total Carbohydrate 27g (Dietary Fiber 3g, Sugars 15g); Protein 1g. % Daily Value: Vitamin A 0%; Vitamin C 8%; Calcium 0%; Iron 4%. Exchanges: 2 Other Carbohydrate, 1 Fat. Carbohydrate Choices: 2

Betty's Kitchen Tips

Success Hint: Frozen berries are available year-round and are often more economical than fresh berries. However, when fresh berries are in good supply, substitute 6 cups of fresh berries for the frozen. Skip the microwave thawing step.

Variation: Substitute 1 cup of blackberries for 1 cup of the blueberries or raspberries, if you prefer.

caramel-apple pie

Prep Time: 25 Minutes
Start to Finish: 3 Hours 25 Minutes
Servings: 8

- 1 box Pillsbury® refrigerated pie crusts, softened as directed on box
- 1/2 cup butterscotch caramel topping
- 2 tablespoons Gold Medal® all-purpose flour
- 8 cups baking apples, peeled, cored, sliced 1/2 inch (6 to 8 medium apples)
- 1/2 cup packed brown sugar

- 2 tablespoons Gold Medal® all-purpose flour
- 1-1/2 teaspoons ground cinnamon
- 1 teaspoon milk
- 2 teaspoons sugar
- 1/2 cup butterscotch caramel topping
- Vanilla ice cream, if desired

1 Heat oven to 400°F. Place cookie sheet on bottom oven rack. Make pie crusts as directed on box for Two-Crust Pie, using 9-inch glass pie plate. In small bowl, mix 1/2 cup topping and 2 tablespoons flour; spread in bottom pie crust.

2 In large bowl, mix apples, brown sugar, 2 tablespoons flour and the cinnamon. Spoon over caramel. Gently press apples. Cut small shapes from top crust to allow steam to escape. Place crust over apples. Seal edge and flute. Brush crust with milk; sprinkle with sugar.

3 Bake 60 to 70 minutes or until apples are tender and crust is golden brown. (After 30 minutes of bake time, cover entire pie with foil to prevent overbrowning.) Cool about 2 hours before serving.

4 In small microwavable bowl, place remaining 1/2 cup topping. Microwave uncovered on High 30 to 45 seconds or until warm. Top slices of pie with ice cream; spoon topping over top.

High Altitude (3500-6500 ft): No change.

Nutritional Info: 1 Serving: Calories 300 (Calories from Fat 60); Total Fat 7g (Saturated Fat 2.5g, Trans Fat 0g); Cholesterol 0mg; Sodium 190mg; Total Carbohydrate 58g (Dietary Fiber 2g, Sugars 36g); Protein 1g. % Daily Value: Vitamin A 0%; Vitamin C 4%; Calcium 4%; Iron 2%. Exchanges: 1 Fruit, 3 Other Carbohydrate, 1-1/2 Fat. Carbohydrate Choices: 4

Betty's Kitchen Tip

• Small canapé cutters, typically about 1 inch in size, are good for cutting shapes out of the top crust. The cutout shapes can be brushed on the back with water or milk and placed on the top crust for decoration.

apple-pecan crisp

Prep Time: 25 Minutes
Start to Finish: 1 Hour 20 Minutes
Servings: 12

- 2/3 cup maple-flavored syrup
- 1/4 cup Gold Medal® all-purpose flour
- 1 teaspoon ground cinnamon
- 8 large baking apples (about 5-1/2 lb), peeled, cut into 1/2-inch slices (about 12 cups)
- 1/2 cup cold butter or margarine, cut into pieces
- 1 pouch (1 lb 1.5 oz) Betty Crocker® oatmeal cookie mix
- 3/4 cup chopped pecans

1 Heat oven to 375°F.

2 In large bowl, stir together syrup, flour and cinnamon until blended. Add apples; toss until evenly coated. Spread in ungreased 13x9-inch (3-quart) glass baking dish.

3 In same bowl, with pastry blender (or pulling 2 table knives in opposite directions), cut butter into cookie mix until mixture looks like coarse crumbs. Stir in pecans. Crumble mixture over apples in baking dish.

4 Bake 30 minutes. Very loosely cover with foil; bake 10 to 15 minutes longer or until apples are tender.

High Altitude (3500-6500 ft): No change.

Nutritional Info: 1 Serving: Calories 380 (Calories from Fat 130); Total Fat 14g (Saturated Fat 5g, Trans Fat 0g); Cholesterol 20mg; Sodium 220mg; Total Carbohydrate 59g (Dietary Fiber 2g, Sugars 31g); Protein 4g. % Daily Value: Vitamin A 6%; Vitamin C 2%; Calcium 0%; Iron 6%. Exchanges: 1 Starch, 1/2 Fruit, 2-1/2 Other Carbohydrate, 2-1/2 Fat. Carbohydrate Choices: 4

Betty's Kitchen Tips

Do-Ahead: While entertaining your guests, assemble this crisp, and then pop it into the oven as you start dinner. It will be ready to serve warm from the oven for dessert!

Success Hint: The oatmeal cookie mix is the secret ingredient that makes this topping super easy to throw together.

Special Touch: This crisp is delicious served with ice cream or whipped cream.

harvest fruit compote cobbler

Prep Time: 25 Minutes
Start to Finish: 1 Hour 15 Minutes
Servings: 6

Compote

3	medium baking apples (1-1/2 lb), peeled, cut into 1/2-inch slices (3 cups)
3	medium slightly ripe, firm Bartlett pears (1-1/2 lb), peeled, cut into 1/2-inch slices (3 cups)
1/2	cup dried apricot halves, cut in half
1/2	cup dried plums, cut in half
1/2	cup packed brown sugar
2	tablespoons Original Bisquick® mix
2	tablespoons finely chopped crystallized ginger
1/4	teaspoon ground cloves

Topping

1-1/2	cups Original Bisquick® mix
1/3	cup milk
1/4	cup granulated sugar
1/2	teaspoon ground ginger
1/4	cup butter or margarine, melted
1	tablespoon coarse sugar

1 Heat oven to 375°F.

2 In large bowl, mix compote ingredients. Spoon into ungreased 8-inch (2-quart) square glass baking dish.

3 Bake uncovered 25 minutes. Meanwhile, in same bowl, mix all topping ingredients except coarse sugar, using rubber spatula or spoon, until dough forms. Drop dough by spoonfuls over top of hot compote. Sprinkle with coarse sugar.

4 Bake 25 to 30 minutes or until fruit is tender and topping is golden brown and baked throughout.

High Altitude (3500-6500 ft): No change.

Nutritional Info: 1 Serving: Calories 470 (Calories from Fat 110); Total Fat 12g (Saturated Fat 6g, Trans Fat 1.5g); Cholesterol 20mg; Sodium 470mg; Total Carbohydrate 86g (Dietary Fiber 5g, Sugars 53g); Protein 4g. % Daily Value: Vitamin A 15%; Vitamin C 4%; Calcium 8%; Iron 8%. Exchanges: 1 Starch, 1 Fruit, 3-1/2 Other Carbohydrate, 2-1/2 Fat. Carbohydrate Choices: 6

Betty's Kitchen Tips

Success Hint: In this recipe, use pears that are a bit ripe but still firm. If they are too ripe, they'll be mushy at the end of baking.

Purchasing: Crystallized ginger is fresh ginger that has been peeled, diced and coated with sugar. It is sold in the spice aisle.

frozen chocolate-raspberry pie

Prep Time: 10 Minutes
Start to Finish: 3 Hours 25 Minutes
Servings: 8

EASY

- 1 quart (4 cups) raspberry sherbet
- 1 cup hot fudge topping, slightly warmed
- 1 creme-filled chocolate sandwich cookie crumb crust (6 oz)
- 1 cup frozen (thawed) whipped topping
- 1/2 cup fresh raspberries

1 Let container of sherbet stand at room temperature about 15 minutes to soften. Spoon and spread 1/2 cup of the fudge topping carefully in bottom of crumb crust; place in freezer for 15 minutes to set. Place remaining 1/2 cup fudge topping in small microwavable bowl; refrigerate until serving time.

2 Spoon and spread sherbet over fudge topping in crust. Cover with plastic wrap; freeze 3 hours.

3 To serve, microwave fudge topping on High 10 to 15 seconds or until thin enough to drizzle. Garnish individual servings with dollop of whipped topping, drizzle of fudge topping and several fresh raspberries.

High Altitude (3500-6500 ft): No change.

Nutritional Info: 1 Serving: Calories 370 (Calories from Fat 100); Total Fat 11g (Saturated Fat 4.5g, Trans Fat 1g); Cholesterol 0mg; Sodium 270mg; Total Carbohydrate 65g (Dietary Fiber 3g, Sugars 45g); Protein 4g. % Daily Value: Vitamin A 0%; Vitamin C 6%; Calcium 6%; Iron 8%. Exchanges: 1 Starch, 3-1/2 Other Carbohydrate, 2 Fat. Carbohydrate Choices: 4

Betty's Kitchen Tips

Success Hint: To easily cut pies made in purchased crumb crusts in foil pans, cut through the edges of the pan with kitchen scissors and peel away the pan.

Substitution: No fresh raspberries? Top with toasted almonds instead.

peach crumble pie

Prep Time: 35 Minutes
Start to Finish: 2 Hours 30 Minutes
Servings: 8

Crust

1	cup Gold Medal® all-purpose flour
1/2	teaspoon salt
1/3	cup plus 1 tablespoon shortening
2 to 3	tablespoons cold water

Filling

4	cups quartered peeled peaches (8 to 10 medium)
1/2	cup granulated sugar
1/2	teaspoon ground nutmeg
2	tablespoons whipping cream
1	egg

Topping

1/2	cup Gold Medal® all-purpose flour
1/4	cup packed brown sugar
1/4	teaspoon ground cinnamon
1/4	teaspoon ground nutmeg
1/4	cup butter or margarine, softened

1 Mix 1 cup flour and the salt. Cut in shortening, using pastry blender (or pulling 2 table knives through ingredients in opposite directions), until particles are size of small peas. Sprinkle with cold water, 1 tablespoon at a time, tossing with fork until all flour is moistened and pastry almost cleans side of bowl. Gather pastry into ball. On lightly floured surface, shape pastry into flattened disk. Wrap in plastic wrap; refrigerate about 45 minutes or until firm and cold, yet pliable. (If refrigerated longer, let dough soften slightly before rolling.)

2 Heat oven to 425°F. On lightly floured surface, roll pastry with floured rolling pin into round 2 inches larger than upside-down 9-inch glass pie plate. Fold pastry into quarters; place in pie plate. Unfold and ease into plate, pressing firmly against bottom and side. Trim overhanging edge of pastry 1 inch from rim of plate. Fold and roll pastry under, even with plate; press edge with tines of fork, or flute.

3 Place peaches in pastry-lined plate. Mix granulated sugar and 1/2 teaspoon nutmeg; sprinkle over peaches. Beat whipping cream and egg with fork or wire whisk; pour over peaches. Mix topping ingredients with fork until crumbly; sprinkle over peaches.

4 Cover edge of pastry with 2- to 3-inch-wide strip of foil to prevent excessive browning. Bake 35 to 40 minutes or until top is golden brown, removing foil last 15 minutes. Cool 30 minutes. Serve warm.

High Altitude (3500-6500 ft): No change.

Nutritional Info: 1 Serving: Calories 370 (Calories from Fat 170); Total Fat 19g (Saturated Fat 7g, Trans Fat 2g); Cholesterol 45mg; Sodium 200mg; Total Carbohydrate 46g (Dietary Fiber 2g, Sugars 27g); Protein 4g %. Daily Value: Vitamin A 10%; Vitamin C 6%; Calcium 2%; Iron 8%. Exchanges: 1 Starch, 2 Other Carbohydrate, 3-1/2 Fat. Carbohydrate Choices: 3

pear tartlets

Prep Time: 10 Minutes
Start to Finish: 40 Minutes
Servings: 4 tartlets

EASY

- 1 sheet frozen puff pastry (from 17.3-oz package), thawed as directed on package
- 1 ripe pear
- 1/4 cup peach preserves

1 Heat oven to 400°F. Cut pastry into 4 squares. On ungreased cookie sheet, place pastry squares.

2 Peel pear, and cut into quarters; remove seeds. Slice each pear quarter into very thin slices. Arrange pear slices over pastry squares, leaving 1/2-inch border.

3 Bake about 20 minutes or until pastry is puffed and browned. Spread 1 tablespoon preserves over top of each warm tartlet to cover pears. Cool on cookie sheet 10 minutes before serving.

High Altitude (3500-6500 ft): No change.

Nutritional Info: 1 Tartlet: Calories 430 (Calories from Fat 210); Total Fat 24g (Saturated Fat 8g, Trans Fat 2.5g); Cholesterol 75mg; Sodium 160mg; Total Carbohydrate 49g (Dietary Fiber 2g, Sugars 15g); Protein 5g. % Daily Value: Vitamin A 0%; Vitamin C 4%; Calcium 2%; Iron 15%. Exchanges: 1-1/2 Starch, 1-1/2 Other Carbohydrate, 4-1/2 Fat Carbohydrate Choices: 3

Betty's Kitchen Tips

How-To: Thaw the frozen puff pastry on the counter about 15 minutes. The pastry should be chilled but still pliable when you're ready to work with it. If the pastry gets too warm, the butter layers will flatten and the pastry won't puff as high when it bakes.

Success Hint: This is the perfect dessert to make when you're short on time. Keep puff pastry in the freezer for those occasions when you need a quick dessert.

dutch apple-pumpkin crisp

Prep Time: 20 Minutes
Start to Finish: 1 Hour 15 Minutes
Servings: 8

1-1/2	cups chopped peeled apples (2 small)
3/4	cup Gold Medal® all-purpose flour
3/4	cup packed brown sugar
1/4	cup butter or margarine, softened
1/4	teaspoon pumpkin pie spice
1	cup canned pumpkin (not pumpkin pie mix)

1/3	cup granulated sugar
1/4	cup milk
2	tablespoons Gold Medal® all-purpose flour
1/2	teaspoon pumpkin pie spice
1	egg
Whipped cream, if desired	

1 Heat oven to 350°F. Spread apples over bottom of 9-inch glass pie plate. Microwave uncovered on High 4 to 6 minutes or until apples are crisp-tender.

2 Meanwhile, in small bowl, toss 3/4 cup flour, the brown sugar, butter and 1/4 teaspoon pumpkin pie spice until crumbly. Set aside.

3 In medium bowl, beat remaining ingredients except whipped cream with wire whisk until smooth. Pour over apples. Sprinkle with flour mixture.

4 Bake 30 to 35 minutes or until golden brown and set. Cool 20 minutes. Serve warm with whipped cream.

High Altitude (3500-6500 ft): No change.

Nutritional Info: 1 Serving: Calories 250 (Calories from Fat 60); Total Fat 7g (Saturated Fat 4g, Trans Fat 0g); Cholesterol 40mg; Sodium 60mg; Total Carbohydrate 45g (Dietary Fiber 2g, Sugars 32g); Protein 3g. % Daily Value: Vitamin A 100%; Vitamin C 2%; Calcium 4%; Iron 8%. Exchanges: 1 Starch, 2 Other Carbohydrate, 1 Fat. Carbohydrate Choices: 3

Betty's Kitchen Tips

How-To: To peel apples, use a swivel-bladed vegetable peeler. It peels more quickly than a knife and will remove the peel without taking much of the apple flesh. Or use a crank-type apple peeler to save time.

Success Hint: If your brown sugar has become hard, you can soften it in the microwave. Place up to 2 cups of the hard brown sugar in a microwavable bowl, and microwave uncovered on High, checking every 30 seconds, until softened.

vanilla-ginger-pear crumble

Prep Time: 20 Minutes
Start to Finish: 1 Hour 20 Minutes
Servings: 6

Pear Mixture

- 6 medium slightly ripe, firm Bartlett pears (about 2-3/4 lb), peeled, cut into 1/2-inch slices (about 6 cups)
- 1/4 cup granulated sugar
- 2 tablespoons Gold Medal® all-purpose flour
- 2 teaspoons vanilla
- 1/2 to 3/4 teaspoon ground ginger

Topping

- 1/3 cup Gold Medal® all-purpose flour
- 1/4 cup packed brown sugar
- 1/4 cup cold butter or margarine, cut into pieces
- 12 vanilla wafer cookies, crushed (about 1/2 cup)

1 Heat oven to 375°F. In large bowl, mix pear mixture ingredients until evenly coated. Spread in ungreased 8-inch square (2-quart) glass baking dish.

2 In same bowl, mix 1/3 cup flour and the brown sugar. Cut in butter, using pastry blender (or pulling 2 table knives through mixture in opposite directions), until mixture looks like coarse crumbs. Stir in crushed cookies. Crumble over pears.

3 Bake 50 to 60 minutes or until pears are tender and topping is golden brown.

High Altitude (3500-6500 ft): No change.

Nutritional Info: 1 Serving: Calories 300 (Calories from Fat 80); Total Fat 9g (Saturated Fat 5g, Trans Fat 0.5g); Cholesterol 20mg; Sodium 90mg; Total Carbohydrate 51g (Dietary Fiber 5g, Sugars 34g); Protein 2g. % Daily Value: Vitamin A 6%; Vitamin C 4%; Calcium 2%; Iron 6%. Exchanges: 1 Starch, 1 Fruit, 1-1/2 Other Carbohydrate, 1-1/2 Fat. Carbohydrate Choices: 3-1/2

 Kitchen Tips

Success Hint: The pears in this recipe should be slightly ripe, yet firm. See page 330 for a tip on ripening.

Special Touch: For an elegant touch, serve this dessert in a stemmed glass!

nectarine-plum crostata

Prep Time: 20 Minutes
Start to Finish: 2 Hours 30 Minutes
Servings: 8

Crust

1-1/2	cups Gold Medal® all-purpose flour
1	teaspoon sugar
1/4	teaspoon salt
1/2	cup cold butter, cut into pieces
1	egg yolk
4 to 5	tablespoons cold water

Filling

1/2	cup sugar
3	tablespoons Gold Medal® all-purpose flour
1/4	teaspoon ground cinnamon
3	cups sliced nectarines
2	cups sliced plums
1	tablespoon lemon juice
2	tablespoons butter, softened
1	tablespoon sugar

1 Heat oven to 425°F. In medium bowl, mix 1-1/2 cups flour, 1 teaspoon sugar and the salt. Cut in 1/2 cup butter, using pastry blender (or pulling 2 table knives through ingredients in opposite directions), until crumbly. Stir in egg yolk with fork. Sprinkle with water, 1 tablespoon at a time, tossing until ball of pastry forms. Flatten ball to 1/2-inch. Wrap in plastic wrap; refrigerate 30 minutes.

2 On lightly floured surface, roll pastry into 13-inch round, about 1/8 inch thick. Place on ungreased large cookie sheet.

3 In large bowl, mix 1/2 cup sugar, 3 tablespoons flour and the cinnamon. Stir in nectarines and plums until coated. Sprinkle with lemon juice; mix. Spoon fruit mixture onto center of pastry, spreading to within 3 inches of edge. Dot with 2 tablespoons butter. Fold edge of pastry up over fruit mixture, making pleats. Brush edge of pastry with small amount of water; sprinkle with 1 tablespoon sugar.

4 Bake 30 to 40 minutes or until crust is golden brown and fruit is tender. Cool completely, about 1 hour.

High Altitude (3500-6500 ft): No change.

Nutritional Info: 1 Serving: Calories 340 (Calories from Fat 140); Total Fat 15g (Saturated Fat 9g, Trans Fat 0.5g); Cholesterol 65mg; Sodium 180mg; Total Carbohydrate 45g (Dietary Fiber 2g, Sugars 23g); Protein 4g. % Daily Value: Vitamin A 15%; Vitamin C 6%; Calcium 0%; Iron 8% Exchanges: 1 Starch, 1 Fruit, 1 Other Carbohydrate, 3 Fat. Carbohydrate Choices: 3

Betty's Kitchen Tip

• A fruit crostata will keep at room temperature for 2 days; after that, store it loosely covered in the fridge up to more 2 days. In warm climates, always store fruit crostadas in the fridge.

caramel-apple crisp

Prep Time: 20 Minutes
Start to Finish: 1 Hour 20 Minutes
Servings: 6

- 1/2 cup caramel topping
- 1/2 teaspoon ground cinnamon
- 6 large baking apples (about 2-3/4 lb), peeled, cut into 1/2-inch slices (about 6 cups)
- 2/3 cup Gold Medal® all-purpose flour
- 1/2 cup packed brown sugar
- 1/2 cup cold butter or margarine, cut into small pieces
- 2/3 cup quick-cooking oats

1 Heat oven to 375°F.

2 In large bowl, stir together caramel topping and the cinnamon until blended. Add apples; toss until evenly coated. Spread in ungreased 8-inch square (2-quart) glass baking dish.

3 In same bowl, mix 2/3 cup flour and the brown sugar. Cut in butter, using pastry blender (or pulling 2 table knives through mixture in opposite directions), until mixture looks like coarse crumbs. Stir in oats. Crumble mixture over apples in baking dish.

4 Bake 45 to 50 minutes or until apples are tender and topping is golden brown. If desired, serve with whipped cream and additional caramel topping.

High Altitude (3500-6500 ft): No change.

Nutritional Info: 1 Serving: Calories 430 (Calories from Fat 150); Total Fat 16g (Saturated Fat 10g, Trans Fat 0.5g); Cholesterol 40mg; Sodium 210mg; Total Carbohydrate 67g (Dietary Fiber 3g, Sugars 43g); Protein 3g. % Daily Value: Vitamin A 10%; Vitamin C 4%; Calcium 4%; Iron 8%. Exchanges: 1 Starch, 1/2 Fruit, 3 Other Carbohydrate, 3 Fat. Carbohydrate Choices: 4-1/2

Betty's Kitchen Tips

Success Hint: Try to cut all of the apples in this recipe into slices of the same thickness, so they'll cook evenly.

How-To: To test for doneness, simply poke the tip of a sharp knife into an apple, and you'll be able to feel if it's tender.

general index

alphabetical index